P9-DBV-045

The Royal Stuarts

ALSO BY ALLAN MASSIE

NOVELS
Change and Decay in All Around I See
The Last Peacock
The Death of Men
One Night in Winter
Augustus
A Question of Loyalties
Tiberius
The Sins of the Father
Caesar
King David
Antony
The Ragged Lion
These Enchanted Woods
Nero's Heirs
Shadows of Empire
Caligula
Surviving

ROMANCES
The Evening of the World
Arthur the King
Charlemagne and Roland

NON-FICTION
The Caesars
Colette
101 Great Scots
Edinburgh
Glasgow: Portrait of a City
The Thistle and the Rose

THE ROYAL STUARTS

*A History of the Family
That Shaped Britain*

ALLAN MASSIE

THOMAS DUNNE BOOKS
ST. MARTIN'S PRESS
NEW YORK

THOMAS DUNNE BOOKS.
An imprint of St. Martin's Press.

THE ROYAL STUARTS. Copyright © 2010 by Allan Massie. All rights reserved.
Printed in the United States of America. For information, address St. Martin's Press, 175 Fifth Avenue, New York, N.Y. 10010.

www.thomasdunnebooks.com
www.stmartins.com

ISBN 978-0-312-58175-6

First published in Great Britain by Jonathan Cape,
an imprint of Random House

First U.S. Edition: December 2011

10   9   8   7   6   5   4

For Claudia and Matt

Contents

The Genealogy of the House of Stuart

FAMILY TREE I

FAMILY TREE II

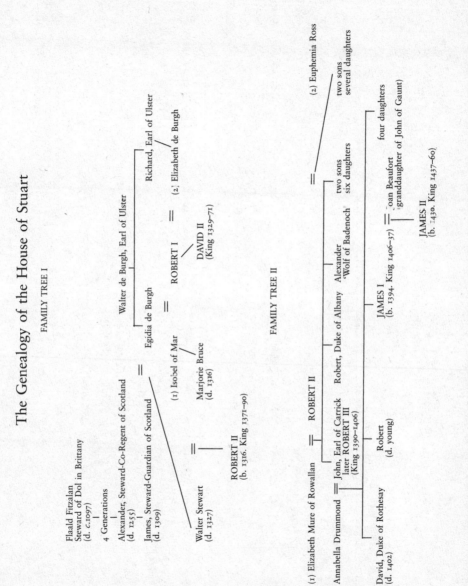

FAMILY TREE III

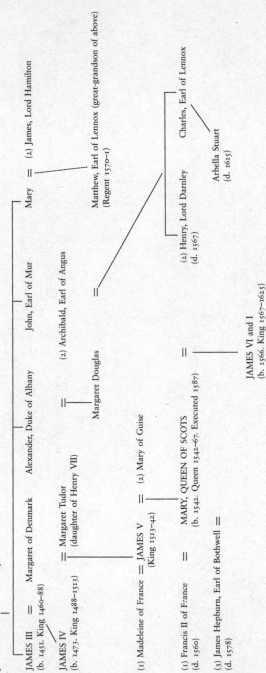

JAMES II ═══ Mary of Gueldres

JAMES III ═══ Margaret of Denmark   Alexander, Duke of Albany   John, Earl of Mur   Mary ═══ (2) James, Lord Hamilton
(b. 1451. King 1460–88)

JAMES IV   ═══ Margaret Tudor   (2) Archibald, Earl of Angus   Matthew, Earl of Lennox (great-grandson of above)
(b. 1473. King 1488–1513)   (daughter of Henry VII) ═══   (Regent 1570–1)

                                                    Margaret Douglas ═══

(1) Madeleine of France ═══ JAMES V ═══ (2) Mary of Guise   (2) Henry, Lord Darnley   Charles, Earl of Lennox
                              (King 1513–42)   (d. 1567)

(1) Francis II of France ═══   MARY, QUEEN OF SCOTS ═══   Arbella Stuart
(d. 1560)   (b. 1542. Queen 1542–67. Executed 1587)   (d. 1615)

(3) James Hepburn, Earl of Bothwell ═══
(d. 1578)

                                                            JAMES VI and I
                                                            (b. 1566. King 1567–1625)

FAMILY TREE IV

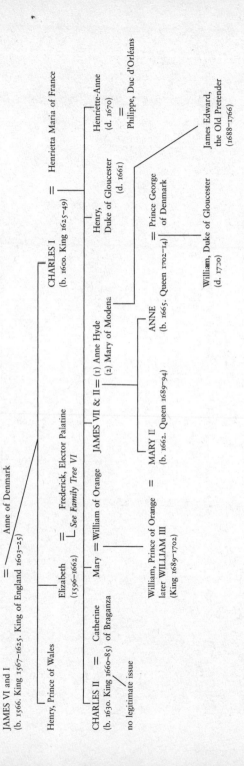

JAMES VI and I
(b. 1566. King 1567–1625. King of England 1603–25) = Anne of Denmark

Henry, Prince of Wales

Elizabeth (1596–1662) = Frederick, Elector Palatine ⌐ See Family Tree VI

CHARLES I (b. 1600. King 1625–49) = Henrietta Maria of France

CHARLES II (b. 1630. King 1660–85) = Catherine of Braganza — no legitimate issue

Mary = William of Orange

JAMES VII & II = (1) Anne Hyde / (2) Mary of Modena

Henry, Duke of Gloucester (d. 1661)

Henriette-Anne (d. 1670) = Philippe, Duc d'Orléans

William, Prince of Orange later WILLIAM III (King 1689–1702) = MARY II (b. 1662. Queen 1689–94)

ANNE (b. 1665. Queen 1702–14) = Prince George of Denmark

James Edward, the Old Pretender (1688–1766)

William, Duke of Gloucester (d. 1720)

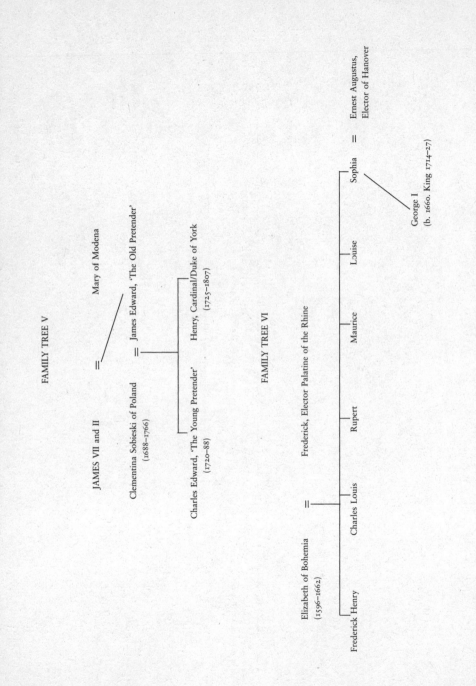

FAMILY TREE V

JAMES VII and II   ==   Mary of Modena

Clementina Sobieski of Poland   ==   James Edward, 'The Old Pretender'
(1688–1766)

Charles Edward, 'The Young Pretender'   Henry, Cardinal/Duke of York
(1720–88)   (1725–1807)

FAMILY TREE VI

Elizabeth of Bohemia   ==   Frederick, Elector Palatine of the Rhine
(1596–1662)

Frederick Henry   Charles Louis   Rupert   Maurice   Louise   Sophia   ==   Ernest Augustus,
                                                                                  Elector of Hanover

George I
(b. 1660. King 1714–27)

The Royal Stuarts

Prologue

It was between ten and eleven o'clock on a July morning in 1685. The condemned man mounted the scaffold with a firmer step than many had expected.

A century and a half later, Macaulay[1] would describe the scene with that relish in executions characteristic of Victorian historians and novelists:

Tower Hill was covered up to the chimney tops with an innumerable multitude of gazers who, in awful silence, broken only by sighs and the noise of weeping, listened for the last accents of the darling of the people. 'I shall say little,' he began. 'I come here, not to speak but to die. I die a Protestant of the Church of England.' The Bishops interrupted him and told him that, unless he acknowledged resistance [to the royal authority] to be sinful, he was no member of their church. But it was in vain that the prelates implored him to address a few words to the soldiers and the people on the duty of obedience to the government. 'I will make no speeches,' he exclaimed. He then accosted John Ketch the executioner. 'Here,' said the Duke, 'are six guineas for you. Do not hack me as you did my Lord Russell. I have heard that you struck him three or four times. My servant will give you more gold if you do the work well.' He then undressed, felt the edge of the axe, expressed some concern that it was not sharp enough, and laid his head on the block. The executioner addressed himself to his office. But he had been disconcerted by what the Duke said. The first blow inflicted only a slight wound. The Duke struggled, rose from the block and looked reproachfully at the executioner. The head sank down once more. The stroke was

repeated again and again, but still the head was not severed, and
the body continued to move. Yells of rage and horror rose from the
crowd. Ketch flung down the axe with a curse. 'I cannot do it,' he
said, 'my heart fails me.' 'Take up the axe, man,' cried the Sheriff.
'Fling him over the rails,' roared the mob. At length the axe was
taken up. Two more blows extinguished the last remnants of life;
but a knife was used to separate the head from the shoulders. The
crowd was wrought up to such an ecstasy of rage that the executioner was in danger of being torn to pieces, and was conveyed
away under a strong guard. In the meantime many handkerchiefs
were dipped in the Duke's blood, for by a large part of the multitude he was regarded as a martyr who had died for the Protestant
religion. The head and body were placed in a coffin covered with
black velvet, and were laid privately under the communion table
of Saint Peter's Chapel in the Tower. In truth there is no sadder
spot than that little cemetery. Death is there associated . . . with
whatever is darkest in human nature and human destiny, with the
savage triumph of implacable enemies, with the inconstancy,
the ingratitude, the cowardice, of friends, with all the miseries of
fallen greatness and of blighted fame.

Thus, incomparably, from the decent security of his study, the
great Whig historian described the botched piece of butchery that
ended the life of the Duke of Monmouth and Buccleuch. It was
to be the last execution of a royal duke, a king's son, in Britain.
Kings, queens, dukes, earls and countesses, all royal, had gone to
the block before him, suffered on Tower Green, in Fotheringay
Castle, outside the Palace of Whitehall and in various castle court-
yards in England and Scotland. But he would be the last, and, his
reputation as 'the Protestant Duke' having faded, is now perhaps
the least remembered.

Some would hold that poor Monmouth was not truly royal, for
he was the illegitimate son of Charles II and a Welsh girl called
Lucy Walter, born in 1650 while the King was in exile. But Charles
acknowledged him as his son, while denying that he had ever been
married to Lucy. The story will be told in full in its proper place.
Suffice to say now that many believed that there had been a
marriage, and Monmouth was almost certainly one of them.

Being illegitimate, he never bore the royal name of Stuart. As a young man he was known as Mr Crofts, taking the name from a gentleman appointed his guardian, and then, after his marriage to Anne Scott, Lady of Buccleuch in the Scottish Borders, he assumed his wife's family name. He was Charles's favourite among his numerous bastards, a young man of grace and charm.

Anthony Hamilton, author of the memoirs of his brother-in-law, the Comte de Grammont,[2] left this description of the Duke:

> His figure and the exterior graces of his person were such that nature never formed anything more perfect. His face was extremely handsome; and yet it was a manly face, neither inanimate nor effeminate; each feature having a beauty and peculiar delicacy; he had a wonderful genius for every form of exercise, an engaging aspect, and an air of grandeur. The astonishing beauty of his outward form caused universal admiration. Those who were before looked on as handsome were now entirely forgotten at court; and all the gay and beautiful of the fair sex were at his devotion. He was particularly beloved by the King, but the universal terror of husbands and lovers.

However, Hamilton adds, while Monmouth 'possessed every personal advantage, he was greatly deficient in mental accomplishments; he had no sentiments but such as others inspired in him, and those who insinuated themselves into his friendship took care to inspire him with none but such as were pernicious. He appeared to be rash in his undertakings, irresolute in the execution, and dejected in his misfortunes.'

Monmouth may never have legitimately borne the name of Stuart; yet in person and fortune, he was in many ways characteristic of that remarkable family: he charmed easily, inspired devotion, failed his followers, showed himself to be possessed of lamentable judgement, and ran headlong to misfortune. He was Stuart through and through; Stuart to the bone.

The man against whom he led a rebellion, the man who sent him to the block, was his uncle, James VII and II, formerly Duke of York. He had played with Monmouth when his nephew was a beautiful and charming boy, but between 1678 and 1681 he had endured attempts by political enemies suspicious of his Roman Catholicism to exclude him from the throne in favour of his brother's bastard. Now he had his revenge.

Chapter 1

The Stewards:
Origins in Legend and History

M acbeth, in his second encounter with the three weird sisters, asks:

Yet my heart
Throbs to know one thing: tell me – if your art
Can tell so much – shall Banquo's issue ever
Reign in this kingdom?

Advised by the witches that for his peace of mind he should 'seek to know no more', he yet insists and is then presented with the apparition of the long line of Banquo's descendants, 'a show of eight kings'.

Macbeth was played before the first Stuart king of Great Britain and Ireland, James VI of Scots and I of England, and this scene served as a compliment to him. Imaginative Scottish historians had long before ascribed a satisfyingly ancient ancestry to the House of Stewart, tracing their descent from Banquo. Hector Boece (*c.*1465–1536), the first principal of the University of King's College, Aberdeen, tells the story, which Shakespeare was to repeat, of how witches met Macbeth and Banquo on a stretch of wild moorland. In Bellenden's translation of Boece's Latin,[1] they promised Banquo that 'you sall never be king, bot of ye sall cum mony kingis quilkes be lang progressioun sall rejose the croun of Scotland'. Macbeth, angered and disturbed by the prophecy, commissioned Banquo's murder, but the victim's son, Fleance, escaped and made his way to France, where he married and so became the founder of the royal House of Stewart.

It was nonsense, an agreeable fiction, but one that by the time of James VI and I was sufficiently widely believed for Shakespeare to retail it. And why not? Most royal genealogies were fanciful, descent being traced from pagan gods or mythological heroes.

The truth was more prosaic. The Stewarts came out of Brittany, land of salt-marshes and moors, saints and dolmens. Nothing is known of any member of the family before the late eleventh century – conveniently for the legend, or fabrication, since Macbeth became King of Scots in 1040. When they emerge into the light of history, it is as steward or seneschal to the Counts of Dol on the south shore of the Gulf of St Malo. In 1097, the then head of the family accompanied the Count and his feudal superior, Robert, Duke of Normandy, eldest son of William the Conqueror, on the First Crusade, and did not return.

He was succeeded in the office of steward by his brother Flaald, whose name was taken by chroniclers to be a corruption of Fleance. One of Flaald's sons, Alan, crossed the Channel in the service of the third Norman king of England, Henry I. He was evidently trusted, for in 1101 Henry appointed him Sheriff of Shropshire with responsibility for the collection of taxes and administration of justice, and the additional duty of guarding the Welsh Marches. The Breton language that Alan spoke is close to Welsh and was probably still closer then; no Normans would have spoken it, and so Alan's ability to communicate with the Welsh tribal chiefs would have recommended him for the post.

One of Alan's sons, Walter Fitzalan, advanced the fortunes of the family further. He entered the service of Henry's brother-in-law, the Scottish prince David, the youngest son of Malcolm III (Shakespeare's Malcolm) and Margaret, the saint-queen, herself a descendant of Alfred the Great and so also of Cerdic, founder of the royal house of Wessex. David spent his adolescent years at the Anglo-Norman court. In 1114 he married a widow some years his senior, and acquired the earldoms of Huntingdon and Northampton. It was doubtless the connection with Henry I that brought Walter Fitzalan to David's notice. He presumably showed himself competent and reliable, and David may have come to look upon him as a friend. At any rate, when David inherited the Scottish throne in 1124, Walter came north with him as a member of his household. He continued to enjoy the King's favour, was granted estates in Ayrshire and Renfrewshire, and was appointed High Steward of Scotland.

The word 'steward' derives from the Anglo-Saxon 'stig', meaning a hall, and 'weard', which is ward, guardian or keeper. In modern usage it has retained, or reverted to, something close to that original sense. In the twelfth century, however, a steward was no mere domestic servant or household official, but a high officer of state, with responsibility in Scotland for the management of the royal revenue and expenditure, while he might also on occasion exercise a military command. The office of high steward became hereditary in the family of Walter Fitzalan, and the third to occupy it seems to have adopted Steward or Stewart (the words being interchangeable) as a family name. Subsequently dependants, retainers and tenants on the various Stewart estates would also go by their lord's family name. No one now supposes that the clan and family names of Scotland necessarily represent blood relationships, though they may often do so of course. When Stevenson, in *Kidnapped*, has his military adventurer Alan Breck Stewart proudly declare, 'I bear a king's name', his boast does not extend as far as claiming a family connection.

The Stewarts were only one among a number of Anglo-Norman or Anglo-Breton families to come by invitation to Scotland in David's reign, or in the reigns of his sons, Malcolm IV and William the Lion. Though descended in the male line from the Gaelic-speaking kings of the Scots,[2] they took the Norman monarchy of England as their model, and, early in the twelfth century, it was observed that 'the more recent kings of Scots profess themselves to be rather Frenchmen [that is, Normans] both in race and in manners, culture and language, and they admit only Frenchmen to their friendship and service'.[3] The Stewarts belonged to that category, as did the Balliols, Bruces and Comyns, and all were welcomed by kings seeking to impose a feudal superstructure on Celtic tribal society, in order to extend and cement royal authority.

We know nothing of the character of any but the last of the men who for seven or eight generations held the office of high steward, serving every king from David I to David II, Robert the Bruce's son. It is reasonable to suppose that they were for the most part able and loyal; able because they were maintained in office; loyal because there is no record of them engaging in open or active rebellion. On the contrary, indeed: they were employed in suppressing rebellions and were rewarded with the grant of forfeited or confiscated lands. We know little of their marriages, though some will have been with the daughters of the old Celtic aristocracy. And we do not even know at what stage they stopped speaking Norman French as their first language, choosing instead to converse in Gaelic or the northern variety of English that would, centuries later, be termed Scots. One of them, Alexander, the fourth to hold the office of high steward, became a Crusader like his first-recorded Breton ancestor, but he was more fortunate and returned home safely. He was sufficiently well thought of to act as regent during the minority of Alexander III (1249–82), and commanded one wing of the army that defeated the Norwegians at Largs in 1263.

His son, James, first to bear the Christian name by which eight of the Stewart kings would be known, was one of the guardians of the realm after Alexander III was killed in a riding accident, and as such was among those who invited Edward I of England to adjudicate between the various candidates, or 'competitors', for the throne when it fell vacant on the death of the late king's granddaughter, the little 'Maid of Norway', in 1286. Edward first compelled the competitors, among them the grandfather of Robert the Bruce, to acknowledge him as overlord of Scotland, and then in 1292 selected John Balliol as vassal king. Balliol soon chafed at his subordinate position, sought to establish his independence, and made an alliance with France. Edward marched north in the summer of 1296, stripped Balliol of his crown, and proceeded to try to incorporate Scotland into his empire as he had already done with Wales.

The Scots resisted, thus sparking the long and heroic Wars of Independence, the proving-ground of Scottish nationality. James the Steward was among those who defied Edward, fighting alongside William Wallace and Andrew Murray at the Battle of Stirling Bridge in 1297. Ten years later, he was one of the first to rally to Robert the Bruce, when he declared himself King of Scots. James married Egidia de Burgh, a daughter of the Norman Earl of Ulster, this alliance offering further evidence that the Stewarts were now in the leading rank of the Scots nobility. He died in 1309, leaving as his heir a young son, Walter.

It is with this Walter that the Stewarts' advance to the throne begins. At the age of nineteen, he fought at Bannockburn, in the division commanded by his uncle, Sir James Douglas, Bruce's chief lieutenant, and in the evening of that famous victory was knighted by the King on the field of battle. He had evidently made an impression, for the next year, 1315, he was married to Marjorie Bruce, King Robert's daughter by his first marriage.

More than two hundred years later, James V, dying in Falkland Palace, was told that his wife, Marie de Guise, had given birth in Linlithgow to the daughter who would come to be known as Mary, Queen of Scots. The disconsolate King is said to have sighed, 'It cam wi' a lass and it'll gang wi' a lass.' As deathbed lines go, this one is at least well invented, even though as a prophecy it was to prove well wide of the mark.

But the lass it cam wi' was Marjorie Bruce, and her short life was as unfortunate at that of any of her more famous descendants. In 1306, after King Robert's hurried and scarcely regular coronation at Scone, she had been sent with her mother and other female relatives, under the guardianship of the King's youngest brother, Nigel, to the presumed safety of Kildrummy Castle, perched above the River Don in Aberdeenshire. But the castle was betrayed, Nigel was killed, and when they tried to flee north, the royal women and their companions were captured and handed over to the English.

King Robert had been one of the many Scottish barons who had accepted Edward as overlord of Scotland and sworn allegiance to him. He may even have been a favourite of the English king. If so, his defiance – rebellion in Edward's eyes – was all the more infuriating, and now Edward, unable to seize Bruce himself, took cruel revenge on the captured women. The Countess of Buchan, who had placed the crown on King Robert's head, and the King's sister Mary were imprisoned in cages hung from the battlements of the castles of Berwick and Roxburgh respectively. Edward ordered that another cage be prepared for the nine-year-old Marjorie in the Tower of London. But when the old king died, his gentler son, Edward II, commuted the sentence, and Marjorie was instead sent to be held in a convent in Yorkshire. She remained there till the year after Bannockburn, when she was returned to her father in exchange for English prisoners taken in the battle; and was straight away married to young Walter Stewart.

Marjorie was King Robert's only living legitimate child, but with the outcome of the war still uncertain, few can have thought a female succession desirable. Accordingly, a parliament meeting in Ayr determined that, if King Robert should die, he should be succeeded by his brother Edward. Marjorie is said to have consented to this arrangement; she would have had little choice but to do so.

Then, in 1316, the pregnant Marjorie fell from her horse, gave birth to a boy, probably prematurely, and perhaps by a Caesarean operation, and died. She was no more than twenty. That child, named Robert after his grandfather, would be the first Stewart king, but he had to wait a long time to inherit the crown. King Robert married again, and his new wife, another de Burgh from Ulster, bore him a son. He would become David II and would reign from 1329 to 1371. He was Robert Stewart's uncle, but eight years younger than his nephew. A Stewart succession still seemed unlikely.

Chapter 2

Robert II (1371–90): The First Stewart King

D avid II's reign was troubled, and the King, a minor when he came to the throne, was in effective control for less than half of it. The early years saw a renewal of the war with England, and of civil strife between the adherents of the Bruces and the Balliols, arising from the young English king Edward III's attempt to install John Balliol's son, Edward, as a puppet king in Scotland. The attempt failed, and Edward III turned his attention to war with France. David, having attained his majority, and faithful to the French alliance, invaded England, but was wounded, defeated and taken prisoner at Neville's Cross in 1346, the year of Edward's great victory over the French at Crécy. He was kept captive there for eleven years, and released only on the promise of a payment of 100,000 marks. Robert Stewart acted as regent in the King's absence, without notable success. He made no attempt to seize the throne for himself, perhaps because he was loyal, perhaps because he was too weak to do so. It was only the King's sudden death at the age of forty-six, when he was about to marry for the third time in the hope of at last producing a legitimate heir, that opened the way to the Stewart succession.[1]

Robert II was fifty-five when he became king, on the verge of old age by medieval standards. He was a great nobleman, head of an extensive family connection, with estates scattered across central and southern Scotland. He was king by hereditary right, but he was never to be more than first among equals.

All medieval monarchies were partnerships. It couldn't be otherwise. No king could govern without the acquiescence of the nobility and the Church. Indeed he required more than acquiescence; he needed collaborators. Kingship might be hereditary; it was also, if only informally, contractual. In Scotland the idea of contractual monarchy had been made explicit in the Declaration of Arbroath, addressed in 1320 to the Pope by 'the Community of the Realm'. Composed in an attempt to persuade the Pope to lift the sentence of excommunication imposed on Robert the Bruce after he murdered his rival John Comyn in Dumfries Abbey before he was crowned king of Scots, it set out its authors' understanding of monarchy. It first recited the pseudo-historical (in truth, utterly mythical) origin of the Scots, who, having come from Scythia by way of Spain and Ireland, had then overcome Picts, Britons, Angles and Norsemen to establish the independence of Scotland under a succession of 113 native kings (most of whom were imaginary). His Holiness was then informed that the Scots had been rescued from the violence of the English by their chosen king, Robert, now compared to the biblical heroes Joshua, son of Nun, and Judas Maccabeus. He was king by the choice of the community of the realm as well as by hereditary right, but the authors of the declaration boldly announced that, should he prove faithless, he would be set aside and replaced by another king: 'for so long as a hundred of us remain alive, we shall never submit or be subject to the English'. This was fine rhetorical stuff, to be regarded in later ages as the definitive statement of Scotch nationality; but in truth all medieval monarchs were in a like position, required to govern in a manner agreeable to the great men of the realm, and might be removed if they failed to do so. In England Edward II would be deposed seven years after this declaration was addressed to the Pope, and Richard II would be replaced by Henry IV in 1399.

For the fact is that, without a regular army, without a police force, medieval government depended on two things: the personality of the monarch and his ability to obtain the consent of the barons, knights, churchmen and merchants who constituted the political class. In this respect Scotland was no different from other countries. Nevertheless, in Scotland the Crown was indeed weaker than in England, principally because the administrative apparatus of the state was far less developed. Building on the organisation of the Anglo-Saxon monarchy, with its effective system of royal writs directed to sheriffs and local magnates, the Norman and Plantagenet kings of England had established a form of government that, in the hands of a capable ruler, was the most efficient in Europe. There was nothing comparable in Scotland. The monarch -- King of Scots, rather than of Scotland – was the leader of a tribal nation. His power was even more dependent on his personality and prestige than was the case in England. It rested very largely on his ability to command respect and approval.

The power of the Crown was indeed very limited. It scarcely existed north of the River Tay, except up the eastern seaboard to Aberdeen and the Moray Firth. The Highlands were largely self-governing, inasmuch as they were governed at all. The Lord of the Isles, controlling the Hebrides and much of the north-west Highlands, was a quasi-independent sovereign, any allegiance to the king being merely verbal. Orkney and Shetland were not yet part of the kingdom, and in name at least were Norwegian dependencies. The Border counties, ravaged by intermittent war with England, were wild and unruly, a debatable land of frontier brigands, scarcely governable, controlled only in part by the heads of the great families established there – the Douglases, Maxwells, Johnstones, Scotts – whose loyalty to the Crown was provisional, their obedience ever uncertain. Every Stewart king, until the Union of the Crowns of 1603, had to scheme and struggle to establish his authority. Success in that struggle was never more than temporary.

The unity of the state was merely political, neither cultural nor linguistic. Suspicion, fear and resentment divided Highland and Lowland Scotland. The fourteenth-century chronicler, John of Fordoun,[2] writing in Aberdeen, had declared that:

The manners and customs of the Scots vary with the diversity of their speech. For two languages are spoken among them, the Scottish and the Teutonic,[3] the latter of which is the language of those who occupy the seaboard and the plains, while the race of Scottish speech inhabits the Highlands and outlying islands. The people of the coast are of domestic and civilized habits, trusty, patient and urbane, decent in their attire, affable and peaceful, devout in divine worship, yet always ready to resist a wrong at the hands of their enemies. The Highlanders and peoples of the islands on the other hand are a savage and untamed nation, rude and independent, given to rapine, easy-living, of a docile and warm disposition, comely in person but unsightly in dress. Hostile to the English people and language, and, owing to the diversity of speech, even to their own nation, and exceedingly cruel.

It is scarcely necessary to remark that John of Fordoun was himself a Lowlander, one moreover who, living close to the Highland line, was even more suspicious of the mountaineers and hostile to them than those dwelling further south might be. But every medieval writer makes the same sort of distinction, John Mair[4] in the early sixteenth century writing of the 'wild Scots' and the 'house-holding Scots'. For others the Highlanders were 'the Irish' (their language generally being called 'Erse') and the Lowlanders the true 'Scots'.

The Scotland of the early Stewarts, scarcely recovered from the destructive Wars of Independence, when the richest part of the country had been ravaged time and again by English armies, with crops ruined and towns burned, was poor and in many respects backward. Though burghs had been growing in number and, inter-mittently, in prosperity since the eleventh century, they mostly remained very small. There was no capital city, no Scottish equiva-lent of London or Paris. Edinburgh did not receive a royal charter till Robert the Bruce gave it one in 1329; there are many more ancient burghs in Scotland. It was only in the time of the later Stewarts that it became a favoured royal residence. The court itself was peripatetic; therefore the administration too, for what we should call the civil service still operated out of the king's house-hold. There was as yet no Scottish equivalent of the English exchequer working from a fixed base. In any case, all medieval monarchs were almost constantly on the move, because this was the only way in which they could exercise justice, and because it was easier to bring the court to food stores than to carry the food stores, in a land with few serviceable roads or navigable inland waterways, to the court. Finally, the royal revenues, drawn from the king's own estates and from the customs duties, were always inadequate, quite insufficient to allow for the creation of a strong state – another reason why the co-operation of the nobility and the consent of the community of the realm, expressed in parliaments, were essential if government was to function at all. Parliament, known usually as 'the Estates', met infrequently, and its members – barons, knights, bishop, abbots and burgesses – were summoned or invited by the king rather than elected.

This parliament, which had a judicial as well as a legislative function, was in a sense an extension of the General Council, which was composed of members of the royal family, leading ecclesiastics, earls and chief barons of the realm, and, significantly, officers of the royal household. The Council advised the king and authenticated the charters he granted. Over the years the influence of the officers of the royal household increased. They had the advantage of being always to hand, unlike the magnates, whose attendance at court might be infrequent, since they were occupied in the management of their own estates and the administration of justice in their baronial courts. The principal officers were: the constable, or chief military officer; the chamberlain, who looked after the king's revenues until this task was taken over in James I's reign by the treasurer; the chancellor, who kept the records and the Great Seal of the Kingdom, required to authenticate royal ordinances, and who was a sort of secretary of state; and the justiciar, or chief law officer. Except for the constable, they were usually, but not invariably, churchmen. Their presence at the heart of government explains why, in several of the minorities of the fifteenth century, men of comparatively undistinguished birth were able to secure possession of the king's person and take control of the government.

It was not only the power of the Crown that was limited. The business of government itself was limited too. Kings were concerned with foreign policy, with administering justice, with maintaining law and order as far as this was possible, with promoting trade by granting charters to burghs (something barons also did on their own estates), with raising revenue and supporting the Church as part of the established order. Laws were indeed passed to encourage some activities and discourage others – as when, for example, James I legislated in 1428 in an attempt to stop people from playing football because it distracted them from archery practice – but there was little that we might recognise as a programme of government in the modern sense. Nor did the common people play any part in politics – less indeed in Scotland than in either England or France, for, partly because of the more limited, and therefore less oppressive, government of the Scottish kingdom, there was no equivalent there of the English Peasants' Revolt of 1381, or the 'Jacqueries', riotous expressions of popular discontent, which disturbed France in 1360 and often subsequently.

Robert II's position was difficult. He lacked prestige and had no military reputation. He had been one of the commanders at Neville's Cross, a quarter of a century back, and was thought to have ordered a retreat with unseemly haste as soon as King David had been taken prisoner. Though seemingly loyal during the eleven years of the King's captivity, he had subsequently engaged in a feeble sort of rebellion with the earls of Douglas and March. No warrior in his prime, he commanded little respect as he approached old age. Other members of the nobility had been accustomed to regard him as an equal, and were not disposed to treat him with greater deference merely because he had now inherited the Crown thanks to his father's fortunate marriage. Nevertheless, whatever his personal failings, he was king and the Crown itself had prestige. Robert indeed was the ninety-ninth King of Scots in descent, according to one version of the manufactured but widely accepted table of genealogy, from the mythical Fergus. Far from being lost in the mists of antiquity, the origins of the Scottish monarchy as recounted in the Declaration of Arbroath were a matter of common knowledge, repeated by bards and heralds on great occasions of state. This ensured that the Crown itself was revered, no matter the failings of the man who currently wore it.

Robert had himself been married twice, and this was to be a cause of confusion, dispute and some danger to the state. His first wife was Elizabeth, daughter of Sir Robert Mure of Rowallan, his second Euphemia, daughter of the Earl of Ross. These were baronial alliances, not royal ones, entangling the new king in a web of cousinship. The Bruces had been short of heirs; the early Stewarts had too many. There was a further complication. By his first wife he had four sons and six daughters, several of whom were born out of wedlock, and were therefore, properly speaking, bastards. They had subsequently been legitimised after their parents' marriage, but the legality of this was open to question, at least in the eyes of the children of the King's second marriage. This had produced two sons and several daughters. The exact number is unrecorded, as is that of other illegitimate children whom Robert fathered, but these seem to have included eight boys. Whatever his deficiencies in battle and his feebleness in the council chamber, Robert was active enough in bed.

Though in fact the succession was secured to the descendants of Elizabeth Mure, the doubt as to the validity of their legitimisation meant that for several decades the descendants of Euphemia Ross could believe that they had a superior claim to the throne. Their resentment would come to a head in the reign of Robert's grandson, James I.

The early Stewarts practised what modern historians have called 'laissez-faire kingship'5, leaving for the most part strong local lords to their own devices so long as they did not set themselves up openly against the Crown. Whether this was policy or necessity is irrelevant, but it is evidence of the weakness of the Crown and the incapacity of Robert II and his eldest son, Robert III. Both were elderly when they became king. It is not surprising that they lacked vigour. In any case an energetic king, seeking to impose himself on his barons, was always likely to run into trouble, as their contemporary Richard II of England discovered when he provoked the baronial revolt that resulted in his deposition and murder. The two Roberts might have been timid or lazy, or merely incompetent, but they survived for a total of thirty-five years without facing any serious threat to their position. This was an achievement of a sort.

We have no portrait of either king. Robert II is said to have been tall and handsome as a young man. The French chronicler Froissart,[6] visiting Scotland, found him unprepossessing in his old age. He had 'red bleared eyes, the colour of sandalwood, which clearly showed he was no valiant man, but one who would rather remain at home than march to the field'. This was a harsh judgement on a man of seventy. By that time indeed his oldest son, John, Earl of Carrick (the old Bruce lordship), had been associated with him in government on the grounds that 'our lord the King, for certain causes, is not able to attend regularly and thoroughly in all things to the execution of the government and the law of the kingdom'. These causes are not specified, but evidently Robert was no longer thought competent to conduct the business of government. He was over seventy, a very old man by medieval standards, and it is possible that he may have suffered the loss of faculties characteristic of senile decay. Certainly, well before his death in 1390, he was king in name only.

Chapter 3

Robert III (1390–1406):
A Troubled Reign

J ohn of Carrick succeeded his father in 1390,when he was
already fifty-three. He chose to be known as Robert III. The
name John was thought unlucky for a king. John of England
had lost almost all the Angevin empire in France and had been
threatened with deposition by his barons. The vassal king John
Balliol, poor 'Toom Tabard' (empty coat), had been notably unsuccessful. John of France had been taken prisoner by the English at
the Battle of Poitiers in 1356. But the change of name hardly ensured
good fortune.

The new king was in poor health. In 1388 a kick from a horse
had left him lame. He soon appeared to be a chronic invalid. Indeed
he was regarded as being so unfitted for government that his younger
brother, the Earl of Fife, who had actually been christened Robert,
was appointed to execute justice and defend the kingdom on account
of the King's 'infirmity'. The exact nature of this is unknown, but
evidently Robert III, though amiable and kindly, lacked the vigour
of the most prominent of his brothers, Fife, and Alexander, Earl of
Buchan. The latter's wildness earned him the sobriquet 'the Wolf
of Badenoch'. His most notorious exploit was the burning of Elgin
Cathedral, described as 'the ornament of the realm, the glory of
the kingdom, the delight of foreigners'; even today in its ruined
state it remains impressive. The Wolf burned the town too; all this
because the Bishop of Moray had had the temerity to command

him to return to the wife he had deserted. He did penance for his crime, but suffered no other punishment, either because the King had an affection for his wayward brother, or, more probably, because he wasn't strong enough to impose any penalty. Alexander continued to flourish as a semi-independent warlord; and, when he died in 1405, was buried in Dunkeld Cathedral, where an inscription commemorates him, with doubtless unintentional irony, as a benefactor of the Church.

The Wolf's activities, and those of his sons who led or organised plundering raids through Angus in 1391 and 1392, highlighted the emergence of a 'Highland problem' that was to persist through the reigns of all the early Stewart kings. To some extent this turbulence may be seen as a reaction to their attempts to establish royal authority throughout a part of the kingdom hitherto left largely to its own devices and to the government of clan chiefs and local magnates. There had, however, been disorder and intermittent clan warfare in Moray for years, and an attempt to settle this took the form of a staged battle between the clans Chattan and Kay (both in fact groupings of a number of different clans) in Perth in 1396. The contest was a macabre parody of the tournament, the favourite sport of chivalry. Thirty men from each clan assembled on the North Inch, a meadow on the banks of the Tay.[1] Stands were erected for spectators,[2] and King Robert, his court and a number of foreign dignitaries graced the occasion. The fierce battle was long remembered: Walter Scott made it the climax of his last successful novel, *The Fair Maid of Perth*. The King's heir, Prince David, acted as umpire, and throughout the afternoon the warriors, denied body armour, hacked at each other until eleven men of Clan Chattan were left on their feet, victorious, while the only survivor of their rivals escaped by diving into the river and swimming free. The pro-Stewart chronicler Bower judged that the day had its desired effect, since 'for a long time the north remained quiet'. His verdict may be received with some scepticism.

Unable to manage his brothers, King Robert was compelled to surrender the effective government of the kingdom to the dominating figure of his sibling Robert, Earl of Fife, whom he created Duke of

Albany in 1398. At the same time, Prince David was made Duke of Rothesay, the title still borne by the eldest son of the sovereign. It would soon be apparent, however, that if the King could not control his brothers, he could not protect his sons either.

In 1399 there was a shift in power. Albany was accused by rival members of the Council of 'misgovernance of the realm', and Rothesay was named as lieutenant-general of the kingdom. Rothesay was an attractive but wild and, by repute, dissolute young man, and soon made enemies, not only among the fathers, brothers and uncles of girls he had seduced. He married a daughter of the Earl of Douglas, in itself a politic move to ally the Crown to the greatest family of the Borders. Unfortunately he had already contracted to marry a daughter of the Earl of March, who, greatly insulted, departed to England. His arrival at the English court, and the news he brought of widespread disaffection in Scotland, persuaded Henry IV to revive the moribund English claim to overlordship. He invaded Scotland, met little resistance, occupied Edinburgh, and then withdrew, having in truth achieved little of substance, but having demonstrated the inability of young Rothesay to defend the kingdom. Discontent was now rife. Albany seized the chance to make a comeback, and compelled the King to consent to his son's arrest. Taken in St Andrews, the young Duke was transferred to Falkland Castle – not yet the fine Renaissance palace that would later be constructed, but a grim keep. Within two months he was dead. The death of his nephew and rival was too convenient for Albany to be allowed to pass without comment, but he obliged the Council to issue a proclamation declaring that Rothesay had 'departed this life through the divine dispensation and not otherwise'. Few can have been convinced, though most kept quiet. A generation later Bower wrote that the Prince had died 'of dysentery or, as some have it, of starvation'. The same explanation had been offered in England two years previously for the death of the deposed Richard II in Pontefract Castle. In *The Fair Maid of Perth*, Scott, basing his account on John of Fordoun's chronicle, has Rothesay murdered by Albany's agents, though in the manner of the murder, they exceed their instructions. The intention had indeed

been to starve the young man to death, but on investigation, 'the
dying hand of the Prince was found to be clenched upon a lock
of hair, resembling, in colour and texture, the coal-black bristles
of Bonthron.[3] Thus, though famine had begun the work, it would
seem that Rothesay's death had been finally accomplished by
violence.' Hector Boece, writing his history of the Scottish kings
more than a hundred years later, was certain of Albany's guilt.
Rothesay was deliberately starved, and 'brocht, finalie, to sa miserable and hungry appetite that he eit, nocht onlie allegedly, the filth
of the toure quhar he wes, bot his awin fingaris: to his gret martyr-
dome'. The last vivid touch, if not true, is well and horribly invented.

Scott's version, based on these chroniclers, is dramatically
convincing and politically persuasive.[4] The King was now over
sixty and in poor health. Rothesay was his heir. Albany's power,
and perhaps his life, had been threatened by the prospect of his
nephew's succession to the throne. Rothesay was in his hands, and
Rothesay did not survive. It requires considerable generosity of
mind to acquit Albany of responsibility for his nephew's death.
There can be nothing surprising in his murder, any more than in
the murder of Richard II at the command of his cousin and usurper
Henry IV. Family feeling may easily be extinguished when power
is the prize.

King Robert, too weak to challenge his dominant brother, had
little choice but to accept the official version of his son's death.
He now withdrew to Rothesay Castle on the Isle of Bute, an old
Stewart stronghold, and surrendered the government to Albany.
But he had a younger son, James, a boy of only eight when Rothesay
died or was murdered. Two years later he was made Earl of Carrick,
the old title of the Bruces, and it was decided to send him to France,
ostensibly to complete his education. It is reasonable to suppose,
as men did at the time, that the young heir to the throne was in
fact sent away for his own safety. The King's health was failing
fast. What chance would the boy have with Albany as regent?

This can only be supposition, yet there is some evidence to
support it. Instead of taking ship at Leith, the port of Edinburgh,
the young Prince was brought with an armed escort, commanded

by an old friend of the King's, Sir David Fleming of Cumbernauld, to the Bass Rock off the East Lothian coast, where he was to wait for a boat on its way from Leith to France. (There was then no Scottish navy.) The elaborate scheme suggests that there was some fear he might be prevented from boarding a vessel in Leith. He had to wait a month on the Rock (more often used throughout Scottish history as a prison) until he was able to embark on a ship trading out of Danzig, which was carrying wool and hides to France. He never arrived there. The boat was intercepted and boarded by English pirates off Flamborough Head. They recognised the value of their catch, handed James over to Henry IV and were rewarded with the ship's cargo. Did Albany have a hand in this? There is no evidence either to acquit him or prove his guilt. Is it significant that Sir David Fleming, on his way back from the coast, was attacked and killed by Sir James Douglas of Balveny? Albany may have been responsible; or again, not, with Fleming the victim of a private feud. What is certain is that the young Prince's capture and imprisonment in England suited the Duke very well.

Robert III survived the news of his son's misfortune for only a few weeks. He died requesting to be buried in a midden with the epitaph 'Here lies the worst of kings and most miserable of men'. The cause of death was sympathetically ascribed to that ailment beloved by historians and sentimental romancers but unknown to medical science: a broken heart. But since he was in his seventieth year, the true cause may have been more prosaic.

The two Roberts had been ineffectual kings. Yet the dynasty was well established. James might be a prisoner in England, but his right of succession was recognised. Two months after Robert's death, a Council of the Scottish Estates – the name given to the Scottish parliament at the point – named him king and authorised Albany to continue to act as lieutenant-governor of the realm. The Duke may have hoped to be king himself. If so, he lacked sufficient support. His government was therefore limited and provisional. When he died in 1420, at the age of eighty, he was succeeded as governor by his son Murdoch, who had himself spent some years in English captivity. But the rule of father and son was maintained only with the consent of the most powerful nobles, who made it clear that they owed allegiance to James and would not tolerate the usurpation of his throne. Just as when David II had been a prisoner in England, loyalty to the rightful king outweighed the inconvenience of his absence.

Chapter 4

James I (1406–37): The Poet-King

The great Cambridge historian F. W. Maitland wrote of 'the mournful procession of the Jameses'. The judgement was uncharacteristically sweeping, uncharacteristically unfair also. Stewart kingship was far from being a failure. The times were violent. None of the five Jameses lived beyond the age of forty-three – in marked contrast to the ineffectual Roberts – but they were all men of unusual ability, capable of asserting themselves and subduing recalcitrant nobles. It was the misfortune of the dynasty, though not necessarily of Scotland, that the reigns of four of them began with a minority.

Comparison with England and France serves, however, to put their troubled history in perspective. If two of the Jameses were murdered and two killed in battle, the years between 1399 and 1485 saw three English kings deposed and murdered, one mad, and another – believed to have murdered his own nephews – killed in the Battle of Bosworth Field. Moreover, for thirty years, 1455–85, England suffered intermittent civil war, on a scale far beyond anything Scotland experienced, and three changes of dynasty. Indeed it is arguable that what many constitutional historians have seen as an advantage enjoyed by England but denied to Scotland – the existence of a strong monarchy and a comparatively centralised state – actually provoked this instability. Since the king possessed bureaucratic machinery that might allow him to impose his will

on the great territorial barons, they were more likely, if dissatisfied with the Crown's policies, to combine to resist them and change
the government.

In France, the fifteenth century was even more terrible than in
England. It began with a mad king, Charles VI, and the murder
in the streets of Paris of his brother, Louis d'Orléans, by cut-throats
in the pay of his cousin, the Duke of Burgundy. Civil war between
the Orléanists (or Armagnacs) and the Burgundians followed. Then
came an English invasion, supported by the Burgundians, the
disaster of Agincourt and utter humiliation before a miraculous
saviour appeared in the person of a shepherd girl from Lorraine,
Joan of Arc. Thirty years later, a 'strong' king, Louis XI, found
himself challenged in the 'War of the Common Weal' by a group
of leading nobles, defending their traditional collective rights and
privileges against the centralising policies of the Crown.

The century to which the Dutch historian Huizinga gave the
name 'the Waning of the Middle Ages' was disordered, bloody,
violent. In Scotland, England and France alike, the penalty of
political failure was often death by the dagger, sword or heads-
man's axe.

Nothing in Scotland, however, matched the horrors perpetrated
in Paris in the summer of 1418 after the Burgundians seized control
of the city and took their revenge on their Armagnac rivals. First,
Bernard d'Armagnac, the Orléanists' leader, and his associates in
government were hacked to death. Two months later the fury of
the mob was directed, not spontaneously, at foreigners: Bretons
and Gascons, Lombards and Genoese, Catalans and Castilians, 'in
the absence', as one French historian sardonically puts it, 'of Jews.
Stripped, mutilated, profaned, impaled, their bodies were thrown
into the middle of the street as if they had been swine.' The next
year the Armagnacs had their revenge. The Duke of Burgundy was
murdered by adherents of the Dauphin, the King's eldest son, on
the bridge over the Seine at Montereau; he had come there to negotiate a peace. There were like horrors in England: the murder of
Richard II in Pontefract Castle in 1399, the summary execution
of Richard, Duke of York, after the Battle of Wakefield; the murders

of Henry VI, the Duke of Clarence and (almost certainly) the boy king Edward V and his younger brother Richard. All this should be borne in mind as the story of the five Jameses unfolds.

When Henry IV was told that his young captive Prince James had been travelling to France only to further his education, he replied that this was unnecessary because 'I speak good French myself.' Actually it is probable that James could already speak the language: his mother, Annabelle Drummond, had been accustomed to correspond with his elder brother, David of Rothesay, in French. This need occasion no surprise. The now long-standing French alliance, as a result of which many Scots served in the French army – one of them, James Power or Polwarth, designing Joan of Arc's banner – meant that the Scottish court and nobility were acquainted with the French tongue and well versed in French culture. Indeed, French influence is evident in many aspects of Scottish life throughout the Stewart period. In church and castle architecture France, not England, supplied the model. Young noblemen were often sent to France to further their education. French words entered the Scots language. The lords' claret was poured from a 'gardevin' (wine jug) into a 'tassie' (cup), and their food was served on an 'ashet' (*assiette*). Scots law diverged from English common law and the foundations were laid in the fifteenth century of a Franco-Roman legal system, which, despite the vast accretions of statute law passed by the United Kingdom parliament since 1707, survives to this day. When universities were founded – St Andrews in 1412, Glasgow in 1455 and King's College, Aberdeen, in 1495 – the model was the Sorbonne in Paris, not Oxford or Cambridge.

Henry's remark may have been a joke, but he did see to it that the education of the captive Prince was not neglected. James soon learned to read Latin for pleasure, and to write fluently. Though he was lodged at first in the Tower of London, where other prisoners included his cousin Murdoch, captured on a raid into England, and Griffith, the son of the rebel Welsh prince Owen Glendower, the conditions of his captivity were not severe. There was the royal menagerie to amuse them, and James was soon allotted his own household servants. He was even on occasion permitted to exercise his regal powers. So, for instance, in November 1412 he issued 'from Croydon' letters confirming two members of the extensive Douglas family in possession of the Border lands of Drumlanrig, Hawick, Selkirk and Cavers. The documents, given 'under the signet usit in selying of oure letters', are declared to be 'rate with oure proper hand', and are the first examples we have of the handwriting of any King of Scots.

Nevertheless, captivity must have been irksome for a young and ambitious prince, especially since his uncle Albany made no effort to secure his release. On the contrary; when Henry IV died in 1413, Albany negotiated the return to Scotland of his own son Murdoch, in exchange for Henry Percy, Earl of Northumberland (who had taken refuge in Scotland after an unsuccessful rebellion), but left the King where he was.

Events turned in James's favour, however, when the English triumph at Agincourt was followed by further successes. The French called for assistance from their Scottish ally, and a force of some six or seven thousand men was sent to France under the command of Albany's second son, the Earl of Buchan, and Archibald, fourth Earl of Douglas, who was married to James's sister Margaret. This army defeated the English at Bauge in 1421, stimulating renewed French resistance.

The presence of the Scots in France persuaded Henry V to take James with him on his next campaign, so that his subjects could be charged with fighting against their king, thus being guilty of treason. James was not reluctant. He admired Henry, had been present at his marriage to Catherine of Valois, and been knighted by him at Windsor. They may even have been friends inasmuch as friendship was possible between kings, or indeed between keeper and prisoner. He was by Henry's side at the siege of Melun and issued an order commanding all Scots in the French army to lay down their arms. The commander, James's cousin Buchan, not surprisingly declined to obey the King's order, but a dozen Scots who had been taken prisoner were hanged for having borne arms against their lawful king. James may have had no choice in the matter. On the other hand, he may well have approved. He had no reason to love Buchan, whose father had been content to leave him a prisoner in England. Certainly such approval would be in keeping with the ruthlessness he would display when at last he returned to Scotland and began to govern.

That day was not far off. In 1422 Henry V died. His son and heir, Henry VI, was still a baby. A council of regency was established. Its chief members were the late king's brothers, John, Duke of Bedford, and Humphrey, Duke of Gloucester, and their uncle Henry Beaufort, Bishop of Winchester. The King's death would have consequences for the war with France, never again prosecuted so successfully, and for the political relations between England and Scotland. The new government saw merit in releasing James. An Anglo-Scottish agreement, even if falling short of an alliance, might lead to the withdrawal of the Scottish army from France. The rapproachement between England and Scotland would be cemented by a marriage. A suitable bride for James was available. She was Joan Beaufort, niece of the Bishop of Winchester. The marriage was undeniably a political arrangement, but, unlike most royal marriages, it may have been a love match too.

For James was not only a king; he was also a poet, and in *The Kingis Quair*, he told, or purported to tell, the story of his romance. It is a long poem of 119 seven-line stanzas, which shows the influence of Chaucer, and though in many ways conventional in theme and imagery, also reads like the product of personal experience.

He tells how he is lying awake in his chamber unable to sleep. So in the manner of insomniacs, he picks up a book: *The Consolations of Philosophy* by the fifth-century Roman Boethius, itself reputedly written in prison and often quoted by Chaucer. He reads for some time, then lays it aside and muses on the mutability of fortune till he hears the bell ring for Matins. He then recounts the story of his youth and capture and years of captivity. This depresses him, and so, in an attempt to lighten his mood, he goes to the window overlooking a garden where a nightingale has been singing.

And therewith kest I doun my eye ageyne,
Quhare as I saw, walking under the toure,
Ful secretly new cummyng hir to pleyne,
The fairest or the freschest yonge floure
That ever I sawe, me thought, before that houre,
For quhich sodayn abate, anon astert
The blude of all my body to my hert.

And though I stude abaisit tho a lyte
No wonder was, forquhy my wittis all
Were so ouercome with pleasaunce and delyte
Only throe latting of myn eyen fall,
That suddenly my hert become hit thrall
For ever of free wyll; for of manace
There was no takyn in hir suete face.

And so it continues, as the poet invokes the aid of classical goddesses
(first, naturally, Venus), visits the Court of Love, seeks advice from
Minerva, Goddess of Wisdom, and travels through an enchanted
land before arriving triumphant at the port of love.

Much of the imagery is trite, but this should be no occasion for
criticism. Poets then did not aim for originality of either manner
or matter. Nevertheless, there is a freshness to the poem, and the
delight that it conveys arises in part from the growing conviction
that this is no mere exercise in verse-making but an expression of
true feeling. The circumstances of that first encounter may be
invented. Seeing a beautiful lady in a garden from a tower window
was a poetic convention dating back to at least the Provençal trou-
badours of the twelfth century. Yet there is a directness in the tone
that gives the impression of sincerity, allowing us to believe that
the marriage of James Stewart and Joan Beaufort may indeed have
been founded in the King's desire and love of his wife. Doubts as
to James's authorship have been raised, for no good reason. Kings
may be poets, even talented ones. At least two of James's descendants, Mary, Queen of Scots and her son James VI, wrote verse of
some merit.

A royal marriage may be a love match, as the poem suggests,

but it can never be only that. Inevitably it has a political significance. Joan Beaufort was not only a lovely sweet-faced girl observed
by a poet as she walked in a garden. She was also a piece on the
political chessboard.

The Beauforts were royal, but dubiously so. Joan was the
granddaughter of John of Gaunt (Shakespeare's 'time-honoured
Lancaster'), the youngest son of Edward III and father of Henry
IV. But her grandmother, Catherine Swynford, had been Gaunt's
mistress before becoming his third wife in 1396, and their children were born out of wedlock. At Gaunt's request, Parliament
legitimised them in 1397, but ten years later the words '*excepta
dignitate regali*' were interpolated; so they were legitimate, but
barred from succession to the throne. Catherine had other children, legitimate ones from her first marriage to Sir Hugh Swynford,
a member of Gaunt's household. One son, Thomas Swynford, had
supported his stepbrother Henry Bolingbroke in the rebellion that
resulted in the deposition of Richard II, and was popularly thought
to be Richard's murderer.

When Henry V died, two Beaufort brothers, Henry, Bishop of
Winchester, and Thomas, Duke of Exeter, were members of the
Council of Regency for the infant Henry VI. They could see advantages in marrying their niece Joan to the King of Scots and restoring
him to his kingdom. It might be a means of breaking the Franco-
Scottish alliance and of establishing peace on the Anglo-Scottish
border, both of benefit to the war effort in France. For James, too,
the advantages of the match were obvious. It might be the only
way, as it was certainly the surest, to obtain his release from
captivity. Even so, there was little enough trust, and burdensome
conditions were attached to his restoration. Scotland was to be
charged £40,000, ostensibly payment for the cost of keeping and
educating the King in England for eighteen years. Since he had not
been there willingly, this might more exactly have been called a
ransom. In recognition of Scotland's poverty and the shortage of
cash in the kingdom, the money was to be paid in four annual
instalments, and twenty-one young Scots of noble birth were to be
sent to England as hostages, surety for the debt. However, with

rare generosity, the Beauforts consented to remit one-sixth of the sum – this to be regarded as their niece's dowry, a bargain for them since it cost them nothing. Not surprisingly, payments were delayed: in the course of James's reign, seventy-two young Scots were to serve time as hostages. He would find this useful, a means of ridding himself for a time of troublemakers and also of keeping their families in line.

It says something for the attachment of the Scottish political class to the concept of their rightful king that, as with David II, there was no usurpation of the throne in the eighteen years of James's captivity, and that the burden of the ransom was assumed, apparently willingly. And this is the more remarkable because there was no shortage of men with a claim to the crown, not only Albany (father and son), but also the descendants of Robert II's second marriage, whose claim was all the stronger, to their mind at least, because of the doubts surrounding the legitimacy of the offspring of the old King's first marriage to Elizabeth Mure. Nevertheless, there seems to have been no attempt to set James aside.

James is the first Stewart of whose character it is possible to form a fair estimate. This is principally because he was far more active than his father and grandfather, more determined to establish his authority, and not particularly scrupulous as to the means of doing so. Yet though many would come to loathe him as a tyrant, his concept of his royal role was laudable, even idealistic. He is said to have announced his determination that 'If God give me life, though it be but the life of a dog, then throughout all Scotland, with His help, will I make the key keep the castle and the bracken bush the cow.' In other words, the rule of law was to prevail, due process superseding arbitrary violence. Within seven weeks of his return north, he summoned a parliament and had it declare that 'ferme and sikkir pece be keepit and haldin throu all the realme'. His sense of the necessity of justice seems to have been sincere – at least where his own immediate interest was not concerned; he even appointed an advocate who was to act in the courts on behalf of poor litigants. It is not perhaps too fanciful to suggest that his English education and his reading of Chaucer and

Langland may have given him some sympathy for the common people, whether they were landless peasants, tenant farmers or townsfolk.

Or maybe it is, for England had taught him a harsher lesson too: that the king's authority must not be challenged by unruly barons if the country was to enjoy security and prosperity. He had observed the ruthless speed with which his friend Henry V had condemned three noblemen – Richard, Earl of Cambridge, Lord Scrope of Masham and Sir Thomas Grey of Northumberland – to death for alleged conspiracy with France; and he would be quick to imitate him.

Even before he was crowned at Scone in May 1424, James arrested Walter Stewart, a son of his cousin Albany, and two other noblemen, on an unknown charge. Stewart was imprisoned on the Bass Rock, where as a boy James had waited for the ship that was to carry him to France. A few weeks later he instituted inquiries into the legal titles to estates that had formerly belonged to the Crown, and arrested Albany's father-in-law, the Earl of Lennox, and Sir Robert Graham, a connection of the descendants of Euphemia Ross, Robert II's second wife, whose marriage had been undeniably lawful. He then moved against Albany himself. imprisoning him along with his youngest son, Alexander, and seizing his castles – Falkland, where the Duke of Rothesay had been murdered, and Doune in Perthshire. The speed and certainty with which he acted suggests he was carrying out plans long brooded on in his years of exile.

Alarm spread among the nobility. Here was a king with a strength of will such as Scotland had not known for a long time. James Stewart, the only one of Albany's sons still at liberty, took up the challenge. He raised a rebellion in the west, burned Dumbarton and killed the governor of its castle, an old Stewart who was the King's uncle or perhaps great-uncle. James responded quickly and effectively. The rebellion was snuffed out. James Stewart and his ally, the Bishop of Argyll, fled to Ireland. Failure though it was, the rising had sealed the fate of the prisoners. They were tried by an assize of nobles in the presence of the King, and condemned to death. Some may have been horrified, few surprised. Walter Stewart, brought from the Bass Rock, was the first to be executed, in the forecourt of Stirling Castle. The next day his father Albany, brother Alexander and the aged Earl of Lennox followed him to the block. The King took possession of their estates, and the Crown was thereby enriched by the revenues of the earldoms of Fife, Menteith and Lennox. James then dispatched Malise Graham, nephew of Robert Graham and great-grandson of Robert II and Euphemia Ross, to England as one of the hostages for the security of his still unpaid ransom. In a few weeks he had made himself more thoroughly master of Scotland than any king since Robert the Bruce. In doing so, he had cut a swathe through the Stewart cousinship and eliminated a number of possible rivals. There was a price to be paid: the King was now feared but also hated.

Previous Scottish kings had mostly been content to select wives and husbands for their children from the ranks of the native nobility. The Stewarts themselves owed their throne to such a marriage. James, perhaps on account of the troubles he had endured and the dangers he had run at the hands of his Stewart cousins, had different ideas. He himself had married into the English royal family; his children should also marry out of Scotland. This would elevate their consequence and the King's also. It would mark him out as being more than 'the first among equals' and leave fewer of the Scots nobility with a claim to the throne. So his eldest daughter Margaret was married – at the age of twelve – to the heir to the French throne, the future Louis XI, a man whose contradictions of character have fascinated and disgusted contemporaries and future historians alike, and are memorably brought to life in the best of Scott's medieval novels, *Quentin Durward*.[1] Margaret, however, did not live to be his queen. She died at the age of twenty, of what one French historian called '*une maladie de langueur*', murmuring '*Fi de la vie de ce monde, et ne m'en parlez plus, et plus qu'autre chose m'ennuie.*'[2] Later Stewarts might fall into melancholy and depression, but Margaret is the only one recorded as dying of boredom.

Her sisters were married to other European nobles – the Duke of Brittany and an Austrian duke among them. There was a single exception. One daughter, Joan, was married to the Douglas Earl of Morton. But it so happened that she had been born deaf and dumb, and so could not be regarded as an asset in the royal marriage market.

James was active, enquiring and energetic. He sought to reform the machinery of the law, commanding, for instance, that no one should come to any court with a band of retainers (who would inevitably be armed). He created a new civil court, which more than a century later would re-emerge as the Court of Session, still the highest civil court in Scotland. He tried to secure the independence of the Scots Church by forbidding churchmen to go to Rome to lobby for benefices in Scotland. At the same time he imitated his mentor Henry V by taking a strictly orthodox line on heresy; at least one heretic was burned in his reign, only the second known to have suffered such punishment in Scotland. He supported the new university of St Andrews, founded by his old tutor Bishop Wordlow, although at one stage he suggested that it should be moved to Perth. St Andrews was remote, at the extremity of Fife, a county cut off to both north and south by the Firths of Tay and Forth and at the same time exposed to attack from the sea. However, he relented, and displayed his approval of the university by attending lectures there himself. James was Scotland's first Renaissance prince, a patron of learning and culture, a stern judge, vigorous ruler, and practitioner of cruelty.

He had an affection for Perth and may even have considered establishing his capital there. It had advantages over Edinburgh, the future capital city. It was in the centre of the kingdom, on the fringe of the Highlands, and was further from the English border and less open to attack. Fixing the capital there might have helped bring together the two Scotlands – the Gaelic-speaking north and Scots-speaking south.

In contrast to his predecessors, who had perforce left barons to act as petty kings in their locality so long as they did not engage in active rebellion, James was determined to establish royal authority throughout the kingdom, even in the Highlands, where obedience to the Crown was an unfamiliar concept. He impressed its advisability on the clan chiefs by leading an army to Inverness, arresting several, beheading two and hanging another. Among those held prisoner were Alexander, Lord of the Isles,[3] and his mother, the Countess of Ross. On their eventual release, Alexander was brought to the King's court, ostensibly to learn manners – in itself an offensive proposition – but principally that he might be kept under surveillance. He disliked what he found there; the southern lords made his dress and accent subject for mockery. He soon escaped and demonstrated his independence of spirit and action by gathering an army and burning Inverness. James could not tolerate such defiance, and marched north to Lochaber in the summer of 1431. Alexander now found the clans that had joined him unwilling to fight against the King in person; the lesson of James's last puni-tive venture north was too recent to be forgotten. So he surrendered and was this time compelled to make his submission public in humili-ating fashion. He was led, in the guise of a penitent, stripped to his shirt and drawers, into the abbey church at Holyrood, where he was required to present his sword to the King before the high altar. This done, the Queen fell to her knees and implored James to spare the young man's life. He graciously consented. It was an impressive theatrical performance. But it could not be said that James had paci-fied the Highlands. He would not be the last king to learn that any success gained there was only temporary.

The two Roberts, content or obliged by their weakness to receive honour rather than obedience, and to leave the nobility to their own devices, had died in their beds. James, far more active in asserting what he conceived to be the rights of the Crown, bore hard on the interest of the nobility. They resented his attempts to extend his power and also his greed for money. Significantly, the bitterest among them were to be found in what remained of the extensive Stewart cousinhood, which had suffered at his hands and feared there might be worse to come.

A conspiracy was formed. Its guiding spirit was Sir Robert Graham, who had been imprisoned by James a dozen years previ-ously. Having escaped, he denounced the King, not without reason, as a tyrant. There were other candidates for the throne if James could be removed: Graham's nephew Malise was still held in England as a hostage at the King's request, but his claim might be thought inferior to that of Walter, Earl of Atholl, the youngest and last legitimate survivor of Robert II's numerous brood. Atholl had been on good enough terms with his nephew the King, but now, though around seventy years old, was persuaded to join the conspiracy, perhaps with the promise of the crown. He may have been influenced by his grandson, Sir Robert Stewart, whose own ambitions extended to the throne. This Stewart was also the King's domestic chamberlain and as such a key figure in the plot.

The King had passed Christmas of 1436 at the Dominican abbey in Perth. The building, which no longer exists, stood on the northern edge of the town, beyond the burgh walls, and was protected by a ditch, originally perhaps the moat of the old wooden castle destroyed in a flood some two hundred years previously. Legend has it that James was warned of danger by an old woman with second sight as he journeyed to the town; but such legends are often the creation of chroniclers or ballad-makers eager to make more dramatic a story that is already strong enough. Since James was a hero to Stewart chroniclers, this wise woman may have been introduced into their story in imitation of the soothsayer Artemidorus who warned Julius Caesar to beware the Ides of March. If, however, there was such a warning, James paid no attention to it.

He remained as a guest of the Black Friars for some weeks – January and February were not inviting months to travel in medieval Scotland. No doubt he conducted business there; he also played tennis energetically, perhaps in an effort to reduce his weight[4] – an ambassador from Rome, Aeneas Silvius Piccolomini (later Pope Pius II), had described him a few years before as 'oppressed by his excessive corpulence'.[5] Irritated by losing tennis balls down a drain that ran from the abbey cellars, the King ordered it to be blocked up. The command would cost him his life.

On the evening of 20 February, the chamberlain Sir Robert Stewart had word from his fellow conspirators that all was ready. He dismissed the guards on some pretext and drew back the bolts on the outer door of the abbey. Under cover of darkness the assassins laid planks across the old moat and crept up to the door. Towards midnight they made their entry unchallenged and approached the chamber where the King was playing chess. Later legend has it that the bolts from that door too had been removed and that one of the Queen's ladies, Catherine Douglas, thrust her arm through the staples on the door frame to check the murderers and give the King time to escape.[6]

Early versions of the story tell of how James, alarmed by the sound of his enemies' approach, tore up some of the floorboards and hid in the vault below, from which ran the drain he had ordered to be stopped. For a little while it seemed that he might escape. The conspirators searched the Queen's apartments and were apparently ready to retire baffled. James then emerged, too soon, from his hiding place, for his enemies returned to find him climbing back into the room. He was in his nightgown and unarmed; yet struggled bravely before being overpowered and dispatched with – accounts vary – either sixteen or twenty-eight dagger wounds. He was buried in the Charterhouse of Perth, which he had recently given the monks of the Carthusian order licence to establish. His heart was removed and taken on a pilgrimage to the Holy Land, and then brought back to Scotland by a knight of the Order of St John. This was a piece of theatrical symbolism, linking the murdered monarch to his great-grandfather, the hero-king Robert the Bruce, whose heart had been carried by Sir James Douglas on crusade against the Moors in Spain.

Told baldly, the story of the murder, drawn from accounts written decades later, is unconvincing, scarcely credible in detail. If James found time to tear up the floorboards, wouldn't he also have had time to seize sword and shield or summon help – not all his retainers or members of his household can have been in on the plot – even put on armour? It seems probable that the version we have is that authorised by his widow, Queen Joan, and that it was framed, or spun, so as to emphasise the wicked treachery of the assassins and the heroism of the King, thus deepening the pathos. The nineteenth-century historian Andrew Lang, who called James 'the ablest and not the most scrupulous of the Stewarts', hints at this: 'the dramatic story of his death had won him a sympathy which his aims deserve better than his methods'.This judgement may be too harsh. Certainly when the citizens of Perth learned of the murder, they hurried to the abbey calling for vengeance. The conspirators, alarmed by this incursion, took flight and made for the hills.

James had been harsh, cruel, overbearing, careless of what his nobles considered to be their rights. He had failed to practise the necessary art of conciliation, had made his determination to exercise his authority to the full all too obvious, and in doing so had rendered his nobles insecure. Yet this was only a murder, not a *coup d'état*, for the conspirators had made no provision to seize power. Perhaps they expected that the murder would be popular. If so, they were mistaken. Within a month, James's six-year-old son was crowned king. Only the decision to hold the ceremony at Holyrood, so much further from the Highland Line and from the estates of some of the conspirators than Scone, traditional crowning-place of Scottish kings, suggests that there was any apprehension about the future of the dynasty.

The murderers were soon rounded up and dealt with. They were first tortured, as an act of revenge, but also in an attempt to discover how widespread the conspiracy had been, and then executed. Sir Robert Graham, the instigator of the murder, defended his action vigorously, declaring that he had renounced his allegiance to King James and was thereby entitled to slay him. His memory would, he said, be honoured as a tyrannicide. But he deceived himself. A popular rhyme expressed the general opinion: 'Robert Graham, / That slew our king, / God Grant him shame!' The aged Earl of Atholl protested his innocence; in vain. It was impossible to believe that he was not privy to the conspiracy, even if he took no part in the actual murder. In fact he admitted that his son, Sir Robert Stewart, had told him of the plot, but pathetically maintained that he had tried to dissuade him. In the belief that the old man had been the designated successor, a crown of red-hot iron was placed on his head. By her swift severity, inspired perhaps by grief for the husband who had celebrated her beauty in his verse, Queen Joan, the regent, not only assured her son's succession; she all but completed the destruction of the Stewart cousinship that her husband had begun with the execution of Albany and his sons thirteen years before. Only Malise Graham, Earl of Strathearn, survived in the male line of descent from Robert II and Euphemia Ross, but he was still a prisoner-hostage in England, and Queen Joan could rely on her Beaufort relations to see that he remained there.

Chapter 5

James II (1437–60):
A Quick-Tempered King

J ames II was known as 'James of the Fiery Face', on account
of a disfiguring birthmark. This was sufficiently well known
to be remarked on by François Villon, poet and criminal, who
wrote of:

> . . . le roy Scotiste
> Qui demy face ot, ce dit on,
> Vermeille comme une amatiste
> Depuis le front jusqu'au menton.

[The Scottish king whose half face, it is said, was bright red like
an amethyst from forehead to chin.]

The mark is evident in a portrait, probably the first authentic like-
ness of a Scottish king, a drawing on vellum made a couple of
years before his death.

James being only six when his father was murdered, Scotland
was condemned to endure a long minority. The chronicler Robert
Lindsay of Pitscottie,[1] writing a hundred years later, expressed what
was no doubt the common opinion: 'so lang as the king is young,
great men reignis at their awin libertie'. If medieval kings were
always likely to find their authority challenged or defied by the
'over-mighty subject', this danger was all the more acute when
the king was a minor. Moreover, no regent or lieutenant-general

of the country could be confident of exercising the royal powers unless he secured possession of the young king's person. Nevertheless, throughout these minorities, the Scottish political class recognised 'the fundamental importance of maintaining the authority of the monarchy'.[2]

The politics of the second James's minority are especially confused. Gordon Donaldson wrote, 'the evidence at the historian's disposal can hardly be called ample. And there are many points where it leaves us at a loss, unable to determine the precise course of events and the reason why things happened as they did. But even if this was not so, the shifting loyalties and alliance and the certainly important acts of men who are little more than names might well leave us perplexed.'[3]

A struggle for control of the King's person inevitably dominated these early years. His mother, Queen Joan, had acted quickly and effectively to ensure his succession and coronation and to avenge her husband's murder, but whatever her abilities, it was generally understood that a woman was incompetent to rule without male assistance. She was therefore first associated in government with Archibald, fifth Earl of Douglas, who was appointed lieutenant-general of the kingdom. But Douglas died in 1439, and Joan then made the mistake of marrying again. The mistake lay less in the fact of remarriage, for that was expected of widows, than in her choice of husband. Sir James Stewart, a distant royal cousin known as 'the Black Knight of Lorne', was a wild and ambitious man with an unsavoury reputation.

Even before this marriage, Joan had lost possession of her son, entrusted by the Council to Sir William Crichton, governor of Edinburgh Castle. Crichton was no great nobleman, but he had been trusted by James I, who had employed him on diplomatic missions and made him a member of his Privy Council, master of his household and chancellor. He has been described as 'an enigmatic figure', but this may mean no more than that little is known about him. He may have thought Joan's English connections dangerous; it is impossible to tell. However, during Crichton's absence on other business, the Queen, along with her new husband, found supporters willing to smuggle the boy king out of Edinburgh Castle, and sailed with the young monarch up the Forth to Stirling Castle. Its governor, Sir Alexander Livingstone, a minor baron from the Lothians, had been another of her first husband's trusted servants, serving for instance on the court that tried the Duke of Albany and his sons and found them guilty of treason. However, either on account of Joan's second marriage, or for some other reason, he too turned against the Queen, and arrested her along with her new husband and his brother, who were both imprisoned. In order to free them, Joan had to surrender custody of her son and was thenceforth forbidden to speak to him alone.

This was the end of Queen Joan as a political force, though she lived another six years and bore her second husband three sons, all of whom would play a part in future reigns. For the moment, the combination of Crichton and Livingstone ruled; Livingstone's extensive family were rewarded with lands and official posts. The pair could not, however, consider themselves secure. The curtain now rose on the central drama of the reign: conflict between the Crown and the House of Douglas.

The Douglases were the dominant family across the Scottish Borders while also holding estates in other parts of the kingdom. There were two branches, the Black Douglases, who held the earldom of Douglas, and the Red Douglases, earls of Angus. Both were descended from Robert the Bruce's general Sir James Douglas (sometimes called 'the Good Lord James'), to whose exploits in the War of Independence the family owed its rise; the Blacks from one of his illegitimate sons, the Reds from a son, also illegitimate, of James, the second Earl of Douglas, killed in the victorious Battle of Otterburn in 1388 and commemorated in a ballad:

> O I hae dreamed a dreary dream,
> Ayont the Isle of Skye;
> I saw a dead man win a fight,
> And I dreamed that man was I.

Since then, the power and reputation of the Black Douglases had grown steadily. The fourth earl had commanded the Scots army that fought against the English in France and had been rewarded with the duchy of Touraine. Moreover, he had married Margaret, daughter of Robert III, while his son Archibald had married Euphemia of Strathearn, herself descended from Robert II's second and unquestionably lawful marriage. Accordingly, Archibald's son, the sixth earl, William, a boy still in his teens, was close to the succession to the throne, should anything befall James; and his claim was all the stronger since he was in the line of inheritance from both wives of the first Stewart king

The young William was attractive and high-spirited, with a touch of arrogance. Not surprising; within the extensive Douglas lands he rode at the head of a thousand horsemen, and his vassals looked to him rather than to the King. Indeed, just as their English rivals, and sometimes allies, the Percys were known as 'the kings of the North', so too in Scotland the Douglases were kings of the Borderland.

To Crichton and Livingstone the young Earl represented a threat; no doubt, they might argue, the royal authority was also challenged and menaced by his power. Certainly, as an adult, James II would make the same judgement of the House of Douglas; but the King was not yet ten. His keepers acted to remove the threat before the Earl came to full manhood. They invited him to a meeting 'that they might confer in all amity and to some purpose concerning the grave affairs of the kingdom'. No doubt he was flattered by this apparent recognition that he was now regarded as being of an age to be consulted about matters of state policy. He accepted the invitation, and, despite the misgivings of some of his entourage, rode to Edinburgh, taking with him his younger brother David. For a fortnight they were guests in the castle, and James was delighted by his new friends. According to one account, he said they would be to him as their ancestor the good Lord James had been to his forefather the Bruce (from whom the Douglas boys were also of course descended). But Crichton and Livingstone had other plans, and what followed became one of the darkest and grimmest of Scottish legends, to be dramatically recounted by Walter Scott:

> Of a sudden the scene began to change. At an entertainment which was served up to the Earl and his brother, the head of a black bull was placed on the table. The Douglases knew this, according to a custom which prevailed in Scotland, to be the sign of death, and leaped from the table in great dismay. But they were seized by armed men who entered the apartment. They underwent a mock trial, in which all the insolences of their ancestors were charged against them, and were condemned to immediate execution. The young King wept and implored Livingstone and Crichton to show mercy to the young noblemen, but in vain. These cruel men only reproved him for weeping at the death of those whom they called his enemies. The brothers were led out into the court of the castle, and beheaded without delay. Malcolm Fleming of Cumbernauld, a faithful adherent of their house, shared the same fate.4

The deed was long remembered in verse:

> Edinburgh Castle, towne and toure,
> God grant thou sink for sinne!
> And that even for the black dinoir
> Erl Douglas gat therein.

It was an appalling crime, murder scarcely concealed by the trappings of a cursory trial. Crichton and Livingstone might argue that the power of the Douglases threatened the Crown. It might indeed have done so, and as an adult, James II would come to that conclusion. Yet the young Earl had done little more than assert his own authority in his own lands and over his own tenants and vassals. It is probable that the two governors acted to protect their own position rather than that of the Crown. Certainly the power of the Douglases was not broken, even if the new Earl – the dead boy's uncle – a fat, lazy man known as James the Gross, did not inherit all the Douglas estates, a share going to the young sister of the murdered boys, Margaret, known as the Maid of Galloway. Fat James made no effort to avenge his nephews. It has been suggested that he may have been complicit in the crime, but perhaps he was merely happy to benefit from it. If he felt any resentment, this was soon appeased when Crichton and Livingstone arranged to have his younger son, Archibald, made Earl of Moray. In any event the Douglases were not long weakened. When James the Gross died in 1443, his son William, the eighth earl, married his cousin, the Maid of Galloway, and reunited the Douglas lands. By doing so, he was in a position to revive any Douglas claim to the throne, no matter whether the rightful king was James Stewart or Malise, Earl of Menteith, who still languished in England. Malise would live to a great age, over eighty – evidence that there was something to be said for being held in the condition of a hostage. Since he never seems to have asserted his claim to the throne, Gordon Donaldson suggests that 'it may perhaps be inferred that he was infirm either mentally or physically'.5 He may, however, simply have been content with his lot.

Throughout the 1440s, there was a truce with England (though such an agreement did not prevent skirmishes either side of the border). The English, embroiled in what was now a losing war in France, had little appetite for renewed conflict in the north, while it was a characteristic of the Stewart minorities that the struggle of various magnates to control the Crown generally precluded an active foreign policy.

The young King was growing up. When he was fourteen, in 1444, a General Council declared his minority at at end. The next year his mother, Queen Joan, died, and her husband, the Black Knight of Lorne, deprived of the protection her name and status had afforded him, decided it was prudent to withdraw to England with their three sons. It is doubtful whether James was yet in control of the government, but the prospect, generally welcome, was alarming for those in office. Crichton was dismissed as chancellor in 1445, probably with the connivance of his rival and sometime partner, Livingstone, who was meanwhile assiduously seeking to strengthen his own position by inserting his relatives in positions of power. One was chamberlain, another controller of the royal finances, a third master of the mint, and the keepers of the castles of Stirling, Dumbarton, Doune and Methven were all Livingstones. Few families had risen so far and so fast in such a short time.

Their fall would be equally swift and complete. First, though, Livingstone tried to ingratiate himself with the young King by arranging a splendid marriage for him in 1449. The bride was Mary, daughter of the Duke of Gueldres and a niece of Duke Philip the Good of Burgundy. Little is known of her character, but with Flanders then economically and culturally the richest and most developed province of northern Europe, it was a good match for the King of Scots. She brought with her a substantial dowry (60,000 crowns in cash) and the promise of commercial links with the rich cities of the Netherlands. The marriage was celebrated with some pomp in Holyrood Abbey and may have been harmonious. At any rate, it produced six children, four boys (one of whom died young) and two girls. The Stewart succession was thus secured, though the presence of royal brothers would be a threat to future domestic peace.

The same year, at the age of eighteen, James assumed full control of the government. If Livingstone had indeed looked for gratitude, he deceived himself. James acted swiftly to break him and destroy the power base he had constructed for his family. Several, including Sir Alexander himself, were arrested and put to death. No pretext was given. No doubt it was felt that none was necessary. But the fact that the Livingstones had been granted, or had granted themselves, royal castles and estates, at least two of which had been promised to the new Queen as her jointure, may have been sufficient excuse. James himself owed the comptroller one thousand pounds, a debt conveniently cancelled by the latter's execution.

The Livingstones were 'new men' with neither an extensive and influential cousinship nor great estates of their own; they were easy to deal with and dispose of. The Douglases were a different matter. In the last years of the King's minority, the eighth earl, William, had been made lieutenant-general of the kingdom. As a youth, the King had been dazzled by him. Now he saw him as a rival, reasonably enough, for across the south of Scotland it was Douglas's writ that ran, not the King's. It was Douglas, not the King, to whom the lesser nobility, barons and knights of the borderland owed their first loyalty. And Douglas was carrying on what amounted to an independent foreign policy and assuming a quasi-royal status. He held something resembling a parliament of his own and even forbade his dependants to attend the legitimate parliament when summoned by the King. In 1451 he formed an alliance, or 'bond' as it was termed, with two northern magnates, the Earl of Crawford, and John, Lord of the Isles. It looked as if he was seeking to encircle the King; perhaps he aimed at the crown himself.

One incident in particular shows his arrogance and determination to be a law unto himself. While still stopping short of open rebellion, he summoned his vassals in defiance of the royal authority. One, by name MacLellan, the tutor or guardian of the young laird of Bombie, refused to answer the summons. Douglas seized him and held him prisoner in his island castle of Threave. This MacLellan was the nephew of Sir Patrick Gray, the captain of the King's Guard, who protested to James. The King sent him to Threave with a letter in which he ordered Douglas to surrender his captive to Sir Patrick. Douglas greeted the royal messenger politely, and quoted the old proverb that it was ill to come between a hungry man and his dinner and that there was no good talking between a full man and a fasting. He invited Gray to sit and dine, after which, he said, he would read the King's letter and they could settle the matter. Meanwhile he sent orders to prepare the prisoner. When Sir Patrick had eaten, Douglas read the letter and said he would grant the King's request. He led him out into the court-yard, where the body of MacLellan lay beside the execution block. 'There is your nephew,' Douglas said, 'but you have come too late, for he wants his head.' Gray contrived to make his escape, waiting till he was safe across the drawbridge before cursing Douglas and promising revenge.[6]

That James now had good reason to distrust, even fear, Douglas is evident. Equally he had to be cautious. If it came to a trial of strength, it was by no means certain that the King would win. It might be that he retained some of the liking and admiration that as a boy he had felt for the Earl. At any rate, he decided to make a personal approach. We know little of James's character, no more than may be inferred from his actions; it is possible that he had the personal charm and magnetism that some of his descendants would display, and that he therefore believed that a meeting might resolve all differences. So he invited Douglas to come to Stirling Castle, in February 1452, and, to allay any fears he might have, provided him with a safe-conduct.

What followed is again dramatically recounted by Walter Scott:

> The King received Douglas kindly, and after some amicable expostulation with him upon his late conduct, all seemed friendship and cordiality between James and his too-powerful subject. By invitation of James, Douglas dined with him on the day following. Supper was presented at seven o'clock, and, after it was over, the King having led Douglas into another apartment, where only some of his privy council and his bodyguard were in attendance, he introduced the subject of the Earl's bond with [the Earls of] Ross and Crawford, and exhorted him to give up the engagement, as inconsistent with his allegiance and the quiet of the kingdom. Douglas declined to relinquish the treaty which he had formed. The King urged him more imperiously, and the Earl returned a haughty and positive refusal, upbraiding the King, at the same time, with maladministration of the public affairs. Then the King burst into a rage at his obstinacy, and exclaimed, 'By Heaven, my lord, if you will not break the league, this shall.' So saying, he stabbed the Earl with his dagger first in the throat, and instantly after in the lower part of the body. Sir Patrick Gray then struck the Earl on the head with a battle-axe and others of the King's retinue showed their zeal by stabbing at the dying man with their knives and daggers. He expired without uttering a word, covered with twenty-six wounds. The corpse did not receive Christian burial.

Scott concludes: 'This was a wicked and cruel action on the King's part; bad if it were done in hasty passion, and yet worse if James had meditated the possibility of this violence from the beginning.'[7]

The King has found his defenders. Eric Linklater, admitting that 'assassination is not a comely or commendable exercise of government', yet wrote that 'if it is the only way – the only possible way – to remove a manifest threat to public safety and preserve peace under legitimate authority, it may be excused, and probably should be pardoned'. In his view, James had little choice when 'faced with the naked intransigence of the most powerful of his nobles'.[8]

The Scots parliament agreed. It declared that Douglas was guilty of his own death, being a traitor and conspirator, and so absolved the King of all blame. No doubt pressure was applied to bring about this favourable verdict, and surely Douglas's friends and allies were either absent from proceedings or chose prudently to keep silent. Nevertheless, it is likely that there were many happy to see him removed.

The murder did not solve the Douglas problem, however, but instead exacerbated it. This was so probable an outcome that it is difficult to believe the crime was premeditated, even though the presence, with battleaxe ready, of Sir Patrick Gray, who had such good recent cause to wish to be avenged on Douglas, suggests otherwise. James may well have had a temper as fiery as the birth-mark on his face.

The Douglas response was immediate and dramatic. The murdered Earl was succeeded by his brother, James. In March, only a few weeks after the murder, the new Earl rode into Stirling at the head of some six hundred horsemen, and beneath the walls of the castle, the scene of the crime, dragged the King's dishon-oured safe-conduct through the streets at the tail of an old grey mare. 'This was the ritual of "diffidatio", by which a vassal formally renounced fealty to his lord.'[9] The Douglas troops then set fire to the town and it seemed as if the blaze might spread across Scotland.

The King, it is said, came close to despair, appalled by what he had done, or at least by its consequences. He even spoke of abdi-cating and withdrawing to France. But this mood was temporary, and his chancellor, Bishop Kennedy, a man revered for both virtue and learning, told him plainly that he was not entitled to abandon his kingdom. Moreover, taking a sheaf of arrows, the Bishop showed him how to defeat his enemies. Banded together, the arrows could not be broken, but each snapped easily if taken by itself. In short, in order to secure victory, the King must first divide his enemies.

So he turned first on the murdered Earl's ally Crawford in the north, and in alliance with the Gordons, a rising family in Aberdeenshire, whose head had recently been made Earl of Huntly, broke his power; Crawford's estates were forfeited, and became available as rewards for loyalty and future bribes to secure support. At the same time, by a mixture of cajolery, promises and scarcely veiled threats, James contrived to detach the other branch of the Douglas family – the Red Douglases, whose head was the Earl of Angus – from their cousins. So, with the support of Parliament, and with the north at least quiescent, he was able to turn against his chief enemy.

He had much need to do so. The Earl and his twin brother Hugh, Earl of Ormond, had formally renounced their allegiance to James, and sent a message to Henry VI of England offering to do homage to him instead. But the suddenness of the King's success against his allies caused the Earl to have second thoughts. For the moment he was prepared to forget his grievances, even forgive the King for his brother's murder. James too, conscious of his own guilt – no matter what Parliament had declared – was ready to make peace. Douglas submitted, gave up his claim to the earldom of Wigtown and promised to make amends and also to do his duty as Warden of the Marches. In return James gave him back that disputed earldom and agreed to support a request that the Pope should grant the Earl a dispensation to permit him to marry his brother's widow, Margaret of Galloway, on the grounds of non-consummation of her previous marriage. This was obtained, though it is likely that few believed that Margaret, a young woman of twenty, was still a virgin. To show his trust, James then sent Douglas to England as his commissioner to renew a truce between the two kingdoms.

His behaviour has puzzled historians, all the more so because the marriage once again reunited all the Douglas lands and gave the Earl the chance to revive, by right of his wife, the claim to the throne of Euphemia Ross's descendants. One explanation that has been offered is that James's lenient treatment of the man who only a few months before had exposed him to public humiliation when he dragged that dishonoured safe-conduct through the streets of Stirling was the result of some impulse of penitence for the murder of Douglas's brother. But it may be that he had merely misread his opponent.

Once over the border, Douglas seems to have forgotten that the King had treated him generously and resumed his intrigues. The state of England was itself disturbed, for that year, 1453, saw an English army defeated in France, at the Battle of Chatillon; and that was the end of the attempt, twice near to success, of the English kings to conquer France. Only Calais now remained in English hands, and as so often, military failure provoked political discontent. The Lancastrian government was weak and discredited, the King, Henry VI, gentle and pious, unfitted to govern. His cousin Richard, Duke of York, had ambitions to supplant him. The sporadic conflict, to be known as 'the Wars of the Roses', was imminent; it would last thirty years. Douglas, seeing an opportunity for himself, approached York and secured the release, after so many years, of the aged Malise Graham, Earl of Menteith. Either he, senior representative of the line of Euphemia Ross, or Douglas himself might replace James Stewart as King of Scots, and York would have an ally, instead of a hostile presence, on the northern frontier. At the same time Douglas sent messengers to renew his murdered brother's bond with John, Lord of the Isles. The King's clemency, it was apparent, had achieved nothing. In the spring of 1455, Douglas crossed the Solway and mustered his forces. The size of his army is unknown; one chronicler credits him with 40,000 men, an impossible figure; in reality it was surely nearer 4,000.

James acted decisively. The time for conciliation was over. Douglas had had chances enough. His power must be destroyed. The Douglas castle of Abercorn in West Lothian was besieged. It held out for a month. In earlier times it might have sustained a longer siege, but there was a new weapon of war: artillery; and it was in the King's hands. The castle was bombarded by 'a gret gun, the quhilk a Frenchemen schot richt weel'.[10] The walls were broken and the castle stormed. The balance of power had shifted. Before the advent of artillery, the advantage in any siege lay with the defenders; now it had passed to the attackers. The gun was not absolutely new. There is mention of one in Scotland as far back as 1384, but James II was the first monarch to have acquired this 'instrument called a gun', or at least the first to understand its value. It has been suggested that as part of his wife's dowry he had obtained guns made by the expert smiths of her native Flanders, and they were, in the words of Gordon Donaldson, 'a weapon to which his subjects could not reply. It is probable that the great gun, Mons Meg, still on display by the ramparts of Edinburgh Castle, was one of his acquisitions; there is a gun of similar size and design at Ghent.'[11]

Douglas may have been unnerved by the taking of Abercorn, which he might have expected to hold out for months. He must certainly have been surprised by the rapidity with which the royal army now advanced against him, through the Ettrick Forest and into the heartland of Douglas territory. One of his allies, Lord Hamilton, quickly decided the game was lost and went over to the King. The Douglas force began to melt away, and the Earl himself followed suit. He fled to England, no doubt with the intention of seeking allies who would enable him to resume the struggle, leaving his brothers meanwhile to carry on the rebellion as best they could. Their best was soon shown to be insufficient. They were defeated at Arkinholm near Langholm, by their distant cousin the Red Douglas Earl of Angus. One brother, the Earl of Moray, was killed there; another, the Earl of Ormond, was wounded and captured. His wounds were patched up to fit him for execution as a traitor. The third, Douglas of Balveny, followed the head of the house to England.

King James was not finished yet. He brought up his guns and took the castles of Douglas and Strathavon. The island fortress of Threave in Kirkcudbrightshire held out for a few weeks before it too fell. It was a signal triumph for the Crown. The fugitive Earl languished in England, a pensioner, 'until', a citation reads, 'he is restored to his heritage, taken from him by him who calls himself

King of Scots'.[12] He would make intermittent trouble for years to come, but he was no more than an irritant. The Douglas power was broken and could not be repaired. James had displayed judgement and ability, and was now more securely master of his kingdom than any monarch since Robert the Bruce himself. The destruction of the Douglases in the spring and summer of 1455 entitles him to be regarded as among the most able of the House of Stewart.

The full extent of his mastery was soon made apparent. The Estates or Parliament, summoned to Edinburgh that August, condemned 'James unquhill Erle of Douglas', his mother and surviving brother as traitors, and declared that any correspondence with them was itself to be regarded as treason. Their estates were forfeited to the Crown, and the Estates declared that 'as the pouertee of the crowne is oftymes the cause of the pouerte of the realme and mony uthir inconvenientis', these lands and castles were to be inalienable Crown property. Since the main source of wealth was then land, this greatly enriched the Crown and for the first time raised the King high above his nobility, as being now by far the greatest landowner in the country. Moreover, the Estates granted him the customs duties for life. There were other enactments in this remarkable session. The office of Warden of the Marches, held by the earls of Douglas for generations now, was no longer to be hereditary, but a royal appointment. The rights of the nobility to private jurisdiction were restricted, and it was decreed that no new 'regalities' were to be created except with the consent of the Estates. All grants of heritable offices made since the accession of James I were revoked.

Though this was all done through the Estates, it is clear that these acts reflected the will of the King and his determination to consolidate by law what he had gained by war. He was aiming to strengthen central government at the expense of the localities, and to move away from the 'laissez-faire Stewart monarchy' towards the ideal of the Renaissance prince, no longer first among equals, but set above his nobility. There should be no surprise if this was so. It was the fashion of the age. His sometime brother-in-law, Louis XI, was pursuing the same policy in France; the Yorkist and

Tudor kings would do likewise in England. But James had the good sense to see that he could best achieve his aim by associating the Estates, which represented the solid interest of the Church, the lesser barons and burgesses, with him. Peace, order, the rule of law, and prosperity, all of which had been threatened or disturbed by the ambitions of the Douglases and other unruly lords, were in the general interest – as the pronouncements of his parliament made evident.

All rebels and disturbers of the peace had been removed, 'no masterful party remaining', and the King was requested to execute the laws passed by the parliament – unnecessarily, one may think, since he had in all probability inspired them – so 'that God may be empleased of him, and all his lieges may pray for him to God and give thanks to Him that sends them such a prince to be their governor and defender'.[13] The flattery may well have been sincere. No King of Scots had stood so high in the esteem of his subjects; none had enjoyed such mastery of the kingdom. The way towards an increasingly autocratic monarchy, on the French or English model, was open.

James was not to live long to enjoy his triumph and establish such a style of kingship. In the late summer of 1460, taking advantage of the unsettled state of England, where the Lancastrian king had been taken prisoner by his Yorkist rivals, he took the opportunity to try to recapture Roxburgh Castle, which had been in the hands of the English for generations. On 3 August, as he stood admiring the firing of one of his great guns, of the type known as bombards, one of the wedges used to tighten the iron bands round the barrel broke loose, flew through the air and, striking the King in the face, killed him. He was not yet thirty, and Scotland was faced with another minority.

Chapter 6

James III (1460–88): A Study in Failure

"**M**y God, sire!" exclaimed Sir Richard, clasping his hands together in impatience; "of what great and inexpiable crime can your Majesty's ancestors have been guilty, that they have been punished by the infliction of judicial blindness on their whole generation.""

This outburst by a loyal Jacobite is directed at the Prince, Charles Edward, in Scott's novel *Redgauntlet*,[1] which features a last – in this case purely fictional – attempt to restore the exiled Stuarts almost twenty years after the cause went down in April 1746 on Culloden Moor, the last pitched battle fought on British soil. It expresses the view, commonly held, romantically inspired, of the Stuarts as doomed to failure and defeat on account of their own obstinacy, 'punished by the infliction of judicial blindness' – that is, by an inability to see the true nature of a case. To many, James III is the first of the line who seems to fit that pattern.

James has been called 'the most enigmatic of the Stewart kings',[2] and the judgement is a fair one, even if a fuller knowledge of his predecessors might reveal them as equally puzzling. We know rather more about James's character, and we have an authentic portrait of him, painted by a Dutchman, Hugo van der Goes, for the Church of the Holy Trinity in Edinburgh, founded in 1462 by the young King's mother, Mary of Gueldres. There is always a temptation to read more into a portrait than is reasonable, but this image suggests a serious and sensitive, possibly troubled, young man. He was perhaps eighteen when it was painted.

Only nine when his father died, the boy king was first entrusted, as was proper, to his mother, who acted as regent in association with Bishop Kennedy. But Mary died in 1363 and Kennedy two years later. Power was then seized by the governor of Edinburgh Castle, Sir Alexander Boyd, a member of an Ayrshire family of no great previous distinction. Boyd and his allies, who included one Hepburn of Hailes, an ancestor of Mary, Queen of Scots' third husband, Bothwell, swooped on the young King at Linlithgow, forced him to mount a horse, and carried him off to Edinburgh, as their prisoner in all but name. Soon afterwards Boyd persuaded or compelled James to issue him with a pardon for what might have been construed as an act of treason. James would not be the last of his family to be rendered suspicious of his nobility by the rough treatment and lack of respect he received at their hands when still a boy.

In 1469, at the age of eighteen, he was married. His bride was Margaret of Denmark, and this marriage completed the kingdom of Scotland, for the islands of Orkney and Shetland were pledged in lieu of a promised dowry and, the dowry never being paid, passed to the Scottish Crown. Margaret was reputed devout, so much so that after her death there was a move to have her canonised, but we know nothing of her relations with James, beyond the fact that they had three children and that he is not recorded as having any illegitimate ones. So the marriage may have been happy. A few of the Stewarts were faithful husbands, even uxorious, though most of them were not.

James was capable of decisive action. Soon after his marriage he disposed of the Boyds. Sir Alexander, despite the pardon he had extracted in 1465, was accused of treason and beheaded, while his brother and nephew found their estates forfeited to the Crown. Sir Alexander's son, Thomas, who had been created Earl of Arran and married to the King's eldest sister, Margaret, escaped to the Continent, where he entered the service of the Duke of Burgundy, who later sent him to England as his ambassador. But if on occasion decisive, James was scarcely persistent, and his attention to the business of government was at best intermittent.

Unlike his vigorous father, he had little enthusiasm for war or for an energetic foreign policy. He was eager to be at peace with England, and was soon criticised for 'the inbringing of Englishmen and to the perpetual subjection of this realm'. This was an easy charge to bring, and a hypocritical one, for his critics did not scruple to seek aid from England themselves when it suited them.

James was easily diverted from the business of government. His interests were primarily artistic and intellectual. His tutor – later secretary – Archibald Whitelaw, who had taught at the University of Cologne, was a scholar and collector of manuscripts and an enthusiast for Roman antiquities, and it is reasonable to suppose that he helped form James's taste. In 1467 James himself commissioned the production of a copy of Mandeville's *Travels*, and possibly also a copy of *The Aeneid* now in Edinburgh University Library.

Two other associates were William Scheves and John Ireland, notable scholars, who greatly disliked each other. Scheves, a graduate of St Andrews, entered the royal household as the King's physician, and within a few years was made Archbishop of St Andrews. He too was a bibliophile, collecting medical books and Scottish chronicles. His learning and interest in science aroused suspicion; sixteenth-century chroniclers would accuse him of gaining influence over the King by his mastery of the occult, a suspicion probably baseless but generated by James's keen interest in astrology. Ireland, educated at the Sorbonne and later a teacher at the College of Navarre, had served Louis XI of France before returning to Scotland, where he became the King's confessor and a member of his council. The presence at court of men like Whitelaw, Scheves and Ireland demonstrates a stirring of intellectual activity, encouraged by the King and reflecting his temperament and tastes.

Despite later criticism, association with such men did no harm to the King's reputation among contemporaries. They were churchmen and scholars, regarded as suitable royal advisers. If the nobility weren't all illiterate, few among them were competent to draw up bills to be presented to Parliament or to engage in diplomatic correspondence with foreign states. The King needed clerks, and only the Church could supply them. He needed advisers as comfortable with the written as the spoken word, and again these were to be found only among ecclesiastics.

It was, however, a different matter when the King chose to consort with social inferiors rather than members of the nobility; still worse if he was believed to be guided by their advice. And this was the case with James III. Most kings have had favourites, those with whom they feel at ease and pass their hours of leisure, but to nobles quick to take offence it seemed scandalous that the King should prefer the company of 'masons and fiddlers'.

The mason in this instance was one Robert Cochrane, certainly close to the King, but probably an architect rather than the mere stonemason as which he was disparaged. James was the first of the Stewart kings to evince an interest in building, which accounts for his patronage of Cochrane, even if the claim that he was responsible for the Great Hall of Stirling Castle is not supported by evidence. But James did commission work at the castle and also at Linlithgow, and promoted the building of collegiate churches, and it is reasonable to suppose that Cochrane had a hand in this. The 'fiddler' was William Rogers – not only a social inferior, but an Englishman. Rogers was in all probability an accomplished musician, and James had sufficient interest in music to have sent a favoured lute-player overseas to further his musical education, and to have presented an organ to the collegiate Church of the Holy Trinity, his mother's foundation in Edinburgh. (These collegiate churches, a recent development, specialised in enriching divine service with choral and instrumental musical accompaniments.) A later, more civil, age would have found nothing reprehensible in such royal patronage of a distinguished musician.

Among the other favourites were Torphichen, a fencing master, Hommyl, described as a tailor, and Leonard, said to be a shoemaker. Again it is likely that the descriptions handed down to us were wilfully derogatory. James was also a patron of poets, among them Robert Henryson from Dunfermline, one of the most accomplished and sophisticated of the so-called 'Scottish Chaucerians'. The names of other poets, whose work has not survived but who were subsequently listed by William Dunbar in his poem 'Timor Mortis Conturbat Me', appear in the treasurer's accounts as recipients of royal pensions. All this suggests that James III's interests were wider than those of most of the nobility, and that the King was something of an aesthete and intellectual, one, moreover, if the association with William Scheves is anything to go by, who dabbled in science. This may render him interesting and even admirable. It didn't in the circumstances of his age equip him to be a successful monarch.

He was unfortunate in another respect; he had brothers of mature years: Alexander, Duke of Albany, and John, Earl of Mar. Albany at least was ambitious, and, as time would show, unscrupulous. Of Mar's character nothing is known, but he does seem to have enjoyed some popularity, which suggests that he may have had an ease of manner and a degree of charm. Both excelled in the manly exercises of hunting, hawking and competing in tournaments, for which the King had little taste, and both were jealous of James's 'favourites', especially if they believed that he preferred their company and advice; likewise the favourites had little love for the royal brothers.

Albany held the office of Warden of the Eastern March and was also governor of Berwick. In this capacity he fell out with some of the Border lords, the Homes and the Hepburns, who were quick to accuse him of treasonable correspondence with England. According to one tale, they persuaded Cochrane to use his influence with the King to destroy Albany. Cochrane, the story goes, then produced an astrologer who declared that a lion would be devoured by its own whelps, the meaning of which was that the King would be killed by members of his own family. The story, it must be said, has every indication of being a later invention.[3]

The King was persuaded. Albany and Mar were arrested, the former charged with treasonable communication with England, the latter with having employed witchcraft against the King. Albany may well have been guilty; certainly his subsequent conduct makes the accusation credible. As for Mar, there is no evidence one way or the other.

Mar died in prison, and there were some ready to hold that he had been murdered by order of the King. There are different versions of the supposed murder. According to one account, the Earl was smothered in his bath; according to another, he slowly bled to death. Equally he may have died of natural causes, and James may have been innocent of any crime. Foolishly, however, he gave some credibility to the rumour by granting Cochrane the revenues from the dead man's earldom and perhaps – accounts vary – the title of Earl of Mar also.

Albany was held in Edinburgh Castle and contrived a dramatic escape. Friends sent him two casks of wine and, concealed in them, a coil of rope, and a letter warning him to act quickly, for the date of his execution had been set. The Duke, who shared lodgings with one of his retainers, invited the governor to dine with him. The governor accepted the invitation and brought a couple of his officers with him. They were settled by the fire and the wine flowed freely, until at last governor and officers were either incapably drunk or asleep. Whereupon Albany and his colleague seized their daggers, murdered them and threw their bodies on the fire. They then unwound the rope to make their escape. The retainer went first, found the rope too short, fell and broke his leg. Albany lengthened the rope with the sheets from his bed, made his descent, and, carrying his comrade on his shoulders, headed for Leith and a waiting ship, which carried him to France.

It is probable that the tale has gained in the telling, but it was quickly disseminated, and may have served the purpose of making Albany appear a bold, even heroic, figure.

It was not long before he was ready to make trouble again. Finding Louis XI of France unwilling to help him (though he did provide him with a noble wife), he crossed over to England and came to an agreement with Edward IV.

In the letter of this agreement, Albany, styling himself 'Alexander R', swore to do homage to the English king for 'my realm of Scotland', to break the old alliance with France, and to hand over

Berwick to England. The next day, either thinking he had not gone far enough to secure Edward's goodwill, or perhaps compelled by the English king, he added much of southern Scotland – Liddesdale, Eskdale, Annandale and Lochmaben – to the gift of Berwick. He also promised to marry Edward's daughter Cecily (who happened to be engaged to his brother James's heir) as soon as he could 'clear himself from all other women'.

This was a remarkable document.

In 1482, at the head of an English army reinforced by dissident Scots, among them the long-exiled Earl of Douglas, Albany invaded Scotland. James, despite his wish for friendship with England, had no choice but to assemble an army to meet the invaders. He did so with difficulty, for many of his nobles were disaffected. They distrusted the King, and resented the influence of his 'low-born' favourites. A particular grievance was a recent devaluation of the coinage, brass and other base metals being mixed with silver to make coins that were supposed to retain their original value. This was held to be the work of the detested Cochrane, and had rendered the King as unpopular with merchants and craftsmen as he already was with the nobility. His critics took advantage of the opportunity and confronted James with an ultimatum: he must dismiss his favourites and restore the value of the coinage, or he could confront his rebel brother without their assistance. Showing characteristic Stewart obstinacy, James refused to meet their demands. They acted promptly, seized a number of his favourites, Cochrane among them, and hanged them in a row from the high bridge at Lauder, where the King had assembled his army. Only one, a sixteen-year-old boy, John Ramsay of Balmain, was spared. The King had begged for his life, but the unusual clemency was more likely prompted by the realisation that young Ramsay was both a Scot and well born.

According to a story that became popular in legend, but that may have a kernel of truth, the dissident nobles, while eager to lynch the King's favourites, nevertheless suffered from cold feet, none daring to make the first move. They therefore found themselves in the position of the mice in the fable resolved to hang a bell round the cat's neck so that they might be warned of his approach, but each reluctant to undertake the dangerous duty. The matter was settled only when the Red Douglas Earl of Angus stepped forward to declare that he would 'bell the cat'. At this moment Cochrane swaggered into the chamber in all his finery, and was seized upon by Angus. The story deserves this much credence: that posterity remembered Angus by the nickname 'Bell-the-Cat'.4

Having disposed of the favourites, the rebel lords then made peace with Albany. The discredited King was kept under house arrest in Edinburgh Castle and Albany was named lieutenant of the kingdom of Scotland. His new appointment did not prevent him from continuing to assure Edward IV of England that he stood by the treaty he had made. However, his ascendancy did not last long, either on account of his incapacity or because rumours of his relations with the English king were circulating and undermining his position. Meanwhile James was cultivating the moderates among his critics and promising to amend his ways. A rightful king who acted in a conciliatory fashion could usually regain ground, such was the innate respect for the authority of the Crown, if not for the individual who wore it. In 1483 Albany resigned, or, more probably, was compelled to resign his lieutenancy, and returned to England. The death of his patron Edward in the same year further weakened his position, and Parliament, prompted by the King, obediently declared his estates forfeit to the Crown. It was perhaps in desperation that Albany led another, largely English, army north a few months later. This time the King's army came to battle and won the victory. Albany's ally, the aged Earl of Douglas, was taken prisoner, but permitted to retire to a monastery, so that, after thirty years of exile, the last of the Black Douglases ended his turbulent career in the odour of piety. Albany himself fled to France, where he was killed in a skirmish a year later: a squalid end to a futile life.

James had seen off his brother, but his position was not secure, though he may have supposed it now was. He acted vigorously rather than wisely. He continued to neglect the nobles, who regarded themselves as his proper councillors, while at the same time threatening their interests. In 1487 he proposed to annex half the revenues of the Benedictine monastery of Coldingham in order to attach them to his own Chapel Royal. His motive may have been admirable. James was personally devout, interested in new developments in the Church, notably the collegiate chapels and their offering of a more refined and spiritual form of worship. The monasteries on the other hand were regarded by some as institutions that no longer served the religious needs of the time. James's action was therefore defensible, in tune with advanced thinking. Unfortunately for him, the revenues of Coldingham had been assigned to the powerful border family of Home, who naturally resented their appropriation. Matters were made worse in January 1488 when James had Parliament threaten action against anyone who opposed this transfer of revenues. This was alarming. If the King was supported by Parliament in this attack on property rights, whose property could be thought secure? The Homes found allies among the disgruntled nobility, notably Bell-the-Cat himself.

James had alienated the greater part of the nobility of southern Scotland, but he could still look for support from nobles north of the Forth. His position was far from hopeless. He held Stirling Castle, the key stronghold of central Scotland, and, leaving his fifteen-year-old son and heir, Prince James, in the charge of its governor, Shaw of Fintrie, crossed the Forth to muster an army. Meanwhile the rebel lords issued a proclamation accusing the King of bringing Englishmen into the country to subvert the traditional liberties of Scotland. More significantly, they bribed Shaw to break his promise to the King and deliver the Prince into their keeping. Then they announced their intention of deposing this unworthy King, who was proving himself a traitor to Scotland, and putting the Prince on the throne in his stead. The charges were false, but James was now so unpopular that many were ready to believe them.

Nevertheless, he was able to raise troops in the north, and the two armies met at Sauchieburn, near Stirling, on 11 June. The battle may have been no more than a skirmish, but the King's men were scattered. James himself, making his escape, was thrown from his horse. A woman drawing water from a well asked him who he was, and got the reply, 'I was your King this day at morn.' He was taken into her cottage, where he asked her to fetch a priest. A man appeared, saying he was indeed a priest, entered the cottage, and stabbed the King to death.[5]

The murderer was never discovered, and it seems that no great attempt was made to do so. It is not even known whether he was a priest or not. The conclusion must be that James's death was so convenient that few, if any, questions were asked. If he was indeed 'the most enigmatic of the Stewarts', then it may be thought appropriate that his death remains mysterious. Yet it is curious that, in comparison with the murder of James I before him, and Mary Stuart's husband Darnley later, this unsolved crime has attracted so little attention.

In some respects James III was an untypical Stewart, evidently lacking the ability possessed by so many members of the family to charm and attract loyalty; lacking also native authority. Clearly too something about him aroused mistrust. In this he bears some resemblance to his descendant Charles I; and like Charles, his virtues were private rather than public. He was a patron of the arts, sincerely religious, and a loving husband; a good man perhaps, but an inadequate king. There was a perceived shiftiness in his character and he evidently lacked the tough masculinity that his position demanded. As a measure of his failure, one may observe that no other medieval Scottish king was confronted with a rebellion apparently led by his own son.

Chapter 7

James IV (1488–1513):
The Flower of the Scottish
Renaissance

There was a fifteenth-century French saying: '*fier comme un Ecossais*',[1] and it might have been coined with James IV in mind. His reign would see the brief flowering of Renaissance Scotland, and James seemed to embody its spirit. He encouraged and patronised the arts, letters and sciences; William Dunbar, the most accomplished virtuoso among Scottish poets, was employed as his court laureate, complaining, however, as writers will, that he was inadequately rewarded. The King built nobly: the Great Hall of Stirling Castle, much of Falkland Palace, Linlithgow Palace, and the first Palace of Holyroodhouse date from his reign. He created a navy – though it is now recognised that his father had set this work in motion. He travelled all over his kingdom, dispensing justice, a duty his father had been accused, rightly or wrongly, of neglecting. The great Dutch scholar Erasmus, employed as tutor to the King's illegitimate son, Alexander, said that James had 'a wonderful intellectual power, and astonishing knowledge of everything, unconquerable magnanimity and the most abundant generosity'.[2] The Spanish ambassador, Pedro de Ayala,[3] reported to his sovereigns, Ferdinand of Aragon and Isabella of Castile, that James was 'of noble stature, neither tall nor short, and as handsome in complexion and shape as a man can be. He speaks the following languages: Latin, very well; French, German, Flemish,

Italian and Spanish.' To these may be added Scots, English and Gaelic; he was the last King of Scots to be fluent in the tongue that Gaels call 'the language of the gods'.4

Kings of course are there to be flattered, and when a king condescends to a commoner, it is natural that he should be praised in return. But Ayala, writing in cipher to his employers, can have had little reason to dissemble. It is fair therefore to conclude that this was indeed the impression that James made on those who knew him. The list of his acknowledged mistresses suggests that he may have been as attractive to women as his descendant Charles II was to be. Like Charles too he cared for his illegitimate children, but while Charles made his bastard sons dukes, James made his favourite among them, Alexander, Erasmus's pupil, Archbishop of St Andrews when the boy was only eleven, and chancellor before he was twenty-one.

There was a darker side to the King's character, however, reflected in the sobriquet 'James of the Iron Belt'. His involvement, whether voluntary or not, in the rebellion that had led to his father's death seems to have weighed heavy on his conscience, and as penance, he wore an iron chain round his waist next to his skin. He made frequent pilgrimages to shrines such as that of St Ninian at Whithorn and St Dutho at Tain, though the austerity of these excursions was alleviated by the company of minstrels and other entertainers, while he broke at least one journey to Tain with a visit to his mistress at Darnaway. Nevertheless, there is no reason to think him insincere in displaying contrition for his part in his father's death. But it is worth remarking that while he immediately paid for Masses to be said for the soul of his mother, Margaret of Denmark, who had died in 1486, it was to be eight years before he did the same for his murdered father.

He had already celebrated his sixteenth birthday when he came to the throne. The circumstances of his accession were awkward, for the rebellion that had resulted in his father's murder had been that only of a discontented faction, members of which now seized, or were rewarded with, some of the great offices of state. Those who had been loyal to James III could not be expected to approve.

The records of the Scots parliament refer to the 'unhappy field' of Sauchieburn, 'in the quhilk the King our soverane lord happinit to be slane'. If this prudently glossed over the murder, it fell short of excusing it. It was perhaps to emphasise the legitimacy of the succession that the young King was crowned at Scone, the historic crowning place of Scottish kings dating back to legendary times, till Edward I of England had taken possession of the coronation stone – the Stone of Destiny – and carried it off to Westminster Abbey. Despite the stone's absence, Robert the Bruce had been crowned at Scone, but neither James II nor James III had been – perhaps because they were only small children when they became king. The decision that James IV's coronation be celebrated there was thus of some significance. Scone would not see another coronation till 1650, when Charles II was crowned there after the execution of his father.

James IV had one advantage over his immediate predecessors, and indeed his successors. He was, at sixteen, old enough to assume control of the government himself. Scotland was therefore spared yet another minority, and James's personal reign of twenty-five unchallenged years was to be the longest of any Scots monarch since Alexander III in the thirteenth century.

In other respects too he was in a much stronger position than any of his Stewart ancestors. Whatever the failings and misfortunes of James III, his reign had not interrupted the process set in motion by James I. It had been that king's intention to elevate the Crown above the nobility, and, despite the minorities and baronial faction-fighting, this had been achieved by the time of James IV. Through the recovery of Crown lands alienated in the reigns of the two Roberts and during the minorities, the confiscation of estates of condemned rebels, and the securing of the payment of customs duties to the Crown, the Stewarts were now far richer than any of their nobility. The King was no longer merely first among equals as the two Roberts had been.

Moreover, by cultivating the smaller landowners and the representatives of the burghs in parliament, and by encouraging trade and prosperity, the Stewarts had associated themselves with the progressive forces in the country, and might now fairly be seen as the representative of these forces and the guarantor of order. This was reflected in James IV's establishment of a permanent civil court, which in his son's reign would become the Court of Session, still today the fount and arbiter of Scots law.

Nevertheless, though James was more powerful than any previous Scottish king, direct royal control was limited to the Lowlands, and did not even extend to the border counties, which remained lawless and anarchic. Scotland was still a country of localities. James tried to ensure that the same law was observed throughout the kingdom and was himself active in dispensing justice, but he still had to rely on the co-operation of the nobility, who continued to hold their own law courts, punish wrongdoers and settle disputes. He made several military expeditions into the Highlands; yet was no more successful than James I had been in establishing enduring royal authority there. He did end the semi-independent Lordship of the Isles, but he had to entrust administration to local magnates – the chief of Clan Campbell in Argyll, Mackenzie of Kintail in the eastern Highlands, and the Earl of Huntly, head of the Gordon family, in the north-east. While serving the King, these men also served their own interests, establishing authority over their neighbouring barons. It could not be otherwise.

James's reign saw the opening of a question that was to dominate the foreign policy of the Scots government for the next seventy years. Ever since the brief reign of John Balliol, Scotland had been allied to France and both countries had been intermittently at war with England. Those wars had been interrupted by frequent truces, but there had been no settled peace. The border counties, either side of the Anglo-Scottish frontier, were the scene of raids and skirmishes, occasionally full-blown battles, even when there was no regular state of war between the two nations. Dissident or disaffected subjects of either the Scots or English king could find a refuge across the border and would be used, as James III's brother Alexander had been, to stir up trouble in their own country.

This pattern persisted in the early years of James IV's reign. John Ramsay, the only one of James III's favourites to have escaped the lynch mob led by Bell-the-Cat at Lauder, was stripped of the earldom of Bothwell his master had granted him, and resentfully departed to the English court, where he proposed to the new king, Henry VII, that he should kidnap James and his brother. Meanwhile Bell-the-Cat himself was in negotiations with England. These dissidents may have received little encouragement from Henry VII, who was keener on peace than war, but their mere presence in England was an irritant.

James responded by taking up the cause of the mysterious Perkin Warbeck, who claimed to be Richard, Duke of York, the younger son of Edward IV and one of the Princes in the Tower, reputedly murdered by order of their uncle Richard III. Perkin had been recognised as her nephew by Margaret of Burgundy, Edward IV's sister, though the identification was not worth much as evidence, for she had not seen Richard since he was an infant. Nevertheless, she acclaimed him as her 'White Rose of York', and this gave the boy credibility – at least among those adherents of the Yorkist cause who were more than willing to be convinced. In any case he was a handsome young man, with some charm of manner, and on his travels through western Europe seeking support he had been welcomed by the Habsburg Emperor Maximilian, whose response was so enthusiastic that he may fairly be said to have fallen in love with the boy. Now Warbeck arrived in Scotland touting his claims and eager to seek James's support for his attempt to win the English throne, which was 'rightfully' his. To his gratification, he was hailed as Richard IV of England.

If the boy wasn't the prince he claimed to be, he yet made a good show of royalty. James in his turn made him welcome. Was he convinced by Warbeck's claim? It's impossible to say. Only one thing suggests that he may have been: he arranged for the boy to marry Lady Katharine Gordon, one of the daughters of the Earl of Huntly. Since she was a cousin of the King, if a distant one, this was tantamount to admitting the young man into the royal family.

Would James have done this if he had been sure that Warbeck was an impostor? Or did the young man's claims and bearing merely appeal to the streak of knight-errantry in the King's character? Whatever the answer, it was clear that Warbeck might be of use either as an ally or at least as a bargaining counter. There were some in the King's Council who were less impressed and asserted that the boy was not what he claimed to be. They were certainly unwilling to engage in war with England on his behalf. But James was not to be deterred from championing his guest. He might have reflected, cynically, that there were advantages either way. If Warbeck was successful, he would owe his throne to the King of Scots; if the war went badly, then Henry might be prepared to pay for the surrender of the Pretender. But James was no cynic, and it is likely that he thought there was a fair chance that the boy might indeed be the Yorkist heir and the legitimate king of England.

It was not impossible to win the throne for his protégé. Henry VII had himself invaded England with only a few thousand troops, met and defeated Richard III at Bosworth, and made himself king. Furthermore, James had another ambition that might be more easily realised. The town of Berwick-on-Tweed, which had changed hands thirteen times in the last two hundred years, was once again in English possession. It might be retaken in even a limited campaign, and Warbeck obligingly promised to hand it back to Scotland and also to pay James 50,000 marks in return for his assistance. Accordingly, even if the campaign achieved nothing more than the recapture of Berwick, James could consider it a success. So by force of argument or personality he overcame the doubters in his Council, and was able to prepare for war.

In the summer of 1496 the army, with the big guns that were James's especial pride, crossed the Tweed at Coldstream and laid siege to Hetton Castle. Warbeck was soon disillusioned and disheartened. None of the support he had expected from Yorkist sympathisers appeared, and he discovered in himself a distaste for the savage warfare of the borderlands. James on the other hand relished it. Ayala, the Spanish ambassador, who had been invited to accompany him on the campaign, thought him braver and more reckless than a king should properly be. When he remarked on this, James replied that he must do anything he required of his soldiers. Ayala was not convinced. Later he was to reflect that James was not a good commander, because 'he begins to fight before he has given his orders'.5 This was to prove a sadly prophetic judgement.

The campaign petered out. When word came that an English army was advancing from Newcastle, James withdrew. Berwick remained in English hands. The invasion had been a gesture, nothing more. Poor Warbeck had preceded the King back to Edinburgh, and James soon abandoned his cause. It seems that the boy's dislike of seeing men killed in battle may have convinced James that he was not of royal blood. Nevertheless, he paid his pension for another couple of years, then gave him a ship to take him from Ayr to Exeter, where he had been persuaded, or had persuaded himself, that enthusiasm for the Yorkist cause ran high. He was wrong again. Taken prisoner in a skirmish, he was carried to London and imprisoned in the Tower. His wife, Lady Katherine, followed him south, evidence of at least some affection, and begged Henry to spare his life. Henry took a liking to the young woman and was at first agreeable. But Warbeck attempted to escape, with a genuine Yorkist heir, the young Earl of Warwick, and this was too much for Henry. Warwick, who lacked some of his wits, was beheaded as was proper for a nobleman and the King's cousin. Warbeck was first beaten up in his prison until he signed a confession admitting his imposture, and was then hanged at Tyburn, a sad end to a strange life in which he may well have come to believe that he was indeed the prince he had claimed to be. His widow, Lady Katherine, remained at the English court.

It was time James himself was married. He was already well on in his twenties and there was need for a legitimate heir to the throne. He was more ambitious than most of his predecessors, among whom only his father had married into another fully royal family. Approaches for a Spanish princess had come to nothing, though. Soon after James's abandonment of Perkin Warbeck in 1497, Henry VII offered his elder daughter Margaret to the Scottish king, and with her the promise of peace between England and Scotland. Margaret was still a child of seven or eight, and despite political considerations, James was in no hurry to marry. He had already fathered a number of children by different mothers, and was now in love with a young woman called Margaret Drummond.[6] She was the youngest daughter of the first Lord Drummond, and if the poet Dunbar is to be believed was graceful, intelligent and beautiful. James's affections were inconstant, though he provided for discarded lovers and for their children, as records of the royal accounts show, but it may be that he felt more for Margaret Drummond than for any other; their liaison lasted six years.

Still, kings must marry and so Margaret Drummond had to be set aside, for the time being anyway. As it happened, she and her two younger sisters all died suddenly, and there was, as there usually is, talk of poison. The rumour was wild and there is no evidence that it had any foundation. No doubt some, eager for the English marriage, may have supposed that the young woman was an obstacle in the way of its achievement. But this is unlikely. Kings may marry where policy dictates and keep mistresses as fancy chooses.

The marriage of the Scottish king and the young English princess, on 8 August 1503, was to be the most significant in British history, for a hundred years later it led to the Union of the Crowns of England and Scotland. But few would have thought this likely at the time. Certainly Henry VII cannot have done so. He had two sons, Arthur and Henry, and the succession to the English throne seemed assured. He hoped only to secure his northern frontier and deter his new son-in-law from any hostile adventures.

James's court poet William Dunbar dutifully celebrated this union of the Thistle and the Rose. In his poem, the Thistle, 'keepit with a bush of spears', is told by Dame Nature that it is his duty to love and protect 'the fresshe Rose of colour reid and whyte' – Margaret being the daughter of a marriage that had itself united the Red Rose of Lancaster with the White Rose of York. Dunbar then, in full panegyric vein, declares the Rose to be of more illustrious lineage than the Lily, which was the emblem of France. So he advises that Scotland's future should lie in this marriage with England and in the abandonment of the 'Auld Alliance'. The poem is a fine one and the poet's message not necessarily more sincere than was normal on such occasions.

James had no intention of renouncing the French alliance, no matter how eagerly his new father-in-law urged him to do so, for that would have been to lose all freedom of action. Nevertheless he did sign a Treaty of Perpetual Peace with England, and this treaty was confirmed by the Pope, which meant that if either party broke it, he would be subject to excommunication. For the moment the question did not arise. So long as France and England were at peace, James could be so also.

His new wife was only fifteen and, not surprisingly, had herself no great relish for the marriage to a husband twice her age. Observers thought she looked sulky and discontented, but she may merely have been shy and nervous. She was in time to prove that she could be as disagreeable as most members of her family. Almost at once she expressed a dislike for her husband's red beard and he obligingly had it shaved. Still, Margaret and James did their royal duty. Six children were born in the ten years of marriage, though only one, the future James V, survived infancy. Since the King had several bastards in rude good health (his favourite among them, Alexander, was, according to Erasmus, extremely short-sighted, though in other respects utterly admirable), James may have held his wife responsible for the high mortality rate of their children. Be that as it may, he did not allow marriage to tie him down but continued to amuse himself with new mistresses.

The King's patronage of the arts and ambitious building in Edinburgh, Stirling and Fife was matched by others whom the prosperity of the times encouraged to be equally munificent: Bishop Elphinstone founded the University of Aberdeen (King's College) in 1495, and James's illegitimate son, Alexander, though barely out of his teens, collaborated as Archbishop of St Andrews with Prior John Hepburn in founding St Leonard's College at the university there. Dunbar was not the only poet the King supported. He also patronised Gavin Douglas, the translator of The Aeneid,[7] rewarding him with the provostship of St Giles in Edinburgh, though it was in his son's reign that Douglas was made Bishop of Dunkeld.

One of James's more eccentric dependants was an Italian alchemist, John Damian: the King financed his attempts to discover the 'elixir of life' for at least ten years. Damian's researches are said to have required the stimulus of brandy and whisky, and he was perhaps under the influence when, wearing a pair of wings of his own design, he attempted to fly from the battlements of Stirling Castle in September 1507. The design of the wings proved inadequate. He plunged into a midden and broke his thigh, to the happy amusement of Dunbar, who resented the money the King had lavished on this imposter and perhaps thought it would have been better given to him.

James was eager to play a more prominent part in European politics than his predecessors – testimony to the security of his position at home. From soon after his marriage he talked of engaging in a crusade against the Turks, even of leading one. Some historians have dismissed this as a mere fanciful project and one that was also out of date. Yet in the circumstances of the time it was not unreasonable. It was only some fifty years since the Ottoman Turks had taken Constantinople and then in 1461 had captured Trebizond, the last outpost of the Byzantine empire. Tension between an aggressive Islam and the West was real enough.[8] James looked to the Pope for approval and encouragement.

It was not forthcoming. His Holiness Julius II had other more pressing concerns. He was not only the head of the Church, but also an Italian prince, occupied with the shifting politics of the peninsula. A hard-drinking and bellicose pederast, the Pope was ready to scandalise the faithful by leading his own troops in battle, but he had no enthusiasm for the idea of a crusade. It was a matter of greater urgency to prevent either Spain or France from achieving a dominant position in Italy, and since the French invasion of 1494, it seemed that the greater danger came from France. So the Pope occupied himself in constructing an alliance to check French ambitions, and the extent of his spiritual interest was limited to calling this a 'Holy League'. James's brother-in-law Henry VIII, married to a Spanish princess, Catherine of Aragon, and eager to revive the old English claim to the throne of France, signed up happily to the alliance. Thus James not only found his ambition thwarted; he was placed in an awkward position.

What was he to do? The Treaty of Perpetual Peace, signed on the occasion of his marriage in 1503, restrained him. On the other hand the alliance with France also imposed obligations. Attempts at mediation came to nothing. He was compelled to choose. He might perhaps have remained inactive, but such a course was alien to his temperament. Reason pulled one way, old loyalties and ambition the other.

Louis XII of France had responded to the Pope's Holy League by issuing a call for a General Council of the Church. This was an old device that had proved a means of calling popes to order in the past. However, it was ineffective now, partly because of the strength of the alliance Julius had constructed, partly because one of his predecessors had decreed that henceforth only the Pope himself could lawfully convoke a General Council. Julius now denounced Louis as a schismatic – one who threatened to divide the Church. James, disappointed in his hopes for a crusade, unappeased by the gift of a sword and hat9 that Julius had blessed, responded by writing angrily to the Pope accusing him of dividing Christendom by his Holy League rather than uniting it against the infidel. Accordingly he renewed the French alliance, despite exposing himself to the risk of excommunication for having joined himself to a schismatic, and breaking the Treaty of Perpetual Peace. Louis for his part promised that as soon as he was able he would give his support to the projected crusade.

Henry VIII was keen to deflate his brother-in-law's pretensions. There were incidents at sea, Scottish ships being boarded and seized by English sailors acting 'in the name of the Holy Father'. The English ambassador told James that all the world knew that his master was acting as a servant of the Church; James replied that Henry was lucky to have found such an obliging Pope whose interests chimed so well with his own ambition.

Throughout the early months of 1513 James tried to negotiate a settlement. In a letter to his uncle, the King of Denmark, he insisted that he had been labouring for two years to keep France, Spain

and England from war. France had indeed requested, or authorised, him to negotiate with England, but Henry now even refused
to grant his ambassadors the customary safe-conducts. James had
offered to renew the Treaty of Perpetual Peace, if Henry agreed to
desist from his intention to make war on France, but the English
parliament, prompted doubtless by the King, was eager for war
with both France and Scotland.

James's diplomatic efforts continued throughout the early summer
months. He told the English ambassador that he wanted to remain
at peace with Henry. All that was necessary to ensure this was for
his brother-in-law to abandon his plan to make war on France.
But he could get no such assurance. In May he sent Lord
Drummond, the father of his late mistress and one of his most
competent servants, frequently employed on diplomatic missions,
to Henry inviting him to agree to be party to the year's truce that
Ferdinand of Aragon – since his wife Isabella's death in effect ruler
of all Spain – had just concluded with the French. He appealed to
Henry to join him in working for the union of all Christian
monarchs against the Turk. The English king, who would a few
years later be granted the title 'Defender of the Faith' by Pope
Leo X, was not interested. He was determined to have his French
war. James was pushed into an intolerable position. Either he stood
aside, deserting his traditional ally and losing face, or he took the
risk of war. To abandon France was to expose himself to humiliation. Moreover, if Henry's French war was successful, he might
then turn his attention to Scotland and seek to reduce the country
to the status of a vassal. Step by step James was forced to the
brink of war. It is unlikely that the plea from the French queen,
Anne, who called on him 'to march three paces on to English
ground as her knight', was the deciding factor, though he wore the
turquoise ring she had sent him as a token of her trust. It was not
romance, but the logic of realpolitik that drove James to declare
war on England in July 1513.

Nevertheless, there were still many in Scotland who thought the
war rash and unnecessary. James's wisest councillor, Bishop
Elphinstone, had argued consistently for peace at any price. So did

the aged Bell-the-Cat, who may have been in English pay. He
put the case against war so fiercely even after the army had been
mustered that James, exasperated, told him that if he was afraid,
he could go home. Whereupon, we are told, the fierce old Earl
burst into tears before departing. His two sons, however, remained
with the army.

Other attempts were made to dissuade the King – or were at
least reported afterwards. The most remarkable is to be found in
the *History of Scotland* compiled by Robert Lindsay of Pitscottie:

> Yet all their warnings, and uncouth tidings, nor no good counsel,
> might stop the King, at this present, fro his vain purpose, and wicked
> enterprise, but hasted him fast to Edinburgh, there to make his
> provisioning and furnishing, in having forth his Army against the
> day appointed, that they should meet in the Boroughmuir of
> Edinburgh: that is to say, seven cannons that he had forth of the
> Castle of Edinburgh, which were called the Seven Sisters, casten by
> Robert Borthwick, the master-gunner, with other small artillery, and
> all manner of order, as the master-gunner could devise.
>
> In this meantime, while they were taking forth their artillery, and
> the King being in the Abbey for the time, there was a cry heard at
> the Marcat Cross of Edinburgh, at the hour of midnight, proclaiming
> as it had been a summons, which was named and called by the
> proclaimed thereof, The Summons of Plotcock, which desired all
> men to compear, both Earl and Lord and Baron, and all honest
> gentlemen within the town (every man specified by his own name)
> to compear, within the space of forty days, before his Master, where
> it should happen for him to appoint, and be for the time, under the
> pain of disobedience. But whether this summons was proclaimed
> by vain persons, night walkers, or drunken men, for their pastime,
> as if it was a spirit, I cannot tell truly . . .[10]

'Plotcock' was none other than Pluto, the Roman God of the
Underworld. Sir Walter Scott observes that 'the Christians of
the Middle Ages by no means misbelieved in the existence of the
heathen deities; they only considered them as devils, and Plotcock,
so far from implying anything fabulous, was a synonym of the
grand enemy of mankind'.

Pitscottie, who was himself born only in 1532 – that is, twenty years after the events narrated – assures us that he had his information from 'a landed gentleman who was at that time twenty years of age, and was in the town the time of the said summons; and thereafter, when the field was stricken, he swore to me, there was no man that escaped that was called in the summons, but that one man alone that made his protestation, and appealed from the said summons; but that all the lave [rest] were perished in the field with the king'.

No doubt the tale had been improved over time; and indeed it is quite likely that the whole thing is an invention after the fact. Nevertheless, if there was such a summons, and we dismiss any supernatural interpretation, it must have been a sort of black propaganda intended to deter the King from his enterprise by arousing superstitious fears. Yet it demonstrates very vividly the strength of opposition to the King's adventure. Scots might serve happily as soldiers of fortune on the Continent; they might engage in skirmishes at home. Borderers were ever ready to make raids into England. But there was rarely much appetite for 'national' warfare.

James himself had not wanted war, but he had no reason to fear its outcome. Admittedly Scottish armies had won few pitched battles against the English; Stirling Bridge (1297) and Bannockburn (1314) had been rare exceptions. More commonly the English longbow had proved the dominant weapon on the battlefield, destroying the massed ranks of Scottish spearmen as it had destroyed the French chivalry at Crécy (1346), Poitiers (1356) and Agincourt (1415). Efforts by successive kings to encourage the practice of archery in Scotland had been generally unsuccessful. There were few bowmen except in the Ettrick Forest. However, battles in the later stages of the Hundred Years War between England and France had suggested that the supremacy of the longbow was nearing its end. The weapon was not yet obsolete, but developments in military technology were providing the means to make it less effective.

The most important of these was defensive armour. This wasn't of course new in itself. Knights had gone into battle wearing heavy armour since at least the tenth century. However, this had for long offered little protection against the longbow – as the French knights had found to their cost. Now it was different. In the words of one modern historian:

> By the late fifteenth century, armourers could produce excellent quality suits of 'harnois blanc' (white armour, meaning full plate armour) which were fully articulated and protected every part of the wearer. Contrary to popular belief, this harness did not make the wearer a lumbering, immobile target, but instead was light and flexible enough to allow considerable freedom of movement. Just as importantly, the curved and fluted shape of the armour was specifically designed to deflect sword-blows and arrows. With a maximum draw-force of 120 pounds, a longbow arrow had to strike plate armour at a 90 degree angle to have any chance of penetration. By 1513 a man wearing a complete harness of plate armour had little to fear from a longbowman.[11]

Most of James IV's army did not have this protection, but his nobles and their retainers did. In 1496 James had established a 'harness mill' at Stirling, and recruited experienced French armourers to supervise production. The King had also imported quantities of armour from France and the Netherlands. The army he led to war in 1513 was certainly far better protected against the longbow than any previous Scottish army had been.

The development of field artillery also threatened the longbow's supremacy. Early guns such as those which James II had procured (and which had cost him his life) were heavy and unwieldy, effective for siege work but not on the battlefield. Guns were now being cast in bronze rather than iron. They were lighter and had a more rapid rate of fire. The small iron ball fired from a bronze cannon was as effective against a castle wall as the heavier stone ball fired from an iron gun, while the bronze cannon could be manoeuvred effectively on the battlefield. James, interested in the new technology, had invested in artillery, and the train he took to war in 1513 was one of the finest in Europe.

The Scots army was still deficient in cavalry, but the best of its infantry was ready to fight in approved modern fashion. For half a century the dominant force on European battlefields had been the highly disciplined Swiss infantry, equipped with eighteen-foot pikes. They fought in phalanxes and advanced in echelon formation. James was determined to emulate them and had been importing pikes to replace the shorter Scottish spear. The evidence of the battle that ensued at Flodden suggests that he had also copied the Swiss mode of advance, for we are told that the Scots came on 'in Allmayne fashion' – 'Allmayne' meaning Swiss-German.[12]

There was another reason for optimism. Henry had taken his best troops to France. His northern army, commanded by Thomas Howard, Earl of Surrey, who had been a guest at James's wedding, was composed of the reserve, feudal levies of bowmen, and infantry armed with the shorter English bill. This had one advantage over the long pike, if the battle came to a standstill at close quarters, for the bill had an axe-head at its side that could be used to hack at the longer pikes and also a hook that could be employed to drag a knight from his horse or grab a foot soldier by the ankle and disable him.

Still, it seemed that the advantage lay with the Scots. Moreover, James's aim was limited. He had no intention of penetrating deep into England; quite the contrary. His intention was only to distract the English and divert their attention away from France. If he could draw Surrey into battle and defeat him, he would win prestige for himself and might compel Henry to abandon his French campaign. Even if the English king then invaded Scotland, which he wouldn't be able to do till the following year, James need have little fear. He could adopt what was now a traditional Scottish strategy: refuse battle, and draw the English army on till it ran out of provisions and was forced to retreat before it disintegrated.

In pursuit of his strategy, James took up a strong position with his back to Scotland on Flodden Edge, only a few miles across the border. This was a saddlebacked hill almost a mile in length. The army's position on one flank was protected by marshy ground, while on the other the ground fell away steeply towards the River Till, a tributary of the Tweed, which as it approached the sea marked the frontier between Engand and Scotland. Awaiting the

English, James had his artillery positioned behind trenches. Surrey could attack only from the south, across rising open country, a hazardous operation.

Too hazardous, indeed. Surrey was an experienced commander, and it was obvious to him that the Scots' position was very strong, so strong as to deter an attack. Accordingly he determined to outflank the Scots, march round behind them, and position his army between them and the Tweed. This manoeuvre was itself risky, for the Scots might choose to attack his line of march. But the alternative for Surrey was to withdraw and refuse battle. That course too was dangerous, all the more so because he was short of provisions, and had reason to fear that some of his levies would make for home if there was no immediate requirement to fight a battle. As it was, he effected his march successfully in the early morning of Friday, 9 September. James responded by abandoning his position on Flodden Edge, turning his army about to take up a position on Branxton Hill. So it happened that the two armies were now in place, the wrong way round as it were, the Scots with their backs to England, the English with theirs to Scotland. This made battle unavoidable. Nevertheless, the Scottish position remained formidable. They held the high ground. Their troops were fresh, while the English were wearied by their march; and they were better provisioned. Surrey would have to launch an attack uphill. That prospect was less daunting than it had been when the Scots were dug in on Flodden Edge, but still unattractive.

James's plan was simple and, in theory, sound. The Scots artillery would open fire, and this would provoke Surrey to attack up the slope of Branxton Hill. When they did so, James would, at the right moment, launch his pike columns forward, in the approved 'Allmayne fashion'. With the advantage of the ground, they would surely push the disordered English back, till retreat turned into rout.

That was the theory. Reality was different. The heavy Scottish guns, designed for siege work, had a slower rate of fire than the lighter English ones. Moreover, the apparent advantage of the ground turned against them. They were firing downhill, and their cannonballs, instead of bouncing and doing damage in the ranks of the English army, embedded themselves in the soft earth. Meanwhile the English gunners, at perhaps 600 yards range (twice the effective distance of the longbow) began to direct their fire at the phalanxes of Scottish pikemen.

James was now confronted by a choice he hadn't expected. He could either withdraw his army behind the ridge of the hill, out of range of the guns, and hope that the English, seeing this, would respond by advancing up the slope. But orderly retreat was a risky manoeuvre, and it was probable he couldn't trust his troops, inexperienced and at best half-trained, to carry it out. The alternative was to order his pikemen to advance in an all-out attack – another risk but one in accordance with advanced military thinking and Swiss practice. 'The best remedy' – for an army under artillery fire – was, according to Machiavelli in his treatise *The Art of War* – to make 'a resolute attack on it [the artillery] as soon as possible'.[13] In theory, again, the advantage lay with the more numerous Scots.

James himself led one of the 'battles', columns of pikemen. He has been criticised for this, on the grounds that it made it impossible for him to direct the course of the encounter. But on the one hand the Scots expected their king and his chief nobles to take the lead in the battle and expose themselves to danger, and on the other, once this sort of battle was joined there was very little that a commander remaining in the rear on the hill could do to influence its course.

As it happened, while the Scots triumphed on one wing and were routed and fled for home on the other, the decisive battle was in the centre, where the King himself was to be found. What determined its outcome was not faulty tactics on James's part, but the lie of the land, for at the bottom of the hill there was a little stream invisible from the top, which the pikemen had to cross to get at the English on the other side. The stream was not wide – a man could leap it – but what is an insignificant obstacle to an individual may be formidable to an army. The momentum of the advance slackened, then was lost altogether. Instead of charging into the English ranks in a powerful column, the Scots did so irregularly, and the battle in the centre became a desperate hand-to-hand encounter in which the versatility of the English bills had an advantage over the long Scottish pikes. At some point, perhaps quite early in the struggle, the men in the rear of the Scottish columns seem to have lost heart, and fled. This enabled the English archers, previously ineffectual (partly because the wind and rain reduced their range), to get round the Scottish flank and fire from close range into the heaving mass.

So the battle turned against the Scots. Instead of the promised comprehensive victory, they were now under huge pressure, fighting for their lives and with no obvious way of retreat to Scotland. James himself is said to have led a charge – perhaps by now a desperate one – against the spot where Surrey's banners flew, and to have been 'slain within a spear length from the said Earl of Surrey'. In the thick of the fighting few probably saw him fall. The struggle went on till night fell, while beyond the field English cavalry pursued fleeing Scots.

In the words of the old poem:

> For all the lords of their land were left them behind,
> Behind Brymstone in a brook breathless they lie
> Gaping against the moon, their ghosts were away.[14]

Besides the King, his favourite bastard son, the Archbishop of St Andrews, Alexander[15] was killed, as were the Bishop of the Isles, two abbots and the Dean of Glasgow. Nine of Scotland's twenty-one earls fell at Flodden, and fourteen other lords of Parliament. At least 300 knights and lairds were among the dead. The Royal Burgh of Selkirk sent eighty men to Flodden; only one returned home.[16]

James's body was found with 'diverse deadly wounds'. It was stripped and taken to Berwick, where it was embalmed and placed in a lead coffin, which was later brought to London and placed in the Carthusian monastery of Sheen, near Richmond, until Henry VIII decided where his brother-in-law, the King of Scots, should be buried. It seems to have been a matter of no great moment to him, and the coffin was left at Sheen in a storeroom. It disappeared when that monastery was dissolved more than twenty years later, and no one knows where the bones of Scotland's Renaissance king found their last resting place.

Chapter 8

James V (1513–42): People's King or Tyrant?

J ames V was the first Scottish king for five generations to die in his own bed, which he did abruptly, aged only thirty, of no discernible cause. It is perhaps proper that his death should have been mysterious, for much in his life is baffling. His character, like that of his grandfather James III, was enigmatic; all the more so because, although we have more information about the fifth James, it is difficult, even impossible, to determine what manner of man he was.

On the one hand he was remembered fondly by the common people, stories about his habit of travelling in disguise among them being told for generations after his death. On the other hand he frequently showed himself to be harsh to the point, it has been suggested, of sadism, bitterly resentful, unforgiving to his enemies, greedy and covetous, willing to pervert justice when his interest was at stake. He alienated most of the Scots nobility, and eventually found himself unable to assemble a loyal army. 'Taking into account his vindictiveness, his ruthlessness and his cruelty, as well as his acquisitiveness, he must,' Gordon Donaldson judged, 'have been one of the most unpopular monarchs who ever sat on the Scottish throne.' He quotes an observer who, in 1537, declared: 'So sore a dread king and so ill-beloved of his subjects, was never in that land. Every man that hath any substance fearing to have a quarrel made to begin therefore.'[1]

Only eighteen months old when his father was killed at Flodden, he never knew what it was not to be king. His mother, Margaret Tudor, was made regent and tutrix – that is, guardian – of her infant son. This testifies to her strength of character, given that her husband had been killed in a war against her brother. As regent, her power was provisional, her authority necessarily more limited than that of a king. Unlike a reigning monarch, an unpopular or incompetent regent could always be removed without threatening the stability of the state. All kings had to pay heed to the opinions of their Council, but a regent, being no more than first among equals, could be successful only if he or she pursued policies that had general approval.

The position of a female regent was especially precarious. There was no tradition of being governed by a woman, and it was generally accepted that a widow who had inherited great estates would marry again. When the widow was a queen and mother of the infant king, her choice of husband was politically important. Margaret married again in 1514, with what some considered indecent speed. Her new husband was Archibald Douglas, Earl of Angus, the grandson of old Bell-the-Cat. Few had much regard for him; one of his uncles had called him 'a young witless fool'. The marriage was immediately unpopular with other magnates. Prompted by them, the Estates formally demanded that Margaret be deprived of both her position in the Council and the guardianship of the young King. In her place they summoned John Stewart, Duke of Albany, from France, where he had lived all his life, and appointed him governor of Scotland. He was the son of James III's turbulent brother Alexander, and so the great-uncle of the little King. Fortunately Albany was a very different man from his violent and treacherous father, being sensible, public-spirited and trustworthy. Though he was heir presumptive to the throne, he had no ambition to occupy it, partly perhaps because he had been brought up speaking French and was fluent in neither Scots nor English. Next in line of succession was James Hamilton, Earl of Arran, another grandson of James II, but he did not dispute the appointment of Albany and may indeed have been one of those who proposed it.

Flodden had been as disastrous a battle as any in Scotland's history, but it did not lead either to panic or a change of policy. Indeed, before Albany's arrival from France, there were even tentative plans to renew the war the following year, though in the weeks after the battle, the Council, fearing an English invasion, gave orders for the fortifications of Edinburgh to be extended. A new wall was built that enclosed the suburbs on the southern side, including the convent of Greyfriars, the church of St Mary-in-the-Fields, and the country houses of rich merchants, lawyers and other notables. Portions of this Flodden Wall still stand, but the precautions proved unnecessary. Surrey made no attempt to follow up his victory. He had cleared the Scots out of England and that was enough. Besides, his own army had been badly mauled too, and he at once dismissed most of the feudal levies, smugly telling King Henry how much money he had saved him by doing so. In Scotland, talk of a new campaign evaporated, rendered unnecessary, even if ever practical, by the announcement of a peace treaty between England and France.

The years of James's minority were dominated by the shifting alliances among the nobility. Inasmuch as any consistent thread can be discerned, it took the form of argument between those who held by the French alliance and those who favoured an accommodation with England. Some were motivated by patriotism, a consideration of what was best for Scotland; others, perhaps more numerous, by personal ambition. Those who promoted an English alliance could expect to be well rewarded by Henry. Given his background, it is natural that Albany should have stood by the Auld Alliance, but it is characteristic of the confusion and uncertainties of the time that the Queen Dowager, Margaret, should have belonged first to one party, then the other. In 1515, after her unpopular marriage, she and Angus withdrew to England, where she gave birth to a daughter, Lady Margaret Douglas.[2] However, while Albany was temporarily absent in France, where he had gone to attend to his estates, Margaret and Angus were able to return to Scotland, hoping to re-establish their political position and leaving their infant daughter in the care of her uncle, Henry VIII.

Soon, though, a quarrel broke out between the couple, partly because Angus had seized control of his wife's revenues, partly because of his infidelity. They separated, the Queen Dowager now expressing her hatred for her husband,[3] and despite being English herself, she joined the pro-French party. This weakened Angus's position as a rival to Albany, but as a great nobleman and the chief agent of the English king in Scotland, he retained a deal of authority. Yet being wayward and quick-tempered, he soon fell out with almost everyone, even the Earl of Arran, despite their shared preference for an English alliance. In 1520 the feud betwen the two noblemen boiled over with a running battle in the capital between their followers, when Arran's men were driven out by the Douglases; it became known as 'Cleanse the Causeway' and was symptomatic of the turbulence of these years of the King's minority.

Albany returned, revived the pro-French party, made two unsuccessful raids into England, which cost him much support among the nobility, and in 1524 left Scotland for ever, returning to France, where he would act as the Scottish ambassador till he died in 1536. But he also served the French king, Francis I, acting as his envoy to the Pope, and arranging the marriage of the Dauphin, the future Henry II, to the Pope's niece, Catherine de Medici (previously proposed as a bride for the young King James). While there he also obtained papal approval in 1527 for the annulment of Margaret's marriage to Angus. Her brother, Henry VIII, already embroiled in his attempt to secure an annulment of his own marriage to Catherine of Aragon, which would enable him to marry Anne Boleyn, must have envied the ease with which his sister had been freed of an unwelcome husband.

Angus, however, was not finished. In Albany's absence he dominated the Council, and as the head of the pro-English party became in fact, though not in name, regent. He was powerful enough by 1526, the year before the annulment of his marriage, to take possession of the young King, now aged fourteen, and to make a treaty with England. A previous Council decree had stipulated that the King should reside in turn with four great magnates – Angus, Arran, the Earl of Lennox and his own mother – but Angus felt

powerful enough to disregard this decree and refused to surrender
the King's person. Meanwhile, he sought to bolster his position by
granting lands and the principal offices in the state and the royal
household to his supporters and members of his extended family.
According to Pitscottie, 'The tyranny of the house of Douglas
became every day more intolerable to the nation. To bear the name
was esteemed sufficient to cover the most atrocious crime, even in
the streets of the capital; and during the sitting of parliament, a
baron who had murdered his opponent on the threshold of the
principal church, was permitted to walk openly abroad, solely
because he was a Douglas.'4

Angus's supremacy did not last. It provoked the resentment of
the young King, of all those nobles excluded from power and influence, and of the pro-French party, now headed by James Beaton,
Archbishop of St Andrews and chancellor from the year of Flodden
until he was displaced by Angus. The young King, eager to escape
the Earl's control, contrived to resume communication with his
mother, now married to her third husband, Henry Stewart, Lord
Methven.5 She held Stirling Castle, and as soon as James was
assured of a welcome and refuge there, he made plans to escape.

In the late summer of 1528, Angus had left him at Falkland
Castle in Fife, under the guard of his own uncle, Archibald, his
brother George, and another kinsman, James Douglas of Parkhead,
captain of the guard. A few days after Angus's departure, Archibald
went to Dundee on private business and George to St Andrews,
apparently to investigate some matter connected with the finances
of the diocese, leaving the King in the charge of James Douglas
and a hundred-strong guard. The King then proposed that they
should spend the next day hunting and that invitations be sent to
certain Fife lairds, for, he said, 'he was determined to slay a deer
or two for his pleasure'. He asked for his 'disjeuner'6 to be served
at four in the morning, and urged James Douglas to go to bed
early so that he might rise the sooner. Then, when all was quiet,
he eluded the sentries – one wonders if they were bribed or perhaps
drunk – and with only two servants, one a stable boy named Jockie
Hart, who provided the horses, escaped and rode hard for Stirling,

reaching the castle as dawn was breaking. The gates were closed behind him, in case of a pursuit, and the captain of his mother's guard 'laid the King in his bed, because he had ridden all that night'. Pitscottie in his chronicle takes up the story:

> We will lat him sleep in his bed, and return to George Douglas, who came home to Falkland at eleven hours at night, and required at the porters what the King was doing, who answered that he was in his own chamber sleeping, who was to rise tymous to the hunting, and right so said the watchmen. George hearing this went to his bed, till on the morn that the sun rose. Then came Patrick Carmichael, Baillie of Abernethie, and knocked at George Douglas's chamber door, and inquired of him what the king was doing. George answered that he was not waked as yet in his own chamber. The Baillie answered: 'Ye are deceaved; he is along the bridge of Stirling this night.' Then George Douglas gat up hastily and went to the porters and watchmen and inquired for the King, who still answered that he was sleeping in his own chamber. Then George Douglas came to the king's chamber door and found it locked, and dang it up, but found no man in it. Then he cried, 'Fye, treason, the King is gone.'[7]

Pitscottie's account is vivid and suitably dramatic, yet open to question. How, one wonders, could Baillie Carmichael have had the information he relayed? And if he did somehow know that the King had ridden to Stirling, it was surely bold to the point of rashness to reveal it to George Douglas. Moreover, there is some confusion in his narrative, for he goes on to relate that some said the King had slipped out 'to visit a gentlewoman' at Bambriefe. This seems to have been thought credible, for though James was only sixteen, it is said that Angus had not neglected to supply him with women who might serve as a distraction – and indeed he would have at least three illegitimate children before he was twenty. But the Douglases' hope was soon disappointed. The bird had indeed flown. Angus was sent for urgently and hurried from his castle of Tantallon on the other side of the Forth, and then they mustered their forces and headed for Stirling in a desperate attempt to retrieve the situation.

They were met with news that a herald had been sent to the town cross to proclaim a royal decree that neither Angus nor any of his company should approach within six miles of the King upon pain of death. Some would have defied the command, but perhaps they were too weak; perhaps the Earl's nerve cracked. At any rate they withdrew to Linlithgow to await events. By this time other nobles were congregating at Stirling protesting their loyalty, among them Archbishop Beaton. A few months earlier he had been so fearful of Angus that he had gone into hiding disguised as a shepherd. Then he had apparently made peace with the Earl, resuming control of his diocese and entertaining Angus and the King for the Easter feast. It may be, however, that he already knew of the King's plans and had perhaps detained George Douglas at St Andrews in order to facilitate the escape. Certainly some must have been apprised of it; otherwise it is difficult to see how so many of the nobility could have rallied so quickly to the King.

James made his way to Edinburgh where he summoned a Council that proclaimed Angus, his brother and uncle to be traitors, forbidding anyone to have intercourse with them or offer them help or risk being held as their accomplices. The King laid forth all the grounds of his complaints. The Douglases were dismissed from all offices and the Council sent an envoy to England to inform Henry that the government of Scotland was now in the King's own hands. For a few weeks Angus held out in Tantallon Castle, but his position was hopeless. He sued for peace, surrendering the castle in return for a promise (which, surprisingly perhaps, was kept) that he should be allowed to go into exile in England. Other members of the family would be less fortunate. Angus's brother-in-law, the Master of Forbes, was charged with plotting to kill the King and was executed. The Earl's sister Lady Glamis was condemned for conspiring to poison James and was burned. (She had previously been acquitted of an attempt to poison her own husband.) James Douglas of Parkhead, the jailer the King had outwitted, was also put to death, and other members of the family, including the young Earl of Morton, found their estates forfeited.

The reversal, which may even be described as a royal coup,

had political consequences. Angus, inasmuch as he had any political aims other than the securing of his own power, had been the leader of the pro-English faction. It was natural that James, in his detestation of his former stepfather, should be confirmed in his preference for the French alliance. Andrew Lang, nineteenth-century historian, essayist, poet and collector of folklore, marked its significance:

> James became implacable to the whole Douglas name. But to shake off and break down the Douglases, a thing desirable in itself, was to turn away from England, the patron of the Douglases, to turn away from Protestantism, to court France, and to choose the doomed cause of Catholicism in the north . . . These dull and squalid intrigues of a selfish, sensual termagant [Margaret Tudor] and her unscrupulously ambitious husband Angus, determined the fate of the Stuart line. They were to lean on France and lose three crowns for a mass. Exile, the executioner's axe, and broken hearts were to be their reward in a secular series of sorrows flowing from the long minority and unhappy environment of James V.[8]

This was to read history backwards, or to interpret it in deterministic fashion. The fate of the Stuart line would indeed unfold in the manner Lang describes. But it need not have done so. There were to be many moments in the following two centuries when different decisions might have been taken, different policies pursued. What happened – the ultimate failure of the Stuarts – was the course history took. Nothing can alter that. Yet one does not have to be a devotee of what is called counter-factual history to believe that the course of the river of history might have been diverted into other channels.

Freed from the control of the Douglases, James, at the age of seventeen, took charge of the government himself. His first aim was to restore the authority of the Crown and to bring the country to a degree of order. With this intention he made an expedition in 1529 into the notoriously lawless Borders. That country had been ravaged by the recurrent wars with England, and the Border clans or families made raids indifferently across the frontier, into the

Lowlands, and on each other. They were thieves and murderers, but not lacking in a certain glamour, and their wild way of life is immortalised in the great 'Riding Ballads' of the borderland.

James was determined to pacify the Borders. The exercise was billed as a 'justice ayre' (or eyre), but was really a punitive miliary expedition. He seized several of the most prominent Border barons, among them the Earl of Bothwell, Scott of Buccleuch, lords Home and Maxwell, Ker of Fernihurst, and various Elliots, and imprisoned them. Then he summoned one of the most celebrated reivers (brigands), Johnnie Armstrong of Gilknockie, to meet him at Carlinrig on the road between Hawick and Langholm. Armstrong was a notable scoundrel, guilty of many thefts and murders either side of the border – a sixteenth-century mafioso; but one with a style and panache that had won him the admiration of many. According to a ballad published by Scott in *The Minstrelsy of the Scottish Border*, the King had sent him a promise of safe conduct:

> The King he wrytes a loving letter,
> With his ain hand sae tenderly;
> And he hath sent it to Johnnie Armstrong,
> To cum and speik with him speedily.[9]

Armstrong, trusting in the promise and confident of his own prowess, swaggered to the meeting, richly dressed, at the head of some fifty men. The King remarked on his splendour and then accused him of many crimes. The reiver defended himself boldly, arguing that he was a good Scot, a loyal subject of King James, and no traitor. Then, becoming aware that he was in imminent peril, he exclaimed that King Henry of England would 'downweigh my best horse with gold to know that I was condemned to die this day'.

As Alistair Moffat writes in his history of the Borders, Armstrong was 'missing the subtleties of the political reality behind his situation. Henry would have paid dearly; that was the point.'[10] James had no wish to be on anything but good terms with his uncle of England; suppressing the reivers was good policy.

So the noose was slipped round Armstrong's neck as he sat his horse. It was attached to the overhanging branch of a tree, the horse given a whack on its rump, and Johnnie was left swinging in the air. The same treatment was meted out to his followers. But the ballad-maker gives Johnnie the last word, and it is a fine one:

> To seik het water beneath cauld ice,
> Surely it is a greit folie;
> I have asked grace at a graceless face
> But there is nane for my men and me.

Asking grace of a graceless face, and being refused it; that is one picture of James V, and it is a fair one. Yet the other side of the King's character should not be forgotten, the side that caused him to be remembered in song and story with affection by the common people. If he aroused the animosity, even hatred, of many of his nobles, this was at least in part because of his determination to enforce laws to protect the weak against the oppression of the strong. His care for justice was sincere, and he would be remembered as the 'King of the Commons' and 'the Gudeman of Ballenguich', this latter the name he reputedly assumed when travelling the country incognito so that, as Scott puts it in his *Tales of a Grandfather*, 'he might hear complaints which might not otherwise reach his ears, and, perhaps, that he might enjoy amusements which he could not have partaken of in his avowed royal character'.

It is in this guise that he appears as a character in Scott's poem *The Lady of the Lake*, and in one of the notes appended to the poem Scott wrote:

The two excellent comic songs, entitled 'The Gaberlunzie Man' and 'We'll gae nae mair a-roving', are said to have been founded on his amorous adventures when travelling in the guise of a beggar. Another adventure, which had nearly cost him his life, is said to have taken place at the village of Cramond, near Edinburgh, where he had rendered his addresses acceptable to a pretty girl of the lower rank. Four or five persons, whether relations or lovers of his mistress is uncertain, beset the disguised monarch as he returned from his rendez-vous. Naturally gallant and an admirable master of his weapon, the king took post on the high and narrow bridge over the Almond river, and defended himself bravely with his sword. A peasant, who was threshing in a neighbouring barn, came out upon the noise, and, whether moved by compassion or natural gallantry, took the weaker side, and laid about so effectively with his flail as to disperse the assailants. He then conducted the king into his barn, where his guest requested a basin and a towel, to remove the stains of the broil. This being procured with difficulty, James employed himself in learning what was the summit of his deliverer's earthly wishes, and found that they were bounded by the desire of possessing, in property, the farm of Braehead on which he laboured as a bondsman. The lands happened to belong to the Crown, and James directed him to come to the palace of Holyrood, and enquire for the Gudeman (i.e. farmer) of Ballengiech, a name by which he was known in his excursions, and which answered to the Il Bondocani of Haroun al-Raschid. He presented himself accordingly, and found, with due astonishment, that he had saved his monarch's life, and that he was to be gratified with a crown charter of the lands of Braehead, under the service of presenting a ewer, basin and towel, for the king to wash his hands when he shall happen to pass the Bridge of Cramond.[11]

The tale may have no basis, or little basis, in fact: neither the date of this remarkable occurrence nor the name of the King's mistress is known, though Scott does attempt to give ballast to the story, one of several such he recounts, by assuring us that 'this person was ancestor of the Howisons of Braehead, in Mid-Lothian, a respectable family, who continue to hold the lands (now passed into the female line) under the same tenure'.

That such stories, no matter how fancifully embroidered over the years, were told about James V testifies to the hold he had on popular imagination, and suggests that the harsh judgements made by some contemporaries and later historians should be tempered by a more generous appreciation of the King's character.

James's personal rule would last for fourteen years, years domin-ated by deepening controversy about the direction Scotland should take with regard to foreign policy and in matters of religion. In 1528 the Protestant Reformation – or Revolution – set in motion in Germany by Martin Luther eleven years previously, had scarcely touched Scotland, or indeed England. Nevertheless, communications between the east-coast towns and Germany already gave the authorities some cause for alarm. In 1525 the Estates had passed a law prohibiting the import of Lutheran books, and in 1527 a letter was sent to Rome affirming the determination of the King of Scots (then still, as we have seen, detained by Angus) to prevent the Lutheran heresy from infecting his people. James himself followed this up as soon as he was in control of the government, and assured His Holiness that he would 'banish the foul Lutheran sect'. In return he asked the Pope to confirm the privileges of the Scottish Crown. Two years later he would reap the reward of his orthodoxy when the Pope authorised him to collect a tax of £10,000 a year from the Scottish Church, and a levy for three years of one-tenth of all Scottish ecclesiastical revenues. The pretext for the former was to establish a College of Justice. Actually the Court of Session was already in being, and the only change was that its judges were now termed (as they still are) Senators of the College of Justice. We may assume that the name 'senator' sounded impressive to Roman ears. There is, however, no reason to believe that James ever intended to spend as much as £10,000 on the College of Justice.

The Pope had good reason to be generous to James, for in England Henry VIII was moving – uncertainly, till Thomas Cromwell became his chief minister – towards the breach with Rome. Henry would never himself become a Protestant – indeed, he prided himself on his doctrinal orthodoxy, and would burn Protestants as heretics as happily as he sent obstinate papalists like Sir Thomas More and Bishop Fisher of Rochester to the block as traitors; but by 1534 he had first made it illegal for anyone to appeal to Rome against a decision of the English courts, and had then had himself declared, by Act of Parliament, Supreme Head of the Church in England. Within a few years Cromwell would organise the Dissolution of the Monasteries in England, transferring their property and wealth to the Crown and subsequently to its favoured servants, himself chief among them. Henry would urge his nephew James to follow his example, but James remained obdurate.

For one thing he was already doing well out of the Church, since in addition to the taxation the Pope had authorised, His Holiness had granted him the right to appoint all Scottish bishops and abbots. He made good use of this – from his point of view anyway – giving nominal authority over several abbeys, and real control of their revenues, to at least four of his illegitimate sons (though they were still children) as well as to favoured nobles. This nepotism and disregard for the true interests of the Church brought the ecclesiastical system into disrespect and turned some who were seeking a spiritual reformation towards Protestantism.

The King's orthodoxy may have been sincere. Like his father he displayed devotion to shrines and relics, and he patronised the Observant Friars, a reforming order within the Catholic Church. At the same time he was close to Sir David Lindsay of the Mount, his former tutor, who attacked the vices of the Church in his play *Ane Satyre of the Thrie Estaites*, which James himself ordered to be performed before him at Linlithgow. But anti-clericalism can sit easily with orthodoxy; and criticism of clerical vice had been a commonplace for centuries. Chaucer and Langland in England, Henryson and Dunbar in Scotland had all expressed such criticism in verse, without their orthodoxy being questioned. James upheld the authority of the Pope in all spiritual matters, and was happy to persecute heretics who challenged it. When the English ambassador told him that Cromwell's examination of monasteries, friaries and convents had revealed them to be nurseries of vice, James merely smiled and said that if members of the religious orders in Scotland did not live well, he would amend them, and then changed the subject. In the last year of his life he demonstrated his commitment to Catholicism by having Parliament pass an act that decreed the death penalty for anyone who argued against the Pope's authority or in any way impugned it. Another act declared that it was unlawful for any except 'theologians appointed by famous universities, or admitted thereto by those who have lawful power' to hold conventicles in order to dispute the Holy Scriptures, and unlawful too for anyone to give lodging to a known heretic. Such measures might be difficult to enforce; their intent is, however, clear.

Kings must be married, and the search for a suitable wife for James occupied several years. A daughter of the Emperor Charles V was at one time proposed; and then the offer was withdrawn. Henry suggested that James might marry his elder daughter, Mary, and even held out the hope that this might enable him to be his successor as King of England. This was surprising, for Mary was loyal to her mother, the discarded Catherine of Aragon, and committed to the Roman Church. However, since her fond father had, after he had rid himself of Catherine, declared the Lady Mary to be illegitimate, the proposal was less flattering than it seemed; and James rejected it. There was talk of a French princess, Madeleine, daughter of Francis I, but her health was poor – she was indeed consumptive – and Francis was reluctant to let her go to Scotland. In 1537, though, James himself went to France to inspect a daughter of the Constable de Vendôme. Disliking what he saw, he moved on to the French court, saw Madeleine, and, it appears, fell in love with her and she with him. At any rate, he charmed Francis, or at least persuaded him to approve the match. They were married in the Cathedral of Notre-Dame, and a few months later took the five-day voyage from Dieppe to Leith. On arrival the Queen fell to her knees and kissed the earth, expressing her gratitude that she had survived the voyage and come safe to her husband's land. She would have little experience of it, for a few weeks later her condition deteriorated sharply, as tuberculosis often does, and she died. So James was soon in the marriage market again. This time his choice fell on Marie de Guise, daughter of the house whose members would be the chiefs of the Catholic party in the French Wars of Religion that broke out twenty years later. Henry VIII, when between wives as he so often was, had proposed himself as her husband, but she had declined the offer, remarking that she had only one neck, if a pretty one, and preferred to keep her head attached to it.[12] However, she was happy to accept James, and so the French alliance was once more secured. It soon seemed that the future of the dynasty was also assured, for Marie bore James two sons within the first three years of their marriage.

James was covetous to the point of rapacity, resuming Crown lands granted with dubious legality during the years of his minority; this was a prime cause of the disaffection of the nobility that became apparent in the last years of his reign. If the King was grasping, he was also extravagant, spending lavishly on castles and palaces. Stirling, Holyrood, Linlithgow and Falkland were all enlarged and embellished at his command and at his expense; he brought craftsmen and artists from France and the Netherlands to work there. He looked to the future in other ways too, importing stallions and mares from Denmark to improve the native breed of horses and provide himself with a more formidable cavalry.

James seemed a strong and masterful king. In 1540, when word came of a minor revolt or rebellion in Skye, he responded by sailing in a fleet of twelve ships around the northern isles, where his favourite Oliver Sinclair, from an old Anglo-Norman family, was installed as Sheriff of Orkney, and on to the western isles. The rebellion, probably not very significant, was crushed, and a number of Highland chiefs whose loyalty was doubtful were arrested. The following year he visited Aberdeen. Its citizens were always pleased to see the wild Highlanders kept in check, and the university was delighted to honour the royal couple and to entertain them with plays and addresses 'in Greek, Latin and other languages'.

Yet in just a few months James's rule crumbled. He rejected attempts by his uncle Henry VIII to wean him from the French alliance, and when Henry condescended to travel to York, further north than he had ventured in his thirty years as king, in order to meet him, James, having first accepted the invitation, then changed his mind, probably because he distrusted Henry and feared he would be taken prisoner. The insult infuriated the English king and the next year, without any formal declaration of war, he made to invade Scotland, only to suffer a further humiliation: defeat at Haddon Rig, near Berwick. However, another detachment burned Roxburgh and Kelso. Meanwhile Henry denounced James as the aggressor.

Now the Scots king learned the cost of having alienated so large a part of his nobility, for when he proposed to march into England, he found that he could not command their support. They would fight on the defensive, they said, but would not cross the border. Pitscottie tells us that they asserted that the war 'was not grounded upon no good cause or reason, and he was ane better priests' king nor he was theirs, and used more of priests' counsel nor theirs. Therefore they had the less will to fight with him, and said it was more meritoriously done to hang all such as gave counsel to the King to break his promises to the King of England, whereof they perceived great inconvenience to befall.'[13]

James accused these nobles of cowardice. They turned aside. Some distrusted him, others had good cause to resent him; some, no more than a few perhaps, disapproved of the French alliance, believed that Scotland should be on good terms with England, and were attracted to the new reformed religion. And there were those who were either already in English pay or looked for some personal advantage from England.

The King did not give up immediately. There was still fight in him. He gathered another smaller army, and made to invade England by the western route, across the Solway. The army marched in two divisions, one commanded by the King, the other by Oliver Sinclair. But the borderland through which they advanced was hostile. James's punitive expeditions against Armstrongs, Elliotts and Scotts had been neither forgotten nor forgiven. While James halted at Lochmaben, waiting for the ebb tide that would let him cross into England, Sinclair's division encountered the English Warden of the Marches, Sir Thomas Wharton, at Solway Moss. It was scarcely a battle. The Scots army was rounded up – like cattle, it was said – with the help of the Liddesdale men, who had rich experience in cattle-rustling, and who had opportunely changed sides, having come to an accommodation with the English for the time being.[14]

James now suffered a moral collapse. Only a few months previously he had been secure in his power, rich, married to a beautiful and capable princess, father of two sons. Then the boys had died within a week of each other, and now failure in war and the hostility of leading nobles saw his authority washed away, like a sandcastle before the incoming tide. His favourite Oliver had disgraced both himself and his master. 'Is Oliver fled? Is Oliver tane?' James asked repeatedly. 'Then all is lost.' He spent a few days in Edinburgh, then in Linlithgow, where his queen was about to give birth, then withdrew to the palace of Falkland, where Angus had held him prisoner, and whence he had escaped to begin his personal rule. There they brought him news that the Queen had given birth to a daughter. This was no consolation. Remembering Marjorie Bruce, by way of whom came the Stewarts' right to reign, he sighed and muttered the words that became famous: 'it cam' wi' a lass and it'll gang wi' a lass' – a prophecy that would not be fulfilled.

And then he died. No cause of death has been identified. He seems simply to have lost the will to live. It is the most mysterious of Stewart deaths, for this was a king regarded as being strong in body and resolute in will. He died as an old dog might, hiding itself away to die; but James was only thirty, not old at all.

Chapter 9

Mary (1542–67):
Scotland's Tragic Queen

Mary Stuart's effective reign lasted barely six years and was therefore far shorter than that of any of her Stewart ancestors. Yet the drama of her life, the horror of her death, and the courage and dignity with which she met it have made her a figure of romance, the best known of her family, and the subject of many novels, plays and films. When in Edinburgh, on their way to the Hebrides, Boswell spoke to Dr Johnson of his regret that since the Union of 1707, 'our independent kingdom was lost', the old English Tory flared up in dismissive contempt: 'Sir, never talk to me of your independency, who could let your Queen remain twenty years in captivity, and then be put to death, without even a pretence of justice, without your ever attempting to rescue her; and such a Queen too! as every man of any gallantry of spirit would have sacrificed his life for.'[1] We shall see why there was no such attempt, why the Scots acquiesced in Mary's execution. But Dr Johnson's indignation on her behalf speaks eloquently of the power of the Marian myth. Though many of her contemporaries thought her wicked, and some historians have dismissed her as foolish, no amount of critical investigation of her career, or psychological enquiry, can alter the popular perception of her as the glamorous, unhappy and much abused queen. That is the myth, and it cannot be easily argued away.

Rightly so, for there is always some truth in myth, and this was the case with Mary. Had it not been so, she could have won neither the devotion of many in her lifetime nor the partisan loyalty of posterity. Yet the reality of her story is at least as compelling, and perhaps more deeply interesting, than the myth.

She was first, inescapably, a politician, if in the end a singularly unsuccessful one, 'whose political folly was', in the words of one of her modern biographers, Dr Wormald, 'seemingly unlimited'.[2] She was all but born a queen, being only a week old when her father took to his bed and died, and from the first she was a cause of discord. She represented, through her mother, Marie de Guise, the French interest in Scottish affairs. Consequently those who favoured an English alliance were ranged against her. This opposition was rendered the more acute by the ideological disputes that disturbed and divided Europe. On account of Henry VIII's marital difficulties, England had rejected the authority of the Pope and broken away from the Roman Catholic Church. Though it was not yet certain in 1542 that England would become Protestant, it was probable. France remained predominantly Catholic, but there was a strong Protestant party (the Huguenots), and some of the greatest noble families, especially in the south-west, were adherents of the Reformed religion. Intermittently, throughout Mary's adult life, France was ravaged by civil war, in which the chief Catholic champions were her maternal relations, the great House of Guise, while the last Valois kings, dominated by their mother Catherine de Medici, tried to steer a middle course between the Huguenots and the Catholic League. Scotland was still Catholic in 1542, but Protestantism was winning converts and supporters, some religious enthusiasts, others noblemen who enviously watched their English counterparts enriching themselves on the spoils and property of the Church.

For Henry, held at a distrustful distance by James V, the accession of the infant Queen offered an opportunity to detach Scotland from France. The Earl of Angus (Margaret Tudor's second husband and therefore, till their divorce, Henry's brother-in law) had been resident in England since James V had escaped his control in 1528. Henry now sent him back to Scotland, along with a number of noblemen taken prisoner at Solway Moss, who obtained their liberty in return for promises to further the English interest. The regent or governor of Scotland was James Hamilton, second Earl of Arran, who, as a great-grandson of James II, was next in succession to the baby Queen. A man of no great strength of character or constancy of purpose, he would swither between the French and English parties. For the moment, though, he allowed himself to be dominated by Angus. Cardinal Beaton, Archbishop of St Andrews, anti-English and pro-French, was imprisoned. Henry now proposed a future marriage between his only son, Edward, who was then not quite six, and the Scottish queen. His offer was accepted. In July 1543, a treaty was drawn up at Greenwich, which provided for peace between the two kingdoms, and for the betrothal of Mary and Edward. Arran ratified it the following month. However, he soon changed his mind and reversed his policy. One reason for doing so was Henry's stipulation that the little Queen should be sent to be brought up in England till she was of marriageable age; this suggested an intention of incorporating Scotland into the kingdom of England. Arran was also influenced by his half-brother John, Abbot of Paisley, who had only recently returned to Scotland from the Continent, and who exercised considerable influence over the governor. 'What the English lords decide him to do one day, the Abbot changes the next' was the judgement of one observer. Finally, Arran's second thoughts may have been prompted by the hope that his own son, the Master of Hamilton, might make a better husband for Mary than the English prince. So Cardinal Beaton was released from prison and the pro-French party was once again in the ascendant.

Henry's hope of a marriage that would lead to the union of the two kingdoms was not yet lost, but he contrived to destroy any chance of success by characteristic brutal stupidity. Abandoning diplomacy, he turned to force, sending an army north to burn and ravage the southern counties of Scotland. The Scots called this a 'rough wooing' and watched helplessly but angrily as the great Border abbeys of Jedburgh, Kelso, Melrose and Dryburgh went up in flames. Then in 1546 Cardinal Beaton was murdered in the castle

of St Andrews. Ostensibly this was revenge for the execution of a
popular Protestant preacher, George Wishart; his crime was heresy,
but he may also have been an English agent. The Cardinal's assassins, among them John Knox, the future leader of the Scottish
Reformation, held the castle for some months till it was bombarded
by a French fleet.

Henry died in January 1547, but his policy was still pursued by
the Duke of Somerset, Lord Protector to his nephew, the boy-king
Edward VI. He led another army north and defeated the Scots at
the Battle of Pinkie in Musselburgh. It is a measure of the resentment provoked by English aggression that the commander of the
Scots at Pinkie was the Anglophile Earl of Angus. The Scottish
Council now sought further help from France, and an army of
6,000 men was provided. In exchange the French stipulated that
the little Queen be sent to France for her own safety and betrothed
to the Dauphin, heir to the French throne, as a guarantor of this
renewal of the Auld Alliance. Thus the ill-temper and impatience
of the old ogre Henry VIII determined Mary's future. She would
be brought up as a Frenchwoman.

The Sieur de Brantôme[3] was a French soldier, member of an old
noble family, who took to writing after he was crippled by a fall
from a horse. Two years older than Mary, he knew her at the
French court and was one of the company who sailed with her
when she returned to Scotland in 1561. In old age he wrote a brief
memoir of her. More than half of it recounts the circumstances of
her death, which he knew second-hand from written accounts and
the testimony of two of her ladies-in-waiting, but the first part of
his memoir is the more interesting. He adored her and thought her
well-nigh perfect.

As time went on and the child grew older, her great beauty began
to be manifest and her virtues increase, to such an extent that when
she was fifteen her fairness shone bright as the sun at high noon;
nay, so bright as to eclipse the sun at its brightest, so radiant the
beauty of her person.

Yet the beauty of her mind was equally bright. She had made
herself most learned in the Latin tongue. At the age of thirteen or

fourteen, she recited publicly, in the presence of King Henri, the Queen, and the entire court, in a room of the Louvre, a speech in Latin composed by herself, sustaining against the common belief the thesis that it is becoming in women to be acquainted with literature and the liberal arts. What a rare and admirable thing it was to see this beautiful and learned Queen speak thus in Latin, which she understood and spoke exceedingly well! For this I can vouch, for I heard her on that occasion myself.

She was likewise so deeply interested in suchlike matters that she had Antoine Fouquelin, of Chauny in the Vermandois, write a French Rhetoric, which still exists, in order than she might understand the language still more perfectly, and prove more eloquent than if she had been born in France . . . There was no field of human knowledge in which she could not intelligently discourse, but she loved poets and poetry before all else, and her favourite poets were M. de Ronsard, M. du Bellay and M. de Maisonfleur, who all wrote beautiful verses and elegies for her. When she departed from France, I was present (both in France and later in Scotland) when such poems, being read to her, drew tears from her eyes and sighs from her heart . . . She even wrote verses herself, some of which I have seen.

In conversation she spoke quietly, with a charm of manner exceeding agreeable, yet majestic – a mixture of discretion and modesty, with a notable grace. She spoke her own language – naturally barbarous-sounding, crude and harsh to the ear – so gracefully that hearing it spoken by her one might imagine it a beautiful tongue. Behold how the virtue, beauty and grace of this woman were able to transform so much crude barbarism into what was delicate, courtly, and civilized. Yet this is not so marvellous as that when she was dressed like a savage (as I have seen her) in the barbaric fashion of her country, she still shone forth like a goddess.

Extolling her beauty and kindness, he insists on her love of France and on her virtue. She is, in his tender memory, the princess of innumerable fairy tales; but it is probable that he neither seeks to deceive, nor consciously gilds the picture. This is how he truly saw her: the Mary of romance, of the myth or legend, the image that still exercises its charm across the centuries.

In France, Brantome declares, everybody adored her, from the

King and Queen, who became her parents-in-law, downwards. (Actually Catherine seems to have been jealous of her and was certainly severely critical of much that Mary did after her return to Scotland.) When her first husband, little Francis II, died in 1560, only two years after their marriage, his young brother Charles IX, according to Brantôme, 'was so enamoured of her that when he looked on her portrait, he could not take his eyes off it'. Indeed, 'had he been of age (but he was then both young and small) he was as much in love with her as I have ever seen him at a later date. He would never have permitted her to leave the country and would certainly have married her.'

Throughout her life Mary was indeed adored by those around her, ladies-in-waiting, servants, small children, dogs, and also by many who stood at a distance from her. But though she was charming and amiable, she did not, contrary to the legend, inspire passionate love, and may only once have experienced that emotion.[4] Neither the romantic view of her as a great lover, nor the hostile one that casts her as a sexual adventuress, can be sustained.

Mary might have been the darling of the French court, but while she lived in France, the politics of Scotland became ever more violent and unsettled. Her mother was now regent, but depended much on the support of French troops, regarded by many as an army of occupation. The Protestant reformers continued to gain strength, though from 1553 to 1558 they were unable to look for support from England, where Henry VIII's eldest child Mary Tudor had restored the Roman Catholic Church when she succeeded her half-brother Edward on the throne. Nevertheless, the Scots Protestants were able to present themselves as the patriotic party after their queen's marriage to the Dauphin in 1558, for her father-in-law Henry II had rashly declared that France and Scotland were now one country. This raised the possibility of Scotland becoming a French satellite, or even of being incorporated into France, as the Duchy of Brittany had been when its last independent ruler married Charles VIII of France in 1494.

Mary Tudor died in 1558 and the new queen was her half-sister Elizabeth. Since her father's desire to marry Anne Boleyn had provoked the Reformation in England, their daughter Elizabeth was inevitably identified with the Protestant cause. In Catholic eyes she was illegitimate, since Henry had married Anne while his first wife, Catherine of Aragon, was still alive, and the Pope had refused to annul his marriage to Catherine; Elizabeth was therefore no rightful queen. Accordingly, in Paris, Mary Stuart – she had changed the spelling of the family name to make it easier for the French to pronounce – was proclaimed Queen of England and Ireland as well as Scotland. The following year, on the death of her father-in-law, she was Queen of France too.

The England of Elizabeth and the Scots Protestants now had an interest in common: to break the French alliance. It was not difficult to arrange this, for the regent and the French forces that sustained her were unpopular, and the reformers, led by the Queen's illegitimate half-brother, Lord James Stewart, could pose as representatives of the patriotic cause. In this capacity they called in an English army to expel the French. Its arrival in 1559 was followed by the unexpected death of the Queen Mother in Edinburgh Castle, which deprived those who held to the Church of Rome and the Auld Alliance of their leader. Thus that alliance, which dated from the brief reign of John Balliol three and a half centuries before, expired suddenly and ignominiously. Scots who retain a sentimental affection for its memory often forget, or don't know, that it ended when other Scots, proclaiming themselves to be patriots, invited an English army into Scotland to drive their auld allies out.

A treaty was made at Leith between England and Scotland, the latter represented by the Protestant revolutionaries who styled themselves the Lords of the Congregation of Christ. According to its terms, Mary was obliged to relinquish her claim to be the true Queen of England and to recognise Elizabeth as queen in her stead. Though Mary never signed the treaty herself, she came to acquiesce tacitly in its content, and thereafter concentrated her attentions on trying to persuade Elizabeth to acknowledge her as heir to the English throne. Yet in her own mind she never abandoned the claim. In her last letter, written to her brother-in-law Henry III of France the night before her execution, she spoke of her 'God-given right to the English throne'. This conviction was so strong as to be fairly called an obsession; and it brought her to her doom.

Mary's husband, Francis, had died in 1560, a few months after the Treaty of Leith was made. He was two years younger than Mary, and had always been stunted and sickly. At the age of sixteen he was still little more than a child, but Mary had been fond of him, though perhaps as an elder sister rather than a lover or wife. She might have stayed in France, where she had great estates in Touraine, settled on her at the time of her marriage. There was the possibility of another royal match. The claims of Don Carlos, son and heir of Philip II of Spain, were canvassed, but Philip, who had been married to Mary Tudor, had no desire to antagonise his sister-in-law Elizabeth by allowing such a wedding. It was a happy escape for Mary. Don Carlos was undersized, backward, vicious and mentally unstable. Her Guise uncles, the Duke and the Cardinal of Lorraine, were eager that she should marry the new King of France, her brother-in-law Charles IX. No doubt a papal dispensation permitting the match might easily have been arranged; almost certainly her marriage with poor Francis had never been consummated. But Charles was only ten, and his mother, Catherine de Medici, intended to reduce the power of the Guises rather than enhance it. Indeed, she wanted her daughter-in-law out of France. Everyone adored Mary; few even liked Catherine.

So Mary returned to Scotland, to a country convulsed by the Protestant Reformation, which had there taken the character of a revolution. The historic Church had been overthrown, monasteries and churches sacked, Church property seized, the Mass outlawed, bishops abolished, and a Presbyterian form of Church government decreed. In August 1560 the Estates passed a series of acts in the name of the absent Queen, but without her authority. Like the Treaty of Leith, these acts, lacking Mary's signature, might have been of dubious legality; but questions of legality yielded to revolutionary necessity.

The Estates also published a 'Confession of Faith', twenty-five articles defining correct religious belief and practices. Its author was John Knox. He had had a varied career since participating in the murder of Cardinal Beaton. Taken prisoner when the French stormed the castle of St Andrews, he had spent a year pulling an oar in a French galley. Released, he had made his way to England, where, in the reign of Edward VI, he was offered a bishopric, which he refused prudently, 'in forewight', as he later remarked, 'of trouble to come'. When that trouble indeed arrived in the form of the Catholic reaction, he, prudently again, removed to Geneva, where he came under the influence of John Calvin. There, in what he described as 'the most perfect schole of Christ', he imbibed and accepted the doctrines of Predestination and the Elect, which were to be at the heart of Scotch Presbyterianism. It was from Geneva that in 1558 he delivered the pamphlet entitled *A First Blast of the Trumpet against the Monstrous Regiment of Women*. This was not quite what it seems. 'Regiment' means 'Rule' and his attack was directed at Mary Tudor in England, Marie de Guise in Scotland and (perhaps) Catherine de Medici in France. In private life, Knox was no misogynist. Indeed, he rather liked women, and married twice, the second time when he was over fifty to a girl of fifteen, with whom he had three daughters.5 What he objected to was female government, all the more so because all three were Catholics, enemies of the Reformation to which he was now absolutely committed. This, however, was one occasion when his 'forewight' failed him. He had not considered that a Protestant queen might succeed Mary Tudor. Elizabeth was not amused by his trumpet-blast, and refused to allow him to return to England as he wished. So he came home to Scotland and in May 1559 preached an inflammatory sermon in Perth, which roused what his enemies described as 'the rascal multitude' to storm and sack the town's monasteries and friaries.

Though guided by the Lords of the Congregation, the Reformation in Scotland was a popular movement. It was not, however, universally so – the north-east in particular remaining hostile and attached to the old ways and the Catholic faith for a long time – and its impact was not felt immediately all over the country. There are arguments as to how deep and widespread attachment to the cause of reform was. It was by no means certain in 1560 that it might not be reversed, as had happened in England when Mary Tudor became queen. The vehemence with which it was preached and the incitement of mobs may be taken, in part at least, as evidence of the nervousness and insecurity of the reformers.

Michael Lynch in his *History of Scotland* wrote:

> For many people the Reformation is the central event of Scottish history; it was the point at which they can claim their birthright as a Protestant nation. For them, the Reformation was a kind of 'big bang' – everything happened overnight. In some places it did. In St Andrews, on 11 June, 1559, the citizens went to bed as Catholics and woke up as Protestants, because overnight the Lords of the Congregation – the Protestant army, with John Knox among them – had come into the town, had gone into the parish church and ripped down all the Catholic ornaments, whitewashed the walls and turned it into a Protestant church. The 'big bang' did not happen like that in many places.[6]

Nevertheless, it is undeniable that a great part of Lowland Scotland enthusiastically welcomed the rejection of Rome and embraced the reformed religion with fervent zeal. Mary was apprised of this before she returned to Scotland. On the one hand, the Catholic Earl of Huntly, chief of the great Aberdeenshire family of Gordon, came to her in Paris offering to raise an army of 20,000 men (a boast he could not have made good) to restore the kingdom to proper order and true religion. On the other, her half-brother, Lord James Stewart,[7] advised her to tread warily and to practise discretion. Her Guise uncles, though eager to see Scotland return to the French alliance, counselled likewise, the Cardinal even going so far as to suggest that she might be wise to make a show of Protestantism, at the very least to declare her intention of making no attempt at counter-revolution. This advice was in tune with Mary's own temper, which was essentially mild and generous.

Mary arrived in Scotland on 19 August 1561. If Knox is to be believed, the very face of heaven . . . did manifestly speak what comfort was brought into this country with her, to wit, sorrow, dolor, darkness, and all impiety; for in the memory of man, that day of the year has never seen a more dolorous face of the heaven, than was at her arrival, which two days after did so continue; for, besides the surface wet, and corruption of the air, the mist was so thick and dark, that scarce might any man espy another the length of two butts; the sun was not seen to shine two days before, nor two days after. That forewarning God gave unto us, but alas the most part were blind . . .[8]

Few acquainted with the vagaries of a Scottish August will be as certain as Knox that the foul weather that greeted Mary on her return to Scotland was intended by the Almighty as 'forewarning' that she was bringing 'sorrow, dolor, darkness, and all impiety' to her kingdom.

In fact, even Knox admits that her arrival was greeted with general joy, but he does so to point the contrast, to show how deluded they were, and then how short a time their joy lasted. Mary, while offering no challenge to the reformers, was determined that she should still worship according to the rites of the Roman Church. The news that Mass was to be celebrated in the royal chapel had men asking, if again Knox's account is to be trusted, 'Shall that idol be suffered again to take place within this realm?'; and supplying the answer, 'It shall not.' A demonstration threatened to turn into a riot, with calls for 'the idolatrous priests' to be put to death. At that moment, however, Lord James Stewart, 'the man whom all the godly did most reverence', intervened to guard the chapel door.

The riot may have been spontaneous; again it may not. Lord James may have acted out of respect and regard for his half-sister, the Queen; or he may have staged the whole thing to demonstrate that she must rely on him, that indeed she would find it impossible to govern without his advice and assistance. Mary took the hint, and soon created him Earl of Moray.

Moray, eldest son of James V and his mistress Margaret Erskine, was now a man of thirty, ten years older than his half-sister. He was a sincere convert to the reformed religion and an astute politician.

He was in his way a patriot who believed in the desirability, even necessity, of the alliance with England, which alone could safeguard the Reformation; but he was also in English pay. He may have had an affection for Mary, but, resenting his own illegitimacy, he could not but think he would have made a better king than she a queen. He looked like a Stewart king, tall, dark, serious of expression and mind, and some suspected he had designs on the throne. In 1559 Mary's father-in-law, Henry II, shortly before his death, had commissioned the Constable of France to send Sir James Melville (later Mary's ambassador to the English court) back to Scotland to report on whether there was any truth in rumours that Lord James intended to supplant Mary, then still in France, and seize the crown for himself. Melville's report suggested the rumours were unfounded. He was probably right. Lord James was loyal to Mary, as long as her wishes coincided with his interests, and for a few years she would be guided by his advice.

The Queen's other chief councillor was her secretary – in modern terminology, secretary of state – William Maitland of Lethington, an intellectual whose intelligence provoked both admiration and distrust. (Some called him 'Mitchell Wyllie', a Scots corruption of Machiavelli.) In concert with Maitland and Moray, Mary pursued a prudent policy of conciliation. She had tacitly accepted the doubtfully legal Acts of the Reformation Parliament, which had outlawed the Mass, and when in 1562 the Catholic Earl of Huntly staged a rebellion, which had the intention of reversing the religious changes, she not only suppressed it, but rode with her troops, winning their admiration by her energy, grace and cheerfulness.

Knox, however, was irreconcilable. 'If there be not in her a proud mind, a crafty wit, and an indurate heart against God and his truth, my judgement faileth me.'[9] He and Mary debated matters of religion on several occasions, at length, and by Knox's account he invariably had the better of her. Her version of the argument might have been different. He boasted of having reduced her to angry tears on at least one occasion, which did not greatly disturb him, 'seeing as I have offered unto you no just occasion to be offended, but I have spoken the truth, as my vocation craves'.[10]

Nevertheless, no matter how offended she might have been, Mary continued to pursue the middle way, one of tolerance, unusual, indeed scarcely known, in that time. This, however, was not a quality to commend itself to Knox and his fellow True Believers. Tolerance was laxity and laxity was sin, a defiance of the Word of God as interpreted by Knox.

The other immediate and important question concerned her marriage. Nobody supposed that she could govern effectively without the support of a husband, and she was herself eager to marry again and produce an heir to ensure the future of the dynasty. Elizabeth of England would remain unmarried – or, as she remarked, married only to her country. Her ability to hold out the prospect of a marriage was a valuable diplomatic card. Moreover, she was by nature reluctant to commit herself completely to any course of action and was indeed, to the reiterated anger of her ministers, constitutionally indecisive. But Mary seems never to have contemplated remaining single, and Elizabeth took a close interest in her choice. This was reasonable if she was ever to accede to her cousin's request that she be named as her heir. Whoever Mary married might one day be King of England. That ruled out any foreign Roman Catholic prince – in Elizabeth's opinion anyway.

There was one Scottish candidate, the young Earl of Arran, head of the House of Hamilton. He had been proposed as a possible husband when they were both young children, in the days when his father was governor and was being guided by Cardinal Beaton. Indeed, he had been taken to France with the little Queen in 1548. His father, who had been rewarded for turning against the Treaty of Greenwich with French lands and a French title (Duke of Chatelherault), continued to promote the match, and there was certainly a suggestion that if something happened to prevent the marriage of Mary and the Dauphin, then young Arran would be considered as a future husband. He had a ring that Mary had given him and that he believed was a token of her agreement, and as soon as Francis died he sent it back to Mary to remind her of the promise he thought she had made. Meanwhile, however, Arran had also been paying suit to Elizabeth. Disappointed of both queens, the young man, always nervous, highly strung and erratic, became mad. In 1562 he was placed in confinement, where he would remain, outliving most of his contemporaries, till he died in 1609.

Elizabeth had her own candidate for the position of the Scotch queen's husband: Robert Dudley, whom she had created Earl of Leicester. This might be considered a generous, even selfless, offer, for the world believed that Leicester had been, perhaps still was, her own lover. Worse than that, it was also believed, probably falsely, that he had disposed of his wife, Amy Robsart, in order to free himself to marry Elizabeth. (Amy had died by falling down-stairs – the story is at the heart of Scott's novel *Kenilworth* – but rumour had it she had been pushed by her husband's command.)

Mary regarded the suggestion that she should marry Dudley as an insult. Not only was she being offered Elizabeth's leavings – her discarded lover – but worse still, Dudley was a parvenu. His grandfather, Edmund Dudley, had been a mere lawyer, one of Henry VII's ministers – executed by Henry VIII in a popular gesture as soon as he came to the throne. Then, though Robert Dudley's father John had become in succession Earl of Warwick, Duke of Northumberland and Lord Protector of England during the reign of Edward VI, he too had been executed as a traitor, having attempted to subvert the succession by putting Henry VII's great-granddaughter, Lady Jane Grey (conveniently married to one of Northumberland's sons), on the throne instead of Mary Tudor. So though it was no disgrace to die on the scaffold in Tudor England, the Dudleys were a disreputable lot; and Robert Dudley quite un-acceptable to Mary, Queen of Scots and Queen Dowager of France.

Mary must look elsewhere. She cast her eye about and it lighted on a tall, good-looking boy a couple of years her junior. He was called Henry, Lord Darnley, and he was, she said, 'the lustiest and best proportioned long man' she had ever seen.

Darnley was a cousin of both queens. His mother, Margaret Douglas, was the daughter of Margaret Tudor by her second marriage to the Earl of Angus. So Mary and Darnley shared a grandmother. Since Margaret Tudor was also Elizabeth's aunt, Margaret Douglas was the English queen's first cousin and she stood at one further remove of cousinship from the boy. Margaret Douglas was married to Matthew Stewart, Earl of Lennox, who was himself a descendant of James II. Lennox had been living in England for some twenty years, since taking the English side in the last years of Henry VIII's reign, and young Darnley was more of an Englishman than a Scot. He had a claim also to the English throne, though it was a doubtful one, since in his will Henry VIII had excluded the descendants of his sister Margaret from the succession.

Darnley was a pretty boy with some charm of manner, at least while things were going his way. His parents both adored him and had spoiled him, so that he became petulant and angry whenever crossed or denied his own way. He didn't lack accomplishments: he was musical and wrote verses, danced and fenced well, and had a good seat on a horse. These were his good qualities and they were all that Mary saw. She fell in love with him and felt tenderly towards the boy when he contracted measles, nursing him as she had nursed her first husband, little Francis. It was the one sure romantic impulse of her life, the one time that she fell unreservedly in love. The English ambassador Sir Thomas Randolph reported that 'great tokens of love daily pass' between them, and believed that Mary was in thrall to 'a fantasy of a man'. They were married on 29 July 1565; it was the first great blunder of Mary's life.

The marriage soured relations with both Elizabeth and Moray, though some have argued that Elizabeth expressed her disapproval of the match in order to make sure it went ahead. Darnley had been brought up a Catholic. Moray objected to a marriage that might lead to the re-establishment of the Church of Rome in Scotland. This was not unreasonable; if Darnley was granted what was called 'the Crown Matrimonial', he might prove less moderate than Mary. Moreover, this marriage, unlike one Moray might have approved, would deprive him of power. Finding himself unable to prevent it, he raised his Protestant supporters in rebellion, subsidised by England, though less generously than he had hoped. Mary again rode with her troops. There was no real fighting – the incident became known as the Chase-about Raid – and Moray retired south of the border. The first significance of this inept rebellion is that it shows how insecure the Protestant party felt, how insubstantial their hold still appeared to be; the second is that Mary had turned for support to a Border nobleman, James Hepburn, Earl of Bothwell, whom she now made Warden of the Marches, her lieutenant in the unruly borderlands.

Bothwell, who was some seven years older (and six inches shorter) than the Queen, was a rough, violent man and intensely ambitious. Most of his fellow nobles distrusted him. Some loathed him, others feared him. He was nominally a Protestant but stood apart from the Lords of the Congregation, for he detested Moray, and the feeling was reciprocated. His private life was scandalous. He had had an affair with Janet Scott, the Lady of Branxholm, who was nineteen years his senior and the mother of a quiver of children; and indeed no woman was said to be safe from his approaches. His enemies accused him also of sodomy, but this was a charge more often levelled than proved. He was said to have dabbled in witchcraft and the dark arts while a student in Paris. Yet he was not just a thug. He was fluent in French and knew some Latin and Greek, and Sir Henry Percy, an Englishman who had dealings with him in Bothwell's capacity as Warden of the Marches, found him to be 'wise and not the man he was reputed to be. His behaviour was both courteous and honourable.'[11] Unlike most of the Protestant lords, he steered clear of English entanglements. He was loyal to Mary and would come to seem the one strong man she could trust. Her reliance on him would prove disastrous.

Meanwhile Mary had another confidant or favourite, an Italian called David Riccio or Rizzio. He had come to Scotland in the train of the ambassador of Savoy, and Mary had taken a fancy to him, because he was an accomplished musician and agreeable companion. When the ambassador went home, David remained behind and Mary made him her secretary with responsibility for her extensive correspondence with France. Before the Queen's marriage, he was also friendly with Darnley, with whom he occasionally shared a bed. At a time when it was common enough for men to be required to lie together, beds being in short supply, this does not necessarily mean that they were lovers. Some have indeed thought Darnley bisexual, perhaps because his beautiful face was somewhat girlish, though there were also rumours that he frequented a male brothel in one of the closes off Edinburgh's High Street.[12] It was natural that Rizzio, as an intimate of both Mary and Darnley, should have favoured their marriage, but it was not long before the favour the Queen showed him, and her evident reliance on his advice, aroused anger and suspicion. He was rumoured to be a papal agent, an enemy of the True Religion, and Mary's lover, this last despite his unprepossessing appearance; he was nearer fifty than forty, short, dark and ugly. The suspicion was without foundation. What the Italian offered Mary was agreeable, civilised company such as she had been accustomed to in France and now sorely lacked.

She was already disappointed in her husband. Darnley had a taste for what was called 'low company', and had already acquired a mistress. Nothing contradicts so clearly the picture of Mary as a great lover than her inability to hold the affection of her young husband for more than a few months. He was already piqued because he had been refused the Crown Matrimonial and excluded from government. The young fool was a fruit ripe for plucking by Mary's enemies.

Wild rumours of plots and counter-plots were rife. Sir Thomas Randolph told the Earl of Leicester that Darnley and his father Lennox were conspiring against Mary: Rizzio would have his throat cut and Mary's own life might be in danger. Lennox, he said, had assured Moray that if he supported Darnley, he would receive a pardon for his recent rebellion and be able to return to Scotland.

There was substance to this rumour. Indeed, Moray was in some urgency. A parliament was due to meet and the main item on the agenda would be his condemnation as a rebel and the forfeiture of his extensive estates. So the conspirators moved quickly. Darnley had already been persuaded that Rizzio was his wife's lover, and was easily drawn into the plot. On the evening of 9 March 1566, a troop of men commanded by the earls of Morton and Lindsay, with Darnley in attendance, took possession of the palace of Holyroodhouse. Mary, well advanced in pregnancy, was at supper with her ladies and Rizzio when confronted by the rebel lords, led

by Morton, Lindsay and the grim Lord Ruthven, who was said to
be a warlock and who in his enthusiasm for murder had risen from
a sick-bed, putting on armour over his nightshirt. They seized
Rizzio and stabbed him repeatedly. He called out for mercy. So
did the Queen. She was told to be quiet and threatened with being
'cut in collops' herself. The murder, performed in Moray's interest
and with his connivance and approval, was a direct challenge to
her rule. It was a deed she could never forget or forgive.

She kept her nerve, however. That very night she made peace
with her husband, despite the cruel and ignoble part he had played
in the murder, and detached the silly young man from his confederates, telling him he was a fool if he thought them his friends, or
men he could rely on. As her courage rose, his fell. One of her
ladies slipped out of the palace carrying a message to Bothwell,
who had earlier prudently made his own escape from Holyrood.
Before dawn, the Queen, Darnley and a few servants left the palace
by way of a secret staircase, then out through the kitchens and the
abbey cemetery, to where horses were waiting for them. They rode
hard for Dunbar. At one point they saw a detachment of soldiers
lying, apparently, in wait. Darnley called for more speed, and when
Mary protested that she feared she might miscarry, he told her
crudely that they could well make another child if this one was
lost. Fortunately, the soldiers proved to be Bothwell's men, who
accompanied them to Dunbar. After the night's hard riding, the
Queen cooked eggs for her companions' breakfast.[13]

She then returned to Edinburgh, escorted by several hundred of
Bothwell's Border troops. Revenge may have been in her heart, but
she was governed by her head. She sought once again to concili-
ate her enemies. The alternative was to risk civil war, which might
invite English intervention. Furthermore, she could not be certain
who was truly on her side and who against her. So pardons were
granted. Moray was restored to favour. Darnley's plea of innocence was accepted, doubtless with reservations on her part. Even
evidence that the conspirators had received money from England
was not pursued. Mary did not question Elizabeth's bland assurance that she knew nothing of any such payment.

Three months later Mary gave birth in Edinburgh Castle to the child who would, as James VI and I, fulfil her own ambition and unite the crowns of Scotland and England. 'My lord,' she told Darnley, 'God has given you and me a son, begotten by none but you.' When her ambassador, Sir James Melville, relayed the news to Elizabeth, she 'laid her hand upon her haffet [cheek] bursting out to some of her ladies, how that the Queen of Scotland was lighter of a fair son, and that she was but a barren stock'.[14]

Mary may at this moment have hoped and intended to repair her marriage. Her good nature and kindliness inclined her to do so. In the will she made before her confinement she had left Darnley a diamond ring, noting, 'it was with this that I was wed'. But whatever her intention, she could not trust him again, and nor could anyone else. His participation in Rizzio's murder stuck in her gullet. His desertion of his confederates caused them to hate and despise him. Moray and Maitland of Lethington, restored to influence if not power, were eager to find ways to be rid of him; and so was the ambitious Earl of Bothwell.

It is possible to feel some sympathy for Darnley, though most historians and biographers of Mary have found it easy to resist any temptation to do so, and may not indeed have felt it.[15] Much in his character was deplorable. He has been called vain, conceited, lazy, cowardly, weak-minded and treacherous, and on various occasions his behaviour merited all these derogatory epithets. But he was very young, had been spoiled by his parents, who reared him to think himself perfect, and was married to a wife who had fallen out of love with him very soon after their wedding and who now viewed him with what seemed a settled dislike. Worse still, he had been led into being at least an accessory to Rizzio's murder by as violent and frightening a gang of cut-throats as can be imagined. Then, either because he was afraid or because, just possibly, his better nature asserted itself, he had betrayed them and accompanied his wife when she fled from the palace. If he was now terrified of Moray, Morton, Lindsay, Ruthven and the rest of the murderous gang, he can scarcely be blamed.

There was talk of a divorce, or, more exactly, an annulment.

Mary was seemingly eager to be rid of him, but drew back when she realised that an annulment of the marriage would call into question the legitimacy of her son. That was unthinkable. The matter was shelved.

Darnley himself was eager to get away. He spoke of going to the Netherlands to fight in the Spanish army, then of commissioning a ship and making for France. He did neither, and in any case it would have been illegal to leave the country without the Queen's permission. More sinister rumours surrounded him. He was known, or at least believed, to have been in communication with the Pope. There were again dark mutterings of a Catholic plot, headed by Darnley and his father, the Earl of Lennox. The Queen, it was said, would be set aside in favour of her son, Darnley would become regent, and the Roman Church restored. This was probably no more than wild talk. But the times were uneasy. Rome had put its house in order, and the Counter-Reformation was well under way. Spain was moving to crush a Protestant revolt in the Netherlands, while France was slipping into civil war. Moreover, men like Moray and Morton, who had fomented revolution and organised murder, were naturally wary. When Mary rejected proposals for an annulment, her secretary Maitland of Lethington said, with sinister obscurity, 'We shall find the means that Your Majesty shall be rid of him.'

At Christmas 1566, Darnley fell ill in Glasgow. There was the usual talk of poison, for which there is no evidence, but it was probably smallpox.[16] When he was out of immediate danger, Mary went to Glasgow to nurse him. If it was smallpox, she could do so without fear of infection, for she had contracted the disease while a child in France, though only lightly, as it had left her unmarked. Nursing him again, as she had before their marriage, a spark of affection may have revived. They agreed that he should return with her to Edinburgh as soon as he was well enough to travel in a litter. Her intention was to take him to Craigmillar Castle, a couple of miles beyond the city limits, but he preferred a lodging offered him in what was known as the Provost's House of Kirk o' Field, which abutted on the Flodden Wall on the south side of the city. It belonged to one Robert Balfour, a canon of Holyrood, and was made ready for Darnley by Robert's brother, Sir James Balfour.

James Balfour was a conspicuous scoundrel, even by the standards of the time. Twenty years previously he had been one of the gang who murdered Cardinal Beaton, and like his fellow in that murder, John Knox, had served time in the French galleys. Knox, however, loathed him. He was 'a man without God', he said, and indeed he was known to many as 'blasphemous Balfour'. If a man was wanted to commit a terrible crime, there could be no better choice than Sir James Balfour.

The murder of Darnley was the climactic moment of Mary's life. It led to her ruin and was used to blacken her reputation throughout western Europe. Yet she was entirely innocent, innocent of the deed, ignorant of the plot, so ignorant indeed that her first response – and fear – was that she herself had been the intended victim. It is possible that she was. Major-General Mahon suggested in *Tragedy of Kirk o' Field*, described by Antonia Fraser as 'by far the most detailed investigation into the geography and circumstances of the event', that Darnley, who had after all selected the house,[17] himself planned to murder his wife. This is improbable – for one thing he was incapable of keeping any secret – but it is not improbable that the first devisers of the plot meant to kill both Darnley and the Queen.[18]

What happened was simple enough. Around two o'clock on the morning of Monday, 10 February, a huge explosion utterly destroyed Kirk o' Field. 'The blast was fearfull to all about,' remembered John Maxwell, Lord Herries, 'and many rose from their beds at the noise.' It is easy to understand why Mary should have thought the plot aimed at her. After dining with some of her nobles, among them Bothwell and the earls of Huntly and Argyll, she had passed the Sunday evening with Darnley and had intended to spend the night in the house, sleeping in the chamber below his, as she had done more than once in his week of convalescence. It was only at about ten or eleven o'clock that she was reminded that she had promised to dance at the wedding party of Bastien, one of her French servants, who had been married that morning to one of her maids. Darnley, with whom relations had been friendly, even affectionate, since his arrival in Edinburgh, begged her to stay. She might well have done so, but said she must keep her promise to Bastien. Those determined to have Mary as an accomplice in the crime may present her departure to go to the dance as evidence that she knew Kirk o' Field was no place in which to remain. To believe this is to make her a hypocrite as well as a murderess, for she gave Darnley the present of a ring before she left and made arrangements that the next day he would return with her to Holyrood. It is also pertinent to observe that Darnley had written to his father two days previously to tell him that his recovery from illness had been quicker than he expected, thanks to Mary, who had behaved 'like a natural and loving wife'.

Mary was not alone in thinking, as she told the Archbishop of Glasgow, that the explosion had been meant to kill her as well as Darnley. The Venetian ambassador in Paris received information that the murder was the work of heretics 'who designed the same for the Queen'. The charges cannot be easily discounted. Moray and the murderers of Rizzio had cause to wish to be rid of both King and Queen, Darnley because he had betrayed them (as they thought), Mary because they could not believe she had forgiven them. Moreover, despite Mary's tolerance of Protestantism, the fear of a Catholic counter-revolution was real enough.

Darnley, though, was not apparently killed by the explosion. His body, naked under his nightshirt, was found in the garden some way from the ruined house. Beside him was his valet, Taylor, who was also dead, and beside them a chair, a length of rope, a furred cloak and a dagger. There was no mark on the King's body. According to some accounts he was strangled, according to others smothered. I say 'apparently' because it is possible that both men, chair and rope were thrown there by the force of the blast. As Eric Linklater, advancing this theory in an essay, remarked, stranger things were recorded after bombing raids in the 1939–45 war. The more commonly held theory is that

Something frightened Darnley, as he lay within the mined house, and frightened him so badly that he escaped out of the Provost's Lodging in only a nightgown and attempted to make his way across the gardens beyond the town wall to safety. He had had no time to dress himself, and although his servant picked up a cloak, Darnley was not wearing it when he died. They had one dagger between them. The chair and the rope indicate the improvised method of their escape – a chair let down by a rope out of the gallery window into the alleyway . . .[19]

The explanation is persuasive, yet not quite cogent. First, why was the chair near the bodies? Second, if there was indeed no mark on Darnley's body, and he was killed, as is surmised by some of the Douglas men in the service of the Earl of Morton, neither strangling (which would have left marks) nor smothering (which wouldn't) was a mode of murder likely to occur to Morton's men. Use of the sword or dagger would have been more their style.

Some women who lived nearby in Blackfriars Wynd affirmed that they had heard Darnley crying out for mercy: 'Pity me, kinsmen, for the sake of Jesus Christ, who pitied all the world.' They may have heard such cries, but it sounds like an invention after the fact.

The mystery of Kirk o'Field is likely never to be solved.[20] Various alleged accomplices, mostly servants or associates, eventually confessed to their part in the plot, or to knowledge of what had happened. But their confessions were all made under torture or the threat of torture, and though earlier historians who lived in gentler times than ours may have taken them at face value, we have learned that men who are tortured will mostly say in the end what their torturers want them to say. Some of their accounts, designed to incriminate Bothwell – and Bothwell alone – are incredible. In particular, what became the official version of how and when the gunpowder was brought to Kirk o' Field makes no sense at all. There can be no serious doubt that it was stored in the cellars of the house before Darnley arrived there; and in that case the man responsible for arranging this must have been Sir James Balfour, at that time an ally of Bothwell, very soon his enemy.

Bothwell himself was almost certainly the man immediately responsible for lighting the fuse, but he acted, for once, in concert with other nobles: Maitland, Argyll, Huntly, Ruthven, Morton and Lindsay, with Moray cautiously in the background. All had reasons either to hate Darnley or want to be avenged on him for his treachery at the time of Rizzio's murder, or to fear that he was indeed the figurehead, if not the prime mover, of a projected Catholic *coup d'état*. As for Bothwell himself, his subsequent actions make it clear that he intended to take Darnley's place as the Queen's husband. Foreigners had no doubt that many of the leading Scottish nobles had been behind the conspiracy. The ambassador of Savoy, Moretta, pointed the finger at Moray. Both Elizabeth and Catherine de Medici wrote to Mary saying it was imperative that suspects be put on trial and found guilty.

Darnley's bereaved father, the Earl of Lennox, was angrily calling for justice – or vengeance – and had no doubt that Bothwell was the guilty man. Meanwhile placards were posted in the streets of Edinburgh naming Bothwell and Balfour as the murderers. One showed Mary as a mermaid, stripped to the waist, with Bothwell crouched by her side. In contemporary iconography, a mermaid meant a siren, even by extension a prostitute; the implication was all too clear and damning.

The Queen herself was at a loss, near despair, sunk in passivity. It was as if she had suffered a nervous collapse. She could hardly be blamed. She was isolated. One must remember that Darnley was murdered less than twelve months after Rizzio had been stabbed in her presence. Both murders had been the work of members of her nobility, the men with whose help she was supposed to govern the country. She may no longer have believed that she herself had been the intended victim, but she cannot have been sure whom she should trust. The English agent Sir William Drury reported to his master, William Cecil, Elizabeth's secretary of state, that Mary had been 'melancholy or sickly' ever since the murder and had fainted several times.

The Earl of Lennox brought a private petition accusing Bothwell of the crime. Mary agreed that he should stand trial before

Parliament, and he declared himself willing, even eager to do so, that he might establish his innocence. On the appointed day, 12 April 1567, he rode into Edinburgh at the head of a troop of armed men, with Maitland and Morton on either side of him. The formalities of justice were observed, but Lennox failed to appear to make the case for the prosecution, presumably because he was afraid, and so Bothwell was acquitted. Rumours persisted, accusations still flew, one placard denouncing Bothwell as 'the chief author of the foul and horrible murder', but for the moment he was in the clear. He rode to Parliament the following day at the Queen's side, and heard it pronounced that his trial had been just according to the law of the land. The way was now open for his next step: marriage to Mary and the Crown.

For this he needed support, and he had little doubt that he could obtain it. When Mary at Craigmillar Castle the previous December had spoken of her wish for a divorce from Darnley, and Maitland had assured her that they would find the means to free her from her husband in a manner approved by Parliament, it was then thought 'expedient', according to one account, 'and most profitable for the common wealth, by the whole nobility and lords under scribed, that such a young fool and proud tyrant should not reign or bear rule over them; and that for diverse causes, therefore, that these all had concluded that he should be put off by one way or another; and whosoever should take the deed in hand, or do it, they should defend and fortify as themselves'.[21] Actual evidence of this bond has been lost, but it was reputedly signed by Bothwell, Maitland, Argyll, Huntly and James Balfour, later also by Morton, while Moray, according to Maitland, 'looked through his fingers', neither dissenting nor putting his name to it. Bothwell now attempted the same device. He held a supper party at Ainslie's Tavern in the high street. There were twenty-eight guests – noblemen and bishops. At the end of the meal Bothwell produced a document in which, after declaring again his own innocence of Darnley's murder – this must have caused many of the company to smile knowingly – he demanded that if the Queen were to choose him as her new husband, those present were to promise to support and approve the marriage by all means. Eight bishops, nine earls and seven barons obligingly signed. Some may have been drunk, some afraid, some indifferent; a few possibly sincere. Most would soon disclaim or choose to forget their participation, among them Maitland and Morton. Moray was not present at this remarkable supper party, being in London courting Elizabeth's favour.

Mary was in truth at Bothwell's mercy. All the contemporary evidence as to her state of mind in the weeks following Darnley's murder points to the same conclusion: that she was at a loss, incapable of coherent thought or independent action, and frequently in tears. She was still a young woman, not yet twenty-five, and her experiences in the last year had been horrible. If she was now willing to rely on Bothwell, it was because he alone of her nobility had not yet betrayed her. Even so, she must have suspected that he had indeed had a hand in Darnley's murder.

Novelists and playwrights, and some romantically minded historians, have portrayed Bothwell as the great love of her life, even suggesting that she experienced with him a sexual satisfaction she had not known before.[22] There is no evidence of this. She married Bothwell because she could see no alternative, because she was constrained, not because she loved him. First, he was a strong man, and she desperately needed such a husband, one with whom 'she sought to share the strains of the government of Scotland'. He seemed capable of providing her with that necessary support, and he reinforced this opinion by presenting her with the 'Ainslie bond', or a copy of it. Even so, she twice refused his proposal of marriage, till by her account, he forced himself upon her and raped her.[23]

She submitted. Bothwell quickly arranged to be divorced. His wife – Lady Jean Gordon, Huntly's sister – obligingly accused him of adultery, and asked the court to be 'no longer reuted flesh of his flesh'. It was, however, his counter-suit pleading for an annulment that was approved, on the grounds that the marriage had been 'null from the beginning in respect of their contingence in blood, without a dispensation obtained before'. This judgement was delivered by the Roman Catholic Archbishop Hamilton; in the eyes of both the Catholic Church and the Presbyterian Kirk,

Bothwell was at liberty to marry again.[24] So, on 15 May 1567, a mere four months after Darnley's murder, Mary and Bothwell were married by Protestant rites, something of which Mary would later be bitterly ashamed. Whatever she hoped for, she found neither happiness nor security. In the weeks after the marriage – the few weeks in which they were together – she was often in tears, and once asked for a knife so that she might kill herself.

Worse still, it was soon clear that his fellow nobles would not submit to Bothwell's authority. The assurance offered by the Ainslie bond proved delusory, its signatories reneging on their word. Mary and Bothwell were faced with armed rebellion. The two armies met at Carberry Hill outside Musselburgh on 15 June, and Bothwell's melted away. Mary submitted to the opposition lords on a promise of safe conduct for her husband, a promise scarcely worth the air it was spoken in. Her spirit was not yet altogether broken. When she caught sight of the Earl of Morton, she called out, 'How is this, my lord? I am told that all this is done in order to get justice against the king's murderers. But I am told also that you are one of the chief of them.' Morton turned away, but this was the last show of spirit from the Queen for a long time. Much worse was to follow for her. She was led back to Edinburgh as a prisoner, with an angry mob surging around her shrieking insults and calling out 'burn the hoor'. She was alone, afraid and compelled to realise that she had lost the love of her people as surely as the loyalty of the nobility. In the city she was lodged in the Provost's house rather than in the castle or at Holyrood. The next morning, after a miserable night, she appeared at the window, calling out that she was being held a prisoner by subjects who had betrayed her. She was hauled away, but the people had already seen their young Queen, her hair disordered, her clothes torn open, distraught, looking like a madwoman.

The nobles, Moray and Morton chief among them, were determined to be rid of her. They too were nervous. Bothwell was still at large. He might raise troops. The Hamiltons, in the west, were still loyal to Mary, and were Moray's sworn enemies. The fickle Edinburgh mob might turn against them, especially if they learned that the Queen was now demanding a parliamentary inquiry into Darnley's murder. That was something Morton, Maitland and Sir James Balfour, all party to the conspiracy, were anxious to avoid. Better to remove Mary from Edinburgh to some secure place where she would be alone, unprotected, without friends, at their mercy.

They fixed on Loch Leven Castle. It was ideal in several ways. First, the castle itself was situated on a little island in the middle of the loch. This would make any attempt at rescue by Mary's friends difficult, well nigh impossible. Second, it was the property of Moray's half-brother, Sir William Douglas. He was the son of Moray's mother (James V's mistress) Margaret Erskine by her lawful husband, Robert Douglas; also the nephew of the Earl of Mar to whom the Council had given charge of the baby Prince James, and Morton's cousin. His mother, old Lady Douglas, was resident there and known to dislike Mary.

The Queen was now isolated. Sir Nicholas Throckmorton, who had been the English ambassador in Paris when Mary was Queen of France, and who had now been sent to Edinburgh by Elizabeth to report on how matters stood, was not only disgusted by the insults he heard levelled at the Queen but convinced that her life was in danger. He seems to have believed that if Elizabeth had not sent him to express her disapproval of the rebellion and the imprisonment of the Queen, Mary would have been murdered like Darnley and Rizzio. His contempt for the rebel lords was acute.[25]

Mary was indeed in danger of losing her life. The rebels had come to a decision: she should be compelled to divorce Bothwell (who had been declared an outlaw) and then to abdicate in favour of her infant son, with Moray to be appointed regent. She refused the first demand, for she was pregnant, and it was only when she miscarried of twins that she was ready to abandon Bothwell. As to the abdication, it was forced on her, the brutal Earl of Lindsay telling her that if she did not sign the paper, they would have no choice but to cut her throat and achieve their ends in that manner. So on 24 July 1567 she submitted, after Moray, the half-brother on whom she had once relied, also threatened her with, as he charmingly put it, being left only with the hope of God's mercy, for there would be none from men.

Gradually her health recovered, her spirits revived, her resolution returned, and she began once more to be capable of exercising her magnetic charm. Even old Lady Douglas softened towards the captive. More importantly Mary made two new conquests: first, the young George Douglas, her jailer's brother, a handsome young man known as 'pretty Geordie'; second, a younger boy, Will Douglas. George fell in love with her – William Cecil later said he was 'in a fantasy of love' – and may have nursed ambitions to be more than her knight. Why not? Bothwell was off the scene, out of Scotland, on the way, though none yet knew it, to his own terrible doom, a prisoner in Denmark chained to a pillar where he would subsequently die raving mad, covered in hair and filth.[26] If Mary was once free and restored to her throne, might she not in gratitude marry her rescuer, who was after all well born, eligible enough, the half-brother of her half-brother? As for young Will, he conceived a romantic devotion to the captive Queen and would continue to serve her for many years. Together the two plotted her escape.

It was neatly and boldly managed. George Douglas found a reason to leave the island, and, once off it, procured horses from stables on the mainland. Meanwhile, young Will found a boat, removed stoppers from the other boats to hinder a pursuit, and obtained the keys of the castle gate from his master as he served him wine. When night fell and the castle was quiet, the Queen, who had given out that she felt unwell and had retired early, slipped out from her room and into the courtyard, where the boy was waiting for her. He led her to the boat and rowed out across the loch. They found George there with the horses and rode hard for the west, where her allies, the Hamiltons, had already been alerted.

Mary still had supporters. The Hamiltons especially were opposed to the new regime. The head of the house, the former governor, Duke of Châtelherault, was, after the infant Prince James, Mary's presumptive heir. His eldest son, Arran, her former suitor, was mad beyond hope of recovery, but there were three other sons.

The Hamiltons could not be pleased by Moray's usurpation of power. Mary was able to gather an army quickly, and it was larger than that which the rebel lords brought against them. On 13 May 1568, they met at Langside, just south of Glasgow, on ground now known as the Queen's Park. The advantage seemingly lay with Mary, but her battle was mismanaged, lost, and she had to flee. Dumbarton Castle was still held by her supporters, and offered a refuge from which she might be able to take a ship to France. But to reach Dumbarton she would have to cross hostile Lennox country. The risk was too great. Following the advice of the faithful Lord Herries, she made for the south-west, still strongly Catholic. There she might hope to find a vessel in the Solway Firth if her supporters failed to muster a new army.

They rode hard, the Queen disguised. It was now clear there was no chance of continuing armed resistance. All the company urged her to make for France, where she would be safe; from there she might hope to be restored to her throne by French arms. But Mary, with that poor judgement and obstinacy that were to seem characteristic of the later Stuarts, insisted on crossing over to England. Surely her 'sister and cousin' Elizabeth could be trusted to defend her rights.

She arrived in England as a refugee, confident that a meeting with Elizabeth would lead to her restoration. She would remain there a prisoner for nineteen years, always denied that interview she first demanded, then begged for.

What Mary did not realise was that her enemies had been busy blackening her name, portraying her as an adulteress and murderer. She saw herself as an innocent victim of rebellion that Elizabeth could not be expected to approve. That might be so, but the men around Elizabeth, notably Cecil and Leicester, saw things differently. From their point of view, what had happened in Scotland was to England's advantage. A Catholic queen had been replaced by a Protestant coup. A queen with close connections with France had been forced to abdicate and a regime eager for an English alliance and dependent for its survival on English goodwill established in Scotland. Whatever their queen's view of the wickedness of rebellion, no matter what sympathy she might feel for her cousin, her advisers saw nothing to be gained by restoring Mary to the Scottish throne.

Elizabeth herself was in a quandary and characteristically played for time. She refused to receive Mary, but at first insisted that she should be kept as a guest rather than a prisoner, to be treated with respect, watched over and guarded. She declared that Moray, whom she knew and for whom she had some regard, must be given the opportunity to explain and defend his actions, while Mary herself must satisfactorily answer any accusations brought against her before there could be any thought of restoring her to her throne. It was accordingly now up to Mary's enemies in Scotland to provide evidence of her guilt.

They were ready to do so, and the evidence they produced came in two forms, both dubious.

While Mary was still a prisoner on Loch Leven, Maitland and Morton, dining together in Edinburgh, had been told that some of Bothwell's former servants were in town. They ordered them to be seized, and one, a tailor called George Dalgleish, after being threatened with torture, told them of a casket – a locked silver box – that he had taken from the castle and which was now in his possession. When this was produced and opened, it was found to contain eight letters written in French and some French sonnets, allegedly composed by Mary. These were subsequently sent to England to be read and examined by the commissioners appointed by Elizabeth to consider the accusations levelled at Mary. If genuine, they seemed to indicate that Mary had committed adultery with Bothwell while Darnley was still alive, that she had foreknowledge of the plot to murder her husband and was therefore complicit in it, and that her alleged subsequent abduction by Bothwell was no abduction but a meeting planned by Mary herself. If they were genuine, that is . . .

Certainly there is no reason to doubt that the papers belonged to Bothwell, but beyond that point formidable doubts rear up. The question is complicated by the fact that the originals disappeared long ago – no one has seen them since the execution in 1584 of the Earl of Gowrie, into whose possession they had come. What we have are copies – English and Scots translations, and also translations from these back into French. The poems, in a clumsy, almost doggerel French, are certainly not Mary's work. They bear no resemblance in style to her acknowledged poetry, and both Ronsard and Brantome, who knew her poetry well, denied that she could have written them. They were most probably written to Bothwell by one of his many mistresses.[27] As for the letters themselves, they are made up of some passages that were very probably written by Mary, but other sections have been interpolated, again clumsily and not always coherently. They are forgeries intended to prove her guilt. This probability is enhanced by a question Moray's secretary, John Wood, put to Elizabeth and her Council: 'If the French originals are found to tally with the Scots translations, will that be reckoned good evidence?'[28] The inference is that the Scots translations had already been supplied, and that the French originals could be altered if necessary.

As it happened, the Casket Letters, over which historians have pored, convinced nobody except those who were already sure of Mary's guilt. Elizabeth herself thought the evidence altogether insufficient. One of the commissioners, Thomas Radcliffe, Earl of Sussex, summed up the situation astutely. If Mary was allowed to appear before the tribunal, she would obviously deny that she had written the letters, and could not be convicted on their evidence. Elizabeth would then have to set her free. If, however, she was not permitted to appear, then the whole thing could be, as he put it, 'huddled up':[29] Moray and his confederates would not be exposed as forgers, but Mary's innocence would not be established, and so Elizabeth could keep her in prison. This was indeed precisely what happened.

The response of another commissioner, the Duke of Norfolk, was more interesting still. He professed himself horrified by the letters. If they were authentic, then Mary must certainly be convicted. But a few days later he changed his mind. He had meanwhile had a conversation with Maitland, who had by now fallen out with Moray and was on his way to being the leader of the Marian party in Scotland. The assumption must be that Maitland had told him that the letters were not what they purported to be, but were indeed in large part forgeries. Soon afterwards, Norfolk proposed himself as a husband for Mary. It is unlikely he would have done so if he believed she had had a hand in Darnley's murder.

However, the case against Mary was also made in another form, one that had both a more immediate and a more lasting effect on her reputation. This was a narrative written by George Buchanan.

Buchanan was the most famous Scotsman of the day, a humanist scholar, poet and playwright. Since he wrote in Latin, despising like other humanists the vernacular language, his work is now little read. But it was highly admired in his own day and for two hundred years after. He was acclaimed as the greatest Latin poet since Virgil. As a writer of Latin prose he was considered the equal of Tacitus. Joachim du Bellay, after Ronsard the finest French poet of the age, said that Buchanan was the first man to demonstrate that a Scotsman need not be a savage. Montaigne, who was his pupil in Bordeaux, called him simply 'this great Scots poet'.[30] He displayed his virtuosity by translating the Psalms into twenty-nine different Latin metres.

Buchanan was born in 1506 in Killearn in Stirlingshire and probably grew up as a Gaelic speaker. Killearn was in Lennox country and this was to be of some significance. He was educated first at St Andrews University, then at the Sorbonne in Paris, in both places studying under the Scots humanist historian John Mair (or Major). Returning to Scotland, he was briefly made the tutor of the King's illegitimate son, Lord James Stewart, later the Earl of Moray. A satire on the Franciscans cost him the post and his liberty, but he escaped, or was released, from prison and made his way to France. For almost thirty years he taught there, in Paris and Bordeaux, and also briefly in Portugal, where he attracted the unwelcome attention of the Inquisition. Back in France, he found employment as tutor to the son of the Catholic Marshal de Brissac, and wrote poems in praise of the Catholic rulers of France and in particular of the leaders of the extreme Catholic party, the great House of Guise. One poem was composed in celebration of the Duc de Guise's recapture of Calais from the English in 1558, another in celebration of Mary's marriage to the Dauphin. When Mary returned to Scotland in 1561, she invited him, as the favourite poet of her Guise relations, to accompany her. He was the chief intellectual ornament of her court, granted a pension of £250 a year. He would read and discuss Livy and other Roman historians with the Queen after dinner, and was appointed principal of St Andrews University.

Little in Buchanan's history to date – and he was now in his middle fifties – suggested he had Protestant leanings. By his own account he began to study the arguments advanced by the reformers only when he was middle-aged. Yet he would soon emerge as one of the chief apologists in Scotland of 'the true Reformed religion' and Mary's most bitter and effective critic.

What caused the change? There seem to have been several reasons. First, there was his own temperament, combative, intellectual, responsive to ideas, and, like many intellectuals, ready to fly from one extreme to another, to move in his case from being the laudator of the Duc de Guise to the propagandist of Calvinism. Sir James Melville, Mary's ambassador to the English court, remarked on this tendency. Buchanan, he said, 'was so facile that he was led with any company that he haunted for the time, which made him factious in his old age'. This need not surprise us, for in our own age there have been many examples of intellectuals who moved from left to right, or right to left, with comparable facility, displaying the same vehemence and certainty in the promulgation of their new opinions as they had in advancing their previous ones.

Then, in 1565, Mary sent him to France on a secret diplomatic mission. He found much changed. Many of his old humanist friends, formerly Catholic conformists, finding that their criticism of the abuses of the Roman Church were now unwelcome in the new spirit of Rome's Counter-Reformation, had become Calvinists.

Moreover, if Mary was one patron in Scotland, another was his old pupil, Moray. As long as the Queen and her half-brother remained friendly and worked in harmony, Buchanan experienced no divided loyalties. His position became less comfortable when Moray moved into opposition.

Finally, there was Darnley's murder. Darnley, despite his English upbringing, was a Lennox Stewart (or Stuart) and Buchanan was a Lennox man. Darnley might have been a Catholic and even perhaps engaged in a plot to restore Catholicism, but for Buchanan, the old tribal loyalties of the Highlands were powerful. His chief's son had been vilely murdered, and he was easily persuaded that Mary had been at least cognisant of the crime, if not an accomplice. Again there need be no surprise. Darnley's parents, the Earl and Countess of Lennox, were equally certain of their daughter-in-law's complicity. (Much later, when Mary was a prisoner in England, the Countess would change her mind, and resume friendly relations with her, if only by letter – one of the surest proofs of Mary's innocence; but that time had not yet come.)

So Buchanan set to work, or was set to work, preparing the case against Mary in his *Detectio*. It was not a case that might be advanced in a court of law. That wasn't the intention. It was a work of propaganda, written with zest and with the skill of the most accomplished man of letters of the time. One charitable judge has found in it 'a feeling of outraged moral fervour', but such fervour is a characteristic of popular journalism, and moral outrage is better not expressed by one who can treat fact with the cavalier disregard Buchanan displays.

One example will suffice. Eager to demonstrate that Mary's wicked passion for Bothwell preceded Darnley's murder by several months, he tells of how Bothwell, wounded in a border scuffle, was confined to bed at Hermitage Castle in Liddesdale. 'When this was reported to the queen at Borthwick,' Buchanan wrote, 'she flew madly, by forced journeys, first to Melrose, then to Jedburgh. Though she learned there on good authority that his life was safe her affection could brook no delay, and she betrayed her infamous lust by setting out at a bad time of the year, heedless of the difficulties of the journey and the danger of highwaymen, with a company such as no decent gentleman would entrust with his life and goods.'[31]

This is certainly vivid, its meaning clear. The facts, however, were very different.

Mary was already at Jedburgh, presiding over a court of law, when word came that Bothwell was wounded. Far from flying madly to his side, she waited five or six days till the court's business was done before riding to Hermitage. No doubt she went to express sympathy, but also to discuss the unruly state of the borderland with her Warden of the Marches. She remained there only a few hours and returned to Jedburgh the same day. (It was a round trip of about fifty miles.) Nor was it at a particularly 'bad time of the year'. The date was 16 October, and October is often one of the most agreeable of months in the Scottish Borders. Finally, the 'company such as no decent gentleman would entrust with his life and goods' included her half-brother, Moray, Buchanan's own patron, the man who had commanded him to compose his narrative. The great poet and scholar had a talent for imaginative journalism.

Nevertheless, his *Detectio* had its desired effect. It further blackened Mary's name, and convinced many that she was indeed guilty of the crimes of which she was accused. John Cunningham, nineteenth-century historian of the Scottish Church, believed that 'the casket letters all but prove her guilt', but he could not have arrived at that conclusion without Buchanan's supporting narrative.

Despite the production of the Casket Letters and Buchanan's ingenious and indignant narrative, Mary's guilt could not be proved to the satisfaction of the English commissioners. On the other hand, Elizabeth was not inclined to restore her to her Scottish throne. She might disapprove of the rough treatment Mary had suffered. She deplored rebellion and the deposition of a fellow monarch. She was surely unconvinced by Buchanan's argument that the ancient constitution of Scotland, which was actually an imaginative myth, provided precedents for such action. But the government of Scotland was now in the hands of the regent Moray, a Protestant and a man who had shown himself to be a good friend of England. So Mary must remain where she was, whether her situation was to be described as a guest under restraint or a prisoner. Elizabeth continued to refuse all her cousin's pleas for a meeting, something Mary was sure would lead to a true understanding. It may be that Elizabeth was afraid this would prove to be the case. Or perhaps she merely wished to save herself embarrassment. Nevertheless, she protected Mary for years from the hostility of the more extreme Protestants who sought her death for fear that, if Elizabeth herself should die, Mary's claim to the throne would be supported by English Catholics and foreign powers. If the English Parliament had had its way, Mary would have been put on trial and sentenced to death in 1572, after the discovery of the Ridolfi plot against Elizabeth.[32]

For much of the 1570s and even into the next decade, Mary's confinement was irksome rather than rigorous. She was treated as a queen and served by her own household, at one time as large as thirty people. She was permitted to ride out, hunting and hawking. She was officially denied the comforts of her religion, but at various times disguised Catholic priests held posts within her household. Certainly she was under constant supervision, but some of her jailers, notably the Earl of Shrewsbury, were even friendly. She had her little dogs and cage-birds, and she spent hours doing embroidery, sending samples of her work as presents to Elizabeth with friendly messages. Her servants were mostly devoted to her, and for a while she delighted in the company of her niece Arbella Stuart, the daughter of Darnley's younger brother Charles and Elizabeth Cavendish, whose mother Bess of Hardwick was now married to Shrewsbury. Yet much of her life was a torment of boredom and frustration. She was often in poor health, especially in winter, and by the time she was forty she already moved, and often looked, like a much older woman.

Hope is the prisoner's stay, often illusory. Mary trusted that when her son assumed management of his own affairs he would press hard for her release. Schemes to associate her with him in the government of Scotland were propounded, considered, abandoned, with regret on her part, indifference on his. As the years passed, her contact with the outer world was restricted, her understanding of it clouded. As recompense, her attachment to the Catholic faith, light and even perfunctory in her youth, deepened. She spent hours in prayer, wrote devotional poetry and in 1580 an 'Essay on Adversity'. Though she could not know it, she was preparing herself for martyrdom.

Events beyond her prison conspired against her. Protestant

England was engaged in a cold war with Catholic Spain. Religious civil wars agitated France. Protestants everywhere had been horrified by the St Bartholomew's Night massacre of French Huguenots in 1572; one man who had witnessed it was Elizabeth's spymaster, Sir Francis Walsingham, who had been in Paris on a diplomatic mission at the time. Meanwhile in the Netherlands a Protestant rebellion against their lord Philip of Spain was assuming the character of a war of liberation; in 1584 the Dutch leader William of Orange (known as 'the Silent', because, though normally loquacious, he had on one important occasion held his tongue) was assassinated. In 1570 the Pope had excommunicated Elizabeth and absolved English Catholics from allegiance to her. In response Parliament had passed an act declaring the presence of Catholic priests in England to be illegal. Those who dared to defy the law were, if arrested, tortured and executed – as traitors rather than heretics.

Elizabeth, who disliked bloodshed, except when alarmed, might be, despite everything, well disposed towards her 'cousin and sister', but the men around her were Mary's enemies. They had good reason to be so. Elizabeth was nine years older than the Scots queen. Suppose she died? Suppose she was assassinated? What then? As Protestant patriots, men like Cecil and Walsingham feared the worst for England and for themselves; their own necks might be in danger if Mary survived Elizabeth and became queen. So ingrained is the myth of the sturdy Protestantism of Elizabethan England that their fears may seem fanciful. But they were real enough. Catholics were still numerous, their loyalty doubtful. Mary had supporters and sympathisers, at home and abroad. All the chief men in government had lived through one Catholic reaction – Mary Tudor's. They were determined there should not be another, and to ensure against it they were equally determined to be rid of the Queen of Scots. But they knew that Elizabeth would consent to her death only if she had irrefutable proof that Mary had given her approval to a plot against her life.

At last in 1586 the opportunity presented itself. Anthony Babington was a young idealistic Catholic gentleman from Derbyshire. As a boy he had served as a page in Shrewsbury's household, seen the Queen of Scots, if only from a distance, and conceived a devotion to her. He gathered like-minded young men about him, fervent in the Catholic faith and hostile to the established order. Some of them, like Babington himself, saw Mary as an oppressed and ill-used queen, a figure of romance, a beacon of hope for their fellow Catholics. They fell in love with the idea of her,33 and so they devised a plot: Elizabeth would be killed, Mary rescued and Catholicism restored. It was wild and fanciful and it never had any chance of success.

In the heightened tension of the 1580s, Mary's confinement had become narrower. For some time her communication with the world beyond her prison had been cut off. Now – miraculously, it must have seemed – a new secret channel of communication was opened, and she received Babington's letters. It was no miracle. Walsingham had arranged it, having already infiltrated one of his spies as an agent provocateur into Babington's little group of conspirators. The bait was laid. It only remained for Mary to take it, and the trap would be sprung. At last, in one letter, she assented, or seemed to assent, to all Babington's plans, stipulating only that he must move quickly enough and with sufficient strength to set her free. When this letter – like all her correspondence – was sent to Walsingham, opened, copied and scrutinised, before being passed on to Babington – the spymaster drew a gallows on the paper.

Though it is probable that Mary did approve Babington's plans, it is not absolutely certain. The fatal letter may have been doctored. Mary still wrote by preference in French, her first language – her written English was very poor. Her letters were then translated and put into a cipher by her secretary, and it is just possible that he, believing the correspondence secure, may have thought it wise to make his mistress's approval of the assassination plot explicit in order to fortify Babington's resolution. Alternatively, Walsingham or one of his agents may have done this. Certainly Walsingham added one damaging footnote.

Babington and his friends were arrested, tortured till they confessed, and then executed in the horrible manner of the age.34 They were certainly guilty of their plot, but it had never had any chance of success, for ultimately it was as much Walsingham's conspiracy as theirs, and Elizabeth had been in no danger.

Nevertheless, she was at last convinced. The Queen of Scots must be put on trial. Mary defended herself with spirit, while denying that an English court could have any jurisdiction over her. She offered to state her case, before Parliament, and was refused. She told Walsingham she knew he was her enemy. He denied it, saying he was an enemy only to the enemies of England and his queen. This was casuistry, for he had no doubt that Mary was the enemy of England, as he understood England, and therefore he was indeed her enemy, as she alleged.

The verdict was never in doubt; this was a show trial, in which there was no possibility of an acquittal. Mary was sentenced to death.

Only two questions remained. Could Elizabeth be brought to sign the death warrant, and would Mary consent to submit to the sentence? The answer to the first was in doubt for weeks. Elizabeth hated the idea. She was not cruel and it may be that the idea of sending her cousin to the block, of condemning her to suffer the death inflicted so long ago on her own mother Anne Boleyn, revolted her. Moreover, she was reluctant to take the responsibility of carrying out a judicial sentence on an anointed queen, and she was afraid of the response from Spain and France. Her scruples deserve respect but her next move invites only contempt: she urged Mary's latest jailer, Sir Amyas Paulet, to relieve her of responsibility by arranging the murder of the Queen of Scots himself. To his credit he refused. 'I am so unhappy to have lived to see this unhappy day,' he wrote to Elizabeth, 'in which I am required by direction from my most gracious sovereign to do an act which God and the law forbid . . . God forbid that I should make so foul a shipwreck of my conscience, or leave so great a blot on my poor posterity, to shed blood without law or warrant.'[35] Elizabeth was infuriated by his 'daintinesess', but at last she signed the warrant and her ministers whipped it away before she could change her mind.

Any fear that Mary would offer resistance – a fear that remained even on the morning of her execution – was unfounded. She accepted death as a martyr to the Catholic faith, as she wrote to her brother-in-law Henry III of France on 8 February 1587, in her last letter a few hours before she was due to die, and she played her part in the macabre and horrible drama at Fotheringay as a piece of noble and self-conscious theatre. When the executioner lifted her severed head, it fell away from his hand and he was left holding the auburn wig she had chosen to wear. It was then seen that her hair was grey and the face was that of an old woman, though she was not yet forty-five. A little pet dog, a terrier, had accompanied her into the hall, hidden under the folds of her dress. It now ran out and stood beside her bleeding neck and would not be coaxed away.

Chapter 10

James VI and I (1567–1625):
The King as Survivor

On the ceiling of the banqueting hall in the Palace of Whitehall, Rubens depicted James VI and I as the 'British Solomon' dispensing justice amidst swirling Baroque clouds. Though the most successful of the Stuarts, he has more often attracted ridicule than admiration; the Duc de Sully, chief minister of his cousin Henry IV of France, called him 'the wisest fool in Christendom'. His mother Mary has never lacked devotees. Nor has his son Charles. Their deaths on the scaffold, and the manner in which they met them, lend their memory a nobility their lives frequently lacked. James died, in ordinary and inglorious fashion, in his bed. Highly intelligent, a scholar and poet, he was an unusual man to find on a throne, perhaps the only king of either Scotland or England who may reasonably be styled an intellectual. He liked to call himself 'the great schoolmaster of the realm', and it is easy to imagine him as a university don.

If posterity has found it hard to grant him respect, it is partly because of the picture of him drawn by a malicious court gossip, Sir Anthony Weldon, in his unreliable memoirs.[1] It was Weldon who told how the King's clothes were ludicrously padded to guard against dagger-thrusts, how he fiddled continually with his codpiece, how a weakness in his legs gave him an unsteady gait, how he fawned over his handsome favourites Robert Ker (or Carr), whom he made Earl of Somerset, and George Villiers, who was created

Duke of Buckingham, how he lacked dignity and majesty of person, rarely washed, made unsuitable jokes, and was frequently in liquor.

Moreover, his reign in England has generally been compared unfavourably with the fabled glories of the Elizabethan age. Some of his subjects indeed made such a comparison. But many of the problems James faced first appeared in Elizabeth's last years, and were inherited by him unresolved. Much of what is styled Elizabethan is also Jacobean. It was in James's reign and under his patronage that the Church of England came to its rich maturity, and it was James himself who commanded the making and publication of the Authorised Version of the Bible. If not its begetter, he was its patron and inspiration, and the King James Bible is his richest legacy, a work such as Elizabeth never contemplated, and the great storehouse of the English language.

He became King of Scots when less than a year old, and was crowned in the Church of the Holy Rude in Stirling. John Knox preached the sermon, and the Bishop of Orkney, consecrated according to the Roman Catholic rite but now an energetic reformer, anointed the infant. Then while the little boy's guardian, John Erskine, Earl of Mar, held the crown over James's head (for it weighed three and a half pounds and the baby could scarcely be expected to wear it), the nobles present approached and touched the symbol of kingship in homage. The oath was taken on his behalf in the absence in France of the regent Moray by James Douglas, Earl of Morton, one of the accomplices in his father's murder. It was necessary to do all in order, and in conformity with precedent, since the child was king only because of the *coup d'état* which had resulted in his mother's deposition, the first time this had happened in Scotland since Malcolm III's son Edgar supplanted his uncle Donald Bane in 1097. A good many of those who had joined the confederacy against Bothwell were by no means ready to approve of Mary's imprisonment, her forced abdication, the appointment of Moray as regent and the coronation of the little King. Indeed, the attendance at the coronation was exiguous. Many hesitated to commit themselves to the new regime till they saw how things worked out. Others, Maitland of Lethington among

them, reverted to their former loyalty and became Mary's partisans. Her party grew in numbers and for the first six years of
James's reign there was intermittent civil war. It was a time of great
disorder, of murders, skirmishes, running battles in the streets of
Edinburgh and Stirling. 'All natural ties,' wrote Scott in his *Tales
of a Grandfather*, 'were forgotten in the distinction of Kingsmen
and Queensmen; and, as neither party gave quarter to their opponents, the civil war assumed a most horrible aspect. Fathers, and
sons, and brothers, took opposite sides, and fought against each
other.'

In 1570 Moray was assassinated in Linlithgow, shot in the street
from a window by one Hamilton of Bothwellhaugh. This Hamilton
had been sentenced to death in 1568 after being taken prisoner at
Langside, where he had fought in the Queen's army. He had been
reprieved, but his estate had been declared forfeit. His wife was
turned out of the house she had brought him as her dowry, and
it was given to one of Moray's dependants. Hamilton vowed to
be ravenged on the regent, whom he held responsible for his misfortunes. He waited patiently for an opportunity, and when he had
fired his carbine, calmly mounted his horse and rode away. A few
days later he escaped to France.

Buchanan, in his *History of Scotland*, hailed Moray as the best
man of his age, the inspiration and standard-bearer of the Protestant
cause, a partisan sentiment. He was succeeded as regent by Darnley's
father, the Earl of Lennox. Dumbarton Castle, where Mary's
supporters had been holding out, was captured and the last Roman
Catholic Archbishop of St Andrews, James Hamilton, was hanged
in his episcopal robes on a gibbet in Stirling. Less than a year later,
in 1571, Lennox himself was murdered in the same town, and
James, not yet five, saw his grandfather's bleeding corpse carried
into the castle. The next regent, James's guardian, the Earl of Mar,
died within a few weeks of his appointment, remarkably of natural
causes, and was replaced by Morton, a leader of the gang who
had murdered David Rizzio, who thus crowned a career of treachery,
violence and murder by assuming the government of Scotland. For
all his faults Morton was a man of some ability as well as fierce

determination. He came down hard on Mary's remaining supporters, fewer in number as their cause weakened in the years of her imprisonment in England. At last, in 1573, only Edinburgh Castle remained in their hands. Morton called for assistance from England and was sent a fine siege-train with which he battered the castle walls. The garrison, short of supplies and seeing no hope of relief, surrendered on a promise of pardon. The promise was not kept. The commander, Kirkcaldy of Grange, was hanged. Maitland of Lethington, who in his last years had been as ardent for Mary as he had previously been energetic in opposition to her, committed suicide in prison.

Such was the happy state of Scotland in the boyhood of King James.

His own upbringing was miserable, harsh and often frightening. His father was dead, his mother a prisoner in England, himself in effect an orphan. Buchanan, now rising seventy, was made his tutor. In one respect he did his work well. James was taught Latin before he could write English, and learned his lessons thoroughly, becoming a notable scholar. He learned Greek too, and as an adult would be able to converse in French, Italian and Spanish. But Buchanan was a harsh master, ruling his charge by fear and thrashing him when displeased. In later life James would acknowledge the debt he owed him, while also, by his own account, trembling once at the approach of a man who resembled his old tutor. Buchanan's magisterial methods may be considered disgraceful, but worse still perhaps, in his savage partisanship he taught James that his mother was a wicked woman, an adulteress guilty of his father's murder. It would be years before James could free his mind of the poisonous version of his family tragedy that Buchanan had given him.

The boy was starved of affection. It is a common observation that those denied love in their youth will grow up either harsh and incapable of giving love themselves or conspicuously tender. James, to his credit, was the latter. The fondness he lavished on his favourites, the maudlin sentimentality he displayed in old age, were a consequence of his lonely and loveless childhood, a compensation for its miseries. The experiences of childhood and youth had another result: they bred him to caution.

When he assumed control of the government he would move carefully to achieve his ends, displaying none of the recklessness and indifference to the opinion and personal interests of the nobility that had characterised several of his predecessors and led James I and James V to push their policies beyond what was tolerable. He might be as determined as they had been to assert the rights of the Crown and extend its power, but unlike them, he knew when to compromise, even when to yield. His caution was represented by many as timidity. He was said to have a horror of violence. Some have attributed this to his pre-natal experience when his pregnant mother saw Rizzio stabbed to death in her presence and was herself threatened with being 'cut into collops'. This may of course be true, but actually James didn't lack physical courage – he was a daring rider in the hunting field – and the history of his rule in Scotland at least offers plenty of evidence that he was possessed of an unusual degree of moral courage.

A French visitor to his court, by name Fontenay, gave this description of James when he was eighteen:

Three qualities of the mind he possesses in perfection: he understands clearly, judges wisely and has a retentive memory. His questions are keen and penetrating, and his replies are sound. In any argument, whatever it is about, he maintains the view that seems to him most just, and I have heard him support Catholic against Protestant opinions. He is well instructed in languages, affairs of state, better, I dare say, than anyone else in his kingdom. In short, he has a remarkable intelligence, as well as lofty and virtuous ideals and a high opinion of himself.

I have remarked in him three defects that may prove injurious to his estate and government: he does not estimate correctly his poverty and insignificance but is over-confident of his strength and scornful of other princes; his love for favourites is indiscreet and wilful and takes no account of the feeling of his people; he is too lazy and indifferent about affairs, too given to pleasure, allowing all business to be conducted by others.

He dislikes dancing and music, and the little affectations of court life such as amorous discourse or curiosities of dress, and has a special aversion for ear-rings. In speaking and eating, in his dress and in his sports, in his conversation in the presence of women, his manners are crude and uncivil and display a lack of proper instruction. He is never still in one place but walks constantly up and down, though his gait is erratic and wandering, and he tramps about even in his own chamber. His voice is loud and his words grave and sententious. He loves the chase above all other pleasures, and will hunt for six hours without interruption, galloping over hill and dale with a loosened bridle. His body is feeble and yet he is no delicate. In a word, he is an old young man.

An old young man: the judgement is telling. James never knew the careless exuberance of youth. He was on his guard from the day he was conscious of his position. He had a high sense of the sacred character of kingship, but he could not but be aware that the person of a king might be roughly handled, and his life at risk. Two of his predecessors had been murdered. His mother had been compelled to abdicate, his father assassinated. Mary's English partisans plotted to kill Elizabeth. In 1584 the leader of the Dutch revolt against Spain, William of Orange, was murdered. In 1587 Mary went to the block. Two years later, James's cousin, the Duc de Guise, was stabbed in the presence of another cousin, Henry III of France. Within a few months Henry himself fell victim to an assassin's dagger. Kings might, as James believed, rule by divine right, but dangers surrounded them. If, as the gossip Weldon smirked, fear of assassination led him to wear padded clothes, he had good reason to think this necessary.

His loneliness was relieved in 1579, when he was thirteen, by the arrival from France of a glittering cousin, Esmé Stewart, Seigneur d'Aubigny. He was in fact Darnley's first cousin and, with the exception of an elderly great-uncle (old Lennox's brother), James's nearest living relative on his father's side. Esmé Stewart was a man of about thirty, an accomplished horseman and fencer, and he brought a breath of French sophistication to Presbyterian Scotland. James was dazzled by him and made a hero of him. Others too could see his value. He became a focus for the opposition to Morton, who was arrested in the last days of 1580 and charged with complicity in Darnley's murder, which had for more than a dozen

years cast a dark shadow over the public life of Scotland. When
Morton was executed a few weeks later, almost all those who had
been involved one way or another in the conspiracy against Darnley
were dead.

James created Esmé Earl of Lennox, the title being vacant
since the death of his uncle Charles, Darnley's younger brother,
in 1576. But Lennox, reared a Catholic in France, was suspected
of favouring a Spanish alliance against England, and so provoked
the opposition of the pro-English Protestant party. They responded in traditional style, seizing the person of the King while
he was hunting near Perth, and consigning him to the care of
the Earl of Gowrie, son of another of Rizzio's murderers.
Meanwhile Lennox was exiled or perhaps thought it prudent to
exile himself. James escaped from his captors, found support in
the Catholic north from the earls of Huntly, Crawford and Argyll,
and turned the tables. Gowrie was arrested, charged with treason,
and executed. James was still only sixteen.

To be sixteen was, however, to be of age. His minority was over.
He was ready to rule as well as reign. With the help of an able
chief minister, Sir James Maitland of Thirlestane (a connection of
Lethington's), he would govern Scotland efficiently for twenty years,
pursuing always his mother's dream of the English succession.
Indeed it is no exaggeration to say that establishing himself as
Elizabeth's heir dominated his mind and determined his policy.

It also informed his attitude to his mother. He had little filial
feeling, and this can be no surprise. He had no memory of Mary
and he had been taught that she was guilty of his father's murder.
Even when she was about to be put on trial for her life, he contented
himself with asking that she should be kept in prison. He had
already written to her that he could do nothing for her because
she was 'a captive in a desert'. Now he declined to play the one
card that might have saved her, never threatening to break the
treaty of alliance between Scotland and England, which he had
signed in 1585 and which, he believed, came close to assuring him
that he would indeed be Elizabeth's successor. When Mary was
sentenced to death, he protested, but mildly, and he asked the

ministers of the Kirk to remember his mother in their prayers, requesting 'that it might please God to illuminate her with the light of His truth, and save her from the apparent danger in which she is cast'. That was as far as he went, but even that was too far for the Kirk. The ministers of Edinburgh refused to do as he asked on the grounds that such prayers implied a belief in Mary's innocence and a condemnation of Elizabeth's conduct.

James ordered the court to go into mourning for his mother, and was disconcerted when the Earl of Sinclair appeared in armour and told him this was the proper mourning for the Queen of Scots. But he accepted Elizabeth's explanation that she had never intended that the warrant for Mary's death should be executed (though she had signed it). There was no point, he thought, in disturbing the friendship between the two states. However, when at last he inherited the English throne, he had Mary's body removed from Peterborough Cathedral and a splendid tomb erected in Westminster Abbey. Perhaps this salved his conscience, or such conscience as he had.

The business of government occupied him. Given the history of the last two reigns and his own minority he was remarkably successful in imposing his authority and maintaining order. He had learned from his study of history how unwise some of his predecessors, notably James I, James III and James V, had been in attempting to repress the nobility with harsh severity. So, while preferring to rely on men of comparatively humble birth, such as 'Tam o' the Cowgate', his lord advocate and secretary of state, whom he created Earl of Haddington, he excluded as far as possible the great nobles from the management of affairs of state. He also promoted the royal law courts, which competed successfully with the baronial courts from which the nobility drew so much of their local power. At the same time, however, he conciliated the nobles by confirming them in possession of estates that before the Reformation had been Church lands, and rewarding them with further grants.

Moreover, few nobles were now quite as ardent reformers as their fathers had been. The Kirk's democratic tone was no more to their taste than it was to the King's. When Knox's successor as the most influential figure in the Kirk, Andrew Melville, angrily told James that he was no more than 'God's sillie vassal' – 'sillie' meaning simple, not stupid – it would have been a very dull noble who didn't understand that such a challenge to the King threatened a subversion of the whole social order.

Gradually, with skill and patience, James re-established royal authority over the Kirk and its General Assembly. He even managed to restore the office of bishops, though insisting, both in deference to the opinion of the Kirk, and in his own royal interest, that these must not be the 'proud, papal prelates' of old, but royal servants supervising the clergy and subduing their more extreme opinions.

By the time he inherited the English Crown, James had succeeded in establishing royal authority more effectively than any previous Stuart king. Even so, this remained fragile.

In 1588 James was twenty-two. It was high time he was married. Various brides were suggested, among them a sister of Henry of Navarre, who would become King of France the following year, but eventually Anne, the younger daughter of the King of Denmark, was the chosen candidate. Her portrait pleased the King – she was blonde, blue-eyed, a typical Scandinavian beauty. There was some difficulty over the dowry, which the Danish king couldn't afford, but this was resolved when James, now full of an unaccustomed eagerness, declared that the princess was not a piece of merchandise and he would take her without a dowry. In the one romantic gesture of his life, he sailed to Norway (then part of the Danish state) to meet and marry his bride, already the subject of some of his most ardent, if least competent, verses. Seeing her, he convinced himself he was in love. The marriage took place. It was celebrated with some flourish at the Danish court, where Anne's father told his new son-in-law, that they would soon teach him to drink like a Dane.[2] They spent four months in Denmark, James taking time off from feasting and his new marital duties to attend lectures in Copenhagen, arguing with theologians about the doctrine of predestination and discussing the Copernican theory with the great scientist Tycho Brahe. Anne did not share her husband's intellectual interests, and in later years they would drift apart, but for the time being the marriage went well. They would have seven children, of whom three survived to adulthood. It is probable than Anne was the only woman with whom James slept. Unlike earlier Jameses and his grandsons, Charles II and James VII and II, he left no illegitimate children, at least none of whom there is any record. There is no reason to suppose that, while in Denmark, he enquired about his stepfather Bothwell, who had died, raving mad, in a Danish prison a decade previously. That was all past history, and in any case Bothwell, as far as James was concerned, had been his father's chief murderer.

When he returned home in May 1590, he found that the arrangements he had made for the government by the Council in his absence had worked well and his kingdom had remained at peace, untroubled by rebellion or riot. This is a fair measure of his achievement. Nevertheless Scotland remained a violent country in which the King could not feel secure. Three episodes may be taken as illustration.

There was first the business of the North Berwick witches. The origin of this story may seem ridiculous. Before James himself decided to go and fetch his future wife in person, the plan had been for Anne to sail to Scotland. However, a storm blew up and the Danish fleet had to return to port. Its admiral then expressed his belief that the storm had been stirred up by witchcraft. Soon after the return of the royal party, a coven of witches was discovered at North Berwick. Under examination they confessed to having summoned up the storm. Perhaps they even believed that they had such powers. More probably, they said what their torturers would have them say. James was terrified. Like most in his generation he believed implicitly in the powers of darkness and in the awful possibility that men and women might traffic with the devil. His conviction was such that he would actually write a book on demonology. In later life he would amend his views and conclude that much of what passed for witchcraft was mere fantasy; but for now he was a firm believer. More alarming still was the witches' confession that the leader of their coven was his cousin the Earl of Bothwell, the Lord Admiral of Scotland. This added credibility to the story. Who better than the Lord Admiral to intercede with Satan to call up a storm at sea?

Bothwell was Francis Stewart, like the King a grandson of James V. His father was John Stewart, Mary's favourite among her illegitimate half-brothers; when he had died in 1563, she had cried out that God always took from her those she loved best, and she then made a pet of his infant son, Francis. John Stewart had been a friend of Bothwell and had married his sister, which was how the earldom and the title of Lord Admiral descended to Francis. However charming he may have been as a little boy, he grew up to be wild, unruly, and only doubtfully sane. Unlike the wretched victims of the witch trial, Bothwell was not 'examined'. He was, however, imprisoned in Edinburgh Castle in April 1591, but escaped two months later. In December that year he raided the Palace of Holyroodhouse in an attempt to kidnap the King. Unsuccessful, he again evaded arrest.

He had his allies, among them another cousin, James Stewart, Earl of Moray, the son-in-law of the murdered regent. The King, alarmed by the connection, ordered the Earl of Huntly to hunt them down, at the same time offering Moray a pardon for all offences if he would break with Bothwell. Moray may have intended to do so, but Huntly was too quick for him, besieging him in his castle of Donibristle in Fife and killing him when he tried to escape. Legend has it that he delivered the fatal blow himself. According to the popular ballad inspired by the killing, James had 'bad ye bring him wi'ye,/But forbade ye him to slay'. Be that as it may, Huntly escaped without punishment for the murder, suffering no more than a week's house arrest. The murdered man's mother, Lady Doune, commissioned a painting of her dead son, displaying all his wounds. It still hangs in the Morays' Darnaway Castle.

Bothwell was still at large. Two years later he again broke into Holyrood, on this occasion even forcing his way into the King's bedroom, where he brandished his sword. Servants rushed in, Bothwell fled, and James showed himself in his nightshirt at the window to calm the excited crowd that rumour of the Earl's raid had brought into the streets. This was Bothwell's last fling. He fled the country and went to Italy, where he is said to have scraped a living as a fortune-teller till he died in Naples in 1612. His crazy and dangerous antics make it easy to understand why James was so eager to remove to the calmer atmosphere of England. In Scotland the King lived cheek by jowl with his subjects, for the poor quarter of the Canongate came right up to the gates of Holyrood; in England there was a distance between them more suited to the majesty of royalty.

More mysterious and more dangerous than Bothwell's extravagant wildness was the 'Gowrie Conspiracy'. The official story, as told by the King himself, is quite straightforward. Unfortunately it makes little sense.

On the morning of 5 August 1600, James was at Falkland Palace in Fife, preparing for a day's hunting, in weather that, he said, was 'wonderful, pleasant, and seasonable'. While in the field he was approached by the young brother of the Earl of Gowrie, Alexander Ruthven, who was known as the Master of Gowrie. He was an agreeable, good-looking young man who had already applied for a position at court, where his sister Beatrix was one of Queen Anne's maids of honour. Alexander had ridden over from Gowrie House in Perth with, according to James, a remarkable story: he had come upon a man burying a pot of gold in a field, and suspected that the man was a Jesuit spy. Would James please ride back to Perth with him and question the arrested man himself? The King agreed, and when the hunt was finished, at eleven o'clock in the morning, he set off with the Master, the rest of his entourage following behind.

It was a journey of about fourteen miles, and at one point James asked the Duke of Lennox (son of his admired Esmé Stuart) what he thought of young Alexander, who was the Duke's brother-in-law. Lennox said he was 'an honest gentleman' and the King then told him why they were heading for Perth. The story struck Lennox as thin, but he did not try to dissuade James.

They arrived in Perth and were met by the Earl of Gowrie, who escorted them to the family home. Gowrie House no longer exists

– the Perth Sheriff Court now occupies the site – but it was a fortified house with gardens that ran down to the River Tay. A meal
was prepared, and after a while James and the Master disappeared
upstairs. Some of the King's men made to follow but were told
that James and young Alexander had private business to discuss.

They were absent for some time. Meanwhile the company below
finished their meal and some strolled into the garden and plucked
cherries from the trees. The afternoon wore on until one, Thomas
Cranstoun, the Earl's master-stabler, came out and told them that
the King had already left. However, the porter said he hadn't seen
him go, and Gowrie said he would go back into the house and see
if James was still there. He returned and told the company that
the King had indeed left. Lennox then called for their horses to be
brought, but while they were waiting for them, the King's head
appeared at a window in the turret. There was a hand over his
face, and he seemed to be calling for help.

John Ramsay, the King's favourite page, who had been restless
all afternoon, heard the cry, ran up a turnpike stair (with a hawk
he had been admiring still attached to his wrist) and into a gallery
chamber, where he found James and Alexander struggling together.
'Strike him low,' the King cried. 'He wears a pyne dowlit' (secret
doublet). Ramsay stabbed the Master and pushed him down the
stair where those rushing up finished him off. His last words were
reputedly 'Alas, I had na wyte [knowledge] of it.'

All was now confusion. Gowrie hurried into the house and found
John Ramsay alone in the gallery chamber – the King, for his
safety, having been locked in the next room. Ramsay and the Earl
drew their swords. Someone called out that the King was dead.
Gowrie lowered his point and Ramsay stabbed him. Both brothers
were now dead, and the 'conspiracy' had failed. There was no sign
of the Jesuit or the pot of gold, though the King later claimed he
had indeed seen him, and subsequently one of Gowrie's servants,
by name Henderson, confessed to having impersonated him.
However, he bore no resemblance to the description James had
given, so his evidence seems worthless.

Any attempt to make sense of the 'Ruthven Raid' must start

with the Earl of Gowrie. He was no friend to James and had indeed been involved in rebellion when he was only sixteen. His grandfather had been one of Rizzio's murderers and his father the leader of the group who had taken James prisoner in 1584. That failed coup had cost him his head. Young Gowrie had financial grievances too: James still owed him more than £80,000 (Scots) for expenses incurred by his father when treasurer. It may be that he intended to hold the King in custody till his debt was settled.

On the other hand, his ambitions may have flown higher. Gowrie had only recently returned to Scotland. He had spent five years at Padua University studying law; also, reputedly, necromancy. (After his death, a piece of paper with strange cabbalistic designs and figures was reputedly found in his pocket.) From there he had gone to Geneva, where he had been entertained by Calvin's successor, Theodore Beza. His journey home had taken him to Paris, where the English ambassador described him to Elizabeth's secretary of state, Robert Cecil, as 'a man of whom there may be exceeding good use made'. A visit to the English court followed, and Gowrie is said to have made a good impression on Elizabeth.

Back in Scotland, he established himself as one of the leaders of the extreme Presbyterian party who were displeased by the King's Church policy. No doubt the time spent with Beza gave him credibility. He was certainly popular, at least with those who were dissatisfied with the King – one reason why James's account of the events of 5 August was greeted with considerable scepticism. Moreover, Gowrie had royal connections himself, even if somewhat distant ones. His formidable mother, Dorothea Stewart, was the granddaughter of the Earl of Methven (himself a Stewart), who had been Margaret Tudor's third husband after her divorce from the Earl of Angus. It is not inconceivable that Gowrie aimed at the throne. While his brother Alexander was described as 'a learned, sweet and hurtles gentleman', the Earl was a different proposition.

His intention was to seize the King. Whether James was to be held prisoner or murdered is debatable. The former is more likely, a repeat of his father's 'Ruthven Raid'. There were precedents galore. Whoever held the King might control policy. Only if James proved obdurate would his life be in danger. As to the means intended, these seem clear enough. Alexander was to detain James in the gallery chamber until the Earl could persuade the King's men that their master had already left Gowrie House. The King would then be taken through the garden to a boat and carried to the Ruthven castle of Dirleton in East Lothian, which was being held by the Earl's mother. Alexander's role was to play the dupe.

Why did the King fall into the trap? An answer might be found in two letters he wrote, one to each brother, on 2 August. Unfortunately, these have disappeared, and we know of them only because of the record of a payment made to the messenger who delivered them. So one can only speculate.

The official story about the Jesuit and the pot of gold is improbable in itself. Had there been such a discovery, the obvious course would have been for the King to command that the arrested man be brought to him under guard. Second, James spent much of the afternoon closeted with Alexander, more than enough time to question the mysterious man, who in any case disappears even from the King's version of events and has never been identified. Had he existed, he would surely have been produced to substantiate James's story. Moreover, given that the King was a cautious man, alert with good reason to the dangers of being taken prisoner or assassinated, there must have been some other inducement.

James might be a married man and the father of a family, but Anne had already begun to bore him, and his fondness for handsome young men had already been remarked on. (The current favourite was John Ramsay, who was perhaps not yet twenty.) A plausible explanation for his willingness – even eagerness – to accompany Alexander back to Gowrie House is that he was promised what he had been demanding. The assignation may even have been the subject of the lost letter to the Master. If Alexander showed it to his brother, that would have been enough to set the plot in motion. After the event of course, none of the King's company could explain why they had not been suspicious of the story about the Jesuit without alluding to what they knew of the King's sexual tastes. That knowledge explains also why they do not seem to have been concerned when James disappeared upstairs with Alexander and remained there throughout the afternoon.

Two other pieces of evidence support this version of the day's events. John Ramsay was on edge, unable to keep still. He had reason to be disturbed. Fear that Alexander was about to supplant him in the King's affections was cause enough for jealousy. He at least could have no doubt as to what was happening in the upper room.

Second, more damning still, are James's words to Ramsay when he entered the room to find the King struggling to free himself from Alexander's grip: 'Strike him low. He wears a pyne dowlit.' How could the King know about this doublet if it hadn't already been removed while they made love?

This explanation has the merit, which no others have, of making sense of the day's events. Alexander would keep James in play till his brother had persuaded Lennox and the other member of the King's retinue that he had already left Gowrie House. When they set off after him, Gowrie himself would appear and make James his prisoner. But the timing went wrong. James, having got what he had come for, was himself anxious to be off. Alexander, obedient to his brother's orders, tried to prevent him. James forced his way to the window and called for help, with Alexander holding on and trying to stop his mouth with his hand. The anxious and jealous John Ramsay hurried to the rescue, and the Gowrie brothers were doomed. One would like to think that young Alexander spoke the truth when he cried out that he had no 'wyte' or knowledge of the plot, but that seems unlikely.

The true story could not be told. It was too shameful. So James stuck with his cock-and-bull version. Few may have believed it, but it was rash to call the King a liar.[3]

In March 1603 Queen Elizabeth died after a reign of forty-five years. Till almost the last moment she had refused to name a successor, but few doubted that it must be the King of Scots. All the chief men of her court, notably the secretary of state, Robert Cecil, had been in communication with him for years. Now at last, when she was beyond speech, the question was put directly to her, and she signified by a motion of her hand that she approved. As soon as she was pronounced dead, her cousin, Sir Robert Carey, who held the office of Warden of the Marches, took horse and rode hard for Edinburgh. A fall at Norham delayed him, and when he arrived in Edinburgh he was told that the King had already gone to bed. But he insisted on seeing him.

> I was quickly led in and carried up to the king's chamber. I kneeled by him, and saluted him by his title of England, Scotland, France and Ireland. He gave me his hand to kiss and bade me welcome. After he had long discoursed of the manner of the Queen's sickness and of her death, he asked me what letters I had from the Council. I told him, none: and acquainted him how narrowly I escaped from them [they had wanted someone other than Carey to bring the news north] and yet I had brought him a blue ring from a fair lady, that I hoped would give him assurance of the truth that I had reported. He took it, and looked upon it, and said, 'It is enough; I know by this that you are a true messenger.' Then he committed me to the charge of Lord Home, and gave straight command that I should want for nothing.4

It is appropriate that James VI, the least dignified of the Stuarts, should have learned that he had achieved his life's ambition, uniting the crowns of England and Scotland, when dressed in his nightgown.

He made haste to be off south to take possession of his Promised Land. But before he left he found time to write a letter of fatherly advice to his elder son, Prince Henry, who was with his tutors at Stirling Castle.

> Let not this news make you proud or insolent; for a King's son and heir was ye before, and no more are ye yet. The augmentation that is here like to fall unto you, is but in cares and heavy burdens . . . Look upon all English men that shall come to visit you as upon your loving subjects, not with that ceremony as towards strangers, and yet with such heartiness as at this time they deserve.

The letter, both sententious and affectionate, is typical of James. Yet, while he might speak to his son of 'cares and heavy burdens', he himself was now free of the burden of uncertainty and determined to enjoy himself.

James left Scotland promising to return every three years – one of the many promises he did not keep, though it may have been made in good faith at the time. Though it would not be long before many in England were speaking nostalgically of the days of 'Good Queen Bess', the new King was received enthusiastically. Elizabeth had been long in dying, and the feeling that it was time for a change is not confined to democratic electorates. When he reached York on his journey south, a conduit running from the Minster flowed with claret, to the delight of the citizens, even though the quality of the wine was doubtful. There was good reason for the English to be happy. The fear of a disputed succession such as might lead to civil war had been removed. The new King was an experienced ruler, known also to be a good Protestant. Moreover he was so obviously delighted to be among them that he could be forgiven even his strong Scots accent. He was genial and approachable, and though his extravagance would soon cause concern and put him at odds with his parliaments, it was at first welcome after Elizabeth's mean economy and reluctance to spend any money except on her own adornment.

James and Anne were crowned in Westminster Abbey in July of that year, but it was a hurried ceremony and festivities were curtailed, for plague was rife in London, and the city was not safe to stay in. So King and Queen almost immediately withdrew to a rural retreat.

James retained Robert Cecil, Elizabeth's 'little beagle', as his chief minister, but others who had been out of favour with the Queen now looked for advancement. Chief among these were Cecil's cousin Francis Bacon, and Henry Howard, Earl of Northampton. Both were remarkable men, with qualities to commend them to the King, not least that both were, like him, homosexually inclined. Bacon, scholar, scientist, lawyer and polymath, would have to wait before being rewarded with the high office he believed, with reason, his talents deserved. There were two reasons for this.[5] First, his cousin Cecil was jealous of him and also distrusted him. Second, Bacon had been among the entourage of Elizabeth's last favourite, Robert Devereux, Earl of Essex. James too had admired Essex, Cecil's bitter rival, and when he met his son soon after his arrival in England, embraced him as the heir of the noblest knight England had known. But Essex's career had foundered, and, foolishly, he had raised what seemed a rebellion against Elizabeth. Its failure brought him to the executioner's block, and Bacon had abandoned him and even given evidence against him to save his own career and perhaps his neck. So James first looked on Bacon with suspicion.

Henry Howard was a younger brother of that Duke of Norfolk who had proposed himself as a husband for James's mother, and had suffered for his presumption. Elizabeth had had no time for Henry. His ornate manners repelled her. He was pro-Spanish and believed to be a crypto-Catholic. He was a schemer and a sinister aura surrounded him. But he was highly intelligent, an unusual nobleman, who had actually been a lecturer at Cambridge University. He was a great flatterer who had taken pains to ingratiate himself with the King of Scots, and though James mocked the flowery 'Asiatic' style of his letters, his genuine scholarship commended him to the King. Queen Anne detested him, but Howard shrugged that off, and established himself in James's favour. His machinations would involve the King in the worst scandal of his reign.

James's intentions were good, and he was confident of his ability to put them into practice: 'We are an old and experienced king,' he told the Commons. He quickly put an end to the war with Spain, which had dragged on without either success or much meaning since the year of the Armada. This may not have been popular, but it was sensible. One of James's merits was his preference for peace rather than war. He believed, with some reason, that there were few disputes between states that could not be settled by diplomatic means, and, with less reason, that he himself was a master diplomat.

Two dissident groups looked on the new reign with especial eagerness: the Roman Catholics, who hoped that Mary's son would relax the Penal Laws, which forbade the legal practice of their faith, exposed them to fines for resistance, and made the celebration of the Mass a treasonable act; and the Puritans, who thought Elizabeth's Anglican settlement an insufficiently pure Reformation and who hoped that the king of a Presbyterian Scotland would look kindly on their demands. Both would be disappointed.

Though James was no fanatic, and even, like his mother and his grandsons, the future Charles II and James VII and II, inclined to toleration of religious differences, so long as his legal authority was respected and civil order maintained, he had been reared in the reformed faith and held to its doctrines. He might have little wish to persecute Catholics, but he could not but believe they were in error. When, disappointed in their hope of relief, some of the most fervent Catholics engaged in the conspiracy that goes by the name of the Gunpowder Plot in 1605, he could scarcely be expected to alleviate the unhappy condition of their co-religionists. Nevertheless, the Penal Laws were more leniently enforced than in Elizabeth's time, and when, some years later, Queen Anne herself converted to Catholicism, James did no more than grumble and shrug his shoulders.

As for the Puritans, the King was indeed anxious to restore the uniformity of religion for which Elizabeth's parliament had legislated, but which had gradually crumbled, and he summoned a conference at Hampton Court in 1605 to enable Church of England divines of all shades of opinion to debate matters of religion. But when the Puritans called for the abolition of episcopacy, James, who had struggled successfully to impose bishops on the Kirk in Scotland, would have none of it: 'No Bishop, No King,' he cried, and that was that. Time would render this opinion ridiculous, but in the seventeenth century it made sense. A Church without bishops was a species of republic. Without hierarchy in the Church, you were but a short step away from rejecting the royal authority. In this James was prescient. Episcopacy would be abolished in the 1640s, and within a few years England would indeed be a republic.

James styled himself King of Great Britain and was eager to bring about a more perfect union of his two kingdoms. By this he meant amalgamation into a single state. That had not been achieved by the Union of the Crowns of England and Scotland, so that for more than a century the constitutional reality would be best expressed by the formula 'One King, Two Kingdoms'. James was, he explained in his pawky manner, a Christian king married to his kingdoms, and it was unseemly that he should have two wives. So commissioners were appointed to consider how such a union might be made. The English ones were merely required to examine the means of creating one 'convenient and necessary for the honour of His Majestie, and the weale and common good of both the said realmes', while the Scots were asked to 'consult upon a perfyte union', which should not however derogate from the 'fundamentall lawes, ancient privileges, offices, richtis, dignities and liberties of this kingdome'.

The different instructions show the King's understanding of the difficulty of effecting a union between a large, rich country and one which was much smaller and poorer, for in any such union the former would have little to gain, while the latter would fear that union meant subjection or incorporation. Nevertheless, while the Scots parliament, obedient to the King, actually passed an Act of Union in 1607, it was conditional on English acceptance of the proposal. This was not forthcoming. As far as the English were concerned, the Union of the Crowns was enough; England no longer had a dangerous northern frontier. Meanwhile there were quite enough needy Scots flocking to London and the court in search of jobs and pensions as it was. So the project failed. James was ahead of his time.

The day-to-day business of government bored James and he was content to leave it to Cecil (now Earl of Salisbury) and other ministers. Besides, after his harsh childhood and the dangers he had run as a young king in Scotland, he felt entitled to enjoy himself. He indulged his passion for hunting. Often poor misshapen Salisbury had to trail round the shires trying to catch the King, weary after a day in the field and now perhaps showing the effects of the wine he had been constantly sipping, in order to get him to attend to official business. Most of the time what James wanted from his minister was money, for he was extravagant and generous, and the royal coffers of England were not as well stocked as they had appeared to be from poor Scotland. On the other hand he was happy to address Parliament, in his capacity as 'the great schoolmaster of the realm', and feed them with his wisdom, which his faithful Commons were less and less happy to receive. In other ways too England was not quite as satisfactory as he had expected. When he told the Lord Chief Justice, Sir Edward Coke, a stiff, opinionated man, that he, the King, was the guardian and protector of the law, Coke replied that the case was otherwise; it was the law that protected the King. This was not an answer he could have given either Henry VIII or Elizabeth with impunity, but times were changing, and in any case James, accustomed to the rebukes of the Kirk in Edinburgh, was a less formidable figure than his Tudor cousins.

James's court lacked the dignity and order of Elizabeth's. Sir Walter Scott, who was uncharacteristically unjust to James, and strangely believed this most successful of Stuart kings to have been 'the least talented' of his line, nevertheless gives a vivid and probably accurate picture of the disorderly fashion in which James chose to live. The young hero of *The Fortunes of Nigel* is introduced to the King's chamber, and

> The scene of confusion amid which he found the King seated, was no bad picture of the state and quality of James's own mind. There was much that was rich and costly in cabinet pictures and valuable ornaments, but they were slovenly arranged, covered with dust, and lost half their value, or at least their effect, from the manner in which they were presented to the eye. The table was loaded with huge folios, amongst which lay light books of jests and ribaldry; and notes of unmercifully long orations to Parliament, and essays on king-craft, were mingled with roundels and ballats by the royal 'Prentice, as he styled himself, in the art of poetry, and schemes for the general pacification of Europe, with a list of the names of the King's hounds, and remedies against canine madness.[6]

As for the royal character, Scott found James to be 'fond of his dignity, which he was perpetually degrading by undue familiarity; capable of much public labour, yet often neglecting it for the meanest amusement; a wit, though a pedant; and a scholar, though fond of the conversation of the ignorant and uneducated'.

The King was indeed an oddity, but a more able and attractive one than Scott allows. Moreover, he had one other quality that is rare in monarchs. Though capable of firm, even ruthless action, when he was alarmed or his immediate interests seemed to be threatened, he was essentially kindly.

His interests were also unusually wide. He was a patron of the arts. Shakespeare's theatre company were designated the King's Men, and several of his plays were given command performances at court. *Macbeth*, with its fantasy about the origins of the Stuarts and its promise that as the heirs of Banquo they would reign till 'the crack of doom', may even have been written to please and honour the King. Moreover, in an essay on *Macbeth* and the Gowrie Conspiracy, Arthur Melville Clark suggested that:

> in preconceiving much of the supernatural in his play, Shakespeare was influenced in the direction of contemporary witch-lore by the fact that King James was the author of a notable book on 'Demonology' . . . that the King believed himself to have been a special target of witches and that he regarded himself as possessed of a nose for smelling out practitioners of sorcery and exposing their machinations. And that is why James was so interested in the cabbalistic characters found in Gowrie's pockets, and why the depositions . . . which testify about Gowrie in relation to magic, prognostications, and amulets were published along with the official accounts of the events of 5th August; why the official account itself declared that for many generations the Ruthvens were known throughout the whole land as dabblers in the occult . . . Macbeth and Gowrie were both traitors and both intermeddlers with the diabolical.[7]

But if James patronised drama – *The Tempest*, for instance, being performed on the occasion of his daughter's wedding – the taste of the court ran rather to the lavish spectacle of the masque, gorgeous affairs with the text provided by Shakespeare's friend and rival Ben Jonson, with decor and choreography by Inigo Jones.

One of the most notable of these, *The Masque of Blackness*, saw Queen Anne herself blacked up and arrayed in a beautiful costume fashioned from some of the late Queen's wardrobe of two thousand gowns. The show was set on the purely imaginary banks of the Niger and featured sea nymphs, mermen and mermaids, charming negro children dancing in the old banqueting hall in the Palace of Whitehall, transformed for the occasion into a rich landscape bordered by the sea, and under a blue silk heaven, a silver throne occupied by the moon. It was all very splendid, very popular, very expensive and very silly.

The month-long state visit of Queen Anne's brother, Christian IV of Denmark, offered an occasion for more revelry and even greater extravagance. There was a tournament in which the Danish king rode in the lists like a medieval knight, and this was perhaps the one occasion on his visit that he was even halfway sober. For the rest there was feasting and drinking, and then more feasting and more drinking, with James and Anne matching the Dane glass for glass. It culminated in a banquet and pageant at Theobalds in Hertfordshire, James's favourite country residence. According to the acerbic Sir John Harrington, a godson of Queen Elizabeth, a show displaying the visit of the Queen of Sheba to Solomon saw Sheba lose her footing and collapse with the gifts she was carrying on top of the Danish king. He rose gallantly and would have danced with her, but himself fell over and had to be carried, smeared with wine, cake and jellies, to his bed. Then Faith, Hope and Charity advanced to congratulate King James on his majesty, but Hope was speechless and Faith legless. Only Charity played her part with suitable decorum, but she was followed by Victory and Peace, and they were in much the same condition as Faith and Hope. Victory dissolved into tears and when Peace found her way to the throne blocked by courtiers, themselves the worse for wear, she laid about vigorously with the symbol of her role, an olive branch.[8]

Such was life at court in the merry days of King James.

James and Anne had seven children, of whom four died in infancy. The survivors were Henry, born 1594, who became Prince of Wales in 1603; Elizabeth, born in 1596; and 'Baby Charles', born 1600.[9] By the time he inherited the English throne, James probably no longer slept with his wife, though their relations were mostly friendly, but he was a fond and devoted father. Naturally enough his first care was for Henry as the heir to his crowns, and he wrote for him a book of instruction in the art of king-craft, and in his duties as a man and monarch. Though often pompous in the manner of the day, the *Basilikon Doron* is also full of good sense and keen observation. Among other things, James warned his son against 'the preposterous humility of the proud Puritan' who thinks he is entitled to lay down the law to others – including the King – while resenting any criticism of himself. 'Laws,' the King told his son, 'are ordained as rules of virtuous and social living, and not to be snares to trap your good subjects', advice that modern parliaments and bureaucrats might with advantage ponder.

Henry, like his father before him, received a good education, happily being taught in more kindly fashion than James had been by Buchanan. He was athletic and a keen sportsman, though he disappointed James by being no great enthusiast for hunting. According to the French ambassador, Henry took part 'rather for the pleasure of galloping, than that which the dogs give him'. He was loyal to his servants, taking their side if anyone criticised them, and passionately devoted to ships and the navy. He possessed the characteristic Stuart charm, and is said to have had a delightful smile. But he was also something of a prig, and disapproved of the disorderly court his father kept. He may indeed have nursed a growing contempt for his pacific parent. He was dazzled by the last notable survivor of the heroic reign of Elizabeth, Sir Walter Raleigh; but Raleigh, described in the Queen's lifetime as 'the most unpopular man in England', was a prisoner in the Tower of London, under sentence of death (suspended), on account of his suspected involvement in a plot against James in the first year of his reign. Henry, indifferent to Raleigh's offence, inveighed against his hero's incarceration, remarking bitterly, 'only my father would keep such an eagle in a cage'. Perhaps there were the makings of a feud between father and son, such as were to be characteristic of the

Stuarts' Hanoverian successors, but whereas the Georges all hated their elder sons, James remained tolerant of Henry's independence of mind and his affection was undiminished.

In 1612, however, Henry contracted a fever after a game of tennis. Despite the attentions of the doctors – or perhaps because of the remedies they attempted, applying new-killed pigeons to his shaved head to draw out 'the corrupt and putrid fever' and cockerels, split open, to his feet – he died, asking only for his 'dear sister'. It is tempting to speculate on how different the fortunes of the Stuarts might have been if Henry had lived to be king. Would this strong-willed, energetic, staunchly Protestant young man have won and held the favour of his people and Parliament, taking the country into war on the Protestant side in the great European conflict that broke out six years after his death? Would the Parliament have provided him with the means to execute the 'patriotic' Protestant policy they so often called for – while showing no willingness to pay for it? Such speculation belongs to counter-factual history, but is nonetheless enticing.

James's daughter Elizabeth was, in the fashion of the time, brought up away from court, seeing her parents only occasionally. She learned French and Italian, and spent the afternoons of her childhood on horseback. She hero-worshipped her elder brother, and they sent each other letters almost every day, at times when meetings were impossible. She was waiting, as all princesses must, for marriage, for the day when some foreign match would be arranged and adult life would begin. There was a succession of suitors, among them briefly the recently widowed Philip III of Spain. He was old enough to be her father, reputed virtuous, also deeply stupid. She was spared this marriage when her father settled on a German prince, Frederick, Elector Palatine of the Rhine. (The title of elector meant that he was one of the seven princes who elected the Holy Roman Emperor. In fact, this election was by now little more than a formality; the title had become hereditary in the House of Habsburg.) Frederick was the same age as Elizabeth, a lively but serious young man, as befitted his position as the leader of the German Protestant Union. He was a Calvinist, but not of the most rigid sort. The marriage was arranged, but when Frederick arrived in England, where he fell in love with his bride, as he was doubtless determined to do, Prince Henry died and the wedding had to be postponed. It took place the following year, and the newly-weds sailed to the Netherlands, leaving James in tears, which, in his own fashion, he doubtless enjoyed. Ten months later Elizabeth gave birth to her first child, a boy, christened Frederick Henry. There would soon be a quiver of children, but not before the lives of the young couple were turned upside down.

Of 'Baby Charles', little need be said at this point. He had been a backward child, slow in learning to walk and speak, which latter he did with a disabling stammer. He was small and shy and his brother Henry declared that when he was king, he would make Charles Archbishop of Canterbury.

Meanwhile, before Henry's death and Elizabeth's marriage, King James had himself fallen in love. The object of his affections was a young Scotsman called Robert Ker, or Carr as he was known in England. He belonged to a cadet branch of the Kers of Ferniehurst, one of the great Border families, and he had first come to England with James as one of his 'running pages'. But he had been sent home and then spent some time in France, where his manners acquired a degree of polish. Returning to England, he had the good fortune to break his leg falling from his horse in a tournament, and this brought him to the King's notice. He was confined to bed, where the King visited him and was delighted. Ker was a blond, long-legged boy, deemed handsome (though his portrait suggests that his expression was foxy). He was not very bright but was possessed of an animal magnetism; at least two other people besides James were to be in love with him. James was now in his forties, a time of life when many are ready to make fools of themselves. He made Ker a gentleman of his bedchamber, a post that required him to sleep in or near the King's chamber; in Ker's case, one must assume, in James's bed also. James's interest was not only sexual. He took it on himself to repair the young man's defective education, teaching him Latin. One observer remarked snidely that it would have been a better idea to teach him English, since the boy spoke with a strong Scots accent. But so of course did the King himself. Responsibilities and honours were showered on the young man. He acted as the King's secretary (which enabled James to keep him about his person) and was soon raised to the peerage as Viscount Rochester. Recognised as the reigning favourite, he found courtiers eager to please and flatter him. His elevation must have seemed to him as welcome as it was surprising, always assuming he could bear James's displays of love with equanimity. There is no evidence that he found this difficult. Queen Anne disliked Ker, which was not surprising, but James was indifferent to his wife's opinion. All the warm sentimentality of his nature was directed at the young man, who would soon rise even further, being made Earl of Somerset.

Others sought advancement through Ker's influence with the King. Chief among them was Francis Bacon, who, thanks also to the death in 1612 of his cousin Salisbury, at last achieved office as Attorney-General. Northampton too was quick to make friends with the young man, and soon sought a means of making that friendship firmer. His brother, Thomas Howard, Earl of Suffolk, had a beautiful daughter called Frances. She had been married while still a very young girl to the equally young Earl of Essex. They did not suit. Frances developed a distaste for his person; he disliked and perhaps feared her, for she was strong-willed and dominating, and made no secret of her contempt for him. Now, returning to court, her fancy turned to Somerset. He was flattered but found himself unable to write the sort of love letters she might expect, and enlisted the help of his closest friend, Sir Thomas Overbury. Overbury was a clever young man and something of a poet. He had been the bosom friend, and perhaps the lover, of Ker before he rose to greatness. At first he was happy to do as his friend asked. It may have amused him; perhaps he didn't take the thing seriously. Then he became intensely jealous and advised Ker to break off his courtship of Frances. Politics played a part in his changed attitude. Overbury was opposed to a Spanish alliance, which the Howards favoured. He became a nuisance. It was thought wise to get him out of the way. James was persuaded, easily enough, to offer him an ambassadorship. Overbury refused it. The King was offended; the disobedient poet was dispatched to the Tower as a prisoner.

Meanwhile Frances, advised by her uncle, opened legal proceedings to obtain an annulment of her marriage to Essex, on the grounds that it had never been consummated on account of the Earl's incapacity. This was insulting, and Essex, though disliking his wife extremely, could not be expected to collude in a process that would leave him an object of pity or, worse, mockery. The nullity suit made no progress. There were rumours that Frances was employing witchcraft against Essex. Perhaps Overbury started them, or at least fanned them. Perhaps he threatened to divulge secrets that would prevent the marriage Frances had set her heart on. Then Overbury died. Poison was soon suspected.

Frances obtained her annulment[10] and she and Somerset were married. The ceremony was held at court. There were masques – one paid for by Bacon; it cost him £2,000 which he could ill afford, since he was always deep in debt. Poets, among them John Donne, wrote verses in honour of the occasion and in praise of the happy couple. Some historians have seen James's approval, indeed encouragement, of the match as evidence that his relationship with Robert Ker had never been sexual. Yet this is to misunderstand both him and the age, which approved passionate friendships between men without supposing that this precluded marriage. Besides which, James's first passion for Ker was fading. He had settled into a loving tenderness, and in any case there was always a paternal element to his feeling for the young men he loved.

But now the rumours surrounding Overbury's death became firm allegations. There was indeed evidence of poisoning. A woman called Mrs Turner, reputed to deal in potions and spells, was incriminated, tried and hanged; and Mrs Turner had been a close associate of the new Countess of Somerset.

The governor of the Tower, Sir Gervase Elwes, passed on all he suspected to the King. James was alarmed. The scandal was coming dangerously near the throne. Somerset begged him to have the investigation stopped, but James told him he could not allow such a crime as was alleged 'to be suppressed and plastered over'. He had the good sense to see that a cover-up might be more damaging than anything that might emerge from an examination of the evidence. 'If the delation [accusation] prove false,' he told Robert, 'no man among you shall so much rejoice as I.'[11] Somerset came to the King at Royston where he was hunting to plead once more. In vain. According to one witness, 'When he came to take his leave of the King, he [James] embraced and kissed him often, wished him to make haste back, showed an extreme passion to be without him; and his back was no sooner turned, but he said with a smile, "I shall never see his face more."'[12] One may question the 'smile'.

Somerset hurried back to London to destroy letters from Northampton, who had died a few months previously, which he feared might compromise him.

The minor figures in the case having been condemned and disposed of, Robert and Frances were both arrested and committed to trial. The case was prosecuted, quite gently, by Bacon. Frances confessed her guilt, while affirming that her husband was innocent. He refused to plead guilty. Both were condemned to death, but James commuted the sentences to imprisonment, and the pair remained in the Tower for several years. The reprieve was unpopular: one law for the rich, another for the poor wretches who had been their accomplices. James was convinced of Frances's guilt, even before her confession. He had sent a message to Robert by way of the lieutenant of the Tower, saying: 'If it shall plainly appear that she is very fowle, as is generally conceaved and reported that she is, as being the author and procurer of that murder, then I thinck justice may not be stayed, and he shold have just cause to be glad that he is freed from so wicked a woman.'[13] But when the time came, he could not bring himself to have Frances executed. It would have been difficult to do so without sending Somerset to the block also, despite his protestation of innocence, and James had sufficient lingering affection for him not to do that.

Even before Somerset's downfall, James had a new favourite, a new love. The young man was called George Villiers, and he was both beautiful and charming. James was captivated, more completely in love than he had ever been; he called Villiers 'Steenie', from a fancied resemblance to a portrait of St Stephen, the first Christian martyr. More intelligent than Ker, Villiers took care to ingratiate himself with the Queen, who was soon writing to him in affectionate terms: 'My kind dog, I have received your letter which is very welcome to me. You do very well in lugging the sow's ear, and I thank you for it, and would have you do so still on condition that you continue always a watchful dog and be always true to him, so wishing you all happiness. Anna R.' The young man's rise would be meteoric: Knight of the Garter, Viscount Villiers, Earl, then Duke of Buckingham. The day would come when James would tell his Council that he was 'neither a god nor an angel, but a man like any other. Therefore I act like a man, and confess to loving those dear to me than other men. You may be sure that I love the Earl of Buckingham more than anyone else, and more than you who are here assembled. I wish to speak in my own behalf, and not to have it thought to be a defect, for Jesus Christ did the same, and therefore I cannot be blamed. Christ had his John, and I have my George.' This was the besotted language of infatuation. Buckingham for his part played his game cleverly, making a parade of his devotion while also charming the King with boyish impertinence: 'I kiss your dirty hands,' he wrote. James responded in similar vein. 'Steenie' was his dog, as well as the Queen's, and he celebrated a visit to Buckingham's house in Rutland with one of his occasional verses:

> The heavens that wept perpetually before,
> Since we came hither show theyr smiling cleere.
> This goodly house it smiles, and all this store
> Of huge provision smiles upon us here.
> The Buckes and Stagges in fatt they seeme to smile:
> God send a smiling boy within a while.[14]

Before Buckingham's rise was assured, and while Somerset was caught up in his troubles, the declining favourite had shown himself to be jealous of the rising one. He wearied James with his tantrums and complaints. His Howard relations by his new marriage were also alarmed. They brought a pretty boy, a son of Sir William Monson, under-governor of the Tower, to court, and treated his face with cosmetics (posset; that is, milk curdled with wine) to make him still more delectable. But they had miscalculated. James's taste did not run to effeminate boys, but to handsome and athletic youths like Ker and Villiers. Besides, the King found this blatant appeal embarrassing. The young man was dismissed from the court, and retired, disappointed or perhaps relieved. Henceforth Buckingham had no rival. The King could deny him nothing, and in time came to be dominated by him.

The marriage of James's daughter Elizabeth to one of the leading Protestant princes of Germany had been popular. The King's ambition to secure a Spanish bride for his heir, Prince Charles, provoked opposition. For many Englishmen Spain was the natural enemy, the greatest Catholic power, feared and hated. The King's friendship with the Spanish ambassador, Gondomar, was remarked and disapproved of. As far as James was concerned, the Spanish match was a necessary part of his grand design to stand forth as the Rex Pacificus, the monarch who by the application of intelligence and goodwill would maintain the peace of Europe. It was a noble but impractical ambition.

Then, in 1616, in the wake of the Somerset scandal and perhaps to divert attention from it, James yielded to the demands of the anti-Spanish party and released Sir Walter Raleigh from the Tower. Raleigh himself had a scheme, one which, if successful, promised to make James rich. In Elizabeth's reign he had sailed the coasts of South America, and now proposed to journey there again and mine for gold in the valley of the River Orinoco. He would, he promised the King, abstain from anything that could be construed as piracy. James assented on condition that Raleigh respected the integrity of the Spanish empire and made no war on their forts or settlements. Raleigh accepted the condition, though it was incompatible with his declared intentions. The expedition was a failure. One of his captains attacked a Spanish outpost. No gold was found. Some of the crews threatened mutiny. Raleigh's eldest son was killed. The old adventurer returned in dismay and disgrace.

Gondomar, on behalf of his government, demanded that Raleigh be executed. James set up a board of inquiry, among its members Sir Edward Coke and Francis Bacon. Their report was damning: Raleigh had misled the King, conspired with France and had always intended to plunder the Spanish colonies. He had been under sentence of death since 1605; it was now carried out. He died in 1618 with characteristic panache, remarking that the axe was a sharp physician but a cure for all ills. He had never been popular, but he was a relic of the great days of Elizabeth, and there was deep resentment that he had been beheaded to please the Spaniards. Nevertheless, his death encouraged James – and Gondomar – to believe that an obstacle to the marriage of Charles to an infanta of Spain had been removed.

There had been an uneasy peace in Europe for most of James's reign in England. In Germany the peace had held since the Diet of Augsburg of 1555 had settled the religious question on the basis of the formula '*cuius regio, eius religio*': a state should take the form of its religion from its prince. The religious wars in France had ended in 1598; in 1609 the Dutch rebels had made a twelve-year truce with Spain that effectively secured the independence of the United Provinces of the Netherlands. But now there were rumblings of war, and James's son-in-law, the Elector Palatine, was a central figure in the drama about to unfold.

The Holy Roman Empire was an agglomeration of quasi-independent states, 'neither Holy nor Roman nor an Empire', as Voltaire would declare a century later. The title of emperor was all but hereditary in the House of Habsburg, but the family's power derived from the collection of states – kingdoms, princedoms and duchies, which they ruled directly – and from their alliance with their cousins of Spain. The Habsburg territories were a hotch-potch, and their title to rule varied according to local custom. There was no uniformity, not even of religion. Bohemia (more or less the modern Czech Republic) inclined to Protestantism. More-over, by tradition the crown of Bohemia was elective. Now the heir to the aged Emperor Matthias was his great-nephew, Ferdinand of Styria. He had been educated by the Jesuits and saw himself as the sword of the Counter-Reformation. The Bohemians were alarmed. When the Emperor sent two of his leading officials to Prague to secure Ferdinand's election to the Bohemian crown, his opponents broke into the imperial palace and threw the unfortunate imperial emissaries out of the window. 'Let your Virgin Mary save you now,' cried one, adding in surprise, 'By God, she has,' as the unfortunate man was seen to crawl away. This incident, known as the Defenestration of Prague, sparked off a revolution. The Bohemians refused to elect Ferdinand and instead offered the throne to James's German son-in-law, the Elector Palatine, in 1617.

The King was in a quandary. On the one hand it was certainly pleasing and flattering that his dear daughter Elizabeth should become a queen. On the other hand, if Frederick accepted the throne, it could not be expected that Ferdinand would acquiesce in the loss of one of his kingdoms. A general European war might break out. It did, and the Thirty Years War reduced Germany to a pitiful condition. (Such was the loss of life in these three decades that when peace at last returned, men in some cities and states were temporarily permitted to take more than one wife, so that the land might be repopulated.) The war would draw in all the major Continental powers: Spain, Denmark, Sweden, France and the Netherlands, as well as every German state. In time, the religious divisions that characterised the early years of the war would become blurred, when Catholic France first financed the campaigns of the Protestant Swedish king, Gustavus Adolphus, and then entered the war herself on the Protestant side against the German and Spanish Habsburgs. What had been in its origins an ideological conflict became a struggle between the Great Powers.

Bohemia was, as Neville Chamberlain was to say dolefully four centuries later, 'a faraway country of which we know little'. It was impossible for James to give any help to his son-in-law, even if he had been more eager to do so than he was. But his inaction was unpopular, as anti-Catholic feeling was vented. Indeed many thought it shameful. The reign of Frederick and Elizabeth in Prague did not last long; their forces were defeated at the Battle of the White Mountain in 1620, and they had to flee. They became known as the Winter King and Winter Queen. The glorious promise of their marriage had turned to dust. Worse followed. The army of the Catholic League pursued them, and drove them out of the Palatine itself. They fled as refugees to the Netherlands, where the Stadholder, Maurice of Nassau, a son of William the Silent, gave them sanctuary. They would remain there while the war raged about them, and Elizabeth would have a host of children. The second of them, Rupert, had been born while they were so briefly king and queen in Bohemia.

Many in England clamoured for war. The Protestant cause must be defended. James would have none of it. In any case war was expensive, he was in debt, and Parliament showed no eagerness to pay for the conflict its wilder spirits urged on him. The war cry was futile, an opportunity to vent emotion and feel good, nothing more. England had not mounted a successful campaign on the Continent for two hundred years. James let the cry exhaust itself. Meanwhile he was flattered by a suggestion from Spain that he should act as intermediary and peacemaker. The idea appealed to his vanity, but nothing came of it.

Negotiations for Charles's Spanish match continued, but slowly – so slowly that Buckingham, eager to promote it, devised a madcap plan. He and Charles should go themselves to Madrid, travelling incognito like knights errant, to clinch the deal. They adopted, absurdly, as their aliases Mr Brown and Mr Smith, names that do not suggest chivalry. James, suffering from arthritis and other ailments, for he was ageing fast, reluctantly agreed. He was divided between a touching admiration for the bold romance of the enterprise and fear for their safety. 'God bless you both, my sweet babes, and send you a happy and safe return,' he wrote and sent a chain of 276 pearls from the Orient as a present for the Infanta. She, however, adamantly refused to marry a heretic.

Queen Anne had died in 1619. The love James had felt when she was a young bride had long since spent itself, but they had rarely been on less than good and friendly terms. If his relationship with Robert Ker had displeased her, at least he had been faithful to her in his peculiar fashion. Now that she was gone, he indulged his fondness for cosy domesticity with the female members of Buckingham's family, especially his wife and sister. Indeed the Buckinghams had become the King's extended family and he was happy to arrange marriages for the younger members. His matchmaking was uncritical; one of his dear Steenie's sisters was married to an elderly knight, who had a fine estate but was known hitherto to 'have loved none but boys'.

The King was weary, an old man already in his middle fifties. The storms of his early life were long past. He indulged himself and others. When the Archbishop of Canterbury, Dr Abbott, unfortunately shot a beater while out hunting, James excused him, saying an angel might have made the same mistake. His court remained as disorderly as ever. He had always been capable of being brusque when offended or bothered. 'God's wounds,' he cried once, weary of the attentions of a demanding public, 'I will pull down my breeches and they shall see my arse.' In these final years, he tottered about, often a little drunk, followed by a train of small dogs and hounds, talking endlessly, now about politics, now religion, then sport, the Bible, and the men and women he had known. He was a great gossip and full of jokes, some bawdy, some sly, some very much to the point, and many even funny. A scriptural analogy would be followed by a vile pun, a quotation from Horace or Virgil by an anecdote about his grim youth in Scotland, a blast against 'tobacco-drunkards' by disquisitions on the art of hunting. He remained interested in everything. When he visited Stonehenge, he commanded Inigo Jones to investigate its origins. The conclusion was that it was a Roman temple to the God Caelus.

His dear boys – 'my dog Steenie and Baby Charles' – returned from Spain without the Infanta, but James was too pleased that they had come home safely from their adventure, which he thought 'worthy to be put in a romanzo', to care about the collapse of his foreign policy. Buckingham now had the management of everything. Yet the King's acumen had not entirely deserted him. When Buckingham looked favourably on a move by the Commons to impeach the treasurer, the Earl of Middlesex, James told him roundly that he was a fool and would soon have his fill of impeachments.

In the same way he had long put aside his belief in witchcraft and grown skilled in detecting impostures, and had come to realise that most who pretended to practise the art were deluded.

In March 1625 he fell ill, and met death with a courage he had not always shown in life, affirming, argumentative to the last, that he approved of absolution 'as it is practised in the English Church, but in the dark way of Rome I do defy it'. He had been a king for all but the first months of his fifty-eight years, and had shown a remarkable capacity for survival. Given his forebears' history, it was no mean boast to be able to say, 'Here [that is, in London] I sit and govern Scotland with my pen. I write and it is done; and by the Clerk of the Council now, which others could not do with the sword.' If he had been less successful in England, he had nevertheless contrived to jog along pleasantly enough, and there is no reason to doubt his stated intention to 'govern according to the common weal, but not according to the common will'. The time would come when kings had to take more note of the latter, but not in 'Old Jemmy's' days. The historian should resist the temptation to suppose that Charles I's failure was a bitter harvest sowed by his father. For one thing, James, as a canny politician, knew when to give way, even though he grumbled as he did so. The oddest and most learned of British kings, he also managed, incongruous though it may seem, to combine the conviction that he ruled by divine right and the favour of the Almighty with a robust and sceptical sense of humour.

Chapter 11

Charles I (1625–49):
The Martyr King

I n his twenty-fifth year when he succeeded his father, 'Baby Charles' had overcome the childhood disabilities that had prevented him from walking till he was seven. Yet, probably on account of these ailments, he was very small, not much more than five foot in height. He had learned to control his stammer; indeed it had all but disappeared, emerging only at moments of stress. He had made himself into a fine horseman. Unlike his father he was no scholar, but he was an aesthete, whose collection of paintings would be one of the most impressive in Europe. The great Flemish painter Peter Paul Rubens thought him the most knowledgeable of connoisseurs. Where James had been talkative and emotional, Charles was taciturn and reserved. He stood very much on his dignity; his father had had none. James was highly intelligent, Charles not very bright. They had however one point in common: neither was a good judge of men. Moreover, Charles had inherited his father's conviction that he was the servant of God with a divine right to rule. Unfortunately, while in practice James did little more than talk about this, Charles acted on his belief. The self-assurance it gave him made him a tricky customer, one on whose word few could rely. Deception of others was permissible, because as king he could do no wrong. In matters of policy he was as free from moral scruples as Calvinists, conscious of their status as God's elect, might be in conduct. Charles never understood how untrustworthy he seemed to others.

He was the first monarch to have been raised as a member of the Church of England, and he was utterly devoted to that Church as he understood it. It was his misfortune that his idea of the Church of England was much narrower than that of many of his subjects, and that in their view his commitment to a high and ordered Anglicanism smacked of popery. They were mistaken. He was the only Stuart, with the exception of his granddaughter Queen Anne, to be unwavering in his devotion to the established Church. On the night before his execution he made his two youngest children, Prince Henry, Duke of Gloucester, and Princess Elizabeth, swear that they would remain loyal to the Church of England, and on the scaffold he declared that he died a faithful member of that Church as by law established. To call him the 'martyr King' is not unjust, for if he had been willing to offer a genuine, rather than merely tactical, compromise on the matter of religion, he might well have kept his crown, though with his power curtailed.

The early years of his reign were dominated by Buckingham. Charles had first resented his father's favourite and, not surprisingly, disapproved of him. But Buckingham, conscious that Charles was the rising sun, had exerted himself to charm him, and his charm was compelling. The Prince was soon as devoted to the glittering Duke as his besotted father, though his language to the favourite was more restrained and free of terms of fond endearment, while his behaviour was unquestionably chaste. The quixotic trip to Spain in search of a bride had cemented the relationship, and for the first three years of the new reign Buckingham's will was all-powerful. Charles, shy and still unsure of himself, drew strength from the Duke.

In fact Buckingham's influence and policy were disastrous. He provoked wars, first with Spain, then with France, where he allied England to the French Protestants (the Huguenots), whose privileges, assured by the Edict of Nantes, which had marked the end of religious wars in France, were now being challenged by the new First Minister, Cardinal Richelieu. The Spanish war was fought in support of Charles's sister Elizabeth and her husband Frederick, the deposed Elector, and in defence of the Protestant cause in Germany, something Parliament had long clamoured for. Spain was still the great European power, and its king, Philip III, financed the Catholic armies of his Habsburg cousin, the Holy Roman Emperor Ferdinand. Moreover, the Spanish empire included the southern Netherlands, modern Belgium, throughout history of strategic importance to England. Buckingham recruited an army, mostly composed of German mercenaries, with the intention of deploying it to drive the Habsburgs out of the Palatinate and restore Frederick to his throne. The enterprise was a dismal failure. England had no standing army, and the mercenaries Buckingham hired, though of poor quality, nevertheless expected to be paid. This Parliament was disinclined to do, despite its proclaimed enthusiasm for the defence of the Protestant cause in Europe. The war with France, incongruously following Buckingham's success in arranging a French marriage for Charles in 1626, went no better. Attempts to support the Huguenots, besieged by the armies of the French king in their fortified town of La Rochelle, foundered. Buckingham had neither experience nor skill in generalship, though he fought with conspicuous and reckless courage himself. Despite the failure and the Commons' attempt to impeach him, he was preparing another expedition when he was assassinated in 1628 at Portsmouth by a disgruntled officer called Felton.

Charles was distraught, overcome by grief. Hitherto his relations with his young queen, Henrietta Maria, had been bad. She loathed Buckingham, and there were religious differences, for the Queen was a devout Roman Catholic. Charles was infuriated by her French servants, and, without consulting her, had dismissed most of them and sent them back to France. She made scenes and stormed and raved, and Charles was embarrassed and at a loss; he had no idea how to deal with an angry and passionate woman, or how to appease her. He took refuge in cold reserve and silence. But Buckingham's murder changed everything. In his grief he turned to his wife. She consoled him and he fell in love with her. He would remain in love, never looking at another woman; there was to be not even a rumour of infidelity. He now depended on Henrietta Maria even more completely than he had on Buckingham. She was everything to him. He was guided by her in all matters except his own religion; and it was unfortunate that her advice was nearly always bad. She had no understanding of England, English people or English politics; not only no understanding, but little sympathy for them either.

The first four years of Charles's reign were marked by recurrent quarrels with Parliament. The King and those elected to the House of Commons had different views of Parliament's function. For Charles, the main purpose in summoning a parliament was to obtain grants of money, and if Parliament did not oblige, he was ready to seek other means of raising funds from his subjects, by forced – that is, compulsory – loans or by the revival of feudal rights, many of which had withered from disuse. The Commons on the other hand saw itself as the guarantor of the liberties of the subject and increasingly claimed to be entitled to press policies on the monarch, especially in the field of foreign affairs. Charles's third Parliament, summoned in 1628, presented him with a document called the Petition of Right, which declared taxation without parliamentary consent to be illegal, and protested against imprisonment without trial, martial law, forced loans and conscription – this for the French war that the same House of Commons had demanded. The question, one member said, was whether the King was above the law or subject to it. That question would run like a sore throughout the reign, and Charles's refusal to recognise its validity would eventually destroy him. Equally ominously, another member, by name John Pym, raised the question of religion, expressing disapproval of the doctrine that went by the name of Arminianism, and which, he said, was infesting the English Church. Arminius was a Dutch theologian who, as John Milton would put it, 'set up free will as against free grace', challenging the Puritan belief in predestination; it was, they thought, one step on the downward path that led to popery. Charles determined to bring the parliament to an end, but in defiance of all precedent, for there could be no doubt that the monarch was entitled to dissolve Parliament at will, the Speaker was held down in his chair while the Commons voted that innovators in religion (as they considered the so-called Arminians to be) were enemies of the kingdom, as surely as those who levied taxes without the approval of Parliament. The stormy session was at last concluded. The King dissolved Parliament in 1629 and did without it for eleven years. Parliaments, he said, were 'like cats; they grow crabbit with age'.

Henceforth Charles governed, as the Tudors had governed, through his Privy Council. This was not in itself unconstitutional. Elizabeth, in her reign of forty-five years, had summoned only nine parliaments.[1] Moreover she had been firm in declaring certain subjects – such as foreign policy and the question of her own marriage – to be beyond the remit of the Commons. Others might be discussed only with her express permission. Charles, taking no heed of the changing temper of the political class, saw no reason why he should govern differently, and it was indeed possible to govern without Parliament so long as he had no need to raise revenue additional to that provided by the Crown Estates, customs duties, the profits of justice and traditional feudal dues, though these last were now unpopular and thought by many to be out of date. The King incurred further unpopularity by stretching the power to exact these dues beyond what was thought to be their proper limit. The most notable case was that of ship money. This was a levy raised from maritime counties to be spent on the navy. Charles extended it to inland counties also. In 1635, a former MP, John Hampden, refused to pay the sum demanded of him. The matter went to the courts, and though the judges obediently found in the King's favour, the imposition was regarded by many as unconstitutional, indeed tyrannical.

Two men were particularly associated with Charles in these years of personal rule. The first was Sir Thomas Wentworth, later Earl of Strafford. He was a Yorkshireman who had been an MP in the difficult parliaments of the first years of the reign. A critic of Buckingham, he had later tried to have the presentation of the Petition of Right postponed. His failure, and the mood of the Commons, persuaded him, like Charles himself, that parliaments were an obstacle to good government, for their frame of mind was oppositional. In coming to this conclusion Wentworth was right, and had indeed identified a problem that would persist throughout the seventeenth century, and which would not be solved till Parliament, by encroaching on matters previously believed to belong properly to the royal prerogative, made itself an essential partner in government, and so acquired a sense of responsibility it had hitherto lacked. Wentworth, approving Charles's decision to dispense with parliaments – for the meanwhile, that is – was made first president of the Council of the North, an offshoot of the Privy Council responsible for the administration of the northern counties of England. (There was also a Council of Wales and a Council of the (Anglo-Welsh) Marches.) His efficiency there commended him to the King, and he was then appointed Lord Deputy in Ireland.

Charles was King of Ireland as well as England and Scotland, but Ireland was in a sense a dependency, a species of colony. There was an Anglo-Irish upper class, many the descendants of Norman adventurers who had seized land and settled in Ireland in the twelfth and thirteenth centuries. These were now mostly Protestants, members of the Anglican Church of Ireland. But the native Irish remained Catholic and Gaelic speakers, and had engaged throughout the last twenty years of Elizabeth's reign in sporadic rebellion, sometimes with help from Spain. The heartland of the rebellion was Ulster, but with its defeat and the 'Flight of the (Gaelic) Earls' to Catholic Spain soon after James's accession, a new policy had been devised by the Scottish king. This was the Plantation of Ulster, colonised for the most part by Lowland Scots Presbyterians. Wentworth introduced stern and effective government, but disaffection remained rife, and Ireland was a tinderbox waiting to explode.

The King's other chief associate was William Laud, Bishop of London from 1628 to 1633 and then Archbishop of Canterbury. Laud was a devout man whose view of the Church of England was the same as the King's. Believing in 'the beauty of holiness', he sought to introduce order and more ceremony to Church services. Like the King, he took no account of the range of opinion within the Church, and his persecution of preachers who offended him by too free an expression of opinion provoked many and contributed to the spread of disaffection. Indeed, his hostility to Puritanism, and the close censorship of opinion he tried to enforce in both speech and writing, strengthened the opposition he was determined to suppress. He had no political sense, no understanding of what was possible, confusing this with what he thought desirable; and it was unfortunate that the King he served suffered from the same deficiency. Laud's narrowness of outlook, and sharpness of temper, and especially his use of the Prerogative Court of High Commission to punish dissidents and subversives, contributed to the gathering unpopularity of the royal government. Many thought him likely to convert to Catholicism, which he was far from doing, but confusing his love of ceremony with popery, his critics feared and detested him, thinking him a quasi-papist. His unpopularity was extreme, but Charles trusted him, implicitly, disastrously. Even mockery of the Archbishop was forbidden, though mockery of the powerful is an expression of humanity's good sense. King James had, in the old fashion, kept a court fool or jester, called Archie Armstrong. Now Charles dismissed him for showing disrespect to the Archbishop by calling out 'All praise to God, and little laud to the devil.'

Charles's eleven years of personal rule led, with what seems inexorable logic, to civil war and the fall of the monarchy. Yet, marked though they were by folly and blindness to realities, they were to be remembered by many as a golden age, rather as the Belle Epoque and the long Edwardian afternoon were to be gilded in the memories of those who survived the catastrophe of the First World War. Men as different from each other as the eccentric John Aubrey and Edward Hyde, Earl of Clarendon, historian and Charles II's first minister, looked back on the 1630s nostalgically, as a time of peace and plenty when old habits and customs prevailed – even though Hyde entered politics as an opponent of the King. There was this to be said for their opinion: in comparison with the horrors of the long war in Germany, Caroline England might indeed have seemed a paradisal land.[2]

Charles maintained a court very different from his father's. All was polite, decorous, seemly, well ordered. Very early in his reign the King drew up a list of instructions as to proper conduct, and a copy of His Majesty's Rules might be read in the antechambers of Whitehall, Windsor and Hampton Court. Whereas anyone might have accosted James as he ambled around his palaces, with his arm round the neck of a handsome young man, now audiences with the new King were by appointment only. James had loved an argument and been ready to engage with all and sundry on almost any subject, talking for victory like the university don he might happily, in another life, have been, but Charles detested discussion, replying to an assertion of which he disapproved with a chilly 'Sir, I am not of your opinion' or 'By your favour, I think otherwise.'³ Alternatively he might take refuge in a cold silence, which was capable of dismaying or abashing all around him. James had been careless of his dignity; for Charles, dignity was a defence that must not be breached. James was often tipsy; Charles was abstemious: he is said never to have been drunk in his life.

His domestic life was likewise a model of decorum. Henrietta Maria was a silly woman, whose political judgement was lamentable, but she gave him the confidence he had lacked. Soon they were the happy parents of a brood of children. Nine were born altogether, six of whom lived to be adults: Charles, born 1630; Mary in 1632; James, their mother's favourite, a beautiful blond blue-eyed boy, in 1633; Elizabeth in 1635; Henry in 1640; and last Henriette-Anne, the child of the war years and known in the family as Minette. There had not been such a family of royal children in England since the days of Edward III. In private, with his family, Charles was gentle and friendly; in case of difficulty the children were more likely to turn to their father than to their excitable, unpredictable mother. But his public image was very different. Shy beneath an icy demeanour, he shrank from encounters with the common people, even though, through his Council, he sought to regulate their conduct, not only in religion but in the ordinary affairs of their daily life. His government was paternalist, but, lacking the common touch, his paternalism was more likely to irritate than please. He had little sympathy for human frailties, though in so many respects frail himself. Seeing 'a great lover of pretty girls' at a race meeting, he called out, according to the story related by John Aubrey, 'Let that ugly rascal, that whoremaster, be gone out of the park; else I shall not see the sport.'4 In time his domestic virtues might have commended him to his people and gained him their love, but his public policy, narrow, self-righteous, meddling, and in so many ways thought to be first oppressive, then tyrannical, made this impossible. The years of his personal rule raised up a majority of the politically conscious in both England and Scotland against him. This required no small degree of incompetence and folly. Charles never grasped the truth of his father's observation that 'the prerogative is a secret which ryves [tears] with the stretching of it'. In these eleven years Charles stretched it beyond what was found tolerable, and the fabric tore apart.

The trouble first flared up in Scotland. Though born a Scot (in Dunfermline), Charles had little knowledge of his native land or its politics, and less sympathy with its people and their preoccupations. He began badly, issuing within a few weeks of his accession an Edict of Revocation. This measure, employed by various of his predecessors in Scotland, asserted his right to revoke all grants of land made by the Crown since 1540. At first thought only to refer to what had been Crown lands, it soon emerged that the Revocation might be applied to abbey lands and other properties of the pre-Reformation Church. This threatened the interests of all those nobles whose families had acquired what had been Church property; that is, most of the Scottish political class. So the King's natural supporters, those on whom he relied as partners in government, were alienated.

Second, Charles delayed coming to Scotland. The natural loyalty to a Stuart was undermined by his evident disinclination to visit his northern kingdom and be crowned there. In fact he delayed his first visit to Scotland till 1633, eight years after his accession. When at last he came north, he offended many by insisting on Church of England services in the royal chapel.

Indeed, it was his religious policy that stirred up opposition. James had moved cannily, and had contrived to reassert a degree of royal control over the Kirk. Even bishops had been accepted, however reluctantly. Admittedly the old King's last venture – the Five Articles of Perth (1617), prescribing practices in the form of worship that offended Presbyterian sentiment – had been ill judged, and had provoked a dissident underground movement that held conventicles – services where the more obnoxious requirements of the Five Articles, such as kneeling to receive communion, were flouted. But Charles went further, without consideration being given to the feelings and opinions of the Kirk.

There were mutterings in Edinburgh and throughout Lowland Scotland, but for the moment they were no more than mutterings, and Charles and Laud pressed on regardless. Their aim was clear: to bring the Church of Scotland into conformity with the Church of England, though conformity within the Anglican Church was itself a matter of dispute. Orders were given for the preparation of a new liturgy, 'as near as can be to this of England'. Charles, sure of his own rectitude and confident that his divine right to rule not only empowered but obliged him to order the affairs of the Church in his three kingdoms, was not a man capable of reading danger signals. It was the duty of his subjects to obey him; therefore he would be obeyed.

It was not only the King's ecclesiastical policy that irritated Scotland. An increase in taxation, which saw Edinburgh paying more in tax in the first two years of Charles's reign than in the last twenty of his father's, coincided with a downturn in the economy, and one of the taxes levied on interest payments led to a shortage of credit that brought many nobles to the brink of bankruptcy.

In short, Scotland was a simmering pot ready to boil over, but Charles, sitting on a dais and taking notes when the Scots parliament met in 1633, was determined that his northern kingdom should be brought to heel. He was already removed from reality, for he could not enter into the feelings of others and found it beneath his royal dignity to examine the merits of opinions that ran counter to his own.

Throughout these years of personal rule he had shaped a life that satisfied his refined and private taste. His court was a work of art: dignified, elegant, ceremonious, beautifully ordered. He persuaded the Dutch artist Anthony Van Dyck to settle in England, and Van Dyck's portraits of the royal family and various courtiers testify to the image of perfection Charles had made for himself. Van Dyck was knighted and anglicised his name to Vandyke. Rubens was also given a knighthood and commissioned to paint the ceiling for the banqueting hall that Inigo Jones had designed for the Palace of Whitehall. There has never been a king in England, still less in Scotland, of such exquisite taste as Charles, and his aesthetic pleasure was not confined to painting or the court masques. He was a lover of literature too; indeed, the Puritan John Milton complained, perhaps jealously, that he spent too much time reading Shakespeare. Had Charles been a mere figurehead, a monarch of a later age that had seen the Crown's political power so reduced that it was, in Bagehot's formula, a decorative rather than effective part of the constitution, he might be remembered as among the most splendid of kings.

But that time was far off, and Scotland was near. On 23 July 1637, members of the Scottish Privy Council, the two archbishops and eight other bishops, and most of the senators of the College of Justice assembled in the High Kirk of St Giles for a service which for the first time would follow the form prescribed by the new prayer book, as approved by Charles and Laud. Scarcely had the Dean of St Giles begun to read than a hostile demonstration broke out. A stool was thrown at the Dean, and a large part of the congregation ostentatiously marched out of the church. There were similar demonstrations in the other three churches of the city, and rioting in the streets. The Dean took refuge in an upper room, and the Bishop of Edinburgh's coach was stoned as he trundled down the high street and Canongate to the safety of Holyroodhouse. It was not a mere riot, but a revolution, comparable to the storming of the Bastille in Paris another July day a century and a half later, even if few that day understood the full significance of their actions.

To what extent the riot in St Giles was spontaneous is a matter of opinion. One minister, Henry Guthrie, who disapproved of the new prayer book, though himself an Episcopalian, was sure it had been well prepared. 'This tumult,' he wrote in his memoirs, was taken to be but a rash emergent, without any prediliberation; whereas the truth is, it was the result of a consultation at Edinburgh in April, at which time Mr Alexander Henderson came thither from his brethren in Fife, and Mr Thomas Dickson from those in the west country; and those two, having communicated to my lord Balmerino and Sir Thomas Hope the minds of those they came from, and gotten their approbation, did afterwards meet at the house of Nicholas Balfour in the Cowgate, with Nicholas, Eupham Henderson, Bethia and Elspa Craig, and several other matrons, and recommended to them, that they and their adherents might give the first affront to the book, assuring them that men should afterwards take the business out of their hands.[5]

Yet even if the revolt was stirred up by ministers of the Kirk acting as agents provocateurs, it expressed a national mood. Lowland Scotland was defiant. Only the Highlands, where many clans still held to the Catholic faith, and Aberdeenshire, where Episcopalianism and a tradition of classical scholarship were strong, stood apart, The following February a huge crowd, composed of nobles, lairds, burgesses and the common folk, assembled in the kirkyard of Greyfriars Church in Edinburgh to sign the National Covenant. This document, drawn up by Alexander Henderson and an Edinburgh lawyer, Archibald Johnston of Warriston, runs to great length and it is unlikely that many of the signatories had read it all, or had understood its arguments when it was read out to them, but embedded in its long recitation of history and grievances were two statements on which all might agree. One declared the 'incompatibiltie betwixt Episcopal government and prebyteriall power'; the other called for the 're-establishment of a free parliament and free Assembly of the Kirk'.

It was specifically stated that the Covenant was not a signal to rebellion, for its signatories were not yet ready for that; its argument depended instead on the age-old sophism that the King had been led astray by his advisers. So Scots of all classes swore to maintain both royal authority and true religion; and let this glaring incompatibility go by.

Charles saw it differently. To his mind this was rebellion, naked rebellion, and when the free General Assembly, meeting in Glasgow towards the end of the year, abolished the office of bishop, rejected James's Five Articles of Perth and the prayer book of 1637, the reality of rebellion could scarcely be denied, all the more so because the Assembly had defied the attempt of the King's commissioner, the Marquis of Hamilton, to bring its proceedings to an end, by the simple ploy of hiding the key of the door so that he could not leave. 'Next Hell I hate this place,' he wrote to Charles, with deep feeling and good reason.[6]

A wiser king would have been ready to yield to this expression of national opinion, or to seek a compromise. After Charles was dead, the Reverend James Kirkton, himself a Covenanter, wrote: 'People generally think his greatest unhappiness [misfortune] was, he mistook wilfullness for constancy, granting unprofitably to his people today that which would have abundantly satisfied them yesterday, and the next day that which would have satisfied this day, but all out of time.' A fair and judicious assessment.[7]

So now, even while allowing Hamilton, whose own loyalty was uncertain, for he was as wayward in character as he was lacking in intelligence, to temporise and seek to appease the Covenanters, Charles was preparing to make war on Scotland, trusting that the traditional antipathy of the English to their northern neighbours would be strong enough to secure victory. In truth, the two short Bishops' Wars that followed in 1639 and 1640 saw little fighting. The royal army was ill equipped and worse trained; the Scots had the advantage of a number of officers, including their general, Alexander Leslie, who had fought in the German wars; many, Leslie himself among them, had served in the Swedish army of the Protestant hero Gustavus Adolphus. More importantly, Charles's critics in England were of a mind with the Scots, and entered into negotiations with them. The alliance thus formed between the nascent opposition in England and the Scots was to prove the means of bringing the years of Charles's personal rule to an end. To finance his war, Charles needed additional revenue, and to obtain this he found himself compelled to summon a parliament. It proved unsat- isfactory, refusing supply without redress of grievances. He dissolved it, and summoned another, which proved no better. This 'Long Parliament', as it came to be called, embarked on a programme of radical, indeed revolutionary, reform of both Church and state. Charles recalled his most capable minister, Strafford, from Ireland; Strafford, as an old parliamentary hand, was confident of his ability to manage the Commons. But he was now in the Upper House, and his years in Ireland meant that he was out of touch with political feeling in England and unable to bring his stabilising influence to bear.

Meanwhile the Commons, led by John Pym, proceeded to destroy the basis of the prerogative state that had made possible the eleven years of personal rule. They abolished the conciliar courts – Star Chamber and High Commission – which, as offshoots of the Privy Council, had been employed by the Tudors as effective instruments of government, bypassing the common law of England. (Torture, for instance, was illegal according to common law, but practised, especially in the case of political prisoners, by the conciliar courts.) All extra-parliamentary taxation was declared illegal. Parliament now asserted its right – for which there was no precedent – to sit until it should be pleased to dissolve itself. It passed a root and branch bill to abolish bishops, and Laud himself was arrested, impeached and confined to the Tower. All this was made possible by the presence of the Scots army still under arms in the north of England, until Charles should pay the costs of its occupation, as promised in the Treaty of Berwick. But the King could pay nothing till the English parliament granted him the necessary money, and this it continued to refuse.

The Commons then turned on Strafford and impeached him.[8] In February 1641 he was brought to trial in Westminster Hall. Charles and his queen attended the trial to demonstrate their support for the minister, and Strafford defended himself with skill and spirit, while London was in an uproar. The censorship enforced by Laud and the Court of High Commission had broken down, resulting in a flurry of abusive and inflammatory pamphlets. How far the popular agitation was spontaneous, how far orchestrated by Pym and his adherents, is impossible to determine. The issue of the trial remained for three weeks in doubt. Many in the House of Lords, who were the judges, were sympathetic to Strafford, and it seemed that the case had not been made credibly by the Commons. Then Pym produced what were alleged to be notes taken at a Council meeting in May the previous year. What he had was in truth not the original notes but a copy made by the son of the King's secretary, Sir Henry Vane. According to the notes, Strafford had reminded the King that 'You have an army in Ireland, which you may use to reduce this kingdom.'9 Since at the time Charles was at war with the Scots, it is probable that the words referred to Scotland, not England. But the meaning was sufficiently ambiguous for Pym's purpose. Even so, acquittal seemed more likely than condemnation. The process of impeachment was therefore abandoned, and a bill of attainder, that old Tudor device that dispensed with the necessity of proof, was brought before the Commons, declaring Strafford guilty of treason. It was passed, and Strafford's fate now lay in the King's hands, for the bill could not become law without the royal assent. An attempt to free Charles from his dilemma was made by the Earl of Bedford, who suggested that banishment would be a sufficient punishment, but this was thwarted by the Earl of Essex, who declared, 'Stone-dead hath no fellow.' Essex, Frances Howard's first husband, and humiliated by the divorce that King James had approved, had no love for the Stuarts, no wish to ease the King's position.

Charles fought hard for his most loyal and capable minister. He went to the House of Lords and summoned the Commons to hear him plead that Strafford be found guilty only of a misdemeanour. He also denied having had any intention of employing the Irish army against England. But it was in vain. His intervention raised the temperature rather than cooling it. Then the so-called 'Army Plot',10 an attempt by Catholic officers from the army in the north to rescue Strafford from the Tower, failed, and by failing discredited Charles further, emphasising his untrustworthiness, in his opponents' view.

What remained of the government was now in a state of panic. All his Council, with the honourable exception of William Juxon,

Bishop of London, recommended that Charles yield and give his assent to the bill of attainder. Strafford himself nobly advised him to sacrifice his servant rather than his kingdom. Still Charles hesitated. He had promised Strafford that he would protect him against his enemies, and he was loath to break that promise. Only when a mob was raised to howl round the Palace of Whitehall and threaten the lives of the Queen and her children did he give way and sign the bill. It was to his mind the single dishonourable act of his life, and he regretted it till he himself followed Strafford to the block.

Yet even in this dark hour the King's position was improving. The Scots army had at last been paid and was about to return home. Charles had surrendered to the Covenanters' demands; he might hope that he had done enough to regain their loyalty. Moreover, the opposition in England was breaking up. Moderate Church of England men who had resented the illegalities, as they saw them, of the years of personal rule were now satisfied that their grievances had been removed. They had no desire for revolution, no desire to see their Church stripped of authority and licence given to schismatics whose preaching threatened the social order, and no desire to see the Crown further weakened.

Earlier in the year, one of these moderate men, Sir Edward Hyde, who had entered Parliament as a critic of the King, was shocked to learn the way the wind was now blowing. Leaving the Commons, where he had been complaining of the 'indecency and rudeness' of the member for Huntingdon, Oliver Cromwell, he fell into conversation with his friend and fellow barrister Henry Marten, who advised him against listening to approaches being made to him by the court. Hyde replied: 'I have no relation to the Court. I am concerned only to maintain the Government and to preserve the Law.' He explained his reasons, at some length, for he was a wordy man. In reply Marten said: 'I do not think one man wise enough to govern us all.'[11]

Hyde was taken aback. 'It was the first word,' he related in his *History of the Rebellion*, 'he had ever heard any man speak to that purpose.' With such extreme views being aired, Charles had only to wait and act prudently to see the tide turn in his favour, and his party grow. This, indeed, was the advice he had already received from the master-statesman of the age, the first minister of France, Cardinal Richelieu.

Bizarrely, during the trial of Strafford, the first of the royal children was married. This was Mary, the Princess Royal. She was only nine, and her husband, Prince William of Orange, was fifteen. The wedding took place in the Palace of Whitehall a week after the Commons passed the bill of attainder. At that point Charles still hoped to save his minister. Nevertheless, it is strange to think of celebrations in the palace while Strafford lay under sentence of death, and London was seething with discontent.

After the marriage ceremony, the young Prince was introduced by the King to his girl-wife's bed, where he kissed her three times, lay beside her for three-quarters of an hour in the presence of the Queen and her ladies, then kissed her again when he was told it was time to leave. A fortnight later his young brothers-in-law, Charles and James, escorted him to Gravesend, where he took ship for the Netherlands, assuring them that if his wife didn't follow soon, he would return to fetch her. The marriage itself had been popular; the Dutch prince was a good Protestant.

In the late summer of 1641, Charles went to Scotland. At Newcastle, where the Covenanting army was disbanding, he established good relations with its general, Alexander Leslie, that veteran of the Swedish war in Germany. He created him Earl of Leven, and the new Earl promised not to take up arms against him again. The King was well received in Edinburgh too. He attended a Presbyterian service in St Giles and made no complaint, and presided over a meeting of the Scottish parliament. Yet appearances were deceptive. Charles believed that the concessions he had made had been forced on him, and might therefore be rescinded without loss of honour when he was strong enough to do so. The leading Covenanting noble, Archibald Campbell, Earl of Argyll, was equally determined to hold the King to his word, and to prevent him from building up a royalist party in Scotland. The chief among the moderates, James Graham, Earl of Montrose, was in prison. Montrose had signed the National Covenant and led a Covenanting army against royalists in Aberdeenshire, but unlike Argyll, he had no wish to see the Crown weakened further. Meanwhile Argyll won over the Marquis of Hamilton, who had been Charles's foremost adviser on Scottish affairs. Hamilton was a fine figure of a man, but lacking in both intelligence and consistency of purpose.

In October, while the King was still in Edinburgh, rebellion broke out in Ireland, the native Catholic Irish rising against their oppressors. The news was brought to Charles as he was playing golf on the links at Leith. With characteristic self-control he finished the round before hastening back to London. He arrived there to find the city in a ferment of anti-Catholic feeling. Dublin, it was said, had been taken by the rebels, every Protestant farmer would be dispossessed, every Protestant would have his throat cut, and twenty thousand had already been murdered. The rumours were exaggerated, but they fanned fears of a Catholic plot in England and, with this fear, hatred of the Catholic Queen.

The Irish rebellion was a prime cause of the civil war in England. How, Pym and his colleagues asked, could the King be trusted with command of the army needed to suppress the Irish rebels? Might he not turn it first against his enemies in England, and use it, in Strafford's words, to 'subdue that kingdom'? Since they could not trust the King, it seemed to his opponents that they had no alternative but to deny him command of an army.

This was a revolutionary proposal; in the King's view an invasion of his prerogative. It was reducing him to the status of a doge of Venice. How could he be a king if he did not command his armed forces? There were many who by now agreed with him, and thought, like Hyde, that the dominant party in the Commons was undermining all government and the rule of law. Pym, conscious that support for his radical policy was ebbing away, sought to rally it in November by bringing a document called the Grand Remonstrance before the Commons. Running to more than two hundred clauses, it recounted once again all the faults, crimes and unconstitutional acts of the King's eleven years of personal rule; the intention was to remind waverers of the tyranny from which they had been delivered. But his document included one unprecedented demand: that the King should choose ministers subject to the approval of Parliament. If he failed to do so, then the Commons, disregarding him, would take it upon themselves to subdue the rebellion in Ireland. The debate was fierce, passionate, and went on till darkness had fallen. In the end the Remonstrance was carried on 22 November by only eleven votes, 159–148, clear evidence of how opinion was inclining towards the King. Charles, it seemed, had only to wait; to give Pym enough rope and he would hang himself. (This was how his son would act in a comparable crisis forty years later.) But Charles was an inept politician, unable to see the sense of playing a long game. He now acted precipitously and stupidly. On 4 January 1642 he invaded the Commons at the head of a troop of guards, in order to arrest Pym, Hampden and three other members. His rashness was explicable; there was talk of impeaching the Queen. Nevertheless, it was foolish; he had placed himself on the wrong side of the law. It was an action that success alone might have justified. But, forewarned, Pym and the others had already left Westminster and taken refuge among their supporters in the City. 'I see the birds have flown,' Charles said. A few days later he left London and the Queen sailed to the Netherlands to raise money and supplies for war. Charles would not enter his capital again till he was brought there for his trial in January 1649.

Charles would be held responsible for the civil war that broke out eight months later when he raised the royal standard at Nottingham and prepared to subdue his enemies by force. Yet the impression that he bore the brunt of war guilt was in part illusory. However ill judged his tactics had been, he was driven to that resort by the intolerable demands of his enemies.

They were not admittedly aiming at civil war, though from the King's point of view they provoked it. In the words of the historian Conrad Russell, they 'were following a strategy with precedents going back at least to Simon de Montfort [in the thirteenth century] in which the object was to impersonalise royal authority by putting it into the hands of a Council and great officers, to be nominated in Parliament and answerable to Parliament. As a Parliamentary declaration put it in May 1642, Charles was to be treated as if he were a minor, a captive or insane. Charles's opponents, many of whom were experienced Privy Councillors, believed government was too important to be left to Kings'[12] – just as Henry Marten had intimated to Hyde.

Armies on both sides were raised from the county militias, the trained bands of the cities, and from volunteers. There were officers who had experience of the wars in Germany and the Netherlands. In a surprisingly short time both King and Parliament could put an army of more than ten thousand men in the field. Much of the war was local, without any grand strategy, even though the royalists' principal aim was clear: to regain possession of the capital. The parliamentary side had certain advantages: they found it easier to raise money to pay and supply their troops, for not only the City of London but the machinery of government was theirs. Moreover, the navy, on which Charles had lavished money at the cost of unpopularity, stood by Parliament: the Protestant tradition of the Elizabethan sea dogs held good, and with it suspicion of the Catholic Queen and a foreign policy too friendly to Spain in the years of personal rule. Charles relied more on rich supporters, like the Earl of Newcastle and the Marquis of Worcester, for financial support.

In the early years of the war, the royalist cavalry were superior to their opponents. They were commanded by the King's nephew, Prince Rupert, second son of Elizabeth of Bohemia. Though only in his early twenties, Rupert had studied war, and had some little experience of it. Tall, handsome, dashing, he was an inspiring figure and one who was feared by the parliamentary forces. He was the 'Devil-Prince', his white poodle Boy, who travelled everywhere with him, said to be his familiar spirit by means of whom he communicated with his satanic master. The war might have gone better for Charles had he entrusted its entire management to Rupert. But there were jealousies and divisions in the camp, and the vigour with which Rupert prosecuted the war alarmed those who hoped for a negotiated peace.

The royalists' best chance of victory came and went in the early weeks of the war. The Battle of Edgehill in September 1642 is judged to have been inconclusive, for after Rupert's cavalry had swept their opponents from the field, the parliamentary infantry held firm. Yet though there was no decisive victory for either side, Essex, commanding Parliament's army, withdrew and left the road to London open. Rupert was all for an immediate attack on the capital, but more timid counsels prevailed, and the opportunity to end the war quickly was lost. The following year Rupert stormed Bristol, the second city in England, and again a concerted attack on London seemed possible. But the chance was frittered away. The royalists dissipated their efforts when they should have concentrated them. So in the north, the Earl of Newcastle besieged Hull, in the west the King besieged Gloucester, and Sir Ralph Hopton's victorious Cornish army turned back to their homeland.

The King based himself at Oxford, not yet known as the 'home of lost causes'. He lodged at Christ Church, and the district opposite its gates, St Aldates, was packed with courtiers, royal servants and soldiers. John Aubrey recalled: 'I was wont to go to Christchurch to see King Charles I at supper. Where I once heard him say, "That as he was hawking in Scotland. He rode into the Quarry, and found a Covey of Partridge falling upon the hawk." When I came to my chamber I told this story to my tutor. Said he, "That covey was London."'[13]

Charles's dignity and self-control won him the admiration of those who came close to him in the war years, but he was not a good commander-in-chief. Instead of issuing orders he too often made suggestions, and even those were not always clear. 'Though I may propose many things,' he wrote to Newcastle, who was commanding the royalist forces in the north, 'yet I shall not impose anything upon you; as, for example, I hear General King is come; now I desire you to make use of him in your army. I am sure you have not good commanders to spare, no more than arms, yet I confess there may be such reasons as make this desire of mine impossible' – a letter that may have left Newcastle scratching his head.[14]

His enemies might already call him 'the Man of Blood', but a letter to the mayor of Newbury after the first battle fought there in 1643 shows a tender, paternal side to Charles's nature: 'Our will and command is, that you forthwith send into the towns and villages adjacent, and bring thence all the sick and hurt soldiers of the Earl of Essex's army; and though they be rebels, and deserve the punishment of traitors, yet out of our tender compassion upon them as being our subjects, our will and pleasure is, that you carefully provide for their recovery, as well as for those of our own army, and then send them to Oxford.'[15]

The parties in England were evenly matched – more than a third of the members of the House of Commons, once all but unanimous in opposition to the King, had now attached themselves to the royalist side. Both sought an alliance that might tip the balance in their favour, and so looked to Scotland. Parliament had more to offer, for they seemed willing to satisfy the religious demands of the Covenanters as Charles was not. Like the King, the Covenanters believed in the need for uniformity of religion (which entailed the freedom to persecute those who were not of their mind), and so were convinced that the settlement they had secured as a result of their defiance of the King required that England too should adopt the Presbyterian form of Church government. Accordingly, in the treaty they signed with Parliament, which is known as the Solemn League and Covenant (1643), they bound their new allies, as they supposed, to impose Presbyterianism on England in exchange for military assistance now. The Covenanters' demands were arrogant and unrealistic. While most of the parliamentary leaders favoured the Presbyterian form of Church government, there was no majority for this in England. There was not even a majority for it among those to whom they were now allied, for many in the army were Independents, not Presbyterians; that is, they accepted no overall system of Church government, but believed that each parish or congregation should order worship and practise the faith as it thought fit. This opinion was anathema to the Scots Kirk. Meanwhile, all that held Presbyterians and Independents together was suspicion of the King, antipathy to bishops, and fear and loathing of Roman Catholics.

The Covenanting army crossed the border. It was commanded

now by David Leslie, another veteran of the Swedish army, a distant cousin of the Earl of Leven. Leven served on his cousin's staff, thus breaking the promise he had made to Charles. The arrival of the Covenanters tilted the balance of power in the north. The Earl of Newcastle was besieged in York. Rupert, who had been campaigning in Lancashire, crossed the Pennines to relieve the city. Then, despite Newcastle's reluctance, he sought battle in the hope of winning a decisive victory. Rupert believed this was in accordance with the instructions given him by the King, though Charles's letter had been characteristically ambiguous. But Newcastle was right, Rupert wrong. The royalists were outnumbered and ill prepared for battle. Moreover, the parliamentary army attacked in the early evening when their enemy supposed there would be no fighting till the morning. This was the Battle of Marston Moor, on the evening of 2 July 1644, and was the first in which Oliver Cromwell's newly trained cavalry, the Ironsides, proved their quality. The royalists suffered a shattering defeat. The north was lost. Newcastle, in despair, went into exile, but Rupert rallied his troops and resumed the war.

The advantage had now swung against Charles and would swing further the following year when, on 14 June, he suffered another heavy defeat at Naseby in Northamptonshire, and the war in England was effectively lost. But before then a remarkable campaign in Scotland offered a gleam of light. It seemed for a few weeks that Scotland might be won back for the King. This had appeared highly unlikely; the grip of the Covenanted Kirk was secure. But Charles had made the Marquis of Montrose his lieutenant-general. The appointment had been too long delayed. Indeed, in February 1643, before the Solemn League and Covenant had been signed, Montrose had tried to persuade the Queen, lately returned with supplies from Holland, that, as Henry Guthrie related, 'although the king's enemies in Scotland did not as yet profess so much, they certainly intended to carry an army into England, and to join with the king's enemies there; and, for remedy, offered, that if the king would grant a commission, himself, and many more, would take the field and prevent it'. Unfortunately for the royal cause, the Queen, who disliked Montrose, preferred the advice of the ineffectual Hamilton, who undertook 'that without raising arms for the king, he should make that party [the Covenanters] lie quiet, and not list an army for England'. Hamilton failed in this as in most things he attempted, and so it was only after great damage had been done by the Scots to the King's cause in England that Montrose at last slipped into Scotland with only two companions and made for the Highlands to raise troops.[16]

The 'Year of Miracles' that followed is almost peripheral to Charles's story, for while it briefly revived his hope of victory, it served no purpose in the end. And yet its effect was to be enduring, for the loyalty to the Stuarts displayed in later generations by so many in the Highlands owed much to the memory of Montrose and the legend of his year of astonishing victories.

Montrose was that rarest of political beings: a man hot for moderation. He had been a Covenanter, and he never departed from the view that the National Covenant was justified; but it was not long before he concluded that the Covenant, which was intended to rectify the balance in the state, now itself threatened to disturb it. While Charles had previously exceeded his prerogative, the latter was now being infringed by the Parliament in England and the Kirk and its supporters in Scotland. Montrose's position was therefore the same as Hyde's.

When he crossed the border in August 1644, his enterprise seemed hopeless. He brought no troops; Charles had none to spare him. Somewhere in the west or central Highlands there was, he knew, a force of Ulster Macdonalds, Catholics and rare fighting men. They were commanded by one Alasdair, and were the remnant of a force promised by the Earl of Antrim. Alasdair is the hero of the year in Gaelic legend, and it may be that Montrose's biographer, Wishart, his chaplain, does not give the Ulsterman all the credit he is due. Yet claims for Alasdair are exaggerated. In his career he showed boundless courage, but no evidence of strategic or even tactical grasp, except for his year under Montrose's command.

In twelve months Montrose with his little army, shifting in composition and never amounting to more than five thousand men, won seven battles. The last of these, at Kilsyth, made him master of

Scotland. He planned to summon a free parliament and to lead an army into England to revive the King's battered cause. But now the bubble burst. His army, after the manner of Highland armies, scattered. Alasdair led off his Macdonalds to pursue a private vendetta in the west – though he promised to return. Montrose, hoping to raise more troops in the Borders, had hardly begun the task when on 13 September 1645 he was surprised at Philiphaugh outside Selkirk by David Leslie at the head of a battle-hardened force of some six thousand men. Montrose had perhaps a quarter that number and his little army was scattered. He escaped to the Highlands, while the Covenanters honoured their grim God Jehovah by slaughtering three hundred Irishwomen who had been among Montrose's camp followers. 'The lord's work gangs merrily on,' said one minister of the Kirk. Even Leslie, with his experience of the frightful German wars, was disgusted. 'Have you not had your fill of blood?' he asked another of the ministers. The answer was no.

With Montrose's defeat the last hope vanished. There was little left of the royalists as a fighting force. Rupert went into exile, acquired a few ships, and harried the parliamentary fleet as vigorously as he had led cavalry charges. But this was more like piracy than war. In May 1646 Charles rode out of Oxford in disguise and made his way to Newark, where the castle, still held for the King, was being besieged by the Scots army commanded by Leven since David Leslie's return north. Charles rode into the Scots' camp and surrendered his person, then ordered the garrison of the castle to open the gates. It was the end of the war.

Charles was in effect a prisoner, but he was still king, and treated as such. Throughout the war his enemies had maintained that they were acting in the real interest of the Crown (which Charles mysteriously failed to understand) as well as the country, and Parliament had refrained from giving the title of acts to the measures it had passed, for an act required the royal assent. Instead they had issued what they called 'ordinances of the two houses'. As for the Scots, in whose camp Charles would remain for six months, the affairs of Scotland had been settled to their satisfaction in 1641 when the bishops had been removed and the Presbyterian establishment confirmed. They had entered the war as allies of Parliament because they feared that a royalist victory would see the 1641 settlement overturned again. But there was no danger of that now that the King was beaten. Still, they weren't satisfied. The Solemn League and Covenant had, as they believed, promised that Presbyterianism would be established in England too, and this they regarded as a guarantee that there could be no repeat of the Laudian experiment in Scotland. There should be two kingdoms, but the same style of Church government in each. Their hope remained wildly unrealistic, for the New Model Army of Fairfax and Cromwell continued to consist mainly of Independents. The Scots held the King as a valuable bargaining chip, but they were pursuing a chimera in their insistence that the provisions of their agreement with the English parliament should be enacted. To their mind, indeed, the Covenant was first with God, only secondly with Englishmen. As for the Independents, they were as loathsome to the Kirk as were bishops, for their demands would lead to what the ministers of the Kirk elegantly denounced as 'the vomit of toleration'.

The King endured boredom in the Scots camp, being plagued by lengthy prayers and sermons from the ministers; boredom and loneliness, for he had not seen his adored wife since she departed for France two years ago, was deprived of his children, and surrounded by men he regarded with dislike and suspicion. Nevertheless, he had no cause to despair. The inability of his enemies to come to an agreement offered him an opportunity and reinforced his belief that he was indispensable to any settlement.

The Scots were the first to have had enough. Despairing of achieving their ends, they came to an agreement with Parliament. In return for £400,000 – money they were due under the terms of the Solemn League – they handed Charles over and turned their faces to the north, stipulating only that no harm should come to the King's person. Parliamentary commissioners now took charge of the King and escorted him to Holdenby House in Northamptonshire. Crowds are reported to have cheered him as he passed, further evidence to his mind that no settlement of the divided and war-ravaged state could be made without him.

Parliament and the army were now at odds. The soldiers had many grievances. Their pay was in arrears. There were unwelcome proposals to disband some units and send others to Ireland, where the Catholic rebellion of 1641 had never been effectively suppressed. Yet there was also a difference, and point of disagreement, that ran deeper than these grievances; it was to prove an insuperable obstacle to any constitutional settlement. The Presbyterians were in the majority in Parliament; in the army the Independents. So though Parliament held what was recognised as the chief card – the person of the King – it was one that proved incapable of being a winning one. This soon became evident. Parliament proposed a compromise to the King. Let Presbyterianism be established for a trial period, followed by a general settlement agreeable to all. The idea of a trial period had been anathema to the Scots; how could you make a mere experiment of what God had ordained? The bare suggestion was anathema to the Independents of the army. Charles at least gave the matter his consideration, partly because Henrietta Maria was urging him to agree to it in letters from France. Her father, Henry of Navarre, had converted from Protestantism to Catholicism to end the religious wars that had plagued France for thirty years. Paris, he had decided, was worth a Mass. Surely Charles could be as accommodating?

While he temporised, Cromwell acted. On the last day of May 1647 he dispatched an officer, Cornet Joyce, to Holdenby House to seize the King. When Charles asked the cornet for his warrant, Joyce pointed to the five hundred troopers drawn up in the court-yard. The King, with the calm dignity that never deserted him, smiled and said, 'Indeed it is one that I can read without spelling. As handsome and proper a company of gentlemen as I have seen this many a day',[17] and was led off to Newmarket, where he was received with courtesy by the army commanders. Fairfax kissed his hand and allowed his (Anglican) chaplains to return. Cromwell, in benign mood, declared that the King was the most upright and conscientious man in his three kingdoms.

Charles was now brought to Hampton Court and presented with new proposals, drawn up by Cromwell's son-in-law, General Ireton.

On the ecclesiastical side these were moderate and sensible. Indeed, they anticipated the solution to the problem of the contending parties that would eventually be reached almost half a century later. All three – Episcopalians, Presbyterians, Independents – should be allowed to go their own way, with no compulsion. The Church of England might be governed by bishops, Presbyterians might have their own church courts, and Independents should be free from the government of either. Charles was disposed to agree, if without sincere conviction. It might be the best deal obtainable. He recommended the document to Parliament, but Parliament – or what was left of it – said no and the army was even more hostile. Ireton and Cromwell had miscalculated.

At a general council of officers and men, one trooper, by name Sexby, expressed the soldiers' frustration:

> We sought to satisfy all men. We have laboured to please a King, and, unless we cut our own throats, I think we shall never please him . . . And one thing I must say to General Cromwell and General Ireton themselves. Your credit and reputation hath been much blasted upon two accounts – your dealings with the King, your plan of settlement which was to have satisfied everybody and has satisfied nobody, and your dealings with Parliament. The authority of Parliament is a thing which most here would give their lives for, but the Parliament to which we could loyally subject ourselves has still to be called.[18]

This was the language of social and political revolution. It alarmed Cromwell, who nevertheless recognised the strength of feeling and tacked towards it. It alarmed the King, who now concluded that negotiations with the army leaders were futile, since they could not deliver on any agreement acceptable to him. He was heard to say, 'I really do believe we shall have another war.'

Then, in November 1647, the King was warned of a plot to assassinate him. He slipped out of Hampton Court, where he was only lightly guarded, and having crossed the river at Thames Ditton rode south and reached the Isle of Wight, where he found refuge in Carisbrooke Castle. From there he could probably have escaped to France, but at some point he had given his parole, and the man accused by his enemies of having so often deceived them and gone back on an agreement would not break his word now, when he thought his honour was at stake.

He lived comfortably enough and in relative freedom at Carisbrooke, still convinced, perhaps more than ever, that the division among his enemies meant that no settlement was possible without his approval. He wrote to the remnant of the House of Lords, justifying his flight from Hampton Court: 'I appeal to all indifferent men to judge, if I have not just cause to free myself from the hands of those who change their principles with their condition and with whom the Levellers' doctrine [of social, religious and political revolution] is rather countenanced than punished?'[19] This was a barb aimed at Cromwell.

Not content with having thus alienated the most powerful man in his kingdom, Charles now committed an act of supreme folly.

There had been a change of mood in Scotland. Hamilton, now a duke, was back in the country, and had been forming a party of those who favoured the Covenant, were opposed to Cromwell and the Independents, and supported both the principle of monarchy and, albeit with reservations, Charles himself. Emissaries were sent to meet the King in the Isle of Wight, and entered into what was called an 'Engagement' with him. According to this document Charles agreed to a three-year trial of Presbyterianism in England, in return for which the Scottish Estates (or Parliament) would approve the raising of an army to rescue him from the captivity into which they had sold him eighteen months ago. It was a preposterous scheme, doomed from its inception, for it combined incompatibles – the Solemn League and the King – and had nothing in it to appeal to English royalists, for, as Edward Hyde was to put it in his *History of the Great Rebellion*, Charles had made 'so many monstrous concessions that, unless the whole kingdom of England had been imprisoned in Carisbrooke Castle with the king, it could not be imagined that it could be delivered'.[20]

And delivered it was not. The second civil war in the autumn of 1648 was a brief but bloody affair. The Scots army was defeated and destroyed at Preston. In Scotland the extreme Covenanters, led by Argyll, regained the momentum from the discredited 'Engagers', and Cromwell went north to Edinburgh to ensure that even the lukewarm royalism of the Engagers should be extinguished. (One minister of the Kirk, Mr Robert Blair, found him 'an egregious dissembler, a great liar and a greeting [weeping] deevil'.[21])The King's involvement with the ill-conceived Engagement had done for him. Cromwell now agreed with the extremists that Charles should be put on trial for his life, though Fairfax said that if he was killed, then the rights of the Crown must pass to someone else, and asked who that might be.

It was necessary first to subdue what remained of the parliament elected in 1640, and remove those members who were regarded as unsound. On 6 December 1648, Colonel Pride purged the Commons by expelling its Presbyterian majority, reducing it to a rump of some eighty members. The civil war, which had been provoked by the Commons' attempt to transfer the power of the prerogative from King to Parliament, had ended in the destruction of the institution of Parliament itself. Now it would be the turn of the King. 'We shall cut his head off with the Crown still on it,' Cromwell said.[22]

Charles, brought first to Hurst Castle, and then to Windsor, where he spent Christmas, still insisting on his kingly state, and still indeed being treated as a king, did not even now realise what was being planned. He feared assassination, but did not contemplate a trial. This was not surprising, for such an act was unprecedented. Kings of England had been murdered, deposed, compelled to abdicate, but never arraigned before a court to face a capital charge.

There was another difference. In these earlier cases – Edward II, Richard II, Henry VI – the men who removed the king or compelled him to surrender his throne were themselves either royal or great and powerful barons. Charles was on the point of being judged and found guilty 'as a tyrant, murderer, and a public and implacable enemy of the Commonwealth of England' by men who before the war had been of little standing: country squires and lawyers. It was a revolutionary tribunal before which the King was to be tried. Nothing like it had been seen in England before.

Even so, while his condemnation was all but certain, sentence of death was not. There was uncertainty among his judges. Cromwell himself, despite that expressed intention to cut the King's head off with the crown still upon it, seems to have swithered. In a debate in the rump of the Parliament in the last days of December he said: 'If any man whatsoever had carried on this design of deposing the King, and disinheriting his posterity or if any man had yet such a design, he should be the greatest traitor and rebel in the world. But since the Providence of God hath cast this upon us, I cannot but submit to Providence, though I am not yet provided to give you my advice.'[23] This was characteristically ambiguous. But on one reading at least it implied that Charles, who claimed to be king by divine right, was to be deposed by the will of the Almighty, whose mere instrument Cromwell believed himself to be. Nevertheless, there might yet be a last-minute settlement. It would depend on how the King conducted himself and, importantly, on whether he recognised the authority of the court to try him.

One hundred and thirty-five commissioners were appointed to draw up the charges against Charles, though only fifty-two of them attended on the first day. Essentially he was to be accused of shedding his people's blood in England and Ireland, but not Scotland, where representatives of the English parliament could not plausibly claim any jurisdiction. The gist of the case was that Charles was the sole 'occasioner, author and continuer of the said unnatural, cruel and bloody wars; and therein guilty of all the treasons, murders, rapines, burnings, spoils, desolations, damages, and mischiefs to this nation, acted and committed in the said wars, or occasioned thereby'.[24] This was very obviously something impossible to prove, so weak that it might even have been an attempt to get the King to plead, and thus acknowledge the court's right to try him and the view of the constitution that the trial signified – a view that ran clean contrary to that which he had asserted all his reign. Had he done so, then a number of different outcomes were possible, even now: his restoration as a monarch whose powers were henceforth limited by his admission of the sovereignty of the people of England; deposition and his replacement by his youngest son, the nine-year-old Prince Henry, Duke of Gloucester, who conveniently happened to be a prisoner of the Parliament; more importantly, sentence of death would become unnecessary, because Charles would have yielded the argument, and the sovereignty of the people would have been established.

On the first day of the trial in the Great Hall of the Palace of Westminster, 20 January 1649, the King refused to plead. He would not enter the trap set for him. To do so would have been to deny everything he had stood for. He would not recognise the court's right to try him. He continued to refuse each day the court met. He was fortified in this attitude by the realisation that others were very evidently of his opinion. Fairfax had been appointed one of the commissioners who, having drawn up the charge, were now acting as both judge and jury, but when his name was called, his wife in the gallery cried out, 'Not here and never will be. He has too much sense.'[25] It was also clear from the manner of some of the commissioners who did attend that even they were uncertain of the authority thrust upon them.

The King's case was simple. He was not before a legally constituted court. 'I say, sir, by your favour,' he told its president, John Bradshaw, a lawyer from Cheshire, 'that the Commons of England was never a Court of Judicature. I would know how they come to be so.' Bradshaw could not give the truthful answer: that the court represented naked power. Instead he sidestepped the question, declaring, 'The Court hath considered of their jurisdiction, and they have ready affirmed their jurisdiction,' which was to say, 'We are a lawful court because we say we are a lawful court.'

This was chicanery, though essential in view of the assertion that the court was acting in the name of the people of England. That claim too had provoked an interruption from the bold Lady Fairfax: 'It is a lie! Not a half or a quarter of them.'

By now Charles must have realised that he really was in danger of his life. There had come earlier a moment when his position was revealed to him. S. R. Gardiner, nineteenth-century author of a ten-volume history of the civil war, recounted it in this manner: while the prosecutor was speaking, 'Charles had attempted to interrupt him by touching the sleeve of his gown with a silver-headed cane.

The head of the cane fell off, and Charles, accustomed even at Carisbrooke and Hurst Castle, to be waited on by those who were ready to anticipate his slightest wish, looked round in vain for someone to pick it up. For a moment his loneliness was brought home to him as never before.'[26]

Yet he held his ground, his dignity unimpaired. He demanded trial before a properly constituted parliament of England, and he turned accuser himself. The court claimed to represent the people of England, but: 'Pretend what you will, I stand more for their liberties, for if power without law may make laws, may alter the fundamental laws of the kingdom, I do not know what subject he is in England that can be sure of his life, or anything he calls his own.'

It was the argument of all traditional authority against all revolutionaries, but now, denied the show trial they had intended, his judges proceeded to pass sentence. Dressed in black and wearing the ribbon of the Order of the Garter, the King heard the clerk of the court declare: 'For all which reasons and crimes this Court doth adjudge, that the said Charles Stuart, as a tyrant, traitor and murderer, and a public enemy, shall be put to death by the severing his head from his body.'

It was Saturday, 27 January.

There was still a delay in getting the death warrant signed, and there is a degree of confusion about the signatories, for some of those among the commissioners who affixed their names were not present in court on the Saturday, and some who were present were not among the fifty-nine who signed the document. The delay and discrepancy give some plausibility to a story that the King was approached, sometime that day, or on the 28th, before the warrant was signed on the Monday, by emissaries from the army grandees, with a 'paper book' containing proposals that would, if he had assented to them, have left him with his 'life and some shadow of regality'. If this indeed happened – and the story was reported soon after the King's death – Charles remained true to himself and his principles. He would be a martyr rather than an apostate.

Sometime on the 28th or 29th the King was told when he was to be killed and where the execution would take place. He occupied himself with writing letters, including a long one full of advice to the Prince of Wales, with making his last bequests, and attending to his dogs. Prince Henry and Princess Elizabeth, the two children held captive by Parliament, were brought to him to say goodbye. He told them what was to happen – 'Sweetheart,' he said, taking the eight-year-old boy in his arms, 'now they will cut off thy father's head' – and instructed them to forgive their enemies as he forgave his. He impressed on Henry especially that he must remain true to the Church of England and loyal to his eldest brother, resisting any attempt to make him king in his place. 'I'll be torn in pieces first,' the boy said.[27] Charles kissed them and sent them away. Bishop Juxon came to pray with him, and then it was night.

The morning of 30 January was brisk and cold. Charles wore two shirts, lest the cold make him shiver and people think him afraid. He walked from St James's to Whitehall, and was led to the scaffold through the banqueting hall, passing under the great painting, *The Apotheosis of King James*, with which Rubens had decorated the ceiling. The remnant of the Parliament had hurriedly passed an ordinance forbidding him to name a successor; but there was no need for him to do so. There had been fears that he would offer resistance, and arrangements had been made for him to be tied down, but the fear was ridiculous. The King understood that this was theatre, and, like his grandmother Mary at Fotheringay, he gave a magnificent performance. He had lost the war, been defeated by his enemies; by the manner of his death he would conquer them. 'I shall say but short prayers,' he told the masked executioners. 'Remember,' he said to Bishop Juxon. Then he knelt and laid his head on the block.

The fatal blow was greeted with a groan from the crowd. 'Such a groan,' one young man remembered, 'as I never heard before and desire I may never hear again.'[28]

A troop of cavalry was sent in to disperse the crowd. Someone reputedly picked up a handkerchief stained with the King's blood; it was later said effectively to cure scrofula – the condition known as the king's evil.

In the royalist imagination Charles was transformed into a

suffering Christ, the scaffold at Whitehall his Golgotha. The remote, chilly, correct figure of the years before the civil war disappeared, replaced by the holy martyr king. For Henry Guthrie, 'So ended the best of princes, being cut off in his age, by the barbarous hands of unnatural subjects.'[29]

Not everyone felt like that of course. Cromwell himself was reported to have murmured, 'Cruel necessity' as he stood by his victim's coffin. A fifteen-year-old St Paul's schoolboy, by name Samuel Pepys, remembered his elation when he heard the news of the execution. If he had had to preach a sermon that day, he thought, he would take as his text 'And the memory of the wicked shall rot'.

Beyond London, the news was received with horror. In Paris, the King's heir, the eighteen-year-old Prince of Wales, burst into tears when addressed as 'Your Majesty', and, according to Edward Hyde, fell 'into all the confusion imaginable . . . sinking under the burden of his grief'. Henrietta Maria, who for all her faults and the bad advice she had so often given him, had loved her husband passion-ately, could neither weep nor speak nor move from her chair for many hours when they told her he had been killed. Montrose, exiled in the Hague, fainted. For two days he did not move from his chamber, and when his chaplain and biographer Wishart entered it, he found these verses on the table:

> Great, good and just, could I but rate
> My grief, and thy too rigid fate,
> I'd weep the world in such a strain
> As it should deluge once again.
> But since thy loud-tongued blood demands supplies
> More from Briareus' hands than Argus' eyes,
> I'll sing thy obsequies with trumpet sounds,
> And write thine epitaph in blood and wounds.

He had himself painted wearing black armour, and 'from this moment', John Buchan wrote, 'there is an uncanniness about him, as of one who lives half his time in another world'.[30]

This too is testimony to the manner in which Charles, by accepting death as a martyr, had obliterated the memory of the follies and blunders of the years of personal rule – follies and blunders that had driven this same Montrose to sign the National Covenant and take up arms against the King.

In death Charles conquered even his adversaries. A couple of years after the execution, Andrew Marvell, Presbyterian poet and Cromwellian, wrote a heroic ode celebrating Cromwell's achievements in Ireland, where he had slaughtered his prisoners after the Battle of Drogheda and told the native Irish they might go to 'Hell or Connacht'. Yet in celebrating 'our chief of men', Marvell inserted into his poem these lines describing the King's execution:

> He nothing common did or mean
> Upon that memorable scene,
> But with his keener eye
> The axe's edge did try;
>
> Nor called the gods with vulgar spite
> To vindicate his helpless right,
> But bowed his comely head
> Down, as upon a bed.[31]

The image of the Man of Blood, promoted by his enemies, was expunged. After the Restoration, the revised 1662 Prayer Book of the Church of England provided an order of service for the Commemoration of the Martyr King on the anniversary of his execution.

Chapter 12

The Interregnum and the Scattered Family (1649–60)

T he news of the King's execution shocked the courts of Europe. Few probably would have been surprised, or even distressed, if he had been quietly strangled or poisoned in his prison. Assassination had often been the means of ridding a nation of its unpopular or unsuccessful monarch. But for his subjects to put an anointed king on trial and then strike off his head as if he had been a common criminal, that was another matter altogether, one that struck at the roots of all legitimacy. Nevertheless, it was not long before the dictator Cromwell was treated as an equal by foreign courts, receiving the marks of respect commonly accorded to power. England had been weak, of little account in European politics. Now she was strong. However unsuccessful Cromwell proved at home, where his constitutional experiments all failed and he had no more success in dealing with the various parliaments he devised than Charles had had in his relations with the House of Commons, the Lord Protector, as he styled himself, made England feared and admired abroad. 'I desire,' he said, 'the English Republic to be as much respected as was the Roman Republic in ancient times';[1] and his desire was satisfied. He humbled the Dutch at sea, made successful war on Spain, and formed an alliance with France. Despite the close family ties between the Bourbon monarchy and the Stuarts, the French court went into formal mourning when the great dictator died in 1658.

Meanwhile, throughout the years of his rule, the Stuarts lived in exile and poverty, as did so many of their adherents. Some of the royalist exiles in time despaired and made peace with the republicans, enabling them to return home and in some cases repair their fortunes and regain their estates. No such accommodation was possible for members of the royal family. They were condemned to wait till the wheel of fortune might turn – something that seemed unlikely in the high years of Cromwell's rule.

Those who remained in exile were loyal to the new king, Charles II, as of course were many royalists in England, Scotland and Ireland. He might be a king without a state, but he was still a king, head of a government-in-exile, with ministers who had nothing but the affairs of his peripatetic court to administer. Foreign monarchs too recognised him as king, except when they sought friendly relations with the English republic and found Charles to be an embarrassment.

His mother, Henrietta Maria, as a daughter of France, spent the years of exile in Paris. During the disturbances known as the Fronde – a series of civil wars (1648–50) that seemed light-minded and whimsical in comparison with the grim and bloody constitutional struggle in her husband's kingdoms – her circumstances were often miserable. The Cardinal de Retz, one of the instigators of the Fronde, remembered them when he came to write his memoirs:

Four or five days before the king [the young Louis XIV] removed from Paris [on account of the Fronde] I went to visit the Queen of England, whom I found in her daughter's chamber, who has been since Duchess of Orleans. [This was the youngest child, Henriette-Anne, known in the family as Minette]. At my coming in, she said: 'You see I am come to keep Henriette company. The poor child could not rise today for want of a fire.' The truth is that the cardinal [Mazarin, the chief minister] for six months altogether had not ordered her any money towards her pension; that no tradespeople would trust her for anything; and that there was not at her lodgings a single banknote . . . Posterity will hardly believe that, to get out of bed in the Louvre, and in the eyes of

France, a Princess of England, grand-daughter of Henri-Quatre, had wanted a faggot, in the month of January and within sight of the French court.[2]

The Cardinal arranged for the Parlement of Paris to provide the Queen of England with money for her subsistence.

Other royalists were in a like state of destitution. Sir Edward Hyde, the future Earl of Clarendon, now chancellor of the government-in-exile, in his *History of the Rebellion* wrote: 'The Marquis of Ormonde was compelled to put himself in prison, with other gentlemen, at a pistole a week for his diet, and to walk the streets a-foot, which was no honourable custom in Paris.' On the other hand, Lord Jermyn, the Queen's chamberlain, whom some thought her lover, which is unlikely, was reputed 'to keep an excellent table for those who courted him, and had a coach of his own'. Eventually, when the troubles of the Fronde were over, Henrietta Maria was better provided for, thanks to the intervention of her sister-in-law Anne of Austria, the widow of Louis XIII and mother of Louis XIV.

One member of the Stuart family was in a happier condition, materially at least. This was Mary, the Princess Royal. Married to the Prince of Orange, Stadtholder of the United Provinces of the Netherlands, she had the status and security the exiles lacked. Yet she too was not without her discontents and was often low-spirited. The immediate cause was her husband's frequent and flagrant infidelity. Indeed, his love affairs were so open and notorious that they were made the subject of a play staged in Amsterdam – where republicanism was strong and the Orange family unpopular.[3] Mary was devoted to her brothers, especially Charles, as was, to be fair, her husband. She disliked the Dutch and made her distaste evident – which hardly added to the couple's popularity – and spent a lot of time with her aunt Elizabeth.

Elizabeth knew more of the pain of exile than anyone else in the family. It was now over thirty years since her husband Frederick had rashly accepted the offer of the crown of Bohemia, been driven out first from Prague and then from his own Palatinate. Frederick had been dead for years, and Elizabeth had lost much of the youthful beauty that had led the diplomat Sir Henry Wotton to call her 'the eclipse and glory of her kind'. Wotton, remembered for his description of an ambassador as 'an honest man sent abroad to lie for his country', immortalised her in verse:

> You meaner beauties of the night,
> That poorly satisfy our eyes
> More by your number than your light,
> You common people of the stars,
> What are you when the moon shall rise?

For years Elizabeth had depended on a pension from her brother Charles and gifts from her friend and admirer Lord Craven, who had also provided £30,000 towards the cost of an unsuccessful campaign to recover the Palatinate. At the outbreak of the civil war, Parliament, not surprisingly, stopped her pension; thereafter she relied on the kindness of friends and some assistance from the Dutch government. Fortunately she had lots of friends, for her charm was legendary, though not all of her many children were equally captivated by it. Her eldest son was dead, drowned on campaign; she had quarrelled with the second, Charles Louis. Restored to part of the Palatinate by the Treaty of Westphalia (1648), he refused to allow his mother to return with him. Her favourite son, Rupert, was ranging the seas as admiral of the tiny royalist fleet. His brother Maurice, who had accompanied him to England in 1642 to fight for their uncle, was also dead, lost at sea. Four daughters survived to adulthood. Elizabeth, the eldest, an intellectual, friend and correspondent of the philosopher and scientist Leibnitz, would never marry. Henrietta found a husband in a prince of Transylvania. Sophia, having rejected the less than wholehearted advances of her cousin Charles II, married the Elector of Hanover and lived to a great age, her son George becoming King of Great Britain and Ireland in 1714. Louise, who had much of her mother's charm, though indifferent to her appearance, fell in love with the Marquis of Montrose, who, after the King's execution, was in no mood for romance; eventually she turned Catholic, entered a convent and died as Abbess of Maubuisson. All the girls were often irritated by their mother, Sophia complaining that her dogs and monkeys mattered more to Elizabeth than did her children. This may well have been true; it is just as likely, however, that they were jealous of the apparently effortless manner in which Elizabeth continued in her fifties to attract admirers. Her spirit seemed indomitable. 'Though I have cause enough to be sad,' she wrote to one of her elderly friends, Sir Thomas Roe, 'yet I am still of my wild humour to be as merry as I can in spite of fortune.' Like Louise, she adored Montrose, writing letters full of affection, advice and jokes, all of which he was in sore need of. She commissioned his portrait, and hung it in her cabinet 'to frighten away the Brethren'. She also adored her nephew Charles, relishing his easy manner and dry humour. She might well have been happy to see him marry her daughter.

In Paris, Henrietta Maria had other, more ambitious plans for her son. He should be wed to a cousin on her side of the family. This was her niece Anne-Marie-Louise de Montpensier, the eldest daughter of Gaston, Duc d'Orleans. As the brother of Louis XIII he was addressed as Monsieur, and his daughter as Mademoiselle. (She is usually known as La Grande Mademoiselle, not only because she was a big woman, but because of her martial exploits on the rebel side during the Fronde.) Mademoiselle had many merits: she was brave and kind-hearted, intensely loyal to her slippery flibbertigibbet of a father and loving to her half-sisters. She was also extremely rich, thanks to the early death of her mother from whom she had inherited vast estates; and this commended her to Henrietta Maria. But she was also naïve, rather stupid, and incapable of seeing a joke, all of which did not commend her to Charles. Besides, unlike his mother, he understood that marrying a Catholic princess, no matter how well born and rich, would do him no good in either England or Scotland. He spoiled his mother's plans by pretending to Mademoiselle that he spoke no French; she thought him singularly ill-bred. Nevertheless, the comedy went on for some years.

The Queen's first attempt to make a match between her son and her niece was launched when he was little more than a boy in Paris in the early years of exile before the King's execution. Soon the Prince's time there was enlivened by the arrival of the young Duke of Buckingham and his brother Francis. They had been childhood friends, for King Charles had adopted the Villiers boys a few months after their father's murder. The Duke, George, was almost three years older than Charles, Francis eighteen months. Both had inherited their father's beauty, and the Duke was also very clever, endlessly amusing, witty, irreverent, and a wonderful mimic. He had entranced Charles when they were small and would continue to do so almost as long as they lived. Light-minded and utterly untrustworthy, he had only to exercise his charm to be forgiven. Now the two young men were put to study with the philosopher and mathematician Thomas Hobbes, author of *Leviathan*, regarded by the few who read it as a cynical apology for despotism. Charles almost certainly was not among its readers, though he formed a respect and affection for Hobbes. Bishop Burnet, however, writing half a century later, believed that Hobbes 'laid before him his schemes both as to religion and politics, which made a deep and lasting impression on the Prince's mind'.[4] Perhaps. Buckingham was the readier pupil – Hobbes thought him outstandingly intelligent; yet left off teaching him mathematics when he observed him masturbating as his teacher expounded a geometrical theorem.[5]

Soon Charles had other interests. Visiting his sister at the Hague in 1648, he met a girl called Lucy Walter. She was the same age as the Prince, only eighteen, the daughter of an impoverished Welsh squire. Her parents had separated when she was still a child, and at the age of fourteen or fifteen she became the mistress of a colonel in Cromwell's New Model Army, Algernon Sidney, who paid her 'fifty broad pieces' to surrender her virtue – a word never used in connection with her again. A couple of years later he tired of her and passed her on to his royalist brother Robert, who in 1648 obligingly yielded her to Prince Charles. 'Let who's have her,' he told the Prince, 'she's already sped.'[6] The diarist John Evelyn described her as 'a bold, brown, beautiful but insipid creature'. The first three adjectives were just; 'insipid' Lucy certainly wasn't, unless Evelyn was using the word in some specialised sense. He may simply have meant that she was almost wholly uneducated, barely literate. It wasn't, however, her mind that attracted men. Charles fell in love with her, no doubt about that. She gave him a son, James, the future Duke of Monmouth, whom he loved more than any other among the fourteen children he sired who survived infancy.

The relationship with Lucy lasted on and off – more frequently off – for ten years. It ended in recrimination when he employed agents to remove the boy James from her care, and perhaps even in hatred. Lucy declared that they were married, and it is just possible that they went through some sort of ceremony. She claimed to have papers proving it, but convincing documents have never been produced. The matter remains murky. Charles always denied that they had married, but it was in his interest to do so. Some have suggested any marriage would have been illegal, though it is not clear why – especially if it took place after his father's execution, when as king and head of the family he would not have had to seek permission from anyone to wed. Monmouth may well have believed he was legitimate. His mother had told him so, and later, when he was removed from her, his tutors, a courtier called Thomas Ross and a Catholic convert, Father Goffe, who had previously been one of the King's Anglican chaplains, encouraged him in the belief, Ross apparently because he was so charmed by the little boy's beauty and happy temper that he could deny him nothing and was eager to please him in all things. The rumour of the marriage to Lucy would persist to the end of Charles's life, causing him embarrassment and political difficulty. Sometime in the nineteenth century, Monmouth's descendant, the Duke of Buccleuch, is said to have come on a paper in the family archives that, if not a forgery, gave credence to the story. He sensibly – if, from the point of view of the historian, irritatingly – threw it into the fire.

As for Lucy, her lively career, which had included on a brief return to England a stay as a prisoner in the Tower of London, and at least half a dozen lovers after Charles, ended in 1658. According to the memoirs of Charles's brother James, Duke of York, the cause of death was 'a disease incident to her profession. She was very handsome,' he added, 'with little wit and some cunning.'7 As king, James would send Monmouth to the block, so he may have been prejudiced against Lucy.

James himself had arrived in France in 1648, making his escape from England disguised as a woman. He was his mother's favourite child, and made a better impression at the French court than Charles. La Grande Mademoiselle certainly found him more impressive, for he spoke to her in fluent French. 'Nothing,' she declared, 'detracts from a man so much as not being able to converse, and the Duke talked very well.'8 (But then he had no fear that his mother was trying to marry him off to the lady.) Still, with his fair hair, fine complexion, good manners and graceful bearing, he was generally found to be very agreeable. He was allowed to join the French army, showed himself to be very brave, and won the approval of the greatest commander of the day, Marshal Turenne. In these days of his youth, Burnet wrote in his *History*, James 'really clouded the king and passed for the superior genius'. This view, however widely held, was mistaken. Though in Burnet's words 'candid and sincere', and intensely loyal to his brother, James was not very bright. A more acute observer than the Bishop remarked: 'The king could see things if he would; the duke would see things if he could.'

The last member of the family to arrive in exile was young Henry, Duke of Gloucester, usually called Harry. He was a lively, intelligent and affectionate boy whom everyone seems to have liked. In 1652 Cromwell released him from prison and sent him to the Hague, in the charge of a tutor. He may have done so out of a native kindliness, or because of suggestions that England's constitutional dilemma might be best solved by making the boy king, subject to the sort of close limitations of power his father had rejected.

Henrietta Maria was naturally eager to be reunited with her youngest son, whom she hadn't seen since he was three or four. Charles was reluctant to accede to her demands, because he knew she would try to convert Harry to her Catholic faith. When she promised to refrain from doing so, he gave way and the boy was sent to Paris. Whereupon his mother broke her promise. Charles was furious. Harry was distressed. He remembered how his father, in that last terrible meeting the night before his execution, had adjured him to remain true to the Church of England, and he had also conceived an intense devotion to his brother. On the other hand, starved of female affection for years, with the horrible memory of his father's words and also of the death from consumption in 1650 of his only companion, his sister Elizabeth, he was delighted to be part of the family again, with his mother and little sister Minette, and anxious to please the Queen. In the end Charles's will prevailed, as it usually did when he had set his mind to something, and Harry returned to the Hague. He hoped to be a soldier like his brother James. Meanwhile he amused himself with sport, especially tennis. A few years later, in 1658, when money was shorter than usual, it was even rumoured that he was going to earn his keep as a tennis coach. His story is sad, for he died of smallpox a few weeks after his brother's restoration. Burnet says he had 'a kind insinuating temper that was generally very acceptable', and his death was 'much lamented by all, but chiefly by the King; for he loved him better than the Duke of York, and was never in his whole life seen so much concerned as he was on this occasion'.

Chapter 13

Charles II (1649–85):
A Merry and Cynical Monarch

I n May 1640, a couple of weeks before his eleventh birthday,
Charles, Prince of Wales, was sent in a coach to the House
of Lords, the bearer of a letter from his father requesting the
two Houses of Parliament to commute the sentence of death passed
on Strafford to imprisonment, which, said the King, 'would be an
unspeakable contentment to me'. It was Henrietta Maria's idea to
entrust the mission to the Prince. Surely the sight of the boy coming
to plead for his father's minister would soften the hearts of
Strafford's enemies? She had miscalculated. The letter was refused,
returned unopened, and Charles was sent home. This was the first
humiliation he had experienced in a hitherto cherished and protected
life. He would be compelled to endure many more over the next
twenty years. Before he was sixteen, he was an exile, a refugee,
dependent on others for mere subsistence.

In January 1649, when word came that the King was to be put on
trial, Charles sent Parliament a letter signed by himself, otherwise
blank, along with a note offering to make whatever concessions might
be demanded in order to save his father's life. He got no reply. A few
days later he was a king without a kingdom.

Or perhaps not. The Scots had not been consulted about the
King's trial and sentence. For all but the most extreme Covenanters,
it was a breach of the agreement they had made when they handed
him over to the English parliament, with the stipulation that no

harm should come to his person. Moreover, Charles had been King of Scotland as well as England, and it was their king who had been so barbarously and, in their view, illegally put to death. Accordingly, on 4 February, as soon as the news of the King's execution reached the Scottish capital, Charles II was proclaimed king by the Chancellor of Scotland, the Earl of Loudoun, at the Mercat-cross in Edinburgh. A wave of feeling, indignation mixed with loyalty, ran through the land. The indignation was intensified a few weeks later when the Duke of Hamilton, who had led the Engagers so disastrously to defeat at Preston, followed the master he had served so inconsistently and incompetently to the block. Hamilton had been an erratic and ineffective figure. In *The Tale of Old Mortality*, Scott puts this epitaph for him into the mouth of an old woman: 'That was him that lost his head at London. Folks said that it wasna a very guid ane, but it was aye a sair loss to him, puir gentleman.' Nevertheless he was a Scottish nobleman, a descendant of Scottish kings, and the treason with which he had been charged was no treason either to Scotland or its monarch.

So Scotland offered hope and opportunity to the young Charles II, a better chance certainly than Ireland of regaining his thrones, though his mother with characteristic lack of political sense was urging him to declare himself a Catholic; 'Only so you can win Ireland,' she said.

Yet the hope Scotland offered was of an uncertain nature, for the land and its people were divided and distracted. There were essentially three parties. All were prepared to set up Charles as king, but beyond that their aims were incompatible, and they were moreover riven by personal enmities and distrust.

Charles had to deal with three parties whose aims were inconsistent even while they proclaimed themselves ready to accept him as king: first, the zealots of the Covenant led by the Marquis of Argyll, who would accept Charles if he in turn would swear by the Solemn League and Covenant and undertake to establish Presbyterianism in England; second, the Engagers, led by John Maitland, Earl of Lauderdale, and Hamilton's brother and heir,

previously Earl of Lanark – the Engagement had split them from
the rigid Covenanters, on account of their willingness to dilute the
terms of the Solemn League; and third, the royalists, whose chief
was Montrose, and who had realised that the Solemn League and
Covenant was wrong in principle and futile as practical politics,
since it was unacceptable to England and would make co-operation
with English royalists impossible. This last party had sense on its
side, and was the only one whose loyalty to the new King was
unconditional. Unfortunately it was by far the weakest of the three
in Scotland, where Montrose himself had been under sentence of
death since his campaign in 1644–5 and was consequently, like his
king, in exile.

Charles was inexperienced and beset by conflicting advice.
Edward Hyde, for example, as one who knew the temper of
England, was against any agreement with the Covenanters. Yet the
young King was ready to negotiate with them all. This was foolish
and dishonest, and he was to pay a terrible price for it. He would
have done better to listen to his Aunt Elizabeth, whose judgement
of Covenanters, Engagers and the schemers surrounding her nephew
was that 'they are all mad, or worse'.

Charles named Montrose captain-general of Scotland and authorised him to raise troops and make a landing in the north, even
while he was negotiating with the Covenanters and preparing to
submit to their demands. No doubt he hoped that Montrose would
secure Scotland for him before he himself signed the detested
Covenant, and regarded the negotiations with the Covenanters as
an insurance policy if Montrose should fail. But he should have
realised that the news of these negotiations, which obviously could
not be kept secret, would render Montrose's already difficult venture
impossible. For why should men come out to fight alongside him
when the King was known to be considering an agreement with
the Marquis's bitter and implacable enemies? Montrose's chances
had never been good; Charles's trafficking with the Covenanters
doomed his most loyal servant. He might as well have put the
noose round Montrose's neck with his own hands.

The Marquis sailed to Orkney, raised a sadly inadequate army, was defeated, betrayed, taken prisoner, carried to Edinburgh, and hanged. Meanwhile, before he learned of his captain-general's fate, Charles promised to sign the Covenant as soon as he arrived in Scotland, allow the establishment of Presbyterianism in both his kingdoms, and enforce the Penal Laws against Roman Catholics. The promise made him miserable; even one of the Kirk ministers had second thoughts. Feeling sorry for 'that poor young prince', he thought he should not have been forced to sign the Covenant, 'which we knew he hated in his heart'.[1] It was too late, it seemed, to draw back. Charles wrote to Montrose telling him to lay down his arms, and apparently believed that he had secured from his new allies, who were really his captors, a promise of indemnity for the Marquis and other royalists. He was soon deceived. Before he sailed from Holland in the first week of June 1650, he received news of Montrose's execution. 'This is for Your Majesty's service,' he was smugly and dishonestly assured.[2] The months that followed were the bitterest of Charles's life.

John Nicoll was an Edinburgh lawyer and something of a time-server, his opinions veering in accordance with the prevailing wind. This makes him, however, a useful barometer of opinion: 'The news of his landing coming to the knowledge of the estates of Parliament, sitting here at Edinburgh, upon the 26th of June, late at night, all signs of joy were manifest through the whole kingdom; namely, and in a special manner, in Edinburgh by setting forth of bonfires, ringing of bells, sounding of trumpets, dancing almost all that night through the streets. The poor kail-wives at the Tron sacrificed their payments and baskets and the very stools they sat upon to the fire.'[3]

At first all was hope. Though Charles would not be crowned for several months, a flavour of the Covenanters' habit of mind may be caught by the account by the Reverend Robert Baillie of the eventual coronation:

> This day we have done what I earnestly expected and long desired, crowned our noble King with all the solemnities at Scone, so peaceably and magnificently as if no enemy had been among us.

This was of God; for it was Cromwell's purpose, which I thought easily he might have performed, to have marred by arms that action, or at least the solemnity of it . . . Mr Douglas, from II Kings, XI, Joash's coronation, had a very pertinent, wise and good sermon. The King swore the Coronation Oath; when Argyll put on the crown, Mr Robert Douglas prayed well; when the Chancellor set him in the throne, he exhorted well; when all were ended, he [Douglas] pressed sincerity and constancy in the Covenant on the King, dilating at length King James's breach from the Covenant, pursued yet against the family, from Nehemiah v.13, God's casting the King out of his lap, and the 34th of Jeremiah, many plagues on him if he does not keep the oaths now taken. He closed all with a prayer, and the 20th Psalm.4

Baillie, it may be remarked, was one of the more liberal ministers, and one of the few inclined to be sympathetic to the young King.

Very soon after his arrival in Scotland, Charles had a taste of the humiliations in store for him. Most of the royalist friends who had accompanied him were dismissed, Buckingham and Henry Seymour the sole exceptions. Buckingham remained characteristically light-hearted. It didn't matter what he signed, he told Charles; he could repudiate everything once he was king in fact as well as name. Meanwhile the King was afflicted by the ministers of the Kirk, who broke in upon him at all hours to lecture him on the duties of a covenanted king and the iniquity of his parents, his grandfather (James VI) and his Catholic ancestors. He had to attend church four times on Sundays and listen to long sermons couched in the vigorous and violent language of the Old Testament. Jehovah, the Lord of Hosts, was the Covenanters' God; they cared little for Jesus and the Gospel message of forgiveness. 'It was,' Charles said later, 'a miserable life. I saw no women, and the people were so ignorant that they thought it sinful to play the violin.'5 'Sinful' was indeed the ministers' favourite word.

All this might be borne, and Charles did indeed bear it with admirable self-control, swallowing insults and sharp criticism. More worrying was the way in which the bigoted intolerance of those now around him narrowed the base of support for the war against

Cromwell, which must be won if he was to be restored in both his kingdoms. It was no national movement he nominally led. The true royalists, all those who had been associated with Montrose, were anathema. Even the Engagers were spurned, and Lauderdale and the new Duke of Hamilton dismissed; they had compromised the Covenant, were lukewarm, and so the true Covenanters spewed them, like the Laodiceans of the Book of Revelation, out of their mouths. (Even so, some of the Covenanting zealots in the western counties would have nothing to do with this dubiously Covenanted king.)

The most important man in Scotland was not the King, but Argyll. Archibald Campbell, eighth Earl and first Marquis, was in his way as remarkable a man as his great antagonist Montrose. Chief of the powerful Clan Campbell, he was a Douglas on his mother's side, and, through the Douglases, as he liked to remind people, eighth in succession from Robert the Bruce himself. His wayward father, with whom he had been at odds, had converted to Catholicism, and encumbered his estates with debt. So, as a young man, Archibald was principally concerned with getting his lands in order and repairing his financial position. Then, during the momentous General Assembly of the Kirk at Glasgow in 1638, he had experienced a religious awakening. In modern terms he was 'born again', from that day on committed to the Covenant and to the establishment of a theocracy, guided however by the wisdom of godly nobles, of whom he was chief. His political course was erratic, his aim constant. He had assured Cromwell he would prevent Charles from coming to Scotland, then engineered his arrival. Unprepossessing in appearance, slight, dark, thin-lipped and with a cast or squint in his left eye, Argyll was also notably intelligent and capable of exercising considerable charm. Charles soon found him the one man among the Covenanters with whom he could converse agreeably. Nevertheless, he didn't trust him.

In August Cromwell marched north with his veteran army, accustomed to victory, to suppress the insubordinate Scots. Charles, though a proclaimed, if not yet crowned, king, was forbidden to join the army. Instead the ministers urged the necessity of purging it of 'malignants', for the Almighty was offended by their presence among the troops. A hundred officers and three thousand men were dismissed. Either the sacrifice was insufficient or they had misread their divinity's mind, for the battle that followed at Dunbar was disastrous. The ministers themselves were at fault. The Scots army had been drawn up in a good position on a commanding height. Meanwhile Cromwell, outmanoeuvred, was in sore straits, supplies running out. The Scots had only to exercise patience, to adopt the traditional course of refusing battle till the English invaders were further weakened. Instead the ministers commanded that they should advance and 'smite the Amalekites'. This was a mistake, and the battle was lost. Cromwell moved to occupy Edinburgh.

It was now proposed to raise a new army, including Engagers and any royalists who would, like the King, accept the Covenant. Argyll was alarmed. 'You have done wickedly,' he told the King, 'in admitting malignants.' 'I know not what you mean by malignants,' Charles replied. 'We are all malignants to God.'[6]

Preparations for the coronation continued. Argyll sought to bind the King more tightly. 'I cannot serve Your Majesty as you desire,' he said, 'unless you give some undeniable proof of a fixed resolution to support the Presbyterian party – which I think would best be done by marrying into some family of quality that is known to be entirely attached to your interest. This would take off the prejudice upon your mother.'[7]

The bride he had in mind was his own daughter, Lady Anne Campbell. Charles asked for time, and spoke of the need to get his mother's approval. He was becoming adept in the art of prevarication. The young man who had seen off La Grande Mademoiselle was not going to be hooked by Lady Anne. He would play the bitter comedy to the end.

At last he was crowned, on New Year's Day 1651, after a prayer that the Crown should be 'delivered from the sins and transgressions of those preceding His Majesty King Charles II'. At the subsequent banquet, Charles expressed 'much joy in that I am the first Covenanted King of Scotland'. He kept a straight face, and a few days later, at Stirling, consented to pray with Argyll for several hours. Both wept. Argyll was overcome by the high emotion of the night. His wife told him the King had shed only 'crocodile tears'. 'This night,' she added, 'will cost you your life.'[8]

At the price of humiliation, deceit and hours of boredom, Charles had achieved his first aim: to be a crowned king. He now proceeded to gather a new army, from which no faction would be excluded; and the Kirk, weakened by the disaster of Dunbar, was unable to prevent him from doing so. Eight months later, in August, he crossed the border at the head of eight thousand foot, two thousand horse and with a small train of rather outdated artillery. He looked to English royalists to rise in support, but the news that he had signed the detestable Covenant and promised to impose Presbyterianism on England – a betrayal of his martyred father – deterred them. They had not yet learned that the son was of a different temper and that his word was not to be relied on. Scotland had taught him hypocrisy; he had learned the lesson well, and never forgot it. Privately, he had already concluded that Presbyterianism was 'no religion for a gentleman', one indeed that he absolutely detested.

The army marched south. David Leslie, general-in-chief, grew more despondent with every mile they travelled into England. He knew too well the quality of Cromwell's men to entertain optimism. When Charles asked him why he seemed so melancholy, he replied that, no matter how well their army looked, it would not fight. He was wrong there. When Cromwell trapped them in Worcester, and they tried to break out, many of the royalists fought with the greatest courage. Charles put himself in the vanguard – as his cousin Rupert had been accustomed to do – and had two horses killed under him. But Leslie was not quite mistaken: his own cavalry took no part in the action. Some have seen treachery in this, even evidence of an understanding with the absent Argyll. The charge is improbable. Leslie was more anxious to get his men safely back to Scotland. In any case, if he had indeed betrayed Charles, he was ill rewarded, for Cromwell clapped him into the Tower of London, where he remained till the Restoration. Charles himself did not regard Leslie as a traitor; he gave him a peerage in 1660, while Argyll was executed, ostensibly for collaborating with Cromwell.

Worcester was fought on 3 September 1651. Cromwell called it his 'crowning mercy'; the King's cause lay trampled in the blood-stained dust. Charles was all for fighting to the last. When Buckingham and his gentleman of the bedchamber, Henry Wilmot, who had fought on the royalist side throughout the civil war and would prove himself Charles's most steadfast friend, urged him to escape, he cried out that he would rather be shot. But either their arguments prevailed, or they succeeded in leading him away from the lost battle.

The next six weeks were the most extraordinary, the most dangerous, the most dramatic, and yet also, in memory at least, the most exhilarating of Charles's life. He was a fugitive, with a price of £1,000 on his head. His wanderings took him over the west Midlands and the south of England. Everywhere he found loyalists ready to risk their lives to protect him and set him on the next stage of his journey. Many were Catholics, and if, in later life, Charles was indeed drawn to Rome, it may partly have been because of the memory of how so many abused, marginalised and persecuted adherents of the proscribed faith had ventured all to see him to safety. He travelled disguised, now, his face and hands stained with walnut juice, as a woodcutter (though he could not master the local accent and was advised to keep quiet – difficult for so talkative a man); now as a groom riding behind the daughter of his supposed employer.

Everywhere there was danger. He had to trust people he had never met before, any of whom, for all he could know, might be tempted by the reward offered, or, if arrested, betray him under torture or its threat. The government proclamation was widely circulated: 'Take notice of Charles Stuart to be a tall man above two yards high, his hair a deep brown near to black, and has been cut off. Expect him under disguise.' That disguise was not easy. Charles, with his height – six foot two inches – his swarthy complexion, inherited from his Medici ancestors, and his grace of manner, did not look like an English countryman. He found difficulty too in walking like a peasant or woodman. He was recognised several times, once by the butler in a house where he lodged; the man, by name Pope, had been falconer to a Cavalier gentleman. A Mrs Hyde, widow to a cousin of his chancellor, knew him straight away, though she had seen him only once when he was still a boy. But nobody betrayed him. One of his early rescuers, Francis Yates, was hanged for refusing to give any information as to where the King had gone or might be found. Yates was brother-in-law to Richard Penderel, whose Catholic family ran terrible risks to save Charles. 'If I ever come into my kingdom,' he said to them, 'I will remember you.'9 Charles, a man who broke promises as easily as he gave them, did not break this one. Very soon after the Restoration, the whole Penderel family were invited to Whitehall, received pensions, and heard the story of his adventures after they had parted from him.

There were several narrow escapes. He spent one day concealed in an oak tree, while Roundhead soldiers searched the woods below him. On another occasion, near Stratford-upon-Avon, while he was riding behind Jane Lane as her groom, they took a roundabout route to avoid a troop of Cromwell's horse, only to find them already in the town. Humour was not always missing from the tales the King would tell of his escape. When his horse cast a shoe and he asked the smith 'What news?' the reply came: 'None that I know of since the good news of the beating of the rogue Scots.' 'Are none of the English taken, that joined with them?' Charles asked. 'I did not hear that the rogue Charles Stuart was taken – some of the others, but not Charles Stuart.' 'If that rogue were taken,' the King said, 'he deserves to be hanged more than all the rest, for bringing in the Scots.' 'You speak like an honest man,' the smith said, holding out his hand. On another occasion a drunken Cavalier squire took Charles for a Roundhead, and pressed drink on him, swearing lustily when the King was reluctant to match him glass for glass. Charles held up his hand, and imitating the characteristic Puritan whine said, 'O, dear brother. Swear not, I beseech you.'

He journeyed now with one companion, now with another,

sometimes joined by Wilmot and sometimes without him when he had gone ahead to seek information. From Worcester he had gone north by way of Kidderminster and Stourbridge, hoping and failing to cross the Severn into royalist Wales. They had then doubled back to Stratford, then south by Cirencester to near Bristol, where they hoped to find a ship, then by way of Castle Cary to Bridport on the same quest. Unsuccessful there, the King was compelled to lie up for twelve days at Trent House, the property of Sir Francis Wyndham. Thence they made their way east, pausing at Stonehenge (where Charles disproved the popular notion that you could not count the stones twice and arrive at the same total) before at last arriving at Brighton, where they learned of a ship berthed at Shoreham chartered by a merchant ready to carry the King to safety. The merchant, Francis Mansell, brought the ship's captain to the inn where they had put up. After they had eaten, the captain, Tattersall, told Mansell he had not dealt fairly with him: 'That is the King. I know him very well.' Mansell denied it, but Tattersall was not convinced. Again he said, to Charles when he boarded the vessel, 'I know Your Majesty very well.' The innkeeper had recognised him also; he proved to have been one of Charles I's household servants. At five o'clock the following morning, 15 October, the King and Wilmot were put ashore at Fecamp on the coast of Normandy. Captain Gunter, the Sussex landowner who had secured Mansell's services and escorted the King to the harbour, was riding home at around the same hour when he was stopped by a troop of Roundhead horse, searching for 'a tall black man, six foot two inches high'.

A few days later Charles arrived in Paris and had to borrow a clean shirt. His mother was delighted to see him safe, but told him he would have to pay for his own dinner, since she couldn't afford to do so.

His weeks on the run provided him with a story that he would tell, again and again, for the rest of his life. It fascinated those who heard it for the first time. On the ship bringing Charles back to England in 1660 the young Samuel Pepys was enthralled when granted the privilege of hearing of the King's adventures. Twenty years later he recorded the story again at Charles's dictation. Those closer to the King soon found the repetition of the narrative to be an appalling bore. But at first everyone was astonished that a king should have had to undergo such experiences. In conversation with Hyde, however, Charles did not conceal that he had sometimes come close to despair. 'I thought that I was paying too high a price for my life.' He added that he owed most to the persecuted Catholics, without whose help he must surely have been taken.[10]

The years that followed were often wretched, full of disappointments. Charles was impoverished, living from hand to mouth, surrounded by men who were themselves frequently lonely, disgruntled and quarrelsome. Projects for royalist risings were brought before him. He encouraged few of them, knowing how little chance they had of success. He watched Cromwell win the respect of European monarchs while he himself was disregarded or insulted, at best employed as an expendable pawn on the diplomatic chessboard. According to the moves of that game, he was at various times made to realise he was unwelcome in France and the Netherlands, and compelled to move on. Cromwell's spies infiltrated his household. Some of his followers made their peace with the dictator. Buckingham, for instance, contrived to return safely to England, where he married Fairfax's daughter, lived off his father-in-law, and posed as a reformed and pious character, acquiring merit among the Independents. To please his new friends, he would say that Charles had shown himself a coward at Worcester. All this came to Charles's ears and was bitter to hear. Nevertheless, he would forgive the Duke; he wasn't a man with whom Charles could ever be angry for long. Sooner or later Buckingham would jest himself back into favour.

The King's character was formed in these years of exile – more accurately, it was deformed. The blithe and affectionate boy became a hardened cynic, taking pleasure where he might find it. Women came easily to him, and he took them as he found them, but none since Lucy Walter captured his heart. The bitterness with which he pursued her in his attempt to get possession of their son was unlike his behaviour to any other of the many women in his life;

evidence that she alone had the ability to hurt him, that perhaps she was the only one he ever truly loved. Now, in his cynical disillusion, masked only by perfect manners, he reserved his affection for the children in the family – his son James, Harry of Gloucester, Minette, William the little Prince of Orange – and his spaniels. None of them plagued him with impossible demands or presented him with impractical plans; none had let him down.

Cromwell died in September 1658. (At the French court La Grande Mademoiselle was the only person to refuse to wear mourning in honour of the dictator.) There was great excitement among the royalists, but this soon died down and was replaced by frustration, for Richard Cromwell took his father's place as Lord Protector. Richard, however, was in office, but not in power. The army had no respect for him, and he soon gave way and retired into private life. The remnant of the old 1640 Parliament, the Rump, was recalled, amidst general derision, expressed in London by a craze for roasting the rumps of cattle, sheep and pigs. General Monk, who had himself been a Cavalier before he was a Roundhead, marched his army from Scotland, and, after much hesitation and sounding of opinion, summoned what was known as a free parliament, elected by the traditional constituencies. By now it was evident in which direction the tide was running, and the parliament, at Monk's request, appointed commissioners to go to the Netherlands and bring the King back. Charles meanwhile had issued a declaration, drawn up by Hyde, in which he promised to defend the Protestant religion. There should be 'liberty of conscience, and a free and general pardon for political offences'.

In these weeks before the offer of restoration was made, Charles had maintained an appearance of impassivity. It was as if he dared not trust his luck. But at last all was confirmed. General Monk had declared for him; so had Parliament and so had the navy, whose commander, Montagu (later Earl of Sandwich), was deputed to bring him home. So rapid had been the transformation that the ship in which Montagu sailed was still called the *Naseby*; it would soon be renamed the *Royal Charles*. Once aboard, the King became animated. He could not keep still but walked the deck and talked and talked. (It was now that he told Pepys the story of his adventures after Worcester.)

They landed at Dover, where Monk awaited them. Charles, dressed in a new dark-coloured suit, but with a scarlet plume in his hat, took Monk in his arms, kissed him on both cheeks, and called him 'Father'. York also kissed him and young Harry Gloucester threw his hat in the air and called out, 'God bless General Monk.' In a few days Monk would be made Duke of Albemarle, and his dumpy wife, Bess, who had once worked as a washerwoman, a happy duchess. Now the Mayor of Dover presented Charles with a Bible. 'It is the thing I love above all things in the world,' the King said.

They paused at Canterbury, where Charles invested Monk with the Order of the Garter, and found time before he went to bed to write a little note to his darling Minette. 'Monk, with a great number of the nobility almost overwhelmed me with kindness and joy for my return. My head is so dreadfully stunned with the acclamations of the people that I know not whether I am writing sense or nonsense.'

On the afternoon of 29 May, which happened to be his thirtieth birthday, Charles entered London by way of Blackheath, and rode past Temple Bar, along the Strand to Westminster, where the two Houses of Parliament were assembled to receive him. John Evelyn, watching the procession make its way along the Strand, was amazed: 'And all this without one drop of blood, and by that very Army that rebelled against him. Such a Restoration was never seen in the mention of any history, not so joyful a day and so bright.'[11]

Charles came to Whitehall and paused by the gateway of the banqueting hall, looking up at the window from which his father had stepped out to the scaffold. Then he met the parliamentarians, and after their loyal and adulatory addresses, he gave utterance to the most honest words he had spoken that crowded day: 'The laws and liberties of my people and the Protestant religion – next to my life and crown – I will preserve.' Few probably caught the full significance of the words 'next to my life and crown', but in them Charles gave vent to the one principle he would maintain throughout his reign: his determination never – no matter what happened – to go on his travels again.

A little later, in the palace, he looked round the assembled throng and smiled: 'I doubt it has been my own fault I have been absent for so long – for I see nobody that does not protest he has ever wished for my return.' He paused, to allow the embarrassed laughter to die away, and then, striking the note of irony still more clearly, asked, 'Where are all my enemies?'

The King was back, but the restored monarchy was that of 1641, not 1640. The measures passed in the first year of the Long Parliament that had been granted royal approval, however reluctantly, were not rescinded. The prerogative courts, those instruments by which the Tudors and the first two Stuarts had been able to practise authoritarian government, had been abolished, and were not revived. The principle that taxation required the consent of Parliament was firmly established. The right to those old feudal dues by means of which Charles I had so vexatiously raised extra-parliamentary revenue was surrendered. In exchange, Parliament guaranteed the King an income (mostly from customs and excise), which regularly amounted to £1,200,000 a year. (It was never enough till, in the last years of the reign, a trade boom brought in more than expected.) Divine right was dead, even though the Church of England clergy now taught that it was sinful to resist the royal pleasure. Nevertheless, the fact remained that, though Charles was king by hereditary right, he had been recalled to the throne by his people, and his survival required that he should never forget the significance of the civil war and his father's trial, condemnation and death.

He had promised indemnity for his enemies, and that promise was for the most part kept, an exception being made only for the regicides, those who had signed the warrant for the King's execution. (Even so, some escaped death, among them Henry Marten, who had shocked Hyde so long ago by questioning the right of any single person to govern the country.) Compromise was necessary, for those who had effected the restoration were servants of the republic. So, for instance, royalists whose estates had been confiscated regained them, but those who had sold them, whether from financial necessity or by compulsion, did not. The new parliament, though composed largely of Cavaliers and Church of England men, was induced to pass an Act of Indemnity and Oblivion; 'Indemnity for the King's enemies and oblivion for his friends,' some said bitterly. There was to be no purge.

Yet the Cavalier Parliament, as it was to be called, took its revenge in its own manner. A series of acts were passed that severely restricted the freedom of those who were now known as Dissenters or Nonconformists – Presbyterians and Independents. The Cavalier squires had been frightened and humiliated, and were determined to take care that their enemies should be afflicted in their turn, and their own supremacy confirmed by law. This was not to the King's taste. In matters of religion he was indifferent. He once told Burnet that he was no atheist, but did not think God would damn a man for taking a little pleasure. Nor were these acts approved by the chancellor, Hyde (now made Earl of Clarendon), though historians were to give them the name of the Clarendon Code; good Anglican though he was, he had too much sense.

There was a new mood in the country. After the discord of the civil war and the moral rigour of the republic, it was a time for licence. The King himself set the tone: 'Cuckolds all awry, the old dance of England.' He spent the first nights of his reign in bed with the luscious Barbara Palmer, wife of a Cavalier squire. Their liaison would last a dozen years; Barbara would bear him five children and become, successively, Lady Castlemaine and Duchess of Cleveland. Neither was faithful, nor demanded fidelity, though Barbara might be jealous of rivals. Her own lovers included a celebrated tight-rope dancer, Jacob Hall, whom she had picked up at Bartholomew Fair, and a young officer, John Churchill, scarcely out of his teens. On one occasion, when the King knocked at his mistress's door, Churchill had to gather his clothes and leap out of the window. On another, Charles caught the pair 'in flagrante delicto', but forgave Churchill because, he said, 'you are a rascal but you do it for your bread'. Barbara was extravagant and ill-tempered, fond of making scenes, something the King detested; so he generally gave way to avoid them or calm her.

A rival to Lady Castlemaine appeared. This was Frances Stewart, whose grandfather, Walter Stewart (later Lord Blantyre), had been a schoolfellow of James VI, subjected like him to the stern discipline and sharp tongue of George Buchanan. Later he had been Lord Treasurer of Scotland, and one of the commissioners charged with drawing up plans for the complete union of Scotland and England. Frances had been brought up in France and spoke French better than English. Recognising the challenge she posed, Lady Castlemaine made a friend of the newcomer, inviting her to all her entertainments and often keeping her overnight, so that when the King made his regular morning call on his mistress, he often found the two beauties in bed together. 'It was hardly possible,' Anthony Hamilton wrote of Frances, 'for a woman to have had less wit or more beauty . . . She was childish in her behaviour, and laughed at everything, and her taste for frivolous amusements, though unaffected, was only allowable in a little girl of about twelve or thirteen years old . . . "Blind man's buff" was her most favourite amusement'[12] – but she was also very fond of building card houses. Nevertheless, she had wit enough to hold the King off,[13] and eventually married the Duke of Lennox and Richmond, a grandson of James VI's cousin and favourite, Esmé Stuart. Her beauty attracted praise from all, and was such that she sat for the King's engraver of the Mint and was represented as the figure of Britannia on the copper coinage.

Meanwhile the King had married. His bride was Catherine of Braganza, a Portuguese princess with little but her birth and dowry (which included the gift of the city of Tangier) to recommend her. She was a devout Roman Catholic, spoke no English on her arrival and never learned the language properly. Her eating habits were said to be disagreeable. She played little part in the life of the court, was never suspected of infidelity, and failed in the principal duty of queens, which is to produce an heir. Nobody could doubt, given the frequency with which the King's mistresses gave birth, that the incapacity was hers. In time she fell in love with Charles, as most women did, and he displayed a tolerant affection for her. She loathed, and probably feared, Lady Castlemaine.

The theatres, closed down by the Puritans, had reopened, and for the first time women appeared on the professional stage. The King delighted in plays, as did so many of his subjects, among them the amorous Pepys. Nobody then expected virtue of actresses – old-fashioned folk thought them little better than common prostitutes – and the King was not long in finding that the stage could supply him with lovers every bit as agreeable as might be found at court. There was, for example, Moll Davis, whose singing of 'wild and mad songs' charmed the King. She held his affections for some time, a daughter who was to marry the Earl of Derwentwater being born in 1673.

More famous than Moll Davis was the cockney girl Nell Gwyn. She was said to have been born in a night-cellar, to have sold oranges at Covent Garden (or alternatively to have hawked baskets of fish round the streets), to have wandered from tavern to tavern amusing the company by her songs, before going on the stage, where she excelled in comic parts. She was light-hearted, gave herself no airs and was, according to Burnet, 'such a constant diversion to the king, that even a new mistress could not drive her away'. Castlemaine made scenes, but Nell made Charles laugh, which was the secret of her hold on him.

The years of exile had promoted a strong family feeling, though Charles had found his mother intensely irritating; and the Restoration promised them all a scarcely looked-for happiness. But Harry Gloucester died of the smallpox in 1661, and his elder sister Mary, the Princess of Orange, of the same disease shortly afterwards. Elizabeth of Bohemia returned to the England she had left on the occasion of her marriage half a century ago, and her favourite child, Prince Rupert, the King's boyhood hero, came back too. But Elizabeth died in 1662, and Rupert, an amateur scientist, preferred his laboratory to the frivolity of the court; he too took up with an actress, Margaret Hughes, said to be the first woman to have played the part of Desdemona in *Othello*, with whom he had a daughter, Ruperta. The adored Minette was still in France, married to Louis's brother Philippe, Duc d'Orleans. It was not a happy marriage. Monsieur, effeminate, bejewelled, wearing high heels (for he was very short) and rouging his cheeks, was in love with the Chevalier de Lorraine rather than his wife, while Minette engaged in a flirtation with Louis, till she realised his target was one of her ladies-in-waiting, a charming girl called Louise de la Vallière, whose religious scruples did not permit her to surrender her virtue to the King till her confessor assured her it was her duty to do so.

Of the brothers and sisters only James, Duke of York, was left in London, and he was giving trouble. He had got the chancellor's daughter, Anne Hyde, pregnant, and, as a well-brought-up girl, she was holding out for marriage. Henrietta Maria came hurrying over from France to try to put a stop to this unsuitable match; apart from Anne not being royal, the Queen had long detested Clarendon and had had many fierce arguments with him during the years of exile. As it happened, Clarendon himself was appalled. But Charles, perhaps with a touch of mockery, insisted his brother do the right thing: marry the girl, or, since she claimed they were already wed, own up to the marriage. So it went ahead, and James might indeed have done much worse, for Anne was a sensible woman. They had two daughters, Mary and Anne, and things might have gone better for James if she had not died in 1671.

Almost from the day of the King's return, his court acquired a reputation for debauchery and dissipation. In August 1661, Samuel Pepys, who had not yet shaken off his Puritan upbringing, thought that 'things are in very ill condition, there being so much emulation, poverty, and the vices of drinking, swearing and loose amours, that I know not what will be the end of it but confusion'. But for young men and women from a less severe background, it was a merry place, and these were wonderful times. In any case it is hard to blame the returned exiles for revelling in the long-hoped-for but scarcely expected turn of fortune.

The King seemed idle. He often was idle, preferring to chat with his mistresses or play with his spaniels, to stroll in St James's Park, play tennis or ride at Newmarket, rather than attend to the business of government. But he had his serious side too. He cared deeply for the condition of the navy, as did York, Lord High Admiral, to whom little Mr Pepys had attached himself at the beginning of a career that would see him become an exemplary, honest and industrious civil servant. Charles was no aesthete like his father, but he took more than a layman's intelligent interest in science. In the last years of the republic, a group of learned men and amateurs had formed the habit of meeting to discuss scientific matters. Charles was interested in their work, gave them his patronage, and the Royal Society was incorporated in 1662. The King became a member, joining Christopher Wren, Robert Boyle, Earl of Cork, who defined the chemical element as an entity that could not be decomposed into constituents, and a little later, the greatest scientist of the age, Isaac Newton. Some of the members, such as Prince Rupert, John Aubrey and indeed Pepys, who was elected a fellow in 1664, might be fairly described as dilettanti (though Pepys was to be the Society's president in 1684); but the foundation of the Royal Society may be accounted one of the most notable and important acts of Charles's reign.

Charles might dislike business, prefer to pose as a flaneur, and for the first years of the reign leave most of it in Clarendon's capable hands; he might dismiss criticism with a jest and when presented with Rochester's[14] mock epitaph – 'Here lies our Sovereign Lord the King, / Whose word no man relies on; / Who never said a foolish thing / And never did a wise one' – lightly acknowledge its truth with the quip that his words were his own, but his acts were his minsters'; but in reality he had perfected a technique that suited his harshly acquired habit of dissimulation. Always approachable, always affable, apparently living for pleasure, idling the hours away, he concealed a powerful will, a shrewd determination to have his own way, and a distrust of Church and Parliament. Even his contempt for religious or political enthusiasm was expressed with a sunny irony. Only occasionally did the mask slip, but even then he usually lied his way out of trouble.

Much routine business might be neglected; it bored him. But foreign policy was, to his mind, his own affair. Fortunately in the early years of the reign, the King and Parliament were of one mind on the subject. The enemy were the Dutch, England's chief commercial rivals. In opposing them there was continuity with Cromwell.

The First Dutch War (1652–4) had been fought by the republic; the second one broke out in 1665. At first it went well. The fleet, commanded by York, won a convincing victory off Lowestoft, and Dutch colonies in America were seized. But that summer plague broke out virulently in London. It was followed in September 1666 by the Great Fire, which destroyed old St Paul's and raged from London Bridge to Fleet Street decimating the medieval and Tudor city. There was also a financial crisis. Parliament, though it had clamoured for war, refused further supplies. The Dutch sailed up the Medway and towed away the *Royal Charles*. Recovery the next year, when Monk and Rupert fought a battle in the Downs and drove the Dutch fleet back to its own ports, scarcely assuaged the bitterness of the previous year's humiliation. The terms of the peace treaty signed at Dover in 1667 met with disapproval, though England kept her transatlantic conquests and New Amsterdam became New York. The Commons was in an uproar, and Clarendon, blamed for the treaty, was sacrificed to appease them. He retired grumbling to France, to resume work on his *History of the Great Rebellion*, a work more valuable to posterity than anything he might yet have accomplished as a minister.

The new administration was known as the Cabal, a sobriquet formed from the first letter of the names of its five leading members: Clifford, Arlington, Buckingham, Ashley, Lauderdale. The term, suggestive of close, even secretive, collaboration, is misleading. Each minister had his own duties. They did not work together, and the principle of collective ministerial responsibility would not emerge for another hundred years. The group had only one thing in common: none was a member of the Church of England. Clifford had been born, and remained, a Catholic; Arlington, as Henry Bennet a companion of the King during the years of exile, was a Catholic convert; Buckingham, since his marriage, posed as an Independent, the champion of the sects – Charles now nicknamed him 'Alderman George'[15]; Ashley, later the Earl of Shaftesbury, was a Presbyterian who had served in Cromwell's administration; Lauderdale was a Scotch Presbyterian. This was not a ministry to commend itself to the orthodox Anglicans of the Cavalier Parliament.

Charles since his unhappy experiences there disliked, even detested, Scotland. Certainly he had no intention of ever returning, and was content to leave its management to Lauderdale. Uncouth in manner, red-haired, greedy, hard-drinking and with the unpleasant habit of 'bedewing all he talked to', because 'his tongue was too big for his mouth', Lauderdale was also intelligent and widely read, 'not only in Latin, but also in Greek and Hebrew'. He was deeply versed in theology, but in the Chapel Royal a preacher once cried out to him, 'My lord, my lord, you snore so loud you will wake the King.' Charles trusted him, saying he would 'venture Lauderdale with any man in Europe for prudence and courage'.[16] He had been a Covenanter, an Engager, and then a royalist. Imprisoned in the Tower after Worcester, he had read Hobbes's *Leviathan*, and, surveying the confusion of Scotland, had concluded that the government of the saints could be as regardless of law and custom as any absolute king. Monarchy, supported by a loyal aristocracy, offered the best chance of stability. He was happy to impose bishops on the Kirk to secure discipline. His policy met with some success, but the extreme Covenanters could not be appeased. Rejecting the royal government, they were subject to intermittent persecution, and responded by rebellion and acts of terrorism, chief among them the murder of James Sharp, Archbishop of St Andrews, by a gang of zealots acting in the name of God and the Covenant.

France had been allied to the Dutch, if not very effectively, in the recent war, and the King was now eager to bring about a reorientation in foreign policy. He envied his cousin Louis's absolute mastery in his state, though mocking the extreme formality of the French court – 'He cannot piss,' he said, 'but someone must hold the pot for him.' Negotiations for a French alliance were opened, and went so well that in 1670 Louis sent Minette to Dover to sign a treaty on his behalf. Charles was delighted to see his little sister again and all went swimmingly. The public treaty sealed an alliance between the countries and cousins; secret clauses provided Charles with a French pension in exchange for a promise to declare himself a Catholic and re-establish Catholicism in England. This

promise was to be fulfilled when Charles judged the time to be
ripe. It never would be; Charles knew the temper of his people too
well to believe it possible. But promises cost nothing and he needed
the money. Perhaps it also pleased him to please Minette.

It was his last opportunity to do so. She died very soon after
her return to France, only eight hours after being taken ill. There
were, as usual, rumours of poison, administered, it was said, by
the order of her jealous husband. The little Duc de Saint-Simon in
his *Memoirs of Louis XIV and the Regency* declared that the guilty
men were two friends of Monsieur's lover, the Chevalier, who had
been exiled and was then in Rome. Asked whether Monsieur himself
had been involved, they said, 'No; it was well-known that he was
incapable of keeping any secret.'[17] Voltaire, in his history of Louis's
reign, thought the story ridiculous. 'Human malice and the love
of the extraordinary were the sole reasons for this general persuasion.' Minette 'had long suffered from an abscess in the liver. She
was in a very bad state of health, and had also been delivered of
a still-born child . . . Mankind would indeed be unhappy were it
as common to commit atrocious crimes as to believe them,'[18] he
added, speaking with the voice of eighteenth-century sceptical
Reason. Be that as it may, her death cast a gloom on both the
French and English courts. The incomparable letter-writer Madame
de Sevigné said that 'All happiness, attractiveness and pleasure have
gone out of the Court with her.'[19] They had even more surely gone
from Charles's life. The family was contracting sharply. Their
mother, Henrietta Maria, had died the previous year in the French
convent to which she had retired, and now only the King and York
were left.

The King, however, had a new mistress. Louise de Kérouaille
had come to Dover as a member of Minette's household. Charles
was immediately taken by her baby-faced beauty, and when she
returned to England a few months after Minette's death, originally
at the suggestion of Buckingham, who thought he could use her
to control the King, Charles quickly took her to his bed. He called
her 'Fubbs' and made her Duchess of Portsmouth; while a son,
born a couple of years later, was given the titles of Duke of

Richmond and Earl of March in England, and Duke of Lennox and Earl of Darnley in Scotland, the previous holder of them, Frances Stewart's husband, having conveniently died without a male heir.[20] 'Fubbs' was unpopular, regarded as a French spy, which she may well have been, for Louis XIV made her Duchess d'Aubigny (a title held by the Lennox Stewarts), ostensibly as a mark of his friendship for his cousin of England. Nell Gwyn laughed at the new Duchess's pretensions, and once, when her coach was stoned by a crowd who mistook it for Louise's, thrust her head out of the window and told them they were making a mistake because she was 'the Protestant whore'.

The treaty provoked suspicion. 'The public articles are bad enough,' said one Member of Parliament. 'What then may the secret articles be like?'[21] Only the two Catholic ministers of the Cabal had known of them. Disgruntled, Shaftesbury and Buckingham resigned office, and drifted into opposition, steadfast in Shaftesbury's case, characteristically whimsical and flippant in Buckingham's.

The first crisis year of the reign was 1672. France attacked the Netherlands, threatening to overrun the country, which alarmed English Protestants, who from now on saw France, rather than Spain, which was in decline, as the menacing Catholic power, and accordingly questioned the alliance made at Dover. Then there was revolution in Holland, directed against the pro-French republican oligarchy, whose policy of appeasement had failed to prevent war. Its leader, Jan de Witt, and his brother Cornelius were murdered by a mob, and Charles's nephew, William, Prince of Orange, was made Stadtholder at the age of twenty-two and given command of the army. Though he was no great general, William's courage, tenacity and committed defiance of Louis XIV would make him the centrepiece of coalitions resisting French aggression for the next thirty years, and the hero of Protestant Europe.

With unusually poor timing, Charles chose this moment to issue a Declaration of Indulgence, suspending repressive religious laws, and offering freedom of worship to Protestant Dissenters and Roman Catholics alike. The Commons, dominated by Anglican squires, was furious. Even the Dissenters were suspicious. Like the Trojan, they feared the Greeks even when bearing gifts. Enough was now known, or at least suspected, of the secret clauses in the Dover treaty to make the Declaration seem like the first steps in a plot against Protestant England. Charles, knowing, as his father had not, when to yield, withdrew the Declaration. Parliament responded by passing a Test Act in 1673, which required anyone holding public office or a commission in the army or navy to take communion according to the rites of the Church of England and to affirm their belief in its Thirty-Nine Articles of Religion. Charles gave his assent to the act as the only means of getting Parliament to grant sufficient money to enable him to continue to put the Fleet to sea against the Dutch. Despite a victory gained at Southwold Bay in May 1672, the war was inconclusive. It was also increasingly unpopular, for there were many in Parliament who had come to believe that it was the French rather than the Dutch who now offered the most serious threat to England's interest. Meanwhile Clifford, fearing impeachment for his part in the Dover treaty, cut his own throat. York, as a Catholic convert, was compelled to resign the office of Lord High Admiral. Charles bent with the wind and appointed the Anglican Lord Danby as his chief minister.

Three years later, in 1676, Danby, preferring a Dutch to a French alliance, arranged a marriage between York's elder daughter, Mary, and William of Orange. Charles consented happily enough. In the years of exile, he had been very fond of William as a small boy, finding him pretty, intelligent, spirited and original. He called him 'Piccinino' and would have been happy to spoil him, until the boy's mother, Charles's sister Mary, made a jealous scene about his interest in her son. Something of his affection for him may have remained, though he may also have found it difficult to recognise the pretty child who had amused him in the chilly and reserved manner of the young man.

The political nation was restive, many displeased by the King's reluctance to enter into an effective alliance to check French expansionism, though it was difficult to see how this threatened British interests, and it was in any case brought to a temporary halt when a treaty was signed at Nimuegen in 1678. Others were alarmed by the prospect of the succession of the Catholic Duke of York to his brother's throne. The opposition politicians led by Shaftesbury began to talk of seeking a means either of changing the succession or of imposing new limits on the power of the Crown. They were now known as Whigs, the name taken from the Scotch Covenanting rebels, while the loyalists began to be called Tories – Irish Catholic brigands. It was into this inflamed and excitable atmosphere that there now entered the extraordinary figure of Titus Oates.

Oates was a scoundrel, a pathological fantasist and liar, whose career had hitherto been erratic. Ordained as a clergyman of the Church of England, he had been imprisoned for falsely accusing a schoolmaster of indecent relations with his pupils. He had then secured a chaplaincy in the navy and been dismissed from that post on suspicion of sodomy. He converted, or pretended to convert, to Catholicism, studied at a Jesuit college at Valladolid in Spain, from which he was also duly expelled, and then from another at St Omer in France. Now in 1678, claiming to be a doctor of divinity from the University of Salamanca, he reappeared in London and declared that he had evidence of a vile popish plot to assassinate the King and massacre Protestants. He laid information before a magistrate, Sir Edmund Berry Godfrey, who, a few days later, was found stabbed to death on Primrose Hill. The crime was never solved. (It would be nice to think Oates himself had killed Godfrey to add credibility to his outrageous lies.) London was in a fever of excitement. Oates appeared before the Privy Council. The King cross-questioned him and caught him out in lies and contradictions, but it was to no avail. The Salamanca doctor was the hero of the hour, hailed as a Protestant hero. Catholics were arrested, tried and convicted by excited juries on Oates's evidence. Among them was York's Jesuit chaplain, Father Coleman, whose papers did indeed suggest that he looked forward to the day when his Catholic master should sit on his brother's throne. But that was all. Charles, temporising till the fire died down, signed death warrants for innocent men, reluctantly but reprehensibly. 'Let the blood lie on those who condemned them, for God knows I sign with tears in my eyes.'[22]

It was a witch-hunt, the fires stoked by the Whigs. For the moment everything seemed to be going their way. In Scotland the extreme Covenanters were now in open rebellion, though this was checked by the royal army commanded by the Duke of Monmouth, already with military experience in the Dutch army led by his cousin, William of Orange; he further enhanced his reputation by displaying moderation in victory and unusual humanity to the defeated. Meanwhile in London there were echoes of 1640–41 as the opposition seemed to be carrying all before them. But Charles, unlike his father, knew how to give the impression of yielding without in fact doing so, and played for time. Danby had been impeached on charges of corruption by the Whigs and sent to the Tower. Charles dissolved Parliament to halt the impeachment, and called a new one in which, however, the Whigs were still in the ascendant. He made known to those around him his distrust of Shaftesbury, whom he called 'Little Sincerity'. Attending a perform-ance of *Macbeth*, the King loudly remarked when the murderers came on the stage, 'Pray, what is the reason that we never see a rogue in a play, but – odds fish – they always clap on him a black periwig, when it is well known the greatest rogue in England wears a fair one?'[23] And he warned Shaftesbury himself: 'My lord, let there be no self-delusion. I am none of those that grow more timorous with age – rather, I grow more resolute; the nearer I am to the grave, I intend to take a greater care of my own preserva-tion – and that of my people.'[24] He resisted even Tory suggestions that he might defuse the crisis by divorcing his wife and marrying again in the hope that a new wife would provide him with a legit-imate son: 'She is a weak woman,' he said of Catherine, 'and has some disagreeable humours, but, considering my faultiness towards her, I think it a horrid thing to abandon her.'[25] He knew the popish plot was nonsense: 'Brother,' he told York, 'I am sure no man in England will take away my life to make you king.'[26] He was loyal to his brother and determined to secure his succession. So he continued to temporise.

Then Shaftesbury blundered. If York was to be excluded, then the crown should pass to his elder daughter Mary, wife of the

Protestant hero William of Orange. But Shaftesbury had inherited the Cromwellian hostility to the Dutch, and was also himself in receipt of a pension from Louis XIV (for the French king in Machiavellian style played both sides, to keep England in turmoil and preclude the danger of effective intervention on the Continent). So 'Little Sincerity' promoted Monmouth, the Protestant duke, as his candidate for the throne, and his supporters spoke enthusiastically of 'the Black Box' in which were lodged papers that would prove Charles had married Lucy Walter long ago and that Monmouth was therefore his legitimate son and heir.

Charles had always denied the marriage; he continued to do so. Monmouth might be his favourite child. He had always delighted in his beauty, charm and high spirits, but he had no great opinion of his judgement, intelligence or good sense. He was displeased to see the young man being used by his enemies, and making a tour of the West Country, where he was received with joy and acclamation. Moreover, Charles knew that the Whigs' aim was not only to change the succession, but to weaken the Crown. He had already sent James away, first to Holland and then to act as his viceroy in Scotland. Now he ordered Monmouth to go abroad too, while assuring him privately that he would always love him.

He offered the Whigs a compromise. He would agree to limitations being placed on his successor's power. In making this offer he followed the advice of a new minister, the Earl of Halifax. It is probable that Charles was not sincere, equally likely that he made the offer in the certainty that it would not satisfy the Whigs, now determined on passing an act to exclude James from the throne. If so, he had calculated well. The offer was refused, and moderate opinion shifted against Shaftesbury. Royal propaganda became more effective. John Dryden, Poet Laureate since 1668, published *Absalom and Achitophel*, a masterpiece of political satire, in which he pointed up the parallel between the Whigs' plotting and the Old Testament account of the rebellion against King David, nominally led by his favourite son, Absalom. Shaftesbury and Buckingham were vigorously lampooned. Shaftesbury, as 'the false Achitophel, A name to all succeeding ages cursed': 'Great wits are sure to madness near allied, / And thin partitions do their walls divide.' As for Buckingham, he appeared as Zimri: 'Stiff in opinions, always in the wrong, / Was everything by starts, and nothing long.' A near insane fanatic and one who 'in the course of each revolving moon, / Was chemist, fiddler, statesman, and buffoon': these were the chiefs of the Whig party, as presented by the King's poet.[27]

The tide was now running strongly against the Whigs. In 1681 Charles called a new parliament to meet at royalist Oxford, away from the influence of any London mob that Shaftesbury might stir up. 'Remember your royal father and keep the staff in your own hand,' one called out as he rode into the city. 'By God I shall,' replied the King.[28] But there was no danger now, no need for force. The storm had blown itself out, the turbulence was spent. Charles made his determination clear – there would be no Exclusion – and dismissed the parliament. Shaftesbury fled to Holland, where he died in 1683: Buckingham, reputation gone and fortune going, dwindled into insignificance, and would also soon be dead. Monmouth remained in exile. York returned to London, and Charles strolled with his spaniels in St James's Park.

For the last four years of his reign, the King ruled without Parliament. At last he had money enough, thanks partly to payments from Cousin Louis, partly to the revival of trade and the consequent increase in revenue from customs. He had achieved his aim. There was no fear that he would ever have to go on his travels again (though he expressed his suspicion that his brother might). Only the occasional threat from Barillon, the French ambassador, to reveal the terms of his agreement with his master in Versailles could disturb the King's equanimity, and for the most part life was good. In 1683 a wild conspiracy to assassinate the royal brothers as they rode to Newmarket – the Rye House Plot – was discovered, and Charles used this to further stabilise his position. A number of Whigs, not all closely connected with the plot, were executed. London, always troublesome, had its charter called in, revised and reissued in such terms as to ensure the election of a Tory corporation. When a deputation of gentlemen from Berkshire urged the King to call a Parliament, he smiled and said, 'I marvel that my neighbours should meddle with my business – but we shall agree better when we meet over a cup of ale at Windsor' – and they departed, flattered by his attention, won over by his charm, if also puzzled to reflect that they had come away from his presence happy though they had received nothing.[29]

Charles had suffered a mild stroke at the height of the furore over the Popish Plot and the Exclusion, but his health still seemed good except that he was inclined to fall asleep after dinner. He walked in the park without guards and rode his horse at Newmarket, and was ready to converse with anyone on any topic. He still told his stories, though many of them were old, and his bored courtiers had heard them too often. He paid polite attention to his Queen and more agreeable attention to his mistresses, as if the shadows were not lengthening. But Rupert had died in 1682, Buckingham was no longer there to amuse him, and Monmouth could not safely be brought home. York remained, of course, but though Charles was fond of his brother, he had seldom found much amusement in his company.

Then on 1 February 1685, he had another stroke. The doctors averred he could not live more than a few hours. But he rallied, and bells were rung to celebrate his recovery. Prematurely; another stroke days later and he began to sink, rousing himself only to apologise for being 'such an unconscionable time a-dying'. Still, when the Anglican clergy surrounding his bedside urged him to receive the sacraments of the Church, he said, 'Time enough' and dismissed them.

A Roman Catholic priest, Father Huddleston, was brought to him. He had been one of those who had aided Charles's escape in the first days after Worcester, and had now been living in the Palace of Whitehall for some sixteen years. 'Here,' said York, 'is a man who once saved your life, and is now come to save your soul.'[30] So in his last hours, the great sceptic was received into the Church of Rome and given absolution. He had at last kept one part of the promise he had made to Minette and Cousin Louis when he signed that treaty at Dover, but the England he left behind was still as overwhelmingly and defiantly Protestant as he had always known it to be. Was he sincere in this deathbed repentance and conversion? Perhaps. A twentieth-century convert to Catholicism, G. K. Chesterton imagined that in this last act of his life Charles expressed his perfect scepticism: 'The wafer might, or might not be, the Body of Christ; but then it might, or might not, be a wafer.'[31]

'Let not poor Nelly starve,' Charles said to his brother, and asked him to tell Fubbs, the Duchess of Portsmouth, how much he loved her. He requested to be lifted up so that he might see the day break once more, and soon afterwards, the most intelligent, charming and deceitful of Stuart kings was dead.

Chapter 14

James VII and II (1685–88): Author of His Own Tragedy

There was an old saying in Scotland that the Stewarts were like the horses reared in the Aberdeenshire district of Mar, excellent when young, deteriorating more quickly than most. Few of the kings after the two Roberts lived to be old; nevertheless, signs of rapid deterioration were evident in James I and James V, while in the last years of his reign, James VI and I was evidently no longer the energetic and capable king he had been in Scotland. To none of the family, however, is the judgement more surely applied than to James VII and II.

James inherited a secure throne, thanks to the skill, determination and loyalty of his brother. He was even popular at first, for there was a strong reaction in his favour. Yet in less than four years he had lost the support of the Crown's fervent defenders, the Church of England men; provoked some of his greatest, or at least richest, subjects to enter into treasonable negotiations with a foreign power and solicit the invasion of England; then found himself deserted by those in whom he had placed most trust; lost his nerve and fled his kingdom. For all this to happen demanded a quite remarkable degree of folly.

As we have seen, James when a young man was highly thought of. He was known to be brave; he was believed, quite rightly, to be honest, a man of his word unlike his charming brother. Nobody thought him intelligent, but he was loyal, affable, and proved himself, as Lord High Admiral, to be a capable and conscientious administrator. Highly sexed, like most of the family, he had a succession of mistresses. There was nothing remarkable in that, except perhaps that they were generally thought unattractive, even ugly. After York's conversion to Catholicism, Charles joked that he thought his brother's mistresses must be given to him by his priests as a penance; but it is more likely that James was shy and maladroit, and found it easier to seduce plain women than beautiful ones. The most famous of his mistresses was Arabella Churchill, daughter of a West Country Cavalier squire and Member of Parliament, Sir Winston Churchill. Anthony Hamilton described her as 'a tall creature, pale-faced, and nothing but skin and bone'. He revised his opinion, however, when she fell from her horse, and those who crowded round 'found her in a negligent posture; they could hardly believe that limbs of such exquisite beauty could belong to Miss Churchill's face'.[1] James had three children by her: James, who was made Duke of Berwick and became a marshal of France; Henry, who was made titular Duke of Albemarle after the revolution of 1688; and a daughter, Henrietta, who married Lord Waldegrave. More important however was Arabella's brother, John Churchill, whom we have met as the lover of Lady Castlemaine and who would much later become famous as the Duke of Marlborough and England's greatest commander. James regarded him with affection, treated him as his protégé, and advanced his career.

The most significant event of James's early life was his conversion to the Roman Catholic faith. He had been a zealous Church of England man; he was now an utterly devoted Catholic. His sincerity cannot be questioned. His faith nearly caused him to be excluded from the succession; his determination to further the interests of his Church as he understood them cost him his throne. There was nothing in him of his brother's cynical flexibility or of the temper that had led their grandfather, Henry of Navarre, to slough off his Protestantism and convert to Rome in order to win acceptance as Henry IV of France. Had James remained a Church of England man, he might have had a successful, even glorious reign, for he was unquestionably patriotic, and in character and narrow range of interests far more in tune with Cavalier Tories than his sceptical brother had ever been. Indeed, he was as stupid as any rude country squire.

He was popular in the first months of his reign. Many were relieved that the succession had passed off without incident. Others felt ashamed that the country had come so close to depriving James of what was his by right. So his first Parliament was as easy as any parliament of any Stuart king, and it happily voted him a larger revenue than his brother had ever been granted.

Nevertheless, two rebellions broke out in 1685, one in Scotland, led by the Marquis of Argyll, son of the Covenanter who had crowned Charles II at Scone and been executed after the Restoration; the other in England led by Monmouth. Both were futile, ill prepared, ill co-ordinated, and both, as it proved, found negligible support. Argyll's was quickly suppressed; he followed his father to the block. Monmouth had been living in Holland, but understandably received neither encouragement nor support from William of Orange, whose own wife Mary was James's legitimate heir. The rebellion was an act of utter folly, for Monmouth was a sufficiently experienced soldier to know how little chance a hastily raised army could have against regular troops. If he had any expectation that the Whig nobility who had supported his claim to the throne during the Exclusion crisis would now support him, he was sorely deluded. But still he made the venture, and, on landing at Lyme in Dorset, issued a proclamation that made assertions no reasonable man could believe. Apart from declaring his own legitimacy, he accused James of being responsible for the Great Fire of London, with engaging in conspiracy against Charles (the Popish Plot), with commissioning the murder of Sir Edmund Berry Godfrey, and with poisoning his own brother, Monmouth's father. This was a tissue of absurdities. He further declared that the King's religion debarred him from the throne, that three successive parliaments had voted for his exclusion, and that the present parliament was no true representative of the nation. Finally, he declared himself to be the rightful king.

The rebellion was a wild gamble. Probably there was never any chance of success. Failure was however made more certain by Monmouth's indecision. Instead of marching with such support as he had gathered to Bristol or Exeter, cities with a Roundhead tradition, he delayed at Lyme, doubtless hoping that some men of standing would join him. But this hesitation allowed the government to bring troops from Scotland and time for the arrival of an English regiment from the Dutch service, which the Prince of Orange had dispatched to assist his father-in-law. Eventually when the royal army was assembled at Sedgemoor under the command of Lord Feversham and John Churchill, Monmouth resolved on a night attack. The ground had been incompetently reconnoitred, the attack foundered at an open ditch, all was soon seen to be lost, and Monmouth fled. He was taken prisoner three days later, found in a ditch, miserable, hungry and wholly demoralised. He was brought to London, where Parliament had already passed an act of attainder against him. He sought an audience with his uncle the King, which was granted. He protested that he had signed his declaration without reading it, said he had been led on by evil men, and offered to convert to Catholicism if the King would spare his life. James was ready to send him a priest, but refused to commute the sentence.

Macaulay's account of this interview is indignant and scornful: 'The King cannot be blamed for determining that Monmouth should suffer death . . . But to see him and not spare him was an outrage on humanity and decency.' Yet Monmouth himself had begged for the meeting and, as Macaulay recorded, had claimed to be in possession of 'a secret which he could not entrust to paper, a secret which lay in a single word, and which, if he spoke that word, would secure the throne against all danger'.[2] There was in truth no such secret, but it is unreasonable to blame James for granting an interview in which it was, apparently, to be divulged. As for the poor Duke, the historian condemns his 'pusillanimous fear' and writes contemptuously of his abject behaviour. No doubt Monmouth behaved badly, worse than many of his wretched followers. But historians have rarely had their own courage and resolution put to such a test, or found themselves in danger of having their head struck off by an axe.

Punishment for the rebels was harsh, rendered obnoxious by the savage relish with which they were pursued and condemned by the Lord Chief Justice, Jeffreys. Given the feebleness of the enterprise, leniency might have been a wiser, as well as more generous, policy than the use of the law as an instrument of revenge. But James could not forget the innocent Catholic victims of the Popish Plot, the attempt to deprive him of his rightful throne, the Whig conspiracy to murder him and his brother. The so-called 'Bloody Assizes' held by Jeffreys were cruel and horrible, as cruel and horrible as Cromwell's massacres in Ireland.

The lack of support Monmouth had attracted and the ease with which the rebellion had been suppressed encouraged James to try to repeal the Test Act, which excluded his Catholic co-religionists from holding public office or commissions in the army or navy. Debate in Parliament was fierce. Burnet, a Scots Episcopalian and by no means an unprejudiced witness, summed it up as follows.

> The truth is, all who argued for the repeal had no more to say than this – that it was against the rights of the Crown to deny the King the service of all his subjects, and an insufferable affront done him to oblige all those whom he should employ to swear his religion was idolatrous; whereas those on the other side declared that the Test was the best fence they had for their religion, which, if once given up, all the rest should follow; and that if the King might by his authority supersede such a law . . . it was in vain to think of law any more; the Government would then become absolute and arbitrary.[3]

Both arguments had some validity, but from James's point of view the Test Act was an abomination. When passed, a dozen years previously, it had compelled him to resign the post of Lord High Admiral in which he delighted; now it deprived him of the service of his fellow Catholics, who were his most loyal subjects. He set out to circumvent the act by use of the royal prerogative, claiming the right to dispense with the law in individual cases and, more generally, to suspend any law. This was alarming, especially to those who believed that the stability of the state depended on the ability of the Anglican ascendancy to exclude Roman Catholics and Protestant dissenters from public life. To their mind, defence of the liberty of England required that freedom be denied to all whose view of true religion differed from theirs.

James now tried to construct an alliance between all those excluded, and to cultivate the Protestant dissenters. Given that it is improbable that he should have supposed there was any chance of making England Catholic again, he may well have been sincere in proposing the suspension of discriminatory laws and advocating toleration. He was a devoted Catholic, but not a bigoted one. Among his friends was the leading Quaker William Penn; he supported Penn's establishment of a colony (later named Pennsylvania) in America.

Yet his policy was unrealistic, for in general the Protestant dissenters were even more fiercely anti-Catholic, and disposed to believe in popish plots, than the dominant Anglicans. They were the heirs of the opposition to Charles I, and they had supported Shaftesbury's attempt to exclude James from the throne. They eyed the approaches the King made to them with suspicion. Moreover, like the Anglicans, they were alarmed by the army James was creating, stationed at Hounslow Heath on the outskirts of London, and staffed by an ever-increasing number of Catholic officers. What was its purpose if not to advance the Catholic interest and suppress opposition to the King's lack of respect for Parliament and the law?

Events in France now further inflamed Protestant opinion. The French religious wars of the sixteenth century had ended with a compromise, which, while maintaining Catholicism as the official state religion, had granted liberty of worship to Protestants. But Louis XIV had been persecuting Protestants for years, provoking a rebellion in the Cevennes, suppressed with a deal of brutality. Now, urged on by his bishops and his second wife (the devout Madame de Maintenon), he was on the point of revoking the Edict of Nantes, which had secured the French Protestants their rights. Many chose to emigrate rather than submit. They flocked to the Netherlands, to Prussia and to England. Their arrival inevitably intensified suspicion of the policies being pursued by a Catholic king, for if Louis so viciously persecuted Protestants, whose liberty of worship had previously been guaranteed by law, might not James follow suit?

In the years since the Restoration, Church of England divines had proclaimed a doctrine of 'non-resistance'. Inspired by their memories of the civil war, they held that it was sinful to offer opposition (resistance) to an anointed king. James now put their sincerity to the test. First he challenged them in the citadel of High Anglicanism, the ostentatiously royalist University of Oxford. He appointed a Catholic as master of Magdalen College, and when the college fellows objected, expelled them and replaced them with Catholics. This was stupid and provocative, though no doubt to his mind it was only just that Catholics should no longer be excluded from the university, or at least from one of its colleges. Foolishly self-confident, he pressed on, disregarding the hostility with which his measure was greeted.

Next, in 1687, he issued a Declaration of Indulgence, suspending the Penal Laws against Catholics and the acts known as the Clarendon Code, which had imposed restrictions on the Protestant dissenters' freedom of worship. The failure of Charles II's similar 1672 declaration should have been a warning, but James was now deaf to reason. He ordered that the declaration be read from every pulpit on two successive Sundays, and when seven bishops, including the Archbishop of Canterbury, refused to do so, he had them arrested and charged with seditious libel. Their counsel argued that the King could legislate only through Parliament, and that his attempt to bypass Parliament was illegal. There was general rejoicing in London when they were acquitted.

In July 1688, while that trial was still undecided, the Queen gave birth to a son. James had married Mary of Modena in 1673, three years after the death of his first wife. She was then only fourteen, and had not welcomed the prospect of a husband twenty years her senior. Indeed, she was in tears when she arrived in England and found she much preferred her brother-in-law to her husband. Charles, she said, 'was always kind to me, and so truly amiable and good-natured that I loved him very much'.[4] As an Italian and a Catholic she was never popular in England, but at least till 1688 she had not threatened the liberty of Protestant England by producing an heir, her happy failure to do so making it likely that on James's death the throne would pass to his Protestant daughter Mary. Now, to general dismay, there was a male heir who would undoubtedly be reared as a Catholic.

A rumour quickly spread: the child was not the Queen's at all. Her own had been born dead, and a substitute brought into the palace in – it was asserted – a warming-pan. The story was widely believed. Burnet, who was in the Netherlands at the time, and whose information was therefore derived at second or third hand, declared in his *History* that 'if a child was born, there are further presumptions that it soon died, and another was put in his room. The Queen's children were all naturally very weak, and died young.' It was further insisted that the only people allowed into the Queen's bedroom were Catholics, and that the Protestant Princess Anne had been ordered to Bath by her father to take the waters. The story took some time to die, though no one encountering the new Prince of Wales, James Edward, in adult life could have doubted for one moment that he was a Stuart.

Rebellion was simmering even before the child was born, though the men who plotted treason did not dare to make a move themselves. Instead they sent the Whig Admiral Russell to the Netherlands (where he had the excuse of visiting a sister) to sound out the Prince of Orange. William made it clear that he would require something in the nature of a formal invitation if he was to venture on an invasion of England; meanwhile he sent an envoy to London to congratulate the King, who was both his uncle and his father-in-law, on the birth of the little Prince of Wales. Throughout the summer, rumour and counter-rumour flew, and more English grandees, some of them Tories, committed themselves, if cautiously, to William. Meanwhile Louis XIV, learning of the Dutch military movements from spies, sent a warning to James and with it an offer of French troops. This was rejected. James declared his confidence in his loyal army.

Eventually William sailed with an army of some 24,000 men – the largest force ever to invade England. He had issued a declaration recounting James's breaches of the law and proclaiming his own intention to restore the liberties of England – though he also stated that he had no intention of deposing his father-in-law. A wind that held the Royal Navy – itself less than wholly loyal – by the Essex coast blew the Dutch through the Channel and William landed safely at Torbay. His admirers called it 'a Protestant wind'.

If James had moved swiftly and decisively, he might well have checked the invasion, for the grandees who had issued the invitation to William had not yet dared to join him, and it is probable that they were unwilling to act till all risk had been removed, for they were comfortable men with great possessions and much to lose. But James was now himself moving from the ridiculous overconfidence of the previous year by way of self-doubt and distrust towards despair. He remained in London while his army advanced slowly to the west. Soon there came word of the first defection: the young Lord Cornbury. He was of no great significance himself (and failed to persuade his men to cross over to the enemy with him), but as a son of the second Earl of Clarendon, he was James's nephew by marriage. His desertion dealt a notable blow to the King's crumbling morale.

James was in a state of high nervous tension. When he joined his army, he suffered a succession of nosebleeds. It was not surprising, for he no longer knew whom he might trust, and the same uncertainty disturbed even those who remained loyal to him. Nevertheless, at this critical moment the King behaved like a man of honour. He told Clarendon that he would not hold either him or any other members of his family accountable for Cornbury's treasonable desertion. Then he called his generals and senior officers together, among them Churchill, the Duke of Grafton (one of Charles II's bastards), and generals Kirke and Trelawney. Macaulay, so hostile to James, wrote that:

> he addressed the assembly in language worthy of a better man and a better cause. It might be, he said, that some of the officers had conscientious scruples about fighting for him. If so, he was willing to receive back their commissions. But he adjured them as gentlemen and soldiers not to imitate the shameful example of Cornbury. All

seemed moved; and none more than Churchill. He was the first to vow with well feigned enthusiasm that he would shed the last drop of his blood in the service of his gracious master: Grafton was loud and forward in similar protestations; and the example was followed by Kirke and Trelawney.[5]

Macaulay's account of this meeting was derived from a biography of James, compiled during his exile, which is based, if only in part, on memoirs written by him in his own hand. Given Macaulay's antipathy to James, anything he recounts favourable to the King may deserve to be trusted. However, his dislike of Churchill and contempt for him were also intense. Churchill's partisans may therefore choose to reject this story. His descendant, Sir Winston, in his five-volume *Life of Marlborough*, does so. Others, including A. L. Rowse and Marlborough's most recent biographer, Richard Holmes, make no mention of it at all.

Be that as it may, it is clear that Churchill was already planning to abandon the King who had been his patron and to whom he owed so much. All that was necessary was to choose the right moment, and to co-ordinate his desertion with that of the Princess Anne, his wife Sarah's closest friend. Any immediate intention was however put on hold when the King joined his army. Churchill then suggested that James should inspect the outposts of the army at Warminster. He was about to do so when he was overcome by another violent nosebleed, and it was three days before he fully recovered. Subsequently the King was to ascribe this to Providence, having become convinced that there had been a plot to seize him at Warminster and carry him over to the Prince's camp.

While James was incapacitated, Churchill and the Duke of Grafton rode off to join William. Churchill left behind a letter in which, while admitting that he owed everything to James, he asserted that his devotion to the Church of England made it impossible to remain in his service. 'Churchill's conduct at this crisis for the nation needs no defending,' wrote Rowse, 'and we need waste no time upon it. He was bound to suffer the charge of ingratitude, then and for ever afterwards; but the responsibility was James's.

In leaving him Churchill was doing what was best for the nation.'[6] Or, of course, for John Churchill. The ship was sinking, and he ratted. 'Est-il possible?' said Princess Anne's husband, Prince George of Denmark, on hearing of Churchill's desertion. 'Est-il possible?' he asked again, in perhaps simulated surprise, before he and Princess Anne followed Churchill's example.

James's nerve now cracked completely. He had already sent his wife and baby son to France, and was anxious to follow them. His first attempt failed. He was recognised by some fishermen, endured their insults, and was brought back to London. In fact he was in a stronger position than he realised. William was determined to be king, despite his protestations to the contrary, as the only sure way of bringing England into his Grand Alliance against France; and the last thing he wanted was to have his father-in-law in his hands. If James had held his ground, there might have been a compromise, with James retained as king but deprived of control of the government, and with a council of regency established. That would have been an unstable situation, capable of being reversed in the future. The possibility was not to William's taste. Moreover, James and William, uncle and nephew as well as father-in-law and son-in-law, had previously been on good, even friendly terms. It would have been embarrassing for William to have had the King as his prisoner. So he ordered that James should be given the chance to flee again. This time he succeeded in getting to France.

Louis XIV received him with kindness and courtesy. The Palace of St-Germains was put at his disposal. The Queen made a good impression. 'She is judicious and sensible in all she says,' Madame de Sevigné wrote. However, 'her husband is quite different; he is courageous but his intelligence is only mediocre. He recounts all that has happened in England with such indifference that that is all one can feel for him.'[7] Nevertheless, she thought him 'a decent sort of man'. Other judgements were more severe. The Archbishop of Rheims, brother of Louis's war minister, Louvois, remarked: 'There goes a simpleton, who has lost three kingdoms for a Mass.' Whatever might be the fear of Catholicism in England, European politics were no longer determined by religious divisions. William's

Grand Alliance against France had the Catholic Habsburg emperor and Catholic Spain among its members. Indeed, when William sailed for England, the Spanish ambassador at the Hague had caused Masses to be said for a successful voyage.

The revolution in England would be called 'Glorious' and 'Bloodless'; there had been almost no fighting. It wasn't bloodless in Scotland or Ireland, where the King retained support.

Despite criticism of his enthusiasm for watching the torture of Covenanting prisoners, James had been quite popular when dispatched to Scotland by his brother during the Exclusion crisis. Fifty years later, Robert Chambers remembered that 'old people used to talk with delight of the magnificence and brilliancy of the Court which James assembled [at Holyrood] and of the general tone of happiness and satisfaction which pervaded the town'.[8] He had revived the old royal bodyguard, the Company of Archers, created the Order of the Knights of the Thistle, become patron of the Royal College of Physicians and extended his support to the Physic Garden in the grounds of Trinity Hospital. But however welcome his sojourn had been to the nobility, gentry and intelligentsia, the old spirit of the Covenant and suspicion of Catholicism were still alive. When the revolution broke out and the chancellor, the Catholic Earl of Perth, prudently fled from Edinburgh, a mob attacked and destroyed the abbey chapel at Holyrood, which James had converted to Catholic use.

However, the King had supporters in Scotland who, unlike those in England, were prepared to fight for him. Their leader was John Graham of Claverhouse, whom James had made Viscount Dundee. He was a professional soldier who had served in the Dutch army, once indeed saving William's life when he was unhorsed in battle. He had later commanded the royal army in Scotland against the Covenanting rebels, and now resolved, as Sir Walter Scott's ballad has it, that 'Ere the King's crown shall fall, there are crowns to be broke; / So let each Cavalier who loves honour and me, Come follow the bonnet of Bonnie Dundee.' As a Graham and a cousin of the great Marquis of Montrose, Dundee had influence with the Highland clans, especially those hostile to the Whig Clan Campbell.

He raised an army that met the professional Anglo-Scottish-Dutch troops commanded by General Mackay in the Pass of Killiecrankie on the border between Highland and Lowland Scotland. The Highland charge swept all before them, but a bullet hit Dundee and he died in the hour of victory. No one could take his place. King James's cause was lost in Scotland, but the exiled Stuarts would find support there for more than fifty years to come.

Ireland was even more promising territory for James. The native Irish were Catholic, and James's deputy in Ireland, Richard Talbot, Earl of Tyrconnell (and Churchill's brother-in-law) commanded a large predominantly Catholic army. He marched against the Protestant stronghold of Londonderry. It was almost taken straight away, saved only by the prompt action of thirteen young apprentice boys, whose names suggest a Scottish origin, who closed the Ferry Gate against the attackers. The siege lasted 105 days – days of hardship and near starvation – before the city was relieved and a tradition of Protestant defiance was established that has coloured and, some would say, prejudiced the subsequent history of Ulster.

James himself now arrived in Ireland with French troops provided by his cousin Louis, but William defeated him at the Battle of the Boyne in 1690. James, blaming the indiscipline of the Irish for his defeat, left them to their fate, which was miserable, and retired in depression to France. He would live another ten years there at St-Germains, in frequent correspondence with English and Scots politicians anxious to maintain some relations with the exiled King, in case a turn of Fortune's wheel should see him back in Whitehall. Churchill, rewarded for his treason with the earldom of Marlborough, was only one of many, both Whigs and Tories, to keep a line to St-Germains open. No wonder William looked on his leading subjects in England with suspicion and contempt.

As for James, he devoted himself to the practice of the religion that had cost him his throne, and to the recital of complaints about the treachery of his subjects. His mood was morose, his life gloomy. He wrote memoirs full of self-justification and self-pity, and enjoyed only the occasional lighter moment provided by a bottle of his favourite champagne. Some thought the court of St-Germains the most miserable place in France with the exception of the Bastille. He died in 1701, and a few Irish Jesuits maintained that miracles had been performed at his tomb. They might think him a martyr to his faith, but the Pope, more anxious to check the ambitions of France than to restore a Catholic king to the thrones of England and Scotland as a pensioner and ally of Louis XIV, had ordered the bells to be rung in Rome to celebrate James's defeat at the Boyne, and was indifferent to requests that he be considered as a candidate for canonisation.

Chapter 15

William III (1689–1702) and Mary II (1689–94): Revolution Settlement and Dutch Rule

D espite the disclaimer in the declaration he published before invading England, William was determined to be king. He would not act as regent, either for his exiled father-in-law, as some High Church Tories wished, or for his wife, the legitimate heir if the fiction about the warming-pan baby was accepted. So he held out for sovereignty, and the Convention Parliament,[1] having conveniently decided that James's desertion had left the throne vacant, named William and Mary as joint king and queen. William's determination was reasonable. Only as king could he achieve his aim of bringing England – and Scotland – into his Grand Alliance against Louis. He was content to share the throne with his wife, because they were now on reasonably good terms; he could be sure she wouldn't interfere, would do as she was told, and might usefully smooth his relations with the English politicians whom, with good reason, he distrusted and despised. He cared not a jot for the so-called liberties of England he had been invited to preserve. He wanted the English army and navy, and money to finance his wars against Louis, and he made sure he got all of these.

His father had died just before he was born in 1650, and he had been brought up by his mother, Mary Stuart. He had been a sweet-tempered small boy, a favourite of his uncle, Charles, whose pro-French policies he would come to deplore. But the charming affectionate child was soon soured by experience. Mary died when he was only ten, and, with the government of the United Provinces of the Netherlands in the hands of severe republicans who detested the House of Orange, he learned self-sufficiency in his youth. He grew up chilly and reserved in manner, distrustful of all but a handful of intimate friends, chief among them a Dutch nobleman of his own age, William Bentinck, whom he regarded as a brother. The French invasion of 1672 and the revolution in the Netherlands that followed it determined the course of his life. Though only twenty-two he was appointed Stadtholder of the United Provinces and commander of the armed forces, a position less than royal, more than presidential, held by members of the House of Orange since William's great-grandfather had inspired and led the revolt of the Dutch against Philip II of Spain. Henceforth he devoted his life to the struggle against Louis XIV. He was not a great general, though conspicuously brave in battle, but he was a great leader.

He hoped that the marriage to his cousin Mary would lead to a reorientation of English foreign policy. When his uncle Charles showed no inclination for this, but preferred friendship with France, and the pension Louis paid him, William soon lost whatever interest he had had in his wife. He can scarcely be blamed for this. Mary was doubtless a good woman – Bishop Burnet certainly thought so – but she seems to have been a singularly dull one, with less character than any of the rest of the Stuart family. She talked a great deal, but not to any point, and practised her religion faithfully. William was soon bored and took mistresses, chief among them Elizabeth Villiers, whom he would make Countess of Orkney. She was a distant cousin of the Duke of Buckingham, a lively conversationalist but no beauty, disfigured by a hideous squint. Their affair may have been more companionable than sexual. Unlike his uncles, Charles and James, William fathered no children, legitimate or illegitimate. Some thought him homosexually inclined, and he did indeed prefer the company of young officers to ladies. But his friendship with Bentinck was no more than friendship, and only late in life, when he made a favourite of Arnold Joost van

Keppel, a pretty young man with, as Macaulay says, a sweet and obliging temper, was there any relationship that might give substance to this rumour; and this principally because Bentinck, now Earl of Portland, was so manifestly jealous of the young man, who had been one of William's pages and was now made Earl of Albemarle and a Knight of the Garter. The favour shown Keppel 'furnished the Jacobites with a fresh topic for calumny and ribaldry',[2] but Macaulay could not bring himself to suppose that the calumny was other than baseless. He was probably right, though even Burnet found the young man's progress unaccountably quick. Yet it is not difficult to explain. Keppel was unfailingly cheerful and light-hearted, eager to please, whereas Portland had become stiff and peevish. Keppel was indeed generally popular; even the English nobility, jealous of foreign favourites, liked him. If William had regarded Bentinck as the brother he never had, then his little Joost took the place of a son. Moreover, he was one of the few people who could make William laugh.

William never achieved popularity; the English regarded him as a necessary expedient. The Tory squires resented his determination to involve the country in expensive wars, from which they derived no benefit. Nor, outside Protestant Ulster, where, as King Billy, he enjoys the status of a hero, has posterity remembered him with much pleasure. But for Macaulay he was the greatest of kings, and the Whig historian's verdict is worth quoting:

His name at once calls up before us a slender and feeble frame, a lofty and ample forehead, a nose curved like the beak of an eagle, an eye rivalling that of an eagle in brightness and keenness, a thoughtful and somewhat sullen brow, a firm and somewhat peevish mouth, a cheek pale, thin, and deeply furrowed by sickness and by care. That pensive, severe, and solemn aspect could scarcely have belonged to a happy or a good-humoured man. But it indicates in a manner not to be mistaken capacity equal to the most arduous enterprises, and fortitude not to be shaken by reverses or dangers. Nature had largely endowed William with the qualities of a great ruler; and education had developed these qualities in no common degree . . .

The audacity of his spirit was the more remarkable because his physical organization was unusually delicate. From a child he had been weak and sickly. In the prime of manhood his complaints had been aggravated by a severe attack of smallpox. He was asthmatic and consumptive. His slender frame was shaken by a constant hoarse cough. He could not sleep unless his head was propped by several pillows, and could scarcely draw his breath in any but the purest air. [For this reason, he found it intolerable to take up residence at Whitehall or St James's Palace, preferring Kensington or Hampton Court, distant from the oppressive and foetid air of London.]

Cruel headaches frequently tormented him. Exertion soon fatigued him. The physicians constantly kept up the hopes of his enemies by fixing some date beyond which, if there were anything certain in medical science, it was impossible that his broken constitution could hold out. Yet, through a life which was one long disease, the force of his mind never failed, on any occasion, to bear up his suffering and languid body.[3]

Macaulay admits that William 'passed for the most cold-blooded of mankind'; nevertheless he asserts that 'to a very small circle of friends, on whose fidelity and secrecy he could absolutely depend, he was a different man from the reserved and stoical William whom the multitude supposed to be destitute of human feelings. He was kind, cordial, open, even convivial and jocose, would sit at table many hours, and would bear his full share in festive conversation.'

The historian does not deny William's deficiencies. 'His manners were altogether Dutch'; he had little interest in literature, art or science. He granted favours in a grudging manner, and refused them bluntly. Though he disapproved of religious persecution, and practised a politic tolerance, his own faith was the narrowest and bleakest Calvinism. 'The tenet of predestination was the keynote of his religion. He often declared that, if he were to abandon that tenet, he must abandon all belief in a superintending Providence, and must become a mere Epicurean.' There was however no danger of him doing so.

Macaulay's is the portrait of a hero, all the more convincing because he is ready to admit William's limitations, the narrowness of his mind and his disagreeable manners.

William is usually characterised as a dour Dutchman, fairly enough, even though he had almost no Dutch blood. Yet in his long and intense rivalry with Louis XIV, a rivalry that amounted to obsession, he displayed the obstinate single-mindedness of his grandfather Charles I and his uncle James VII and II. In his case, unlike theirs, it did not lead to disaster because the policy he pursued was practical and found support in both the Netherlands and England.

Yet his position in England was never easy. Parliament responded to the attempts by his predecessors to govern without its consent by imposing restrictions on the monarchy. The Bill of Rights (1689) declared the dispensing and suspending powers as employed by James to be illegal. Charles had governed without Parliament for the last four years of his reign. James had not summoned a Parliament after 1685. Now the necessity for Parliament to meet every year was ensured by the passing of a Mutiny Act (1694), which was required to be renewed annually; without this act, maintenance of a standing army would be both illegal and well nigh impossible, since there would be no lawful provision for enforcing military discipline. With regular parliamentary sessions thus guaranteed, it was made clear to William that an active foreign policy could not be pursued without parliamentary approval. Though the King retained great powers, and was still, in fact as well as name, the head of the government, free to select and dismiss ministers at will, practical politics now required these to have the approval of Parliament and the support of a majority of the House of Commons. William's reign may therefore be seen as a period of transition between monarchical and parliamentary government. This was not perhaps immediately apparent, principally because William was as cautious as he was strong-willed, and did not push his prerogative beyond acceptable limits. But the incapacity, for one reason or another, of his successors would accelerate the process over the next century.

William could never feel secure as King of England. There were frequent Jacobite plots, either to assassinate him or take him captive. His own agents at St-Germains were able to obtain sufficient intelligence to thwart them. Nevertheless, Jacobite agents were always active in England, and the possibility of a successful plot could not be discounted. Equally disturbing was the uncertain loyalty of English politicians. Many of them, Whigs as well as Tories, remained in communication with the exiled James; at best this was an insurance policy against his eventual return should the revolution settlement be reversed, at worst outright treason to William. In 1691, for instance, Marlborough and his closest associate, Godolphin, met with a Jacobite agent, Henry Bulkeley, son of an Irish peer, even though Godolphin was at that time First Lord of the Treasury. According to Bulkeley, whose daughter would later marry James Fitzjames, Duke of Berwick (the exiled King's illegitimate son and also Marlborough's nephew), Godolphin was cautiously uncommunicative, but Marlborough surprised him by appearing 'the greatest penitent imaginable'. He begged Bulkeley 'to go to the king [that is, James] and acquaint him with his sincere repentance, and to intercede for mercy, that he was ready to redeem his apostasy with the hazard of his utter ruin, his crimes appearing so horrid to him that he could neither sleep nor eat but in continual anguish'. Bulkeley may have exaggerated, as secret agents tend to do. Evidence of his report is to be found only in the Jacobite *Life of James II*, and may for this reason be dismissed as unreliable. Yet there is other evidence of Marlborough's dealings with St-Germains, and he remained on good terms with his nephew Berwick, who was, for his part, utterly loyal to his father. In any case the willingness of so many leading men in England to remain in communication with the exiled court meant that William could rely on the absolute loyalty of few but his fellow Dutchmen. Eventually he had to take Marlborough back into his favour (after the Earl had been briefly imprisoned in the Tower), first because he was the most able man and soldier in England, second because his wife Sarah was the bosom friend of the heir to the throne, William's sister-in-law Anne.

William never visited his ancestral Scotland and showed no inclination to do so. Scottish regiments had served in his wars against France and he had close Scottish friends, notably Burnet (who, as an Episcopalian, was made Bishop of Salisbury) and the Presbyterian divine, William Carstares. Carstares had suffered imprisonment and torture under the old regime before escaping to the Netherlands, where he became one of William's chaplains and most trusted advisers. He was principally responsible for the settlement in Scotland that restored Presbyterianism and abolished the office of bishop in the Scots Kirk. Indeed he had so much influence with William that the Jacobites, with resentful mockery, called him 'Cardinal Carstares'. William trusted him, and where he gave his trust, he did so without reservations.

The King was, however, no more popular in Scotland than in England, and indeed his indifference to the country made it impossible that he should be so. His reign was marked by the atrocity known as the Massacre of Glencoe. After Dundee's death at Killicrankie saw the immediate Jacobite threat fizzle out, the Scottish government resolved that all Highland chiefs should be required to take an oath of loyalty to the new King and the new regime. One McIan, or McKean, of Glencoe, chief of a small clan who were a sept of the more powerful MacDonalds, delayed doing so. He was an old man, and after hesitation made his way with difficulty in wintry weather to Fort William to take the oath. But he was late, and since his little clan had a notorious reputation as thieves and troublesome brigands, the Scottish Privy Council resolved to make a fearful example of them. A detachment of Campbell soldiers was sent to Glencoe. They were received with hospitality and remained there as guests for some days till the order to exterminate the McIans was confirmed. Then, at night, they set upon their hosts. Some escaped to the snowy mountains, but others, including the chief, were killed. Not only the murders but the breach of hospitality appalled many. William had no share in the planning of this crime, but he had signed the order for it, and must be held ultimately responsible. According to Burnet, he signed it indifferently. Disliking paperwork, he had the habit of allowing it to pile up, and then disposing of it often without proper consideration. While other chiefs took note, as was intended, of the severity with which the government would punish those suspected

of treasonable disloyalty, the atrocity deepened the hatred felt
for the Whig Campbells and confirmed many in their resentment of the new regime.

More serious was William's role in the failure of the Darien Scheme.
Scotland was still a poor country, and the 1690s, years of weather
vile even for a Scottish summer, saw a succession of poor harvests,
and famine in several counties. It was not surprising that, with the
economy foundering, there was an enthusiastic response to a project
proposed by William Paterson, an imaginative entrepreneur who had
been the moving spirit in the foundation of the Bank of England in
1694 and the Bank of Scotland the following year. This was for the
creation of the 'Company of Scotland' and the establishment of a
Scottish colony at Darien on the Isthmus of Panama. The location
would enable the company to set up a trading post, which would
serve as an entrepot for trade between east and west, the Pacific and
the Atlantic. Superficially attractive, Paterson's scheme met with an
extraordinary response in Scotland. One-third at least of the available liquid capital of the country was invested in the new company,
and the first colonists set off with high hopes. Paterson and his fellow
projectors had however failed to take obstacles into account. First,
Spain considered Panama to be within the orbit of its American
empire. Second, the City of London was hostile. Trade with the east
was the monopoly of the East India Company, and they had no intention of seeing that monopoly broken or even threatened. Add to this
the fact that the goods the first colonists brought for sale were quite
unsuitable for a tropical climate, and the failure of the scheme was
all but certain. It was indeed a disaster, and brought ruin to many
who had invested all they could raise in the company. William was
held responsible, in part at least. He was King of Scotland, but in
this great Scottish enterprise he had sided with the City of London,
failed to give the colonists the protection of the Royal Navy, and so
doomed the most ambitious scheme of economic regeneration ever
to be launched in Scotland. Resentment festered. Hostility to William
and the English was intense. It is no wonder that William's advocacy
of a more complete union between England and Scotland met with
no response. Only the Jacobites could be happy.

In 1694, Queen Mary died, of smallpox. She had been more popular than her husband, if only because she was a member of the Church of England as he was not. She had never been a significant political figure, but as a native-born Englishwoman had smoothed the King's relations with some at least of his subjects. (William spoke English, but with a strong accent and often incorrectly; his closest friend, Bentinck, never mastered the language, despite being given an English peerage and, with it, membership of the House of Lords.) Mary's death therefore left William more isolated than before. In her last years she had experienced guilt, intermittently at least, on account of her role in the rebellion that had driven her father from his throne. The Jacobites were delighted by her death, assuming it would weaken William's position. But their hopes were as usual disappointed.

Though William achieved no significant victories in battle, his Grand Alliance had fought France to a standstill, and Louis was happy to make peace in 1697. The strain and expense of continual war had come close to exhausting his resources, and though he continued to offer hospitality to King James, he was now prepared to acknowledge William as King of England, Scotland and Ireland. The peace was popular in England. The war had been expensive. The National Debt, invented to finance it, was high. Interest on the debt, paid for by a land tax, imposed burdens on the Tory squires. Only the City men (who had invested in the debt) seemed to have benefited from the war. People looked forward to a prolonged period of peace.

Peace had been made principally because Louis had been checked. He was in financial difficulties and his country had been impoverished by the war fought for his glory. Moreover, he was now almost sixty, on the verge of old age, and since his clandestine marriage to Madame de Maintenon had become notably devout. Yet it would not be long before occasion for a new war arose.

Spain, not for more than half a century the dominant power in Europe, scarcely indeed to be ranked as a Great Power, remained at the centre of a huge empire. It consisted of Spanish America, the Spanish Netherlands (modern Belgium), where so much of the fighting in the war just ended had taken place, and in Italy both the Kingdom of Naples and Sicily and the Duchy of Milan. But now the King of Spain, Charles II, was dying. In point of fact, his death had been expected for years; he was undersized, deformed, always sickly, and of mean intelligence, ignorant even of the extent of the empire he nominally governed. Nevertheless, he had survived since he assumed the throne from his father in 1665. He had neither children nor brothers to succeed him. One of his sisters had married Louis XIV, another her cousin, the Habsburg emperor. For the whole inheritance to pass to either a French prince or a Habsburg would tilt the balance of power alarmingly. So diplomats came together to negotiate a partition of the empire. There were in fact two partition treaties, because a Bavarian prince who had been granted the bulk of the empire in the first treaty suddenly died. The second treaty, signed by France, England and the Netherlands in 1699, transferred most of the empire to the Austrian archduke, reserving only Italian territories for the French prince – evidence that Louis wished to avoid another war.

Not surprisingly, the Spaniards resented this proposed dismemberment of their empire. Just before his death in 1700 the King was persuaded to make a will, and in it he left the whole empire to Louis's younger grandson, Philippe, Duc d'Anjou, with the proviso that if he refused this inheritance, the empire, complete and unpartitioned, should pass to the Austrian Archduke Charles. Louis was in a dilemma. Should he accept the throne on behalf of his grandson? Should he refuse it, and see the reunion of the two branches, Spanish and Austrian, of the Habsburg family, which would then encircle France as it had done in the sixteenth century? Or should he stand by the treaty he and William had signed, but which the Austrians, wanting the whole empire, had like the Spanish refused to accept? After some hesitation and close debate in his Council, Louis preferred the will to the treaty. He can scarcely be blamed, given the Austrian attitude, though his announcement that the Pyrenees no longer existed was provocative.

At first it seemed he might avoid war. Neither England nor the Netherlands seemed ready to fight for the treaty. Indeed, both countries in February 1701 addressed the young French prince as King of Spain. But the next month, old James VII and II had a stroke, after suffering another nosebleed, and by September he was evidently dying. He did so in exemplary and impressive fashion, publicly forgiving the nephew who had driven him from his throne and the daughters who had betrayed him. As he lay there, his wife, Mary of Modena, implored Louis to recognise her son, the thirteen-year-old James Edward, nominally Prince of Wales, as his father's successor and the legitimate King of England, Scotland and Ireland. Her pleas were seconded by Madame de Maintenon, and though the King's Council advised that it would be folly to antagonise England by such an act, Louis could not resist the temptation to make a grand and selfless gesture, and did as his wife and the exiled Queen of England had asked. It was only four years since, in the treaty made at Ryswick, he had accepted the verdict of the revolution in Britain, and recognised William as King. Moreover, his gesture towards the Stuarts seemed an insult, not only to William but to the English parliament, which only three months previously had passed the Act of Settlement, fixing the succession, after William's sister-in-law Anne, on the nearest Protestant heir, Sophia, Electress of Hanover (the last surviving child of Elizabeth of Bohemia) and her son and heir George Augustus. Now it seemed that the French king in his insufferable arrogance was not only breaking his word but presuming to say who was the rightful King of England. So the mood changed, and Parliament, which had so recently been for peace, was now eager for war. (Few seem to have remarked that ever since the Hundred Years War between England and France, the kings of England had been styling themselves kings of France also.)

War was imminent, though William did not live to fight it. He had been in even poorer health than usual over the winter of 1701–2, but in late February he felt somewhat better and went out hunting in Richmond Park. His horse stumbled over a molehill and threw him. He suffered only a broken collarbone, but fever set in, and a few days later he died at Kensington Palace. For years, Jacobites would drink a toast to 'the little gentleman in black velvet' who had thrown up the earth that brought the 'usurper' down. It was also an article of faith among them that William had been riding that day a horse that had previously belonged to a Jacobite gentleman executed for his part in an assassination plot.

William had been disliked and resented. Yet one doesn't have to be, like Macaulay, a fervent Whig to find him a man very worthy of respect. Voltaire accorded him that respect in his history of the reign of Louis XIV, and compared the two. William, he wrote,

> left behind him the reputation of a great statesman, though he had never been popular; and that of a general to be feared, though he had lost many battles . . . His character was exactly opposed to that of Louis XIV; where Louis was affable, he was melancholy, reserved, serious, cold and taciturn. He hated women as much as Louis was attracted by them. Louis made war as a king, William as a soldier . . . He was proud as Louis but with that gloomy and melancholy pride which repels rather than imposes. Those who value higher the merit of defending his country and the expedience of acquiring a kingdom without natural right, of maintaining his position there without being loved, of ruling Holland with regal power and yet not tyrannising over her, of being the mind and leader of half Europe, possessing at once the resources of a general and the courage of a soldier, of persecuting no one for his religion, of despising all the superstitions of mankind, of being simple and unassuming in his manners – doubtless, such persons will give the name of 'great' rather to William than to Louis. But those who are more impressed by the pleasures and glitter of a brilliant court, by magnificence, patronage of the arts, zeal for public welfare, a passion for glory and a gift for ruling; who are more struck by the arrogance with which ministers and generals annexed whole provinces to France on a simple order from their king; who are more astonished at seeing a single state resist so many powers; who esteem a King of France who succeeds in bestowing Spain upon his grandson, rather than a Dutch stadtholder who dethrones his father-in-law; in a word, those who admire the protector rather than the persecutor of James will give the preference to Louis XIV.

Voltaire, as a French patriot, was scarcely impartial. Yet even he, admiring the glories of Louis XIV's reign, could not withhold respect from the man whose thirty years of resistance to French aggression had stalled Louis's ambition to be the supreme unchallenged power in western Europe.

Chapter 16

Anne (1702–14):
End of an Old Song

Anne's reign was glorious, if victories in war are a test of glory, far more so indeed than either Elizabeth Tudor's or Queen Victoria's. Yet Anne herself is all but forgotten, while they are remembered. Fairly enough, for both the first Elizabeth and Victoria were remarkable women; and poor Anne was not. She presided over a great war and she encouraged the most significant act of her reign – the Treaty of Union between England and Scotland. She was never a nonentity or cipher; ministers had to take her wishes into account. Nevertheless, few can have thought of the government as hers in reality. She was a very ordinary woman in an extraordinary position. On the other hand, she had principles – she was the only Stuart, except for her grandfather Charles I, to be devoted, heart, mind and soul, to the Church of England as by law established. She had affections that in a couple of cases amounted to passions, endured much unhappiness and ill-health with resolution, and had a sense of duty that more glamorous Stuarts lacked.

The younger daughter of James VII and II and his first wife, Anne Hyde, she was the last British monarch till Elizabeth II to have had one parent who wasn't a foreigner, the first since the earlier Elizabeth to have spent all her life in England, except for one visit to Scotland when her father was sent there as viceroy. There was another point in which she resembled the first Elizabeth:

each was the child of a mother who had been a commoner before her marriage. It would be fair to remember Anne as the most English of monarchs since the Union of the Crowns. After she became queen, she scarcely stirred from the south of England, thus setting a pattern followed by her Hanoverian successors until George IV visited first Ireland, and then Scotland.

She was married at the age of seventeen to Prince George of Denmark, an unremarkable man. Charles II's verdict on him has been often quoted: 'I have tried him drunk and I have tried him sober, but there is nothing in him', though this may have been a light quip rather than a considered dismissal. The Prince had some reputation as a brave soldier, having once saved his elder brother's life in battle, and was both hurt and offended when his brother-in-law William treated him with negligent contempt on his campaign in Ireland in 1690. The couple were however well suited, not least in bed. Anne became pregnant time and again, but there were twelve miscarriages, one stillbirth, and four children who did not survive infancy. One boy, William, Duke of Gloucester, gave hopes of living to be grown up, but even he died at the age of eleven. Burnet, who had been entrusted with his education for two years (and reported complacently that he had made 'amazing progress'), tells us that Anne 'attended on him during his sickness with great tenderness, but with a grave composedness that amazed all who saw it. She bore his death with a resignation and piety that were indeed very singular.'[1] It is not to be supposed however that his death, and those of his brothers and sisters, and all the miscarriages, did not make Anne miserable; princesses and queens are not devoid of the feelings natural to women. It may be that this sad history served to forge a close bond between George and Anne. When he died in 1708, she lay on the bed by his side kissing him.

Her relations with her sister Mary were rarely good, partly because Mary as the elder took it upon herself to criticise Anne's conduct and tell her how she should behave, partly because Mary was a chatterbox and Anne naturally taciturn. Like her father, James, she lacked vivacity and was inclined to be gloomy. She had reason to be so.

In compensation, she indulged in passionate friendships with other women, chief among them Sarah Churchill, Marlborough's wife. Sarah was three or four years the elder, but they had played together as children. They were very different in character. Sarah was lively, quick-witted, sharp-tongued, Anne slow and heavy. Sarah dazzled her, and for years until her bossiness and ill-temper became unbearable, she was the person Anne loved most in the world. Some are determined that their relationship was physical, but passionate friendship amounting to love can exist between people of the same sex without them going to bed together. Nevertheless, the judgement of Sarah's most recent biographer, Ophelia Field, that the Princess's 'marriage contained many of the qualities of a friendship, while Sarah's relationship with Anne was developing into a fraught romance'[2] can't be discounted. Certainly some thought Anne's feeling excessive; her father James criticised her 'boundless passion' for Sarah.

Sarah, in her memoirs, written in old age, long after Anne was dead, declared that while royalty generally believed that close association with inferiors detracted from their dignity, 'The Princess had a different taste. A friend was what she most coveted.'[3] She believed too that friends should be on equal terms, and suggested that they should address each other by assumed names, thus eliding the difference in rank. Anne became Mrs Morley and Sarah Mrs Freeman on account of what she called 'my frank, open temperament'. Both detested Anne's brother-in-law William. In their private language he was 'Mr Caliban'.

Anne also disliked her stepmother, Mary of Modena. She may have been jealous of Mary's vivacity – the Queen was her elder by only four or five years – but it was her proselytising Catholicism that she most resented and disapproved of. 'She pretends to have a good deal of kindness for me,' she told her sister, 'but I doubt it is not real, for I never see proofs of it, but rather the contrary.'[4] Her resentment was such that she added that before long it would be dangerous to be a Protestant in England. This was of course nonsense.

The birth of the Prince of Wales in the summer of 1688 infuriated her, and for a time she even subscribed to the belief in the absurd warming-pan story. In later years good sense asserted itself; she recognised that James Edward was her half-brother. But at the time when her father summoned his Privy Council in order to offer them proofs that the baby was indeed his son, Anne chose to absent herself from the meeting, on grounds of ill-health.

Her disaffection was such that she welcomed the Dutch invasion, sending a note of her approval to William. Macaulay declared that she did so because 'she had no will but that of the Churchills', but this is to underestimate her attachment to the Church of England and her undoubted, if exaggerated, fear of popery. When Churchill deserted his master, Anne was alarmed for the fate of her adored Sarah, since they were both then still in Whitehall. She feared that Sarah would be arrested and her papers examined, papers in which there was certainly evidence of treasonable conspiracy. 'Strong affection,' Macaulay wrote, 'braced the feeble mind of the Princess. "I will jump out of the window," she said, "rather than be found here by my father."' Such a hazardous means of escape was unnecessary. Anne and Sarah slipped out of the palace by night, the Princess reportedly still in dressing gown and slippers. When their absence was discovered, the Princess's old nurse cried out that her dear mistress had been murdered by the papists. Wild rumours flew round London: that Anne had been carried off to prison, that she had been beaten by her cruel stepmother, that her life was in danger. It was all nonsense; she was on her way to Nottingham to join the northern supporters of William. Meanwhile, her husband also absconded. When James heard of Anne's flight, he exclaimed: 'God help me! My own children have forsaken me.'

Anne would later repent of her desertion of her father, or at least express repentance. In 1691 she wrote to him asking his forgiveness. James was not impressed; no forgiveness was forthcoming. In any case Anne's sincerity may be questioned. She wrote this letter when Marlborough was also making overtures to the king he had abandoned, and assuring him of his regret and undying devotion.

Likewise it was William's understandable distrust of Marlborough, as much as the King's chilly manner, that occasioned Anne's hostility to her brother-in-law. When Mary died in 1694, William found it expedient to be reconciled to his successor, which in turn made it necessary for him to admit Marlborough once again to his favour. He recognised Marlborough's qualities, and, as renewed war with France became imminent and his own health deteriorated, accepted that Marlborough would be his real successor as the leader of the Grand Alliance against Louis. On her accession, Anne made Marlborough a Knight of the Garter and captain-general of the army; Sarah was in high heaven.

For almost ten years Marlborough, with the assistance of his friend Lord Godolphin on the home front, conducted the most uniformly successful war in British history. His task was never easy. The army he commanded was an allied one. If he had complete command of his English, Scots and Irish regiments, he had to employ rare diplomatic skills to keep on good terms with the Dutch and the various German states joined in the war against France. His charm, courtesy, intelligence and determination usually enabled him to do so. To make a comparison with the 1939–45 war, he was required to combine the diplomatic and managerial ability of an Eisenhower with the fighting qualities of a Patton or Montgomery. His succession of great victories – Blenheim, Ramillies, Oudenarde and Malplaquet – was unprecedented in British military history and has never been matched since. The victory at Blenheim in 1704 was the first great battle won by an English commander on the Continent since Agincourt almost three hundred years previously. Till near the end Anne gave him steady support; that was all that was required of her.

This was the more remarkable because within a few years of becoming queen, her relationship with Sarah began to turn sour. The cause was only in part personal. Certainly Sarah became more demanding, more critical, more assertive and more tiresome than ever. When she found that she was being supplanted in Anne's affections by a distant cousin, Abigail Hill (Mrs Masham), a lady of the bedchamber, her tantrums were insupportable. It is scarcely surprising that Anne, frequently in poor health, became weary of the woman she had once adored, who now increasingly bored and irritated her. But there were political differences too.

Inasmuch as Anne had political principles of her own, she was, as a devout member of the Church of England, inclined to Toryism. As a queen, however, she disliked party, and preferred to promote national unity. Sarah, on the other hand, was a fierce Whig, and insisted that the Tories were all Jacobites – even though Marlborough himself was, as the son of an old Cavalier family, by upbringing and instinct a Tory. Sarah's animus against the Tories was sharpened by their growing disenchantment with the war, a disenchantment that in time hardened into outright opposition. This was partly because the land tax raised to pay for the war bore heavy on Tory squires, but also because only the City of London, and the great Whig families connected with the money power, derived any benefit from continued hostilities. Moreover, the Tories came to believe that the war was being fought in the interests of the Dutch and the Habsburg emperor, and not of England. It seemed that England was fighting, and paying, to put a Habsburg prince on the throne of Spain – something the Spaniards themselves opposed, and which, after the victory at Almanza in 1707 of a Franco-Spanish army, commanded by the Jacobite Duke of Berwick, seemed doomed to failure. As the Tories turned against the war – and in consequence against Marlborough himself – Sarah's attachment to the Whigs grew fiercer and she became quite intolerable to the Queen.

William had found great difficulty in governing two countries with separate parliaments, and advised his successor that the only way to remove the antagonism between them was to effect a union of the parliaments of England and Scotland. The idea was not new. James VI and I had pressed for such a complete union; more tentatively Charles II had appointed commissioners to investigate the possibility of effecting one. Both attempts had come to nothing, principally because the English saw no advantage in the proposal. Anne was of William's mind in this matter. Whether she had come to that conclusion herself or was following his advice is immaterial. In her first speech to her English parliament, made within three days of her accession, she spoke of her desire for a closer union. The English were now ready to consider this proposition. In the past the Scots had been more eager, the English uninterested. Now the positions were reversed.

It was the question of the succession to the throne that brought about the English volte-face. It was now clear that Anne would have no child to succeed her. The English parliament had passed an Act of Settlement in 1701, which declared that the Crown should pass to the nearest Protestant heir of James VI and I – the Electress Sophia and then her son, George. The Scottish parliament had passed its own measure – the Act of Security. This too had stipulated that the monarch must be a Protestant, but had not identified an heir. More alarmingly for the English, it declared that Scotland might choose a king of its own – not necessarily the same person as the King of England – unless particular Scottish grievances were settled and certain assurances given. Since the failure of the Darien Scheme, hostility to England, amounting to Anglophobia, was running high in Scotland. Moreover, there were acknowledged Jacobites in the Scottish parliament. The Scots, from ancestral loyalty to the Stuarts, might even offer the Crown to the 'Pretender' James Edward, whom the Jacobites called James VIII and III, especially if he could be persuaded to turn Protestant. Since he was a pensioner of the French king, this raised the horrid possibility, in the middle of a war with France, of the renewal of the old Franco-Scottish alliance. It was not to be thought of. So English politicians came round to the idea of parliamentary union, because the alternative was the breaking of the regnal union.

The Scots were more divided. The Jacobites opposed union. So did many who feared that the loss of independence – even of the qualified independence Scotland had enjoyed since 1603 – would see Scotland swallowed up by England. The burghs were suspicious; the city mob in Edinburgh and Glasgow fiercely opposed. Yet for many, the prospect of rejecting the proposed union was disturbing. It might even result in an English invasion. Others saw the political and economic advantages of union – security and trade with the English colonies from which Scotland was currently debarred.

Anne appointed commissioners from each kingdom, and the terms of a treaty of union were agreed in 1707. Approval was easily got in the English parliament, achieved with greater difficulty, and after bitter argument, in the Scottish one. Though she saw some of the commissioners privately, Anne achieved her aim without playing any public part in the debates. In effect she had made a treaty with herself, as Queen of England and Scotland. These titles were now extinguished. She was legally Queen of Great Britain and Ireland.

One of the Scots commissioners, Sir John Clerk of Penicuik, had several audiences with the Queen at Kensington Palace, the first in the company of the Duke of Queensberry, who represented her views to the Scottish parliament. 'I twice saw her in her Closet,' Clerk remembered.

> One day I had occasion to observe the Calamities which attend humane nature even in the greatest dignities of Life. Her majesty was labouring under a fit of the Gout, and in extream pain and agony, and on this occasion everything about her was much in the same disorder as about the meanest of her subjects. Her face, which was red and spotted, was rendered something frightful by her negligent dress, and the foot affected was tied up with a pultis and some nasty bandages. I was much affected at this sight, and the more when she had occasion to mention her people of Scotland, which she did frequently to the Duke. What are you, poor mean like Mortal, thought I, who talks in the style of a Sovereign?[5]

On another occasion his reflections were equally sympathetic, even pitiful:

> The poor Lady was again under a severe fit of the Gout, ill-dressed, bloated in her countenance, and surrounded with plasters, cataplasims and dirty-like rags. The extremity of her pain was not then upon her, and it diverted her a little to see company with whom she was not to use ceremonies, otherways I had not been allowed access to her. However, I believe she was not displeased to see any body, for no Court Attenders ever came near her. All the Incence

and Adoration offered at Courts were to her Ministers, particularly the Earl of Godolphin, her chief minister, and the two Secretaries of State; her palace at Kensington, where she commonly resided, was a perfect solitude, as I had occasion to observe several times. I never saw anybody attending there but some of her guards in the outer room, with one at most of the Gentlemen of her Bedchamber. Her frequent fits of sickness and the distance of the place from London, did not admit of what are commonly called Drawing-Room nights, so that I had many occasions to think that few Houses in England belonging to persons of Quality were keept in a more privat way than the Queen's Royal Palace of Kensington.

Despite her wretched health, Anne had her amusements. Chief among them was horse-racing. In the early summer of 1711, while out for a carriage drive, she halted on the common at Ascot, and seeing that it appeared to have been designed by nature for her favourite sport, ordered that a racecourse be laid out, and declared that she would present a challenge plate for the inaugural meeting. The work was done quickly – more quickly than subsequent improvements to the course – and the first meeting was held that August, the Queen driving from Windsor Castle and presenting 'Her Majesty's Plate of 100 guineas' to the winning owner. If little about the poor Queen is memorable, her invention of Royal Ascot at least should not be forgotten.

The war dragged on with no great victories after Malplaquet (1709), a fierce encounter where the allied losses were greater than those of the French. It became more and more unpopular and a Tory ministry came in determined to make peace. Marlborough was dismissed and sent into exile; there was much talk of corruption. Meanwhile the Whigs spoke angrily of peace negotiations being a betrayal of their allies, the Dutch and the Habsburg emperor. But it had proved impossible to dislodge the French prince from Spain, and all the other aims of the war had been achieved. In particular France's power had been given a stiff blow. There would be no French aggression for decades, so badly had this war gone. Jonathan Swift wrote a pamphlet, *The Conduct of the Allies*, which demolished the Whig case for continuing the war – at least in the opinion of the Tories. Swift thought his services to his party deserved a bishopric, but he had to be content with the deanery of St Patrick's in Dublin. He told his favourite correspondent, 'Stella' (Hester Johnson), that he thought it would be a good peace for England, and he was right.[6]

Poor Anne's health continued to deteriorate. Swift went to court and reported to Stella that he had seen the Queen carried in a chair into the garden or to chapel; she had almost lost the use of her legs. Yet she continued to do her duty as she understood it. Though she was queen by the will of Parliament and the old Stuart claim to divine right was dead, she still 'touched' for the king's evil (scrofula), the last monarch to do so. One of those she ministered to in this way was the infant Samuel Johnson.

In 1714 she was failing fast. With the Tories in office the great question was whether they had the will, or the courage, to change the succession and bring back Anne's half-brother, James Edward. Certainly one of the two leading ministers, Henry St John, Lord Bolingbroke, was in communication with the Jacobite court at St-Germains; but he was scarcely on speaking terms with his chief colleague, Robert Harley, Earl of Oxford, the Lord Treasurer. Anne was known to dislike her distant Hanoverian cousins – the Elector, though heir to the throne, had been forbidden to come to England. Many thought she had a tenderness to her half-brother, even if it was provoked by feelings of guilt for her conduct in 1688. Perhaps if he had been prepared to become a Protestant, she might have favoured his succession. But he refused, and Anne's loyalty to the Church of England was stronger than any family feeling. In any case, to change the succession would have required Parliament to amend or repeal the Act of Settlement, and there was no majority for that. Even if Bolingbroke was planning a *coup d'état*, he was prevented by the rapidity of the Queen's decline. Antipathy between him and Oxford was now open. Almost Anne's last act was to dismiss Oxford, who had turned up completely drunk at a Council meeting, and then deny Bolingbroke the treasurer's White Staff, which she offered instead to a moderate Whig, the Duke of Shrewsbury.

Anne died on 1 August 1714. The Protestant succession was assured. The new German king came in, the Whigs were rewarded, Marlborough recalled, the Tories dished, and the Stuart monarchy was at an end – except in the eyes of the exiles and the Jacobite sympathisers at home.

Chapter 17

James VIII and III:
Jacobites

J ames Edward Stuart was born in the Palace of Whitehall and
reared in the gloom of St-Germains. Thirteen years old when
his father died and Louis XIV with rash chivalry hailed him
as King of England, Scotland and Ireland, he would pass all his
life in exile, a king who never ruled. He would be known as the
Chevalier de St-George, as the Pretender (or Claimant) and then
as the Old Pretender; for many in England as well as Scotland he
was 'the King over the water', and in company that was not all
of their opinion, they would pass their glass over the water jug
when invited to drink the King's health. The longer he lived, the
more the hope of a restoration faded, and well before his death
in 1766 he was resigned to failure, piously accepting it as the unfath-
omable will of God.

But it was different in his youth. James was a soldier then and
served in the French army, displaying a courage and disregard of
danger that won him the respect not only of his own commanding
officers but of those whom he considered his rightful subjects now
arrayed against him. Some cheered him when they saw him riding
along the French lines; others were happy to drink his health, if
only in admiration of a brave young man.

Hopes of a restoration were still high, and would remain so as
long as France and Britain were at war. The 1707 Treaty of Union
was known to be unpopular in Scotland, and the Jacobites there
were fierce against union. Their leader, George Lockhart of
Carnwath, whose father, the Lord President of the Court of Session,

had been murdered in the high street of Edinburgh by a disappointed litigant, had been the only out-and-out opponent of union among the commissioners appointed by Queen Anne to consider it. Without union, there was a chance of a Jacobite restoration; this would be much diminished if union was achieved – which was after all the prime purpose of any union in the eyes of the English government.

The treaty was made, but its immediate unpopularity raised Jacobite hopes. Louis was persuaded to sanction an invasion. Six thousand French infantry were put aboard a fleet of more than twenty ships commanded by the Comte de Forbin, a famous privateer. He himself was sceptical, consenting to take the command only when the troops were transferred from slow transports to fast-sailing privateers. He had reason to be doubtful, for British spies were active, and ships of the Royal Navy appeared off Dunkirk, where, by mischance, the young King was confined to bed with measles. But then the wind changed, James recovered, and Forbin consented to sail. He was contemptuous of the quality of the Jacobites on board and declared that the young king – James was not yet twenty – was the only one who showed any courage. Forbin displayed no great spirit himself. His little fleet entered the Firth of Forth, but was shadowed by vessels of the Royal Navy. James begged to be put ashore, alone if necessary, but Forbin would have none of it, and aborted the enterprise.

James had prepared a proclamation to be issued on landing. It would appeal 'to his good people of his ancestral Kingdom of Scotland' to break the parliamentary union. He would leave everything, he promised, to a newly elected Scottish parliament. Such an appeal would have won him support, for implicit in it was an undertaking not to disrupt the Church settlement of 1688–9 that had re-established the Presbyterian Kirk at the expense of the Episcopalians – unless Parliament chose to amend it. But there was no landing.

The danger of invasion and a Jacobite rising alarmed the government. Any noble or laird suspected of Jacobite sympathies who could be apprehended was put under arrest. But most remained at liberty and Edinburgh was almost undefended. The castle garrison was tiny and short of ammunition. Its commander, the Earl of Leven, was ready to withdraw. An English agent reported that the little Scottish home army – most of the regiments were serving under Marlborough in the Netherlands – was 'debauched' and would join the Pretender.

This might have been the best chance the Jacobites ever had. It was the only time when France supplied a sizeable force that came within sight of Scotland. Union then had few supporters in Scotland. If Forbin had landed his troops, James might have been master of his 'ancestral kingdom'. But unnerved by the presence of the English ships that chivvied him up the North Sea, Forbin did not dare to follow his orders. James wept in anger and shame.

Nevertheless, Jacobite hopes rose again as the war became unpopular in England and the Tories – the High Church party – returned to power determined to make peace. Their leaders were even ready to contemplate changing the succession. They were in contact with the exiled court. If James was to change his religion and abjure Catholicism, might he not be more acceptable than his distant German cousin, the Elector of Hanover? But James, though of an amiable temper, had all the characteristic obstinacy of the Stuarts.

Surely, he suggested, his own constancy in this matter was proof that he would keep his promise to maintain the religion of his kingdoms as by law established? This was hardly good enough. Memories of his father's conduct and policies were too recent, still warm. If he became a member of the Church of England, he might be king. While he remained a Catholic, he must remain an exile.

Anne died, and the Elector of Hanover became George I. The Tories, whom the new King disliked and distrusted, were dismissed from office and found themselves in the wilderness. Among those rejected was John Erskine, Earl of Mar, formerly a promoter of union. He took umbrage and became a Jacobite. Now a man of forty, Mar had, like others, already played both sides in his time; nevertheless, his switch surprised many, and his inconstancy would earn him the nickname of 'Bobbing Johnnie'.

His actions may have been prompted by pique, but he was not

alone in being ready to conspire or even rebel. Tory England was rife with discontent. Even the Duke of Ormonde, Marlborough's successor as captain-general of the army, had been dismissed. The Tories were out, and saw no prospect of returning to office while George was king; they might, however, come in again with the Pretender. It was no longer only the wilder spirits among them who were tempted by the Jacobite alternative. Plans were laid for a rising in England, and both Ormonde and Henry St John, Viscount Bolingbroke, were involved. Then Bolingbroke blundered. Highly intelligent, but a poor judge of men, nervous about what might be known of his correspondence with James, he consulted Marlborough, whom he had treated shamefully, and who consequently disliked him. Marlborough, not innocent of communication with St-Germains himself, hinted that Bolingbroke was indeed in danger of arrest – though in truth there was no evidence against him. Alarmed, he now provided the evidence by fleeing to France. By July 1715 he was James's secretary of state, a shadow minister in a shadow government-in-exile.

Unrest was widespread. In May there had been a Jacobite riot in Oxford where the authorities, being themselves sympathetic to the exiled King, took no action. The same month the Foot Guards demonstrated outside St James's and seemed on the point of mutiny. On 10 June, the Pretender's birthday, there were more Jacobite demonstrations: in Manchester, Leeds, Somerset and Gloucestershire. The Riot Act was renewed; impeachments of Tory leaders moved in the Commons. Troops were brought into London and billeted in Hyde Park. The Guards were purged of suspect officers and a colonel in the First Regiment of Foot Guards was arrested, accused of having accepted a commission from the Pretender and of having started to enlist men on his behalf. Ormonde was impeached, though no warrant for his arrest was issued. Then he too slipped over to France to join James at St-Germains.

Such was the mood when Mar came north to his estate on Deeside. He left plans for a simultaneous rising in England. Sir William Wyndham, formerly Secretary at War, Lord Lansdowne and Sir Richard Vyvyan would raise the West Country. Lord Derwentwater, grandson of Charles II, and the actress Mary Davis (and therefore James's second cousin) would lead the Jacobites of northern England along with Thomas Forster, MP for Northumberland; and of course there would be help from France. No wonder there was high excitement in St-Germains, chilled only by awareness of the ubiquity of Hanoverian spies.

In the late summer of 1715, Mar sent out invitations to a hunting party in the hills above Braemar. This was a traditional event at that time of the year, and so provided adequate, if not wholly convincing, cover. Invitations were dispatched to all known sympathisers in the north-east and Highlands. Mar made what a contemporary but hostile historian described as 'a publick speech, full of invective against the Protestant Succession in general and King George in particular'.[1] He explained that though he had formerly been active in support of the Treaty of Union, he could now see his error, and would do what he could to make the Scots again a free people, enjoying their ancient liberties, now, on account of 'that cursed Union', delivered into the hands of the English.

He then displayed his commission from James as major-general of the army in Scotland, and promised French help and a simultaneous rising in England (which some may have thought sat oddly with his promise to end the union); and things were under way – even though James himself had not yet arrived in Scotland.

Under way but not exactly on the move. Mar dithered. Though he had some seven thousand men by mid-October and had occupied Perth, he hesitated to commit his army to battle against the much smaller Hanoverian force commanded by the Duke of Argyll, which was based at Stirling. It should have been obvious that the Jacobites had to defeat Argyll before he received reinforcements from the south, but Mar was no general. One small detachment of the Jacobite army, commanded by Mackintosh of Borlum, crossed the Forth and linked up with the English Jacobites, only to be defeated at Preston. Meanwhile the promised help from France did not appear.

At last, in November, Mar moved towards Dunblane to engage

Argyll at Sheriffmuir in the foothills of the Ochils. The battle was mismanaged on both sides, Argyll, though a veteran commander under Marlborough, making almost as many mistakes as Mar. But the Jacobites had the advantage in numbers and should have won. However, Argyll held his ground and Mar withdrew. Though regarded by both sides and many historians as a drawn and inconclusive battle, Sheriffmuir was in reality a serious strategic defeat for the Jacobites.

Effectively the rising was over, in Scotland as well as England, for Argyll was now reinforced by six thousand Dutch troops commanded by another Marlborough veteran, General Cadogan. Yet there was still a last melancholy act to be played. James himself arrived in Scotland, landing at Peterhead on 22 December, six weeks after Sheriffmuir. He had been delayed, once again, by adverse weather – the Stuarts rarely had luck with the weather – and also by the attempts of the British ambassador in Paris, Lord Stair, to arrange his assassination – a grisly task for which Stair's heredity well suited him, since his father, the first Earl, had been the prime organiser of the Massacre of Glencoe. But James was too late. There was nothing he could do – not even raise the spirits of his army, which was melting away like snow-wreaths in thaw. He left for France early in February, and never saw Scotland again.

Still, he did not give up. The failure of the '15 rising was regarded as a check; no more. Admittedly things were running against the cause. Treatment of the captured English Jacobites had been severe enough to render others cautious in the future, uncomfortably aware that they had a joint in their neck. Moreover, Louis XIV, constant in friendship to James as to his father before him, had died in 1715, and the French government, now headed by his nephew the Duc d'Orléans as regent for the infant Louis XV, was so eager for good relations with Britain that it expelled James from the country and he withdrew to Avignon, still a possession of the Pope. But European politics were lively and there were other possible allies. There was the warrior-king of Sweden, Charles XII, who loathed the Elector of Hanover; but unfortunately a sniper's bullet did for him in 1718. That left Spain, now at odds with France, and with an ambitious chief minister, Cardinal Alberoni, an Italian by birth, who loved intrigue and saw advantages for his adopted country in the restoration of the Stuarts. So James, in disguise and by a tortuous route, to evade English spies and assassins, made his way to Spain. Ormonde joined him there, and in 1719 a new enterprise was hatched.

A Spanish fleet would land Ormonde and Spanish troops in the west of England, while another smaller force commanded by the Earl Marischal of Scotland would be put ashore in the north. Once again the wind turned against the Jacobites. Ormonde's fleet was scattered in a storm. Meanwhile the Earl Marischal had sailed with a few hundred Spanish soldiers. He would be joined by his brother, James Keith, and the Marquis of Tullibardine, son of the Duke of Atholl, with another small force. Tullibardine believed he had a commission to take command, and produced what purported to be one, and the Earl Marischal yielded place. Unfortunately while the Earl Marischal had had a plan of campaign – to march rapidly on Inverness – Tullibardine had none. So though his brother, Lord George Murray, came up with a detachment of the Atholl men, and the outlaw Rob Roy Macgregor appeared with a small band of ruffians, this rising, lacking any sense of direction and winning no new support, never got going. A government force met them in Glenshiel. The Jacobite leaders made off as best they could, while the wretched Spaniards were taken as prisoners to Edinburgh, whence they were in time repatriated. And that was the last Jacobite rising for a quarter of a century.

In 1719 James was thirty-one. He had devoted the dozen years of his manhood to action and had made repeated attempts to launch expeditions to regain his rightful throne. All had failed. He had narrowly escaped capture and assassination. He knew what it was to be surrounded by spies and traitors, to have his every action, and many of his words, reported by the agents of the British Crown. An exile from his own country since infancy, he had been expelled from the once-friendly France, first to Avignon, until the Royal Navy's threat to bombard Civitavecchia in the Papal States had persuaded His Holiness to order James to remove to Italy. For a little while he resided at Urbino, then came south to Rome, where the Pope installed him in the Palazzo Muti in the Piazza dei Santi Apostoli. It is an insignificant building, overshadowed not only by the Church of the Apostles but by the neighbouring palazzi belonging to the Roman noble families, the Colonna and Odealeschi. The Palazzo Muti would be the principal residence of the exiled Stuarts till they were extinct; an inscription within its little gateway records that in 1788, James's younger son, Henry, was there proclaimed King of Great Britain, France and Ireland.

James had recently, with some difficulty, found and married a wife. She was Clementina Sobieski, the granddaughter of the Polish hero-king John Sobieski, who in 1683 had driven the armies of the Ottoman Empire back from the gates of Vienna and so repelled the last attempt of the Turks to expand their empire into the heart of Europe. Stuart and Sobieski made for a rich and foolhardy mix, and Charles Edward, the couple's elder son, born on the last day of 1720, was to display Stuart obstinacy and that disregard for the odds characteristic of Polish gallantry.

Their second child, Henry, followed in 1725, his birth giving the lie to the British government's agent in Rome, the art-dealing Baron von Stosch, who had assured his employers when Charles was born that Clementina could never bear another child. He was not the most reliable of agents, for he had also reported that Charles was deformed; news that was equally welcome and equally untrue.

The marriage was never happy, and, as is usually the case, its unhappiness was the fault of both husband and wife. Clementina was devout, but also light-minded and frivolous, an uncomfortable combination. James was preoccupied with his business of politics. He did not understand his young wife's wish for a lively social life, or if he did understood it, he did not sympathise. She was baffled and bored by his gravity and industry. Moreover, she was angered by his refusal to exclude Protestants from his service. To her, they were heretics; to him, his loyal subjects who had suffered exile for his sake and for their devotion to the cause. He not only felt he owed a duty to them; he knew that a Jacobite restoration was only possible if the fears of the Protestant majority in England and

Scotland were allayed. So he held out against his wife's pious demands, and even persuaded the Pope to grant a dispensation that would allow Protestant rites to be celebrated in the little chapel of the Palazzo Muti.

For James had not abandoned hope of becoming king in reality as he already was by right. His restoration was still the task to which he devoted himself, and hours both by day and night were spent with his secretary, James Edgar, writing letters (many in cipher) to his adherents and sympathisers, and to kings and ministers all over Europe. Other states might have found it in their interest to acknowledge the German elector as King of Great Britain, or been compelled by force of circumstance to do so, but James remained a piece of some value on the chessboard of international politics. He knew it, and felt himself to be more than a mere pawn.

Yet his behaviour after he settled in Rome has puzzled some historians and aroused the contempt of others. The young man who had been so keen and active in his cause now seemed gradually to have sunk into passivity, and, as the years slipped unprofitably by, to display a fatalistic resignation. He never left the Papal States again, but moved with apparent tranquillity between the city and the Palazzo Savelli, the country house His Holiness had bestowed upon him, situated on the outskirts of the little town of Albano overlooking the Roman Campagna.

The explanation is simple. James had not changed; circumstances had. Western Europe was experiencing two decades of unaccustomed peace. In Britain the government was in the hands of Sir Robert Walpole; in France, after the regent's death in 1723, of the aged and pacific Cardinal Fleury. Walpole and Fleury understood each other, and preferred political quiet. Both were committed to a policy of peace.

Peace was bad news for the Jacobites. Only a state of war could persuade France or Spain or any other power to give them military help. Only Britain's danger could be the Jacobites' opportunity. And only war, with the British army engaged on the Continent, could offer a rising any chance of success.

So there was little James could do except try to keep his party in being and his interest alive at other courts. Moreover, with France barred to him, and the British government quick to remonstrate with any state that seemed well disposed to the Jacobite cause, Rome was as good a place as anywhere for him to live. At least the Pope paid him a regular pension, while the pensions granted him by France and Spain were often in arrears, and even the rent due from his investment in the Hotel de Ville in Paris could not always be relied on. He himself paid pensions to many who had lost their estates on account of their loyalty to the cause, Ormonde and the Earl Marischal being only the most distinguished among those who depended on him.

There were some five hundred exiled Jacobites – Scots, English and Irish – in and around James's little court in Rome, and no one knows how many in France and other countries. Some obstinately continued to wait and wait in hope of a restoration. Some, like the Earl Marischal's brother, James Keith, took service in other armies. He became a Russian general before transferring to the Prussian service, where he would be Frederick the Great's most valued marshal. He was the greatest of Jacobite soldiers, but lost to the cause. Others, like Lord George Murray, had returned home and made their peace with the government. Yet James, writing to the exiled Marquis of Tullibardine, never failed to ask him to convey his 'kind compliments' to his brother, Lord George. Whatever his faults, James did not forget the sacrifice many had made for his sake, and was ready to understand and forgive those who had given up hope and accommodated themselves to what seemed to be reality.

As the years passed, it became harder for the King himself to believe in the possibility of his restoration. In 1727 Lord Orrery, reporting to James on the accession of George II, observed disconsolately, 'there do not appear to be many discontented persons'. The next year the veteran Jacobite George Lockhart of Carnwath laid aside his memoirs, concluding that few were now ready to fight for the King, so that the cause 'must daylie languish and in process of time be forgot'.[2] Perhaps this was the will of God, to which James too must resign himself.

James had reason to be pessimistic. Bolingbroke had long since made his peace with the British government and been permitted to return to England on condition that he abstained from politics and was denied his seat in the House of Lords. Mar had done so also; indeed for some years he had been a double agent, reporting to the British ambassador in Paris. There were still Jacobites in England, but they were men of sentiment rather than action. They might, like the Duke of Beaufort, sigh loyally, or, like the heads of old Catholic families in the north and west, speak longingly of the day when the rightful king would come into his own again; but they had nothing but words to offer. Likewise, discontented and impecunious intellectuals like the young Samuel Johnson and his friend, the talented but disreputable poet Richard Savage, might walk the night streets of London talking sedition and Jacobite politics; but to no avail. Years later Johnson would affirm that if England were fairly polled the exiled King would be restored; but then admitted that no one would lift a finger to bring this about. The truth was that Englishmen had too much to risk losing and too little to gain. Only a fantasist could suppose that a rising there had any chance of success.

Nor were Jacobite prospects much better in Scotland. Though there was still discontent and resentment of the Union, by the 1730s its benefits were beginning to be felt. The new regime was attaching the propertied classes to itself by interest, if not affection. Ideas of social and economic 'improvement' were in the air; the first flickers of the Enlightenment were evident in Edinburgh. Lowland Scotland at least was putting the political and religious quarrels of the seventeenth century behind it, and looking towards the dawning of a prosperous new age.

Jacobite sentiment survived among the nobles and lairds of the Episcopalian north-east, and in parts of the Highlands, but even there it was weaker than it had been. A hundred years previously, during the civil war, Montrose had been able to call on the support of clans accustomed to warfare. This was no longer the case. In the words of a modern historian, 'the great clan wars had blown themselves out well before even the '15'.3 Even the chiefs of clans traditionally loyal to the Stuarts were paying more attention to the development of their estates than to thoughts of a new rising. The father of Donald Cameron, Younger of Lochiel, had been an exile since the '15, but the son managed his estates as a commercial enterprise. He was an enthusiastic and efficient forester, was involved in the West Indian trade, and had business interests on the mainland of North America in partnership with his cousin Euan Drummond of Balhaldie. So if the cause was not yet dead, it seemed moribund, and James's resignation is understandable.

His elder son, Charles Edward, was of a different temper, and in 1745 he would embark on a desperate adventure for which he had been preparing himself since boyhood. His enterprise was as thoughtless as it was audacious, and would have tragic consequences for those who responded to his appeal. He has been blamed for this by historians unwilling to make the leap of imagination needed to understand that he lived in the certainty that it was his duty and destiny to regain the thrones of England and Scotland for his father.

Charles was reared in Italy. His spirit had survived his upbringing in a quarrelsome, often melancholy, court. He knew himself to be surrounded by spies; could never be certain who was trustworthy and who had been recruited by his enemies. Some of the errors he made in his great year of action may be attributed to the suspicions engendered by his youthful experience of treachery.

As a child he was vivacious and attractive. The Marquis of Blandford, Marlborough's grandson, pronounced him to be 'a really fine, promising child',[4] though the boy was only six months old at the time. More interestingly, Blandford had several conversations with James on this visit to Rome, and found that the exiled King 'talks with such an air of sincerity that I am apprehensive I should become half a Jacobite, if I continued following these discourses any longer'. Most of the Stuarts had personal magnetism – unlike the Hanoverians, who had none – and neither James nor Charles was an exception.

Charles grew up speaking English, French and Italian indiscriminately, and there is some evidence that he always spoke English with an Italian accent. He was no scholar, and early showed an aversion to Latin. He spelled abominably in all three languages, but few young noblemen of the time were secure spellers.

James saw to it that the Prince should not be educated only by Catholics: any restoration depended on winning the trust of the Protestant majority. In any case, 'It should never be my business to be an Apostle,' he declared, 'but a good King to all my subjects.' Clementina thought differently. She once said she would kill her children with a dagger rather than see them apostasise. Charles in fact grew up with no feeling for religion at all, unlike his younger brother.

By 1730, when Charles was nine, James was so weary of his wife's behaviour that he was wishing he could find 'some prudent means of separation'. Indeed, she had left him once and retired to a convent, from where she persuaded the Pope to send a bishop to accuse James of infidelity and of intending to bring up the princes as Protestants. James replied that if he had taken this message seriously, the Bishop, 'would have run the risk of leaving the house by the window rather than the staircase'.

One can't judge what effect the unhappy marriage of his parents had on Charles, and any attempt to do so is likely to lead to absurdity. One modern biographer surmises that 'he was old enough to have witnessed many quarrels, and, like many children of parents who separate, perhaps he felt in some way responsible'5 – a peculiarly twentieth-century interpretation. The Palazzo Muti was small, but it was not a suburban villa, and it is improbable that as a small boy Charles saw much of either parent.

Nevertheless, James was not only attentive to his heir's education – so far as that went – but showed himself affectionate. He called his son by a pet name, Carluccio, and even when they were estranged in later years, his concern for him remained constant, reproofs being administered in a tone of sorrow rather than anger – which may of course have made them harder to bear.

James may have preferred his younger son, Henry, Duke of York. He was a pretty, affectionate, intelligent and tractable child, and Charles himself seems to have thought Henry his father's favourite.

There were five years between the boys, too wide a gap for real intimacy perhaps, this being anyhow precluded by their different interests and tastes. But they were close enough for Charles to tease his younger brother and call him a '*cacciatore di pan' bianco*' – a white-bread hunter or sportsman (the English equivalent might be 'fair-weather'). This clearly became a family joke. In February 1745, Charles wrote from France to his father saying, 'It is now two months I have not handled a gun, because of the bad weather and the cold, for which I would be called "cacciatore di pan' bianco" by the Duke, if he knew it, in revenge for my calling him so formerly.'[6]

The two boys won general admiration. Their cousin, the Duke of Liria (Berwick's son and heir), described the six year-old Charles as of 'great Beauty . . . remarkable for dexterity, grace, and almost supernatural address'.[7] James Edgar called the Prince 'the admiration and joy of everybody. You would be surprised to see him dance, nobody probably does it better.' One of his favourite pastimes was 'the Golf. It would very agreeably surprise you to see him play so well at it.'[8]

Charles's aversion to study was noted. The Earl Marischal observed that at the age of thirteen he had 'got out of the hands of his governors', but his passion for field sports was held to be to his credit. Not only was this a suitably royal diversion – his distant cousin Louis XV was miserable if he missed a day's hunting – but it trained his body for the rigours of war. During the hunting season he spent every day on the Alban Hills. 'I doubt if you could find many that would not tyre with the constant fatigue and exercise he takes,' his father marvelled. It was certainly more to his taste than being cooped up in the Palazzo Muti – 'no place for an honest man', in the Earl Marischal's opinion.

In 1734, aged fourteen, Charles had his first experience of war. The Kingdom of the Two Sicilies had been awarded to the Austrian Habsburgs in 1713 by the Treaty of Utrecht, but Spain was supporting a rebellion there, and a Spanish prince, Don Carlos, was installed as king. However, the Austrians still held several fortified towns, and Charles's cousin Liria, now after his father's death

Duke of Berwick, was laying siege to Gaeta. The Prince left Rome, with his father's blessing, to join the army, accompanied by his old tutor, Sir Thomas Sheridan (reputedly a grandson of James VII and II), and was greeted with royal honours and made a general of artillery. Eager for action, he was soon in the trenches, and Berwick reported that he showed 'not the least concern at the enemy's fire, even when the balls were hissing about his ears'. Clearly the Prince was marked out to be a hero. His daring was such that Berwick was relieved when the Austrians surrendered. He had found Charles's 'manner and conversation really bewitching' and wished 'to God that some of the greatest sticklers in England against the family of the Stuarts had been eye-witnesses of the Prince's resolution during this siege, and I am firmly persuaded that they would soon change their way of thinking'.[9]

Reports of the Prince's conduct gave his friends cause for pride, his enemies for alarm. The English agent Baron de Stosch took time off from his art-dealing to observe that 'everybody says that he will be in time a far more dangerous enemy to the present establishment than his father ever was'. Don Carlos, now King Charles III of the Two Sicilies, was so taken with the Prince that he invited him to accompany him to Naples. On board the galley, Charles Edward's hat blew into the sea. The sailors made to retrieve it, but Don Carlos cried out, 'Never mind. It floats towards England and its owner will soon go fetch it.' Then he threw his own hat after it, and the whole company followed suit, crying, 'To England, to England.' Reports of this display of boyish high spirits infuriated George II, and the Spanish ambassador was called in to apologise.

Back in Rome, Charles found Henry indignant at having missed the fighting, and his mother dying. Both sons were with her at the end, and the Pope paid for a splendid funeral attended by more than thirty cardinals.

After the excitement of Gaeta, Charles had to fall back on sport. There was no employment for him. When he visited Florence, the Grand Duke, unwilling to offend England, refused to receive him. A visit to Venice led to the expulsion of the Venetian ambassador from London. Charles could only wait and hope. He had no taste for dissipation, despite the urging of the errant Duke of Wharton, Jacobite, spendthrift and profligate, who urged that he be given 'a polite taste for pleasurable vice'. This was not something he would ever learn, and such vices as he did indulge in would bring him little pleasure.

Still, there were visitors to the Muti to keep hope alive. One was the young John Murray of Broughton, full of news of Jacobite stirrings. Charles made him his secretary, and he became his most important link with Scotland. Born in 1715, Murray belonged to the Prince's generation. He had not been soured by years of experience of exile and failure. He was ready to assure Charles that his adherents were as eager for his coming as they were loyal, that the cause was only sleeping, not dead, that the game could still be won. This was what Charles longed to hear, and what James perhaps no longer believed.

At last the long peace ended. In 1742 Britain and France were at war in Flanders and overseas in what would be known as the War of the Austrian Succession. Charles hastened to France, sure that he would receive the military assistance he needed. He was disappointed. There were discussions, negotiations, promises; nothing more. Eventually he chartered two ships from Antoine Walsh, an Irish Jacobite shipowner resident in Nantes, and set sail on a venture that seemed ridiculously quixotic.

He landed on 23 July 1745 on the west coast of the little island of Eriskay between Barra and South Uist. He could scarcely have been further from London, his goal. He had only a handful of companions. The first historian of the rising, the Chevalier de Johnstone, son of an Edinburgh merchant and subsequently the Prince's aide-de-camp, described them with some contempt: 'the Duke of Atholl, attainted and in exile since the year 1715; Macdonal, an Irishman; Kelly, an Irishman, formerly secretary to the [Jacobite] Bishop of Rochester; Sullivan, an Irishman; Sheridan, an Irishman who had been governor to the Prince; Macdonald, a Scotsman, Strickland, an Irishman; and Michel, his valet-de-chambre, an Italian; a most extraordinary band of followers'.[10] To make matters worse, the second of Walsh's ships had been disabled by a Royal

Navy vessel, and limped back to Brest carrying with it all the guns and military stores Charles had managed to acquire. So, almost without equipment and accompanied by no man of note, for the fifty-six-year-old Atholl had never enjoyed possession of his estates, while the dukedom was held by his younger brother James, the Prince was launched on the maddest of gambles. The previous year in Paris, he had told Murray of Broughton that he would go to Scotland if attended only by a single footman. He had not done much better.

He was met with no enthusiasm. The first loyalist with whom he made contact, MacDonald of Boisdale, a sensible hard-drinking man, told him roundly to go home. Charles replied: 'I am come home, sir, and I will entertain no notion of returning to the place from whence I came, for I am persuaded that my loyal Highlanders will stand by me.'[11] Boisdale tried to discourage this belief. So did Bishop Hugh MacDonald, the Roman Catholic Vicar Apostolic to the Highlands, whose office was proscribed by the law of Scotland. Charles brushed him off too. To prove his commitment he crossed over to the mainland and sent his ship back to France with a letter to his father: 'the worst that can happen to me, if France does not succour me, is to die at the head of such brave people as I find here'. He dispatched letters to the chiefs of clans believed to have Jacobite sympathies, informing them of his intention to raise the standard at Glenfinnan on Monday, 19 August.

Cameron of Lochiel was another who believed the venture had no chance of success, and set out to try to persuade the Prince to leave Scotland at once. His brother John, a Glasgow merchant, attempted to prevent him from meeting the Prince, saying that if he did so he would yield to persuasion. Lochiel continued his journey, persevering in his original intention, only to succumb as his brother had said he would.

On 19 August, the Prince was in Glenfinnan to find the glen deserted but for a couple of shepherds. Towards noon, a party of a hundred and fifty MacDonalds appeared. It was about four o'clock when Lochiel led some eight hundred Camerons to the muster, soon followed by three hundred more MacDonalds. A little later the royal standard was unfurled by the attainted Duke of Atholl, who then read out the King's commission appointing the Prince as regent and declaring war on the Elector of Hanover. Few of the Gaelic-speaking clansmen can have understood, but they cheered enthusiastically. The Prince made a short speech, which was also greeted with huzzas.

Among the observers was James More Drummond, a son of the famous Rob Roy. James More, as readers of Stevenson's *Catriona* will know, was a highly dubious character, a professed Jacobite who doubled as a Hanoverian agent. He sent a report of the proceedings to the Lord Advocate. The Jacobite force, he said, was made up of raw young men and a few veterans of the '15. It was short of arms, and such guns as it had 'were in great disorder, some of them with their locks broken and others with broken stocks'. He did not see 'above twenty saddle horses in the camp, but there were a great number of country horses for carrying baggage'.[12]

So, without cavalry, with only '22 Field pieces about the size of one's leg', with a collection of old and broken muskets, and with at most twelve hundred men, the Prince set out to conquer the two kingdoms, united since 1707, and to overthrow the revolution settlement of 1688–9. It was the fourth Jacobite attempt to do so, the least welcome to the adherents of the cause, and the one that, against all odds, came closest to success.

News of the venture brought in more recruits, among them Atholl's brother, Lord George Murray, who was appointed lieutenant-general of the army. He had come out for the Prince with many misgivings. Pardoned for his involvement in the '15, he was living quietly on his estates. He had a wife and children, and much to lose. He did not believe there was much chance of success. Indeed it was only his strong sense of honour that led him to set aside his doubts and fears. Charles never fully trusted him, and this was unfortunate, for Murray had real ability as a soldier. But they were ill-yoked, temperamentally apart. Charles read Lord George's caution as timidity. He questioned his commitment to the cause. Some of the Irishmen around him went so far as to make the unwarrantable suggestion that Murray was a Hanoverian agent and therefore a traitor. Murray of Broughton was another to sow seeds of doubt about Lord George. According to the memoirs of Lord Elcho, he told the Prince that 'Lord George had taken the oaths to the Government, and that he had been looked on for some time past as no friend to the Cause, and in short, his Opinion was that he had joined only out of an intent to Betray the Affair. What Mr Murray said to the Prince upon this Subject had such weight that he ever afterwards suspected Lord George which did his Affairs great harm.'[13]

In 1715 Mar had dithered and thrown away the chance of success. This time the Jacobite army moved swiftly. Slipping by the only government troops in the north, they made straight for Edinburgh and occupied the city (though the castle was still held for King George). One hostile observer, who saw the Prince as he entered the city, thought that his

> figure and presence were not ill-suited to his lofty pretensions. He was in the prime of youth, tall and handsome, of a fair complexion; he had a light coloured periwig with his own [dark red] hair combed over the front; he wore the Highland dress, that is, a tartan short coat without the plaid, a blue bonnet on his head, and on his breast the star of the order of St Andrew. Charles stood some time in the park to shew himself to the people; and, then, though he was very near the palace, mounted his horse, either to render himself more conspicuous, or because he rode well and looked graceful on horse-back.[14]

He dismounted at the gate of the palace and was conducted within by James Hepburn of Keith, who had been out in the '15 and had ever since 'kept himself in constant readiness to take arms'. That afternoon – 19 September 1745 – the Prince's father was proclaimed king and Charles regent, and 'the pretended Union' of Scotland and England was declared to be at an end.

Meanwhile the government troops commanded by Sir John Cope had been shipped from Aberdeen to the East Lothian coast, and were camped by the village of Prestonpans. The Jacobite army marched out against them, took Cope by surprise, and scattered his men within an hour of the autumn sunrise. 'They eskaped like rabets,' Charles informed his father, but he forbade any public celebration of his victory, saying that he was 'far from rejoicing at the death of any of my father's subjects'.

For a few weeks Holyroodhouse became again what it has so seldom been: a royal palace and a brilliant court. The Prince lived there, Elcho wrote,

> with Great Splendour and Magnificence, had every morning a numerous court of his Officers. After he had held a Councill, he dinn'd with his principall officers in publick, where there was always a Crowd of all sorts of people to see him dine. After dinner he rode out Attended by his life guards and review'd his Army, where there was always a great number of Spectators in Coaches and on horseback. After the review he came to the Abbey, where he received the ladies of fashion that came to his drawing-room. Then he sup'd in publick, and generally there was musick at Supper and a Ball afterwards.[15]

But Elcho, who came to dislike the Prince, later claimed to remember that in Council, 'The Prince could not bear to hear any body differ in Sentiment from him, and took a dislike to Every body that did.' This may well be true. Few of the Stuarts could brook contradiction.

The army grew with the enthusiasm of victory and marched south at the end of October. Some were doubtful, but the Prince assured them that they would receive support in England. He may well have believed this. 'His reasons for Thinking so,' Elcho wrote, 'were that in his Youth his Governors and Flatterers amongst his Father's Courtiers had always talked of the Hanover Family as Cruel Tyrants hated by everybody.' He also promised that military help would come from France; and he may have believed this also.

They chose the western route by way of Carlisle because Cumberland and Lancashire had a Jacobite tradition. But the English adherents of the Stuarts were now mostly no more than dinner-table Jacobites, and little support was forthcoming. The choice of the western route was indeed a blunder. The octogenarian

Marshal Wade was at Newcastle with some inferior troops. A victory over Wade on English soil might well have encouraged English Jacobites to be bold, and might have intensified the panic already developing in London, where King George was packing his bags ready to slip away to Hanover.

The opportunity was lost. Instead they marched south as far as Derby, disappointed by the lack of support and uncomfortably aware that George's younger son, the Duke of Cumberland, had brought experienced troops back from the Continent. At Derby, Lord George Murray spoke out in Council. The Scots, he said, had done their bit. They had come into England expecting the promised support, or to join the French if they had landed. But there had been no support and there was no sign of the French. Certainly he had never thought that 4,500 Scots could put the King upon the throne of England by themselves. So in his opinion they should go back and 'join their friends in Scotland, and live and die with them'. Charles was furious and spoke of betrayal, but the weight of opinion and evidence was against him; and he had to yield. The retreat began.

The decision to turn back at Derby has been the subject of argument ever since. It was the reasonable thing to do. Three Hanoverian armies were converging on them. The Jacobites had, as Lord George argued, found no substantial support in England, and there was no sign of the promised French help. Far more sensible to withdraw to Scotland, regroup, and hope that the campaign might be successfully resumed later. On the other hand, the whole venture had been made in defiance of such common sense. It had been an extraordinary gamble from the start. Why change tune now? Make a dash for London, and who could tell what might be the result?

Common sense prevailed, to the Prince's angry disappointment. Having lost the argument, he now lost heart. From being an inspiration on the march south, he became a liability. He sulked and refused to give orders, behaving like a spoiled and petulant child. It was thanks to Lord George Murray's efficiency that the bulk of the army was brought safely back over the border, and indeed won another victory over General Hawley at Falkirk in January 1746.

Murray was for retreating into the hills and waging a summer campaign. The Jacobites were by now however short of the money needed to pay and supply their troops. So, on 16 April 1746, battle was in effect forced upon them, though the ground, Culloden Moor, outside Inverness, was ill-chosen. The battle would probably have been lost in any case, wherever fought. For the first time they came up against experienced professional troops and well-drilled artillery, against which the Highland charge could be only quixotic.

There are two versions of how the Prince behaved when the battle was lost. Elcho had him fleeing from the field, and damned him for 'a cowardly Italian'. 'He never offered to rally any of the broken Corps' – though even Elcho admits that any such attempt 'would have been to no purpose, for none of the Highlanders who escaped ever Stop't untill they gott home to their own houses'. According to the account of a Presbyterian minister, John Cameron, which was collected by Bishop Robert Forbes in his volume of Jacobite letters and memoirs, *The Lyon in Mourning*,[16] Charles fought bravely. He had his horse shot under him, and, when the battle was lost, was urged by those around him to retire, which he did 'with great reluctance and in no hurry'.

After Culloden, the Prince was a hunted man, with a price of £30,000 on his head, and that was a sum such as very few in the Highlands could ever have imagined, let alone have had in their hands. Many knew who he was and where he was to be found during the course of his wanderings, which lasted from the final week of April beyond mid-September, but none was found to betray him. One Ned Burke, from North Uist, whose usual occupation was to carry a sedan chair, was recorded as preferring 'a good conscience to thirty thousand pounds'; and this was the case with all who were in contact with the Prince during his months of wandering. As for him, he showed himself not only physically tough, but of an almost unfailing good humour. Indeed at times he appears to have regarded his predicament as a matter for comedy. The most famous of his helpers was Flora MacDonald, with whom he travelled ridiculously disguised as her maid. When the pair arrived at the house belonging to MacDonald of Kingsburgh, their host's daughter told her mother that Flora had with her 'as very odd, muckle, ill-shaken-up wife as ever I saw'. Then Kingsburgh told his wife that this was the Prince, and her first reaction was: 'we are a' ruined and undone for ever'. But, remarking that 'we will die but ance', he told her to fetch food for the Prince; and when Charles had eaten heartily, he called for brandy, saying, 'I have learned in my skulking to take a hearty dram.' Then he asked for tobacco, saying he had likewise learned to smoke in his wanderings – doubtless first as a deterrent to the Highland midge.

Eventually two French ships evaded the Royal Navy, cast anchor in Loch nan Uamh, and Charles, with a number of followers, including Lochiel, boarded one, and escaped to France. The Prince's Year, as it came to be known in the Highlands, was over, but the Prince himself had another four decades to endure. He had failed in the great ambition of his life, and in the years that followed he found nothing to replace it.

Hope did not die immediately, but withered slowly. When the War of the Austrian Succession ended with a peace treaty signed at Aix-la-Chapelle in 1748, Charles was required to leave France. Refusing, he was briefly imprisoned, before being expelled. He reputedly made a visit, in disguise, to London in 1750, to consult with the surviving members of his party, and expressed his willingness to be received into the Church of England. But it was too late, and futile. He lived some years with a mistress, Clementina Walkinshaw, whom he had met first after the Battle of Falkirk. Many thought her a Hanoverian spy, and she may well have been one. They had, however, a daughter, Charlotte, who would care for her father in old age.

After the failure of the '45, Charles was estranged from his father, whom indeed he never saw again. Blaming Lord George Murray for the decision taken at Derby, and still believing in near paranoid fashion that Murray had betrayed him, he resented James's support for Lord George and his willingness to receive him at the Muti in 1747. He was still more angered by his father's approval of his younger son Henry's decision to enter the Church and accept the Pope's offer to make him a cardinal. Henry had in fact been in

France in 1745 and made efforts to join his brother, but now, like James himself, he accepted that the failure of the rising had extinguished all hope of a Stuart restoration. Charles's obstinate persistence in hope seemed senseless to his father and brother. In any case, Henry's was a softer character: he had the same Stuart charm, but he was more intelligent and dutiful, with a high sense of his position. By inclination homosexual, his only quarrel with his father arose from his intimacy with his 'maestro di camera', which offended James's sense of dignity and (one assumes) morality. But neither the affair nor the quarrel lasted long. No other scandal would touch the Cardinal, though some remarked on the numbers of pretty young men in his household. Made Bishop of Frascati, he resided principally there or at his palace in La Rocca. He became a great collector of books, manuscripts and musical scores – he was himself a competent violinist. As a boy he had been described by Alexander Cunyngham, a Scots physician visiting Rome, as 'very grave and behaved like a little philosopher, I could not help thinking he had some resemblance to his great grd father, Charles the Ist'.[17] This was perceptive: Henry would grow up to be an aesthete like Charles I, though not a philosopher, and in his devotion to his religion and his reserved and dignified manner, he might indeed recall the martyred king.

James died on 1 January 1766. Learning of his illness, Charles Edward had hurried to Rome, perhaps in the hope of being reconciled with the father he had not seen for more than twenty years. But he arrived too late. The Pope granted James a state funeral, but he declined to recognise Charles as the rightful king, addressing him only as the Count of Albany, and requiring the royal coat of arms to be removed from the Muti palace. For some time Charles nevertheless remained in Rome, and enjoyed Roman society. But he soon fell victim again to the alcoholism he had shared with his mistress, or – as the Cardinal put it – to 'the nasty bottle'.

In 1772 he was persuaded it was his duty to marry, so that he might perpetuate the Stuart line. A bride was found in a nineteen-year-old German princess, Louise of Stolberg-Gedern. For a while he stopped drinking, or at least moderated his consumption, and tried to perform his marital duty. But his wife soon found him 'the most insupportable man who ever existed, a man who combined the defects and failings of all classes, as well as the vice common to lackeys, that of drink'.[18] In 1773 the English ambassador to Naples, Sir William Hamilton, reported that Charles was 'universally looked upon as in a great degree out of his Senses and would be deserted if a few people did not go to him out of compassion for his Wife, whom he never quits a moment'.[19] Two years later, refused an audience by Pope Clement XIV, the couple removed to Florence, and there the marriage came effectively to an end after Charles drunkenly assaulted his wife and she left him for the poet Vittorio Alfieri, with whom she had been having an affair.

Charles followed them back to Rome, and was reconciled with the Cardinal, who had never ceased to care for him, and joined by his daughter, whom he created Duchess of Albany. 'The poor old man is almost always asleep,' reported one English observer, '& has I believe but very little sense of his Misfortunes.' The observer, Charles Parker, was mistaken. Far from having little sense of his misfortunes, Charles was obsessed by them. Charlotte warned visitors not to speak of the rising or 'his Highlanders'; such talk reduced the King to tears.

As he lay dying in the Muti, a piper played 'Lochaber No More'. Death came in the early morning of 30 January 1788, but was officially dated a day later, because the thirtieth was the anniversary of the execution of Charles I.

The King's body was carried to the cathedral of Frascati, where he lay in state dressed in royal robes and with a replica of the English crown on his head. The Cardinal said a Requiem Mass, and declared himself Henry IX. He struck a coronation medal that pronounced him king '*non desideris hominum, sed voluntate dei*' – 'not by the wish of men, but by the will of God'.

Charlotte survived her father by little more than a year, dying of a liver complaint.

In 1796 the Cardinal fled from Frascati when the armies of the French Revolution invaded Italy and seized his property. He had already sold much of his private treasure to support the Pope, whose revenues had been appropriated by the French, and lived for some time in penury in Venice. In 1800, however, this was relieved when his very distant cousin, George III, granted him a pension, and he was able to return to Frascati, where two years later he entertained the Pope with some of his old splendour. In 1804 he refused an invitation to accompany His Holiness to Paris for the coronation of Napoleon as Emperor of the French. To have done so would have been a denial of all that the Stuarts had represented; the King of France, his slightly less distant cousin Louis XVIII, might be in exile, but he was still the rightful king, and Napoleon was a usurper.

Henry died in 1807, at the age of eighty-two. He was buried in St Peter's, where Canova's white marble monument commemorates James VIII and III, Charles III, and Henry IX, kings who never reigned. It was commissioned by the Pope, and George IV, as Prince Regent, contributed to the cost.

But there was still one survivor: Charles's wife Louise. With her lover Alfieri she had visited England in 1790 and been introduced to George III's wife, Queen Charlotte. They then established themselves in Paris, and after Alfieri's death in 1803, Louise removed to Florence, where she had lived so unhappily with her husband. She insisted that her servants address her as 'Your Majesty', and that they should walk backwards when leaving her presence. She dined off plates decorated with the royal coat of arms: play-acting to the last, which didn't arrive till 1824, seventy-nine years since Charles Edward had embarked on the disastrous romance that, for all its failure and futility, has ensured that he remains, along with his great-great-great grandmother, Mary, Queen of Scots, the best remembered of his glittering and so often unfortunate family.

Envoi

'It cam wi'a lass and it'll gang wi'a lass.' James V's doleful prophecy was not fulfilled. The second lass, his infant daughter Mary, married her Stuart cousin, Darnley, and the male line was perpetuated. It had indeed come by way of a lass, Marjorie Bruce, but it went with a cardinal. Appropriately enough, for it was the Stuarts' obstinate attachment to the Roman Church that cost them the crowns of England, Scotland and Ireland, and made it impossible to regain them.

It had been a long adventure. If the story of a descent from Banquo was a myth invented to elevate the consequence of this family that had its earliest known origins in the salt-marshes of Brittany, nevertheless by that marriage of Walter Stewart to Marjorie Bruce, the Stuart kings were descended by way of David I of Scotland from Kenneth MacAlpine – who had first in 843 united the little Scottish kingdom of Dalriada with Pictland – and, through his marriage, from the Pictish monarchs whose line stretched back to the mists of Caledonian antiquity. Through David's mother, Margaret, they could boast of descent from Alfred the Great and the old royal line of Saxon Wessex.

James I's marriage to Joan Beaufort, granddaughter of Edward III of England, gave his children a descent from the first Plantagenet King of England, Henry of Anjou, and also, by way of Henry's mother Matilda, from William the Conqueror. Subsequent marriages enriched the royal ancestry of the later Stuarts. James IV was the son of a Danish princess; James V on his mother's side a grandson

of the first Tudor king of England, Henry VII. The marriage of
James VI to Anne of Denmark brought more Danish royal blood
into the Stuart line. Charles I's wife, Henrietta Maria, was the
daughter of the first Bourbon King of France, Henry of Navarre
– himself descended from the long line of Valois and Capetian
kings that stretched back in the female line to Charlemagne and
Charles Martel – and of Marie de Medici, from the great Florentine
family of merchant-princes. James VIII and III had an Italian mother,
Mary of Modena, and his sons, Charles Edward and the Cardinal
of York, could boast of the Polish hero-king John Sobieski as their
maternal grandfather.

Moreover, if the legitimate male line expired with the Cardinal,
the Stuarts themselves were not altogether extinct.

In 1873 Queen Victoria recorded in her journal a voyage she
had made on a little steamer up the west coast of Scotland. Among
her companions was Cameron of Lochiel, and as they sailed into
Loch Arkaig, her private secretary, General Ponsonby, remarked
on the significance of the occasion and setting. It was, Victoria
wrote,

> a striking scene. There was Lochiel, as he [Ponsonby] said, 'whose
> great-grand-uncle had been the real moving cause of the rising of
> 1745 – for without him Prince Charles would not have made the
> attempt – showing your Majesty (whose great-great-grandfather he
> had striven to dethrone) the scenes made historical by Prince Charlie's
> wanderings. It was a scene one could not look on unmoved.' Yes,
> and I feel a sort of reverence in going over these scenes in this most
> beautiful country, which I am proud to call my own, where there
> was such devoted loyalty to the family of my ancestors – for Stewart
> blood is in my veins, and I am now their representative, and the
> people are as loyal and devoted to me as they were to that unhappy
> race.[1]

Victoria was deeply attached to the idea of her Stewart ancestry.
If she owed her throne to the Act of Settlement of 1701 that had
bestowed the crown on her great-great-great grandfather, George,
Elector of Hanover, his own hereditary claim derived from his

grandmother, Elizabeth, the Winter Queen of Bohemia, daughter of James VI and I. Victoria may have been a Hanoverian, child of half a dozen generations of German kings, princes, and princesses, but she felt herself to be Stuart, Stuart certainly rather than Tudor, and indeed declared that she could never forgive Elizabeth of England for 'her cruelty to my ancestress Mary Queen of Scots'.

There are frequent calls for the repeal of the Act of Settlement in order to end its discrimination against Roman Catholics, and on these occasions journalists are required by their editors to write articles suggesting that there are people with a better right to the throne than Her Majesty Queen Elizabeth II. The leading or favoured candidate is the claimant to the throne of Bavaria, being the senior legitimate descendant of Charles I's youngest child Henriette-Anne (Minette). It is all nonsense, of course, a mere game. The British monarchy is a parliamentary one, and has been so since 1688. Arguably long before the revolution of that year, both the English and Scottish monarchies depended as much on consent, as expressed in Parliament or the Council of the Realm, as on strict hereditary right. Indeed, though Charles I at his trial declared that the English monarchy had never been elective, the pre-Norman Conquest Anglo-Saxon monarchy had had at least an elective element, as had the tribal monarchies of Germany, Scotland, Wales and Ireland.

Nevertheless, ever since the Stuart cause was dead, there have been sentimental Jacobites forming societies to honour the exiled family and talk wistfully of a restoration. They have mostly been silly and futile. Compton Mackenzie, though himself inclined to a sentimental attachment to the Jacobite idea, offers a comic picture of the West London Legitimist League in the first volume of his long novel *The Four Winds of Love*. The League's only sensible member is an elderly French aristocrat who, when asked by the young hero whether Jacobitism can ever again become a vital issue, replies: 'If by Jacobitism you mean the restoration of the present Queen of Bavaria to the throne of Great Britain and Ireland, Jacobitism is dead. There are at the present moment over seven hundred people with more right to the throne than Victoria, but there is not a practical claimant among them. Indeed I am quite sure that the large majority are unaware that they have any claim at all. Moreover, the present dynasty of the country is essentially popular . . .'[2]

Seven hundred? There may be more than that number now, but it is of no significance.

Yet if the male line of legitimate descent from Mary, Queen of Scots ended with the Cardinal of York, the number of people with, in Queen Victoria's phrase, Stewart blood in their veins is legion. In Scotland, for instance, the Duke of Hamilton is a descendant of James II (of Scotland), the Duke of Buccleuch and Queensberry a descendant of Charles II, by way of Monmouth's marriage to Anne Scott, Lady of Buccleuch. The Duke of Argyll is descended from the early Stewarts through the Douglas mother of the first Marquis, Montrose's antagonist. The Earl of Moray descends from Mary, Queen of Scots' illegitimate half-brother, Lord James Stewart. The Stuart connection of the Duke of Atholl goes still further back, well into the Middle Ages; and Murrays of Atholl were, as we have seen, engaged in every Jacobite rising. Indeed there is scarcely a single Scottish hereditary peer whose title dates from before the nineteenth century without a Stuart ancestor somewhere in his family tree.

Three English dukes – Grafton, St Albans and Richmond and Gordon – are descended from Charles II and one or other of his mistresses. The eighteenth-century Whig politician Charles James Fox, fierce critic of George III, was another who could claim Stuart blood, for his father Henry Fox had made a runaway love-match with Caroline Lennox, daughter of the Duke of Richmond and a great-granddaughter of Charles II. This was regarded as a misalliance, for Henry Fox was a commoner whose own father, Sir Stephen Fox, though a royal servant who had stood by Charles I on the scaffold, had once been a humble, if unusually ambitious, choirboy in Salisbury Cathedral.

Numerous noble families in Germany, France, Spain and Italy may claim Stuart connections, many by way of Elizabeth of Bohemia, some by way of the late medieval Stewarts who settled in France, others through the illegitimate offspring of Charles II and James VII and II. The most famous of these, James Fitzjames, Duke of Berwick, became a Spanish grandee. His descendants are to be found in South America as well as Spain.

More than ninety per cent of English people are descended from Edward III (king 1327–77), according to a recent biographer.[3] At first sight this appears far-fetched; yet the argument can be made convincingly. It may well be that a comparable percentage of Scots and people with Scottish ancestry are descended from the first Stewart king, Robert II. He had at least fifteen children by his two marriages – probably more, for the number of daughters from his second marriage is uncertain. There were also eight sons among his nineteen known illegitimate children. Even if, on a conservative estimate, only half these thirty to forty children had offspring who lived long enough to be parents themselves, and we grant each of these only two children who lived to be adults, one still has eighty breeding descendants among his grandchildren. In reality the number was almost certainly greater. One can see how quickly his family tree would branch out, and how some of Robert II's more remote descendants would not be noble but might be found at lower levels of society. Admittedly the ruthless policies of the first two Jameses cut a swathe through the extensive Stewart cousinage, but there were many who lived to have children themselves, and these children had to find a place for themselves in the world. Among Robert II's more remote and surprising descendants is Camilla, Duchess of Cornwall. Her husband, the Prince of Wales, is also of course descended from the first Stewart king.

Daughters of the medieval Stewart kings tend to disappear from history, except for the minority among them who made distinguished marriages. Robert II had probably as many as ten daughters from his two marriages, and his eldest son, Robert III, had four. By no means all survived to have children themselves, but the posterity of those who did bear children is mostly unrecorded. James II's daughter Mary married James, Lord Hamilton, and her descendants, the semi-royal Hamiltons, are innumerable.

Moreover, six Stewart kings – the two Roberts, James IV and

James V, Charles II and his brother James VII and II – between them fathered more than sixty illegitimate children, perhaps as many as seventy. Only a small number of the descendants of these sons and daughters born, as the saying went, on the wrong side of the blanket are known to history – not surprisingly, since we are ignorant even of the names of some of these bastard royals themselves. But there can be no doubt that they dispersed the Stewart blood and genes widely. The extensive family of the Stuarts of Bute, for instance, is descended from one of Robert II's illegitimate children; the great Aberdeenshire family of Gordon (Marquesses of Huntley and Marquesses of Aberdeen) from a daughter of James I.

It has been calculated that the population of Scotland at the time of the Union of the Crowns was about 800,000.[4] It was certainly much lower when Robert II became king in 1371, for that was only twenty years after the great outbreak of plague known as the Black Death, which, according to John of Fordoun, may have killed as much as one-third of the population. King Robert, whatever his incapacity as king, played his part in repopulating his country, and the branches of his family tree have spread ever since. Families may die out in the (legitimate) male line, but they seldom do so altogether. Cadet branches continue to flourish; heredity by way of the female line may go unremarked or be forgotten. It is therefore reasonable to suggest that Robert II was as much the ancestor of the Scottish people today – and of the twenty-million-strong Scots diaspora – as Edward III was of the English nation – many of whom will of course also be descended from the first Stewart King of Scotland.

Queen Victoria, reflecting on the misfortunes of the later Stuarts – misfortunes to which, as already observed, she owed her throne – spoke of them as 'that unhappy race'. Historians, especially those of a romantic or Jacobite turn of mind, have endorsed her opinion, which is indeed justified, but also misleading. Certainly the Stuart monarchy ended in failure. James VII and II was forced into exile by the Dutch invasion and the revolution he had provoked. His sons and grandsons were kings in name only, condemned to drag out their lives in the bleak obscurity of their shadow courts. Before them, Mary and her grandson Charles I may also be accounted failures.

Yet to dwell on their follies and misfortunes is to ignore the qualities and achievements of the other members of the family. The two Roberts may not have amounted to much, but they survived and kept their kingdom together. At least five of the first six Jameses were men of quite unusual ability who governed an unruly kingdom effectively. They compare well with their contemporaries who were kings of England and France. They were not only able, but tough, and from the return of James I from English captivity in 1424 to the death of James VI and I in 1625, Stewart kingship in Scotland was remarkably successful despite the interruptions caused by minorities and the turmoil of Mary's brief reign. If James VI's attention to government slackened after he inherited the English throne, and if Charles I by pursuing unwise policies alienated his subjects and provoked rebellion in all three of his kingdoms, Charles II, astute, cynical and determined, re-established the power of the Crown – only to have his legacy squandered by the folly of his brother James.

In the popular imagination the Stuarts may be figures of romance, commemorated in song and myth. Romance is never wholly false or without foundation; that Mary and 'Bonnie Prince Charlie' are the two best-remembered Stuarts is evidence of its potent spell. So too are the gates of Traquair House in the Borders and of Trinity College, Oxford, both closed until the Stuarts return again. So too is the Jacobite lament 'Will Ye No' Come Back Again?'. But romance is only part of the Stewart and Stuart story; the other part is the record of men who established and maintained effective government, welded Scotland together, and then, by means of the chance of inheritance and the cautious diplomacy and political skill of James VI, achieved the regnal union of England and Scotland. It was a long journey from the salt-marshes of Brittany to the gloom of the Palazzo Muti, but a family that maintained itself in power for more than three centuries cannot be dismissed as a failure.

Acknowledgements

This book has been a long time in the making. My first debt is to all those who aroused my interest in history, and those who taught me so many years ago. Most of them are now dead, but my gratitude to them is still alive. The earliest among them was my grandmother, Elizabeth Mary Forbes, who, like Queen Victoria, could not forgive Elizabeth of England for her 'cruelty to poor Mary', Queen of Scots.

Like many who write about Scottish history, I owe a heavy debt to the poems and novels of Sir Walter Scott, and to his *Tales of a Grandfather*, written for his grandson Johnny Lockhart, and favourite reading of mine as a child. Thomas Carlyle wrote that Scott had reminded people that men and women in the past were not abstractions but composed of flesh, bones and blood. I hope I have always remembered this and remained aware that events now in the past were once in the future, the outcome unknown to those who had to determine on a course of action.

Lord Rosebery, Prime Minister in the 1890s, himself a fine historian, once remarked that every Scot was at least half a Jacobite at heart. As a child, enthralled by Robert Louis Stevenson's *Kidnapped* and the Jacobite novels of D. K. Broster, I was wholehearted in my Jacobitism. The commitment faded with the years, but something of it remains.

I am indebted to two other dead novelists, John Buchan, whose biography of Montrose stimulated my interest in the seventeenth century, and Eric Linklater, the finest Scottish novelist of the mid-twentieth century, who showed in his own book about the Stuarts, *The Royal House of Scotland*, that history could be agreeably written with a light hand.

More immediately, I am grateful to my agent, Peter Robinson, to Will Sulkin, who commissioned the book, and to my editors at Jonathan Cape, first Ellah Allfrey and then Alex Bowler, who has seen the book carried forward to publication. I thank both of them for their patience, understanding, enthusiasm and encouragement. I should also thank Noel Gillett for bearing with my technological incompetence and sorting out computer problems.

Finally, my chief debt is, as ever, to my wife, Alison, who has made my life as a writer possible. Without her I would have written less, and worse.

Notes and Sources

Prologue

1 Lord Macaulay, *The History of England* (abridged edition, ed. Hugh Trevor-Roper, Penguin, 1979), pp. 109–11.

2 Anthony Hamilton, *Memoirs of the Count of Grammont*, trans. Horace Walpole, with additional notes by Sir Walter Scott and Mrs Jameson (Swan, Sonnenschein & Co., London, 1904), pp. 332, 334. Grammont was a soldier and courtier; the most interesting parts of the book recount his time at the English court in the decade after the Restoration of 1660.

Chapter 1

1 Boece published his somewhat fanciful *Scotorum historiae* in Paris in 1522. It was translated into Scots by John Bellenden, poet and priest, in 1536. Raphael Holinshed (d.? 1580) drew on it for his *Chronicles* (1577), which Shakespeare used as his source book for *Macbeth*.

2 The Scots were only one of the four peoples who eventually came together to form the Scottish nation. The others were the Picts, who lived north of the River Tay, the Welsh-speaking Britons in the south-west of the country, and the Angles in the south-east Borders and the Lothians.

3 Walter of Coventry, *Memoriale*, ed. William Stubbs. Quoted by Michael Lynch, *Scotland: A New History* (Century, 1991), p. 87.

Chapter 2

1 David Bruce was for a long time regarded or dismissed as a king of lamentable ineptitude, the unworthy son of his great father. Modern historians, engaged on revisionism, have judged him more generously. Michael Lynch in *Scotland: A New History* (p. 136), writes: 'The older picture of a worthless incompetent, attracted to a procession of dominating women, which was encouraged by the moralising censures of pro-Stewart commentators such as Bower, has been replaced by a cooler assessment, based on analysis of the growing activity of the king's administration – a model for later Stewart kings such as James I or II.' Walter Bower (1383–1437), Abbot of Inchcolm, was the author of the *Scotichronicum*, the history of Scotland in his own time.

2 John of Fordoun (*c*.1320–84) was the author of the *Chronica Gentis Scotorum*. Bower's book is a continuation of his work.

3 Gaelic was sometimes called Erse, on account of the Irish origins of the Scots, and sometimes Scots. By the 'Teutonic', John of Fordoun meant the northern variety of Old English or Anglo-Saxon spoken throughout northern England and southern Scotland, originally between the Humber and the Forth, though by Fordoun's time up the eastern seaboard of Scotland to Aberdeen. In the sixteenth century this language would come to be known as Scots or Scottis, to distinguish it from English.

4 John Mair (or Major)(1469–1550) was a historian and philosopher, born in North Berwick, educated at the universities of Cambridge and Paris, and later Professor of Theology at the University of Glasgow. After teaching at the Sorbonne, he bcame provost of St Salvator's College, St Andrews. He was the author of the *Historia Majoris Britanniae* (1521).

5 Jenny Wormald, 'The House of Stewart and the Realm of Scotland' in *Scotland Revisited* (London, 1981).

6 Jean Froissart (*c*. 1333–1405), *Chronicles*.

Chapter 3

1 The North Inch is now a cricket and recreation ground.

2 The stands were erected at a cost of just over £14.

3 Bonthron in the novel is a follower of Sir John Ramorny, Rothesay's Master of the Horse, who turns against him and betrays him.

4 In his customarily extensive notes to the novel (numerous editions), Scott quotes not only the medieval chroniclers, but also the Latin text of the 'Remission' granted by King Robert to Albany and the Earl of Douglas. This was first printed by the Scottish judge Lord Hailes (1726–96), who observed that 'The Duke of Albany and the Earl of Douglas obtained a remission in terms as ample as if they had actually murdered the heir-apparent', such terms indeed as to leave little doubt that they were responsible for Rothesay's death.

Chapter 4

1 Scott's portrait of Louis XI is among the most brilliant of his depictions of 'real historical' figures. In his introduction to the novel he writes that Louis 'was of a character so purely selfish – so guiltless of entertaining any purpose unconnected with his ambition, covetousness, and desire of selfish enjoyment, that he almost seems an incarnation of the devil himself'. He granted him also 'that caustic wit which can turn into ridicule all that a man does for any other person's advantage but his own'. But for his superstition, Louis XI would have been the perfect cynic.

2 '[I am] weary of the life of this world. Don't speak to me of it any more. More than anything I am bored.'

3 The title 'Lord of the Isles' – in Gaelic 'Ri Innse Gall', Ruler or King of the Isles of the Hebrides – goes back to at least the seventh century AD. For much of the early medieval period they were subject to the kings of Norway, until the Western Isles were ceded to Alexander III (1249–86) after his victory at Largs (1263). But it could scarcely be said that they had been incorporated into the Kingdom of Scotland, and the Lord of the Isles, which title became hereditary in a branch of the MacDonald family, was a semi-independent potentate, whose loyalty to the Scottish Crown was doubtful. At times indeed

the Lords of the Isles allied themselves to the King of England. In 1499, in the reign of James IV, it was recorded that 'A great deed was done in Scotland this year by the king of the Scots.' This 'great deed' was the execution on Edinburgh's Burgh Muir of John Mor MacDonald, Lord of the Isles, along with his son and two grandsons. Subsequently the title passed to the heir to the Scottish throne, the Duke of Rothesay. When in Scotland, Prince Charles, though usually styled Prince of Wales, is Duke of Rothesay, Earl of Carrick (the Bruce earldom) and Lord of the Isles.

4 Real (that is, 'royal') tennis, not lawn tennis, which was not devised till the late nineteenth century.

5 Pius II (Aeneas Sylvius) (c. 1405–64) left an account of visits as papal legate to Scotland, England and Germany.

6 There is no contemporary evidence for this story, which first appears more than a hundred years later. Nevertheless, the girl is remembered in legend as Catherine Barlass (the lass who barred the door), and members of the family of Barless or Barles have been known to claim descent from the heroine.

Chapter 5

1 Robert Lindsay of Pitscottie (c. 1532–80) wrote a *Historie and Chronicles of Scotland* in Scots rather than Latin or English. It was a continuation of Boece's *History*, translated into Scots by Bellenden (see Chapter 1, note 1). Pitscottie's work covers the years 1436–1575. Trevor Royle writes: 'Although he has been found to be inaccurate and credulous, his style is vivid and picturesque' (*The Macmillan Companion to Scottish Literature*, London, 1983).

2 This point is cogently made by Jenny Wormald in her essay 'The House of Stewart and its Realm', published in *Scotland Revisited* (Collins & Brown, London, 1991). She also argues that 'the breaks caused by minorities restrained the tendency towards an increasingly autocratic style of kingship, associated with the so-called "new monarchies" of sixteenth-century France, Spain, England; every Scottish king, save Mary, showed

signs of such a move, but none lived long enough nor left an heir old enough to bring it to fruition'.

3 Gordon Donaldson, *Scottish Kings* (London, 1967).

4 Sir Walter Scott, *Tales of a Grandfather*.

5 Donaldson, op. cit.

6 Scott, op. cit.

7 Ibid.

8 Eric Linklater, *The Royal House of Scotland* (Macmillan, London, 1970; Sphere Books, 1972, p. 30).

9 Michael Lynch, *History of Scotland* (Century, 1991), p. 149.

10 Donaldson, op. cit.

11 Ibid.

12 Ibid.

13 Quoted by Donaldson.

Chapter 6

1 In recounting a Jacobite rising that never was, Scott may be said to have devised a new genre: the counter-factual historical novel. Robert Harris's *Fatherland* is one of the more successful recent examples of the genre.

2 Gordon Donaldson, *Scottish Kings* (London, 1967).

3 Sir Walter Scott, *Tales of a Grandfather*.

4 Agnes Mure Mackenzie, *The Rise of the Stewarts* (London, 1935), p. 280.

5 Ibid., p. 293.

Chapter 7

1 'Proud as a Scotsman'.

2 Erasmus's judgements, frequently quoted by historians who have written about James IV, are to be found in his *Letters*.

3 Ayala's reports to the Spanish court, likewise quoted by most historians of the reign, will (I assume) be found in the Spanish Archives. I haven't checked these quotations because they are so well known, and have been frequently cited.

4 George Buchanan (1506–82), scholar, poet and propagandist, took a less flattering view of James's intellectual abilities,

declaring that he was '*ab litteris incultus*', untaught by letters. However, Agnes Mure Mackenzie, in *The Rise of the Stewarts* (London, 1935), p. 294, observes that 'Ayala knew James personally and well; he was a responsible diplomat, writing a secret and confidential report; Buchanan lived nearly a century later [actually half a century] and was writing propaganda against James's grand-daughter and her house in general.'

5 Ayala, op. cit.

6 Margaret Drummond (*c.* 1472–1502) was the youngest daughter of the first Lord Drummond. The rumours of poison arose because she and her two sisters all died after what has been described as 'a suspect breakfast'. If they were deliberately poisoned, the crime may have had nothing to do with the King's intended marriage. Suspicion fell on Lord Fleming, the husband of one of Margaret's sisters. The cause of death may equally well have been food poisoning.

7 Gavin Douglas (*c.* 1474–1522) was the third son of Archibald Douglas, fifth Earl of Angus (Bell-the-Cat). He was appointed Bishop of Dunkeld in 1515. His translation into Scots of *The Aeneid* (*Eneados*) was regarded by Ezra Pound as the finest version of the poem in any variety of the English language. 'In a barbarous age, / He gave rude Scotland Virgil's page': Walter Scott, *Marmion*, Canto VI, Stanza XI.

8 There were good reasons to fear the Turk. In 1526, thirteen years after James's death at Flodden, the Ottoman army defeated King Louis of Hungary at the Battle of Mohacs and Hungary was lost to Christendom, annexed to the Ottoman Empire. In 1529 the Turk even besieged Vienna.

9 The sword may still be seen in Edinburgh Castle, but sadly the hat has long ago been lost.

10 I have taken this anglicised version of Pitscottie's Scots from the notes supplied by Sir Walter Scott to his long poem *Marmion*, which has the Battle of Flodden as its climax: 'The stubborn spearmen still made good / Their dark impenetrable wood, / Each stepping where his comrade stood, / The instant that he fell.'

11 I owe this quotation and the greater part of my account of the Flodden campaign and battle to Niall Barr's masterly *Flodden* (Tempus, 2001). This offers the best analysis of late medieval/Renaissance warfare that I know.

12 Ibid.

13 Niccolo Machiavelli (1469–1527), Florentine statesman and political philospher. Most famous for *Il Principe* (*The Prince*), he also wrote *Discourses on the First Ten Books of Livy* and *Seven Books on the Art of War*.

14 Thomas Percy, *Reliques of Ancient English Poetry* (1765).

15 Sighing over his pupil Alexander's death in battle, Erasmus asked: 'What had you to do with fierce Mars, being destined for the Muses and for Christ?'

16 Flodden gave rise to one of the great Border laments, 'The Flowers of the Forest'. It exists in several versions, the best being that by Jean Elliot (1727–1805). The only Selkirk survivor of the battle, by name Fletcher, returned bearing an English standard, which he lowered in the burgh marketplace. A re-enactment of Fletcher's gesture forms the centrepiece of the closing ceremony of Selkirk's Common Riding Day, held annually on the first Friday after the second Monday in June. After the 'Casting of the Colours', the town band plays 'The Flowers of the Forest', known locally as 'The Liltin', a moment that never fails to be deeply moving.

Chapter 8

1 Gordon Donaldson, *Scottish Kings* (London, 1967).

2 Lady Margaret Douglas would marry Matthew, Earl of Lennox, and their elder son was Henry, Lord Darnley, the second husband of Mary, Queen of Scots. Since Margaret was a granddaughter of Henry VII, her son was in the line of inheritance to the English throne.

3 She spelled his name 'Anguisshe', but whether this is indicative of her feelings or of her defective orthography must be a matter of opinion.

4 Robert Lindsay of Pitscottie, *Historie and Chronicles of Scotland*.

5 She spelled Methven as 'Muffin'.

6 'Disjeuner' for breakfast is further evidence of French cultural influence.

7 Pitscottie, op. cit.

8 Andrew Lang (1844–1912) was a prolific man of letters: poet, essayist, folklorist, biographer, critic and translator. He wrote a *History of Scotland* in four volumes. It remains readable but has been superseded by modern scholarship.

9 Sir Walter Scott, *The Minstrelsy of the Scottish Border*. In the prefatory note to this ballad, he writes: 'The common people of the high parts of Teviotdale, Liddesdale and the counties adjacent, hold the memory of Johnnie Armstrong in very high respect. They affirm also that one of his attendants broke through the king's guard and carried to Gilknockie Tower the news of the bloody catastrophe. This song was first published by Allan Ramsay, in his 'Evergreen', who says he copied it from the mouth of a gentleman called Armstrong, who was in the sixth generation from this John.'

10 Alistair Moffat, *The Borders* (Deerpark Press, 2002), p. 255.

11 Sir Walter Scott, *The Lady of the Lake*, note.

12 Marie de Guise.

13 Pitscottie, op. cit.

14 It is likely that the action of the Liddesdale men owed something to bitter memories of James's punitive expeditions into the Borders, and of the execution of Johnnie Armstrong in particular.

Chapter 9

1 James Boswell, *The Journey of a Tour to the Hebrides* (Everyman's Library edition, 2002), p. 169.

2 Jenny Wormald, op. cit.

3 The Sieur de Brantôme, *Life of Mary Queen of Scots*, trans. Barrett H. Clark (*Great Biographies of the World*, Heinemann, 1929), pp. 516–30, passim. Pierre Ronsard and Jacques du Bellay were the leading members of the group of poets known as 'la Pléiade'. Ronsard himself admired Mary's verses, all written in

French. An edition with translations by the Scottish poet Robin Bell was published in Edinburgh in 2001.

4 The only man with whom Mary fell passionately in love was Darnley, and that did not last. There is no hint of any affair during her years of captivity in England, though there would have been opportunities during the early years when her confinement was not close. If there had been any rumours of an entanglement we cannot doubt that Elizabeth's ministers would have made good use of such rumours further to blacken Mary's reputation. Josephine Tey, in her novel *The Daughter of Time*, has her main character (a Scotland Yard detective) declare: 'Mary Stuart would have made an excellent gamesmistress at a girls' school.'

5 See a perceptive essay, 'Knox and his Relations to Women' by Robert Louis Stevenson, published in the collection *Familiar Studies of Men and Books*: 'For the man Knox was a true man, and woman, the "ewig-weibliche", was as necessary to him, in spite of all low theories, as ever she was to Goethe.'

6 Lynch, op. cit.

7 Lord James's surname is spelled in the old Scottish way, but his descendants, the earls of Moray, sign themselves 'Stuart' – in the manner of his half-sister and victim, Mary.

8 John Knox, *History of the Reformation in Scotland*.

9 Ibid.

10 Ibid.

11 Antonia Fraser, *Mary Queen of Scots*. Fraser's biography remains the fullest and most intelligently sympathetic treatment of Mary's life.

12 There is no firm evidence of Darnley's bisexuality beyond talk of frequenting male brothels in Edinburgh. However, it does now seem to be generally accepted.

13 Fraser, op. cit.

14 Sir James Melville, *Scottish Diaries and Memoirs* (Eneas Mackay, Stirling, 1976) pp. 46–7.

15 His most recent biographer, Caroline Bingham, takes a more generous view than most. Roderick Graham, in his biography

of Mary, *An Accidental Tragedy*, dismisses Darnley as 'a vicious syphilitic bisexual'.

16 Some (see previous note) have suggested Darnley had contracted syphilis. There is no evidence for this. Others have thought he was suffering from scabies, but as Eric Linklater remarked, scabies, however irritating, do not usually require the sufferer to be confined to bed. The illness was probably smallpox, albeit, given the speed of his recovery, in a mild form; or perhaps chicken-pox.

17 The House of Kirk o' Field no longer exists. It probably stood on the site of what is now the Old College of Edinburgh University, one of Robert Adam's finest buildings.

18 That it was Darnley's decision to convalesce in Kirk o' Field lends some credence to the case for Mary's innocence and to the possible existence of a Catholic plot to kill her. Whether there was indeed such a plot or not, there is little doubt that most of the leading Protestant lords saw an opportunity to rid themselves of Darnley. Bothwell may have lit the fuse himself, but the likes of Moray, Morton and Ruthven were in it up to their necks.

19 Fraser, op. cit.

20 The official explanation, given by the Lord Justice Clerk in his report, is incredible. According to it, two of Bothwell's men made two trips from Holyroodhouse to Kirk o' Field carrying the gunpowder in portmanteaus on the back of a horse. It has been calculated by Major-General R. H. Mahon (*The Tragedy of Kirk o' Field*) that this would have weighed about 500 lb. 'Now that quantity of powder, as made in the sixteenth century, was ludicrously insufficient to blow up such a solid building. But there is uncontested evidence that the house was totally demolished, and the implication – impossible to avoid – is that it had been prepared for demolition before that busy Sunday, and perhaps well before it. There were cellars under the whole width of the house and they must have been filled with such a weight of powder that when a fuse was lighted the explosion had the violence of a landmine.' Eric Linklater, *The Royal*

House of Scotland (Macmillan, London, 1970; Sphere Books, 1972), pp. 107–8.

21 Antonia Fraser, op. cit.

22 Far from achieving sexual satisfaction with Bothwell, all the evidence is that Mary was in misery, and often in tears, throughout the weeks of their marriage. 'From her wedding day she was ever in tears and lamentations': Maitland of Lethington. See Fraser, op. cit.

23 Mary told her brother-in-law, Charles IX of France, that Bothwell had taken her by force. Significantly, during her years in England, she kept miniatures of her first two husbands, Francis II and Darnley, but none of Bothwell.

24 Bothwell's wife Jean Gordon brought the divorce suit in a Protestant court, while Bothwell, to make assurance doubly sure, sought an annulment from the Catholic Church. There is no doubt that the two were in collusion. Jean Gordon did well out of the settlement, getting rich estates. She was married twice subsequently, and did not die till 1629, in the reign of Mary's grandson, Charles I.

25 Fraser, op. cit.

26 After Carberry Hill, Bothwell first tried to raise a new army in Scotland, failed and withdrew to Orkney. He then sailed to Denmark, where he was imprisoned, perhaps at the suit of his discarded Danish mistress, Anna Throndsson. At first he was held in honourable confinement, and Frederick II, King of Denmark and Norway, refused requests either to return him to Scotland to be tried again for the murder of Darnley or to have him executed. Eventually, being no longer of any political or diplomatic value, his imprisonment became harsher, and he died, mad, in the manner described.

27 Anna Throndsson, Bothwell's Danish mistress, is the probable author of the doggerel verses. French being not only the language of polite love, but also that in which she and Bothwell may have usually conversed.

28 Linklater, op. cit., p. 111.

29 Fraser, op. cit.

30 There is a brilliant account of Buchanan and an analysis of his arguments in *The Invention of Scotland*, Hugh Trevor-Roper (Yale University Press, 2008).

31 John Cunningham, *Church History of Scotland* (Edinburgh, 1882).

32 The plot was the work of an Italian merchant, Ridolfi, its intention to murder Elizabeth, set Mary on the English throne and marry her to the Duke of Norfolk. A vivid recent account is to be found in Robert Hutchinson, *House of Treason* (Weidenfeld & Nicolson, 2009), pp. 188 ff.

33 After the final defeat of the Queen's Scottish party in 1573, it was Englishmen, not Scots, who saw Mary as a figure of romance and plotted to free her.

34 'The horrible manner of the age': the penalty for treason was to be hanged, cut down before death might mercifully intervene, disembowelled, and then quartered.

35 Fraser, p. 622.

Chapter 10

1 Sir Anthony Weldon was a court offical (Clerk of the Kitchen, 1604, Clerk of the Green Cloth, 1609–17). He was knighted in 1617, but dismissed the same year, by his own account for satirising the Scots. He took his revenge by writing *The Court and Character of James I*, published in 1650, the year after its author's death. Weldon is racy, scurrilous, amusing and unreliable, but everyone who has written about James and the Jacobean court quotes him.

2 The Danes were famous for heavy drinking. See *Hamlet* and the Prince's remark that the drinking of toasts is 'a custom more honour'd in the breach than in th' observance'.

3 Any account of the Gowrie Conspiracy can only be conjectural. An old Scots lady once looked forward to the Day of Judgement in the hope that she would then learn the truth about it. My interpretation owes much to the researches of Christian, Lady Hesketh, in the course of which she discovered this curious sequel: in 1610, ten years after the dramatic events at Gowrie

House, Henry IV of France was assassinated in Paris, stabbed by a lawyer called Ravaillac in the rue de la Ferronerie. The murder weapon was a richly decorated hunting knife with a coat of arms and motto engraved on the blade. The coat of arms was not French. Where had Ravaillac got the weapon? The question was put pressingly in the hope that it would lead to the discovery of an accomplice, but Ravaillac's answer was unsatisfactory: he said he had stolen it in a tavern. The dagger was kept as a souvenir by the future Maréchal de la Force. Some fifty years ago his descendant, the Duc de la Force, made enquiries into its provenance. They led him to Scotland and to the genealogist, Sir Iain Moncreiffe of that ilk. The motto read: '*Haec Dextera Vindex Principis et Patriae*', and was accompanied by the initials I S R and an H surmounted by a coronet. Sir Iain identified the motto as that of John Ramsay, whom James VI and I had made Viscount Haddington in 1606. Ramsay is known to have travelled in France. Perhaps he boasted in an inn that this dagger had slain his king's enemies, and Ravaillac, impressed by the story, stole it. If so, then the dagger that dispatched the Earl of Gowrie and his brother Alexander may have been employed to kill the King of France also.

4 Carey himself wrote an account of his ride north, quoted frequently.

5 Bacon's judgement on his cousin smacks of resentment: 'Fit to prevent things from growing worse but not fit to make them better'; Eric Linklater, *The Royal House of Scotland* (Macmillan, London, 1970; Sphere Books, 1972), p. 145.

6 Sir Walter Scott, *The Fortunes of Nigel*, numerous editions.

7 Arthur Melville Clark, *The Man Behind Macbeth and Other Essays* (Edinburgh, 1981).

8 Sir John Harington, quoted by Linklater, op. cit., p. 248. Harington's miscellaneous writings were not published till 1769.

9 In departing from the family habit of naming his eldest son James, King James bore witness to his attachment to the Lennox side of his family. Henry was his father Darnley's name, Charles that of Darnley's younger brother. The choice of Elizabeth as

his daughter's name was a tribute to the English queen. To have called her Mary might have been regarded as provocative, especially since James's succession to the English throne was not yet assured.

10 The humiliation to which Essex was subjected had sore consequences for the Stuarts. His resentment made him one of Charles I's opponents and the commander of the parliamentary army in the Civil War.

11 Weldon (op. cit.) again.

12 Ibid. Lively and always quoted, but to be regarded with a degree of scepticism.

13 Anne Somerset, *Unnatural Murder* (Weidenfeld & Nicolson, 1997), p. 300.

14 For an examination of James's homoerotic inclinations, see David M. Bergeron, *Royal Family, Royal Lovers: King James of England and Scotland* (Iowa City University Press, 1999) and Michael B. Young, *James VI & I and the History of Homosexuality* (Basingstoke and London, 2000).

Chapter 11

1 See J. E. Neale, *Elizabeth and her Parliaments* (1957), *passim*.

2 C. V. Wedgwood, *The King's Peace* (1955).

3 Hester W. Chapman, *The Tragedy of Charles II* (Jonathan Cape, 1964), p. 18.

4 John Aubrey, *Brief Lives*, various editions.

5 Henry Guthrie, Bishop of Dunkeld, in *Scottish Diaries and Memoirs* (Eneas Mackay, Stirling).

6 David Stevenson, *The Scottish Revolution 1637–44* (Edinburgh, 2003); pp. 116–26 are immediately relevant to this account.

7 The Revd James Kirkton, 'The Secret and True History of the Church of Scotland', in *Scottish Diaries and Memoirs*, op. cit.

8 Impeachment was a legal process in which the House of Commons acted as the prosecution and the House of Lords as judges. In the sevententh century the threat of impeachment was the most effective means of exercising control over the king's ministers. It

fell into disuse in the eighteenth century. Two twentieth-century American presidents, Richard Nixon and Bill Clinton, have been threatened with impeachment. The leaders of the Scottish National Party and Plaid Cymru talked of impeaching Tony Blair over the Iraq war. Nothing came of their threats.

9 Edward Hyde, Earl of Clarendon, *History of the Rebellion*, various editions.

10 For an account of the Army Plot, see essay by Conrad Russell in *Unrevolutionary England 1603–42* (London, 1990).

11 Clarendon, op. cit.

12 Russell, op. cit.

13 Aubrey, op. cit, quoted in Anthony Powell, *John Aubrey and his Friends* (London, 1948).

14 Quoted by Eric Linklater, *The Royal House of Scotland* (Macmillan, London, 1970; Sphere Books, 1972), p. 192.

15 Ibid., p. 193.

16 John Buchan, *Montrose* (World's Classics edition). Buchan is sometimes too generous in his treatment of his hero. Nevertheless his biography of Montrose remains an oustandingly good and readable work.

17 Ian Gentles, *The New Model Army in England, Scotland and Ireland 1645–53* (Oxford, 1992), p. 170.

18 Michael Braddick, *God's Fury, England's Fire* (Allen Lane, 2008).

19 Ibid.

20 Clarendon, op. cit.

21 This observation is quoted by Buchan, op. cit. He ascribes it to John Row's *Life of Robert Blair*.

22 Christopher Hill, *God's Englishman* (Penguin, 1972), p. 98.

23 Hill, op. cit.

24 John Laughland, *A History of Political Trials* (Peter Lang, Oxford, 2008), p. 26.

25 A. L. Rowse, *The Regicides and the Puritan Revolution* (London, Duckworth, 1994), pp. 18–19.

26 S. R. Gardiner, *History of England from 1603–56*, various editions.

27 C. V. Wedgwood, *The Trial of Charles I* (London, Collins, 1964).

28   Ibid.

29   Guthrie, op. cit.

30   Buchan, op. cit.

31   Andrew Marvell, *Poems.*

Chapter 12

1   Christopher Hill, *God's Englishman* (Penguin, 1972).

2   Cardinal de Retz, *Memoirs*, various editions.

3   P. Zumthor, *Daily Life in Rembrandt's Holland.*

4   Gilbert Burnet, *History of His Own Time*, various editions.

5   John Aubrey, *Brief Lives*, various editions.

6   Hester W. Chapman, *The Tragedy of Charles II* (Jonathan Cape, 1964), p. 109.

7   Memoirs of James II, quoted in ibid.

8   Mademoiselle de Montpensier, *Memoirs*, 1729 and later editions.

Chapter 13

1   Diary of Revd Alexander Jaffray (1614–73) first printed 1833.

2   Clarendon, *History of the Rebellion*, various editions.

3   Diary of John Nicoll (?1590–?1667), in *Scottish Diaries and Memoirs* (Eneas Mackay, Stirling).

4   Letters and journals of Robert Baillie (1599–1662), in ibid.

5   Mademoiselle de Montpensier, *Memoirs.*

6   Hester W. Chapman. *The Tragedy of Charles II* (Jonathan Cape, 1964), p. 178.

7   Ibid., p. 174.

8   Ibid., p. 181.

9   Charles told the story of his adventures after Worcester to anyone who would listen. The fullest and most nearly authentic record is that he dictated to Pepys. Even so, this was given and written down, at what was at least the second hearing, thirty years after the event.

10   Clarendon, op. cit.

11   John Evelyn, *Diary*, various editions.

12 Hamilton, op. cit.

13 There were rumours that Charles was so enamoured of Frances that he was prepared to divorce his wife in order to marry her, but this was no more than court gossip.

14 Rochester, rake, poet, playwright and wit, was the son of Henry Wilmot, Charles's companion on the escape after Worcester. Henry was rewarded for his loyalty and friendship with the earldom of Rochester. This, and the young man's own wit, won him Charles's indulgence.

15 Charles delighted in nicknames. He himself was known as 'Old Rowley', the original Rowley being a famous stallion standing at stud in Newmarket.

16 Gilbert Burnet, *History of His Own Time*, various editions.

17 Duc de Saint-Simon, *Memoirs of Louis XIV and the Regency*, 1752 and later editions.

18 Voltaire, *The Age of Louis XIV* (Everyman edition).

19 Madame de Sevigné, *Selected Letters* (Everyman edition).

20 All Charles's acknowledged illegitimate children were given titles. On one occasion, when with the King, Nell Gwyn addressed her son as a 'little bastard' – a reminder that it was time the boy should be ennobled.

21 The MP was Sir William Coventry, who had been secretary to the Duke of York.

22 Burnet, op. cit.

23 Ibid.

24 Ibid.

25 Arthur Bryant; *Charles II* (London, 1930).

26 Ibid.

27 Dryden published the poem in 1681, by which time opinion was already moving against the Whigs.

28 Chapman, op cit., p. 398.

29 Ibid., p. 399.

30 Lord Macaulay, *The History of England* (abridged edition, ed. Hugh Trevor-Roper, Penguin, 1979).

31 G. K. Chesterton, *Essays*.

Chapter 14

1 Anthony Hamilton, p. 320.
2 Lord Macaulay, *The History of England* (abridged edition, ed. Hugh Trevor-Roper, Penguin, 1979).
3 Gilbert Burnet, *History of His Own Time*, various editions, p. 240.
4 Linklater, *Royal House of Scotland*, p. 229.
5 Macaulay, op. cit.
6 A. L. Rowse, *The Churchills* (Macmillan, Papermac edition, 1966), pp. 114–15.
7 Madame de Sevigné, *Selected Letters* (Everyman edition).
8 Robert Chambers, *Traditions of Edinburgh*.

Chapter 15

1 It was called the Convention Parliament because, in the absence of the King, it had not been summoned by royal writ.
2 Lord Macaulay, *The History of England* (abridged edition, ed. Hugh Trevor-Roper, Penguin, 1979).
3 Ibid. Unattractive in many respects as William may have been, Macaulay's admiration seems to me to be justified. If William displayed the resolution of his great-grandfather, William the Silent, hero of the Dutch revolt against Spain, the single-mindedness, to the point of obsession, which he brought to his long war against Louis XIV also calls to mind the obstinacy of so many of his Stuart ancestors.

Chapter 16

1 Gilbert Burnet, *History of His Own Time*, various editions.
2 Ophelia Field, *The Favourite: Sarah, Duchess of Marlborough* (Hodder & Stoughton, 2002).
3 Ibid.
4 Burnet.
5 Sir John Clerk (1676–1755), in *Scottish Diaries and Memoirs* (Eneas Mackay, Stirling).
6 If *The Conduct of the Allies* is one of the most powerful of political pamphlets, the *Journal to Stella* offers an incompar-

ably vivid picture of the ebb and flow of politics in the last years of Anne's reign.

Chapter 17

1 For Mar's character and manouevring see: Bruce Lenman, *The Jacobite Risings in Britain 1689–1746* (Eyre Methuen, 1980) and Daniel Szechi, *1715* (Yale, 2006).

2 George Lockhart of Carnwath, *Papers on the Affairs of Scotland* (posthumously published, 1817).

3 Lenman, op. cit.

4 Blandford was the grandson of the great Duke of Marlborough. His account of his meeting with the Pretender was published in *A Letter from an English Traveller at Rome to his Father* in May 1721. He had of course family connections with the exiled Stuarts, his uncle, the Duke of Berwick, being James Edward's illegitimate half-brother.

5 Susan Maclean Kybett, *Bonnie Prince Charlie* (London, 1984): quite one of the most hostile biographies.

6 Fitzroy Maclean, *Bonnie Prince Charlie* (London, 1988).

7 Ibid.

8 Ibid.

9 Ibid.

10 The Chevalier de Johnstone (1719–*c*.1800) was Charles Edward's aide-de-camp. After the defeat of the rising he became an officer in the French army, and was present at the capitulation of Quebec where other former Jacobites were in the opposing British army. He wrote his memoirs of the '45 in old age.

11 Maclean, op. cit.

12 James More Macgregor Drummond was acting as a government spy reporting to the Lord Advocate. The severe depiction of him in Stevenson's *Catriona* gives a fair picture of his character and chequered career.

13 David, Lord Elcho (1721–87), eldest son of the fourth Earl of Wemyss, was a Jacobite by birth, education and conviction. He met the Prince when he visited Rome in 1740 and served throughout the '45. An admirer of Lord George Murray, he

became very critical of the Prince. After the '45 he lived in exile in France and wrote *A Short Account of the Affairs of Scotland 1744–6*.

14 Alexander Carlyle (1722–1845), Church of Scotland minister and Whig, author of an autobiography.

15 Elcho, op. cit.

16 *The Lyon in Mourning* is a compilation of Jacobite letters and memoirs put together by Bishop Robert Forbes (1708–75).

17 Alexander Cunyngham (1703–85) visited Rome in 1736–7 with the painter Allan Ramsay. They were presented to the Stuart princes by the Jacobite Earl of Dunbar and attended a ball given by a cardinal for Prince Charles's birthday, 'at which most of the English in Rome were present'.

18 The story of Charles's miserable marriage is well told by Maclean, op. cit., unsympathetically by Kybett, op. cit.

19 Hamilton would have his own matrimonial troubles when his wife Emma became Admiral Nelson's mistress. He was however a more accommodating cuckold than Charles Edward.

Envoi

1 Queen Victoria, *Leaves from the Journal of Our Life in the Highlands*, quoted by Eric Linklater, *The Royal House of Scotland* (Macmillan, London, 1970; Sphere Books, 1972).

2 Compton Mackenzie, *The Four Winds of Love* (Chatto & Windus).

3 Ian Mortimer, *Edward III: The Perfect King* (Jonathan Cape, 2006).

4 *Collins Encyclopedia of Scotland* (HarperCollins, 1994).

Notes on Further Reading

This book has been a long time in the making, for I have been reading about the Stuarts since I was a child. My introduction to Stuart history was by way of Scott's *Tales of a Grandfather*, cited in the text, and by various of the Waverley novels in which members of the family feature. Among them are *The Fair Maid of Perth*, *The Fortunes of Nigel*, *The Tales of Old Mortality*, *Waverley* itself and my own favourite, *Redgauntlet*. If anything in this book sends readers back to Scott's novels and to his narrative poem *Marmion*, with its splendid description of the Flodden campaign, they will be well rewarded and I shall be satisfied. Scott is the greatest of historical novelists and all who write about seventeenth- and eighteenth-century Scottish history are in his debt.

As readers will have recognised, this book makes no pretence to be a work of academic history, though I am grateful to many academic historians, and many of the books I have used are listed in the Notes and Sources section. Agnes Mure Mackenzie's *The Rise of the Stewarts* has been superseded by modern historians. It remains, however, a mine of information and entertainment, while her portraits of the Stewart kings are intelligently sympathetic. There are modern academic biographies of all the Jameses, one of the best of which is Norman MacDougall's *James IV*. For a briefer and sometimes highly critical survey, I would refer readers to Gordon Donaldson's *Scottish Kings*.

Mary, Queen of Scots, has been the subject of innumerable biographies, besides novels, plays and films. Among the novels, I remember as a boy enjoying Margaret Irwin's *The Gay Galliard*, which takes an unusually generous view of its hero, Mary's third husband, Bothwell. Some recent writers, notably Professor Jenny Wormald, have been sharply critical to the point of outright hostility. However, Antonia Fraser's life of the queen, though now forty years old, remains to my mind the fullest, most sympathetic and intelligent book about, in the words of her publisher's advertisement, 'the most tragic and romantic figure in British history'. In general, I think she gets Mary right, and I owe much to her work.

Readers will realise that I take a warmer view of James VI and I than many who have written about that odd but able character; indeed, this is one subject on which I part company with Scott, even while relishing his portrait of the king in *The Fortunes of Nigel*. There is also a very good biography of James by David Harris Wilson.

I have named many of the books I have used for Charles I and the Civil War in my notes. Modern historians have covered the ground thoroughly, but for the general reader I would still recommend C. V. Wedgewood's three volumes: *The King's Peace*, *The King's War* and *The Trial of Charles I*. I would also draw attention to my friend Trevor Royle's *The War of the Three Kingdoms* as an excellent survey intended also for the common reader. The best contemporary source remains Clarendon's *History of the Great Rebellion*, rich in perceptive character sketches.

As a boy, I was once given Arthur Bryant's *Charles II* as a history prize. It is doubtless far too indulgent and uncritical, but I revelled in it, and so remain grateful to him. Anyone who wishes to come to a fuller understanding of that charming but shifty character should read Hester W. Chapman's *The Tragedy of Charles II*. Concentrating on the years of exile, it is the story of the education of a cynic.

Macaulay is harsh and unfair to James VII and II, but remains incomparable in his detailed, if biased, treatment of his reign – as he does, of course, in his portrait of his hero, William III. Nobody before Macaulay brought history to his readers as a living thing, and very few have matched him since. The Penguin abridgement of his *History of England*, edited by Hugh Trevor-Roper, offers an excellent introduction, or taste of the work, for those who fear they couldn't stomach the whole.

Another great historian, G. M. Trevelyan, following in his great-uncle Macaulay's wake, gives a marvellously rich picture of the early seventeenth century in his three-volume history of the reign of Queen Anne, though inevitably the poor woman rarely steps out of the background. Nothing gives a more vivid picture of the politics of the reign than Swift's *Journal to Stella*. For a fictional treatment of the time, readers can turn to Thackeray's *The History of Henry Esmond*.

The vast quantity of Jacobite literature is doubtless out of all proportion to the importance of the exiled Stuarts, but offers evidence of the fascination that Prince Charles Edward and the rising of 1745 continue to hold for writers and readers alike. The essence of partisan Jacobite history is still to be found in Bishop Forbes's compilation *The Lyon in Mourning*. The best and most complete modern survey is offered by Bruce Lenman's *The Jacobite Risings in Britain*. It punctures many myths.

Index